D1709235

FOUNDATION PRESS

CIVIL RIGHTS STORIES

Edited By

MYRIAM E. GILLES
Professor of Law
Yeshiva University, Cardozo School of Law

RISA L. GOLUBOFF
Professor of Law and History
University of Virginia

FOUNDATION PRESS
75TH ANNIVERSARY

THOMSON
★
WEST

© 2008 By FOUNDATION PRESS
      395 Hudson Street
      New York, NY 10014
      Phone Toll Free 1–877–888–1330
      Fax (212) 367–6799
      foundation–press.com
Printed in the United States of America

ISBN 978–1–59941–081–4

TEXT IS PRINTED ON 10% POST CONSUMER RECYCLED PAPER

CIVIL RIGHTS STORIES

Introduction

This is a big book. In it, we have taken a broad approach to the idea of "civil rights" in the law. So broad, in fact that the question arises: what makes a case a "civil rights" case? Or, elementally, what are civil rights? Some of the stories describe cases that most Americans would think of as classic civil rights cases—cases concerning the rights of racial minorities, women, the poor, and people with disabilities to the equal protection of the laws. Other stories explore issues that go beyond the archetypal, focusing on cases that raise issues of privacy and bodily integrity. Indeed, the fact that "civil rights" can and does encompass so much makes this legal category all the more contested. We have accordingly included, perhaps most provocatively, cases where both parties to a conflict view themselves as heirs to the civil rights mantle.

Thus, the claimants in these cases are African American and Mexican American; they are women and men, straight and gay; they are abortion protestors and abortion providers; they are members of the Ku Klux Klan, students at military academies, and airline workers. The cases they took to the Supreme Court concern education, employment, voting, sexual autonomy, free speech, and police misconduct. They draw on constitutional and statutory law; take place in states and localities around the country; and span the fifty years between World War II and the beginning of the twenty-first century.

Just as the stories themselves are diverse, so too are the authors' approaches to telling them. All provide a rich background against which to understand the cases, but they do so in different ways. Some regale us with fascinating biographical information. Others edify us with a broad historical perspective. Most reflect the primal force of politics and its role in real civil rights litigation. And all of the stories, we expect, will generate a better understanding of the cases themselves—of how they came about, why they are important and what they meant at the time they were decided.

Taken together, the stories in this volume tend to undercut the dominant myths surrounding civil rights law. In these stories, we see that the relationship between legal pronouncements and social and political realities—between winning or losing a case and creating social change—is rarely direct. Indeed, many of the great civil rights "victories" may contain less than meets the eye. Risa Goluboff, for example, tacks sharply from the traditional civil rights narrative and retells *Brown v. Board of Education* in a way that inspires a sense of regret for the roads not taken—the lost opportunities and overlooked possibilities

FOUNDATION PRESS

CIVIL RIGHTS STORIES

*

Page

for social change. Tomiko Brown–Nagin shows us how great victories may contain the seeds of their own undoing. She argues that the Court's disappointing decision in the 1995 school desegregation case of *Missouri v. Jenkins III* can be traced directly to failings in *Brown* itself.

Other stories show us how legal success may fail to translate into social change. Susan Sturm and Caroline Bettinger–López describe a hard-fought legal victory for pregnant workers in *International Union, U.A.W. v. Johnson Controls*. The authors nonetheless trace the persistence of dangerous workplace conditions in the wake of that watershed ruling. Similarly, Wendell Pritchett reminds us that the Supreme Court in *Shelley v. Kraemer* prohibited only judicial enforcement of racially restrictive covenants, not the covenants themselves. Such covenants continued to be employed as an effective means of residential segregation for decades after that 1948 victory, though the *Shelley* decision spurred fair housing advocates to find other ways of desegregating housing.

Yet other stories describe civil rights "failures"—cases in which the law stymied the claims of civil rights activists and their lawyers. Erwin Chemerinsky tells of the crushing blow to police brutality litigation wrought by the Supreme Court's decision in *City of Los Angeles v. Lyons*. There the Court imposed procedural hurdles to make it almost impossible for plaintiffs to obtain injunctive relief against many types of systemic and deeply entrenched rights violations. William Eskridge's account of *Bowers v. Hardwick* gives texture and context to the stubborn failure of the law to recognize and accept differences in sexual orientation.

These stories teach us that the Supreme Court's opinion in a civil rights case is at most one moment in any process of social change. Much of this volume describes other change agents, those who generally disappear from view in the shadow of the Court: the plaintiffs, defendants, lawyers and organizations that create cases by their actions and then live with them after the Supreme Court has performed its limited role.

Certainly, some of the plaintiffs described in these stories were mere stand-ins, or representatives of the dozens or hundreds or thousands of similarly-situated and affected individuals. The person of James Monroe, for example, fades away in Myriam Gilles's telling of *Monroe v. Pape*, in large part because he could have been any black Chicagoan unlucky enough to have been erroneously picked out of a lineup and illegally arrested by the police, as so many were.

But other plaintiffs in these stories braved ostracism and retaliation to protect their families from a perceived injustice. George Rutherglen tells the story of Mrs. McCrary of *Runyon v. McCrary*. She decided to fight the segregated policies of the private school that wouldn't admit her African American son. In Lynda Dodd's account of *DeShaney v.*

Winnebago County, Mrs. DeShaney challenged the Social Services agency that she believed abandoned her son and allowed him to die at the hands of his father. And Richard Schragger's account of *San Antonio Independent School District v. Rodriguez* describes how Mr. Rodriguez took on the state system of unequal funding for education that left his sons in poorly-financed and managed schools. Sheryll Cashin, meanwhile, paints a memorable and very personal portrait of her father's struggle to start an independent, black political party and field a statewide slate of black candidates in her story about *Hadnott v. Amos*.

The stories also shine a light on the often intrepid lawyers who took on these cases. For law students in particular, the lawyers' stories highlight the dedication and imagination required to use the law as a tool for social change. Some of these lawyers are charter members of the civil rights pantheon—Thurgood Marshall, Charles Hamilton Houston, Charles Morgan, Jr. But most are not well known. Arthur Gochman, a local San Antonio lawyer, took the case of Hispanic parents challenging the Texas school financing system in *San Antonio Independent School District v. Rodriguez* without any prior experience in civil rights litigation. Perhaps less paradigmatic were litigation efforts by public agencies, such as the lawyers in the Departments of Education and Justice who brought a case against the Virginia Military Institute to force the school to admit women, as described in Cornelia Pillard's story of *United States v. Virginia*.

The relationships between lawyers and clients in these stories is not always so straightforward, however. Many of the cases cannot be traced to a single lawyer, organization, or client. The stories in this volume reveal the broad and complicated coalitions behind many of these cases. *Johnson Controls* details the efforts of an alliance made up of labor, civil, and women's rights groups working on multiple fronts to achieve greater workplace equality and safety. Serena Mayeri's story of *Schenck v. Pro–Choice Network of Western New York* similarly describes the creation of the Pro–Choice Network—a partnership of medical providers and lawyers from NOW Legal Defense and Education Fund, the ACLU, and other groups. William Eskridge's story on *Bowers* provides insight into the strategies of the ACLU and Lambda, working together to defeat sodomy laws. Because of the diversity of views, interests, and goals at stake in much civil rights litigation, however, the stories reflect conflict within litigation strategies and within social movements as often as they reflect cooperation.

And then there are the cases where it is more difficult to discern which side properly deserves the title of civil rights advocate. Serena Mayeri's description of the abortion protestors and abortion providers in *Schenck* provides a stark example of a contemporary clash in ideology, resulting in both sides viewing themselves as civil rights crusaders.

Thomas Metzloff's story of *Virginia v. Black* tells of a dedicated legal team made up of an African–American lawyer and a liberal law professor representing Ku Klux Klan leader Barry Black in his struggle for the right to burn a cross under the First Amendment. On the other side of the case were proud Virginians, embarrassed by their state's history and keen on presenting a more liberal face to the nation. In these cases, the history and meaning of "civil rights" are as much part of the debate as the substantive claims of each side.

Taken together, these stories reveal a historical trajectory with some, though hardly well-defined, contours. Vindication of formal rights—like the right not to be taught in segregated schools in *Brown*— has been easier to obtain than vindication of rights requiring more complicated remedies. As civil rights cases moved away from formal racial equality and toward claims involving material equality, sex, poverty, disability, and sexual orientation, the cases became messier and effective remedies became harder to devise. Sam Bagenstos makes this point well in *Barnett v. U.S. Airways*, where an accommodation for a person with disabilities came into direct conflict with the airline's seniority system.

Civil Rights Stories, then, offers readers a broad look at American civil rights law. In choosing to present such a wide variety of cases, approaches, methodologies and insights, this volume aims to suggest the multiplicities of civil rights that coexist in American law today. While neither the individual stories offered here nor the volume taken as a whole conclusively define "civil rights," we are confident that *Civil Rights Stories* will stimulate rich and robust debate toward answering that complex question.

Myriam Gilles

Risa Goluboff

1

Wendell E. Pritchett*

Shelley v. Kraemer: Racial Liberalism and the U.S. Supreme Court

In 1944, Swedish social scientist Gunnar Myrdal published his path-breaking book, *An American Dilemma*. The book, which was the product of more than six years of work in collaboration with dozens of American scholars, exceeded fifteen hundred pages and provided the most comprehensive examination of black America ever produced. Although the book was the product of immense scholarly study, its purpose was not as an intellectual exercise but rather to promote what Myrdal called "social engineering." Historian Walter Jackson described the book as a "modern jeremiad to white Americans concerning the race issue." Myrdal told Americans, "At bottom our problem is the moral dilemma of the American—the conflict between his moral valuations on various levels of consciousness and generality. . . . The Negro has not yet been given the elemental civil and political rights of formal democracy." Among the many aspects of discrimination Myrdal highlighted was the shame of residential segregation, promoted by government policies and "restrictive covenants." Sixty years later, the book remains a primary source for understanding the rise of racial liberalism in this country.[1]

* I would like to thank Risa Goluboff and Myriam Gilles for their comments and suggestions.

[1] GUNNAR MYRDAL, AN AMERICAN DILEMMA: THE NEGRO PROBLEM AND MODERN DEMOCRACY LXXI (1944); WALTER A. JACKSON, GUNNAR MYRDAL AND AMERICA'S CONSCIENCE 186–87 (1990); *see also*, DAVID W. SOUTHERN, GUNNAR MYRDAL AND BLACK-WHITE RELATIONS: THE USE AND ABUSE OF AN AMERICAN DILEMMA (1987).

The impact of the book was immediate and powerful, in large part because it was released when other trends were moving towards the belated acknowledgement that all American citizens were not equal. The ordeal of World War II, a conflict that laid bare the intellectual bankruptcy of theories of racial difference, forced the American public and its political leaders to begin to face the fact of discrimination at home. At the same time, emboldened by the contributions of millions of African Americans to the war effort, and (relatively) flush as a result of the war-produced economic boom, civil rights advocates in 1944 were ready to step-up their legal, economic and political attacks on Jim Crow.

One central front in the war for equality was the battle against discrimination in housing. Several million African Americans had migrated to the urban North during the war to labor in industry and service jobs. When they arrived, they joined their colored brethren in the already crowded ghettoes to which almost all black residents were restricted. Housing discrimination, supported by government agencies, and enforced through legal and illegal methods in neighborhoods across the nation, prevented even those African Americans with money from securing decent shelter. The segregated communities in which blacks lived were not equal, and they suffered from inadequate schools, health care and other problems. Civil rights leaders argued that freedom of residence was crucial to the achievement of full citizenship for African Americans.

The battle against restrictive covenants—agreements among property owners that they would not sell or rent to African Americans and other racial minorities—which resulted in the Supreme Court's 1948 decision in the case of _Shelley v. Kraemer_, was a critical part of the legal attack on segregation in America. Although the decision itself had only marginal impact on residential segregation in this country, the case and its companions brought together public interest lawyers from around the country, fostered a complex and deep collaboration with social scientists and contributed to the rapid expansion of capacity in civil rights advocacy groups at the national and local levels. The legal struggle, which provided a model for the attack on school segregation, represents a seminal moment in the history of civil rights law. By expanding the definition of "state action," the decision represented a (limited) re-envisioning of the government's role in structuring the country's race relations.

The Racial Restrictions on Housing and Urban America

By World War II, government and private efforts to limit the mobility of blacks had a long history. During much of the 1800s, restrictions on black residence were informal, and particularly in the South, whites and African Americans lived in close contact. However, during the early 1900s, as Jim Crow rules were established to cover many aspects of race relations, efforts to establish separate residential districts increased. During the 1910s, several cities used the still-fledgling institution of zoning to mandate racial exclusivity, particularly in newly developed middle-class communities. However, such efforts, which divided cities into racial zones, conflicted with deep-seated notions of private property. In the 1917 case of *Buchanan v. Warley*, the U.S. Supreme Court held that the city of Louisville's racial zoning statute violated the Fourteenth Amendment. The case was the result of a convergence of interests between white homeowners who wanted to sell their property without restraints on potential buyers and NAACP lawyers. In its opinion, the Supreme Court declared that the government could not require the residential separation of the races.[2]

Other, more "private," efforts to promote racial exclusion were more successful. Beginning in the late 1800s, many property owners resorted to servitude law to "protect" their communities from the entrance of blacks and other undesirables. The covenants they adopted were private agreements—often included in property deeds—that bound the owners to refrain from transferring their property to persons other than those of the "Caucasian race." Frequently, the covenants were written into the original sale agreements for new housing. In other cases, homeowners joined together to reach such agreements after they purchased their housing. Restrictive covenants gave each participant the power to sue a party violating the agreement for an injunction or damages and prevented whites (even those who may have wanted to sell to blacks) from transferring their property to blacks. Proponents of racially restrictive covenants argued that they were necessary to protect property values, which declined, they claimed, when blacks or other minorities moved into a neighborhood.

These agreements were often legally suspect, as they did not meet all of the technical legal requirements to be binding.[3] But courts ignored

---

[2] Buchanan v. Warley, 245 U.S. 60 (1917); David E. Bernstein, *Philip Sober Controlling Philip Drunk: Buchanan v. Warley in Historical Perspective*, 51 VAND. L. REV. 797 (1998); CLEMENT VOSE, CAUCASIANS ONLY: THE SUPREME COURT, THE NAACP AND THE RESTRICTIVE COVENANT CASES 2 (1959).

[3] Under common law, a party seeking to enforce a covenant (who was not one of the original parties to the agreement) must show that there was "privity" in the creation of the agreement and its subsequent transfer. The rationale behind this requirement (and others imposed on covenants) was to ensure that the use of covenants was limited, because such agreements conflicted with the general philosophy that owners should be able to transfer their property freely. There are two types of privity; horizontal privity and vertical privity. Horizontal privity, which requires that, at the same time they enter into the covenant, the original parties transfer the covenanted property, was, in theory, a major legal obstacle to the enforcement of restrictive covenants. If, as was in the case in the *Shelley* covenant, the parties were homeowners who entered into an agreement AFTER

these flaws or found ways around them, frequently upholding restrictions based on the law of equitable servitudes. As a result of court acquiescence to race-based restrictions, the number of properties subject to such covenants rose substantially during the 1920s, particularly in large cities. By that time a significant portion of housing in most northern cities (primarily in middle-income neighborhoods) was subject to such covenants.[4] Although the Supreme Court did not consider a case that directly addressed the enforceability of restrictive covenants against subsequent purchasers, in the 1926 case of *Corrigan v. Buckley,* the Court expressed its approval of such agreements. Responding to a claim that such race-based restrictive covenants violated the constitution, Justice Sanford called the petition "so insubstantial as to be plainly without color of merit."[5]

Restrictive covenants also had the imprimatur of the public and private institutions that shaped American housing policy. From the Federal Housing Administration (FHA) down to the local realtor, the real estate industry held as one of its central tenets that people of different races should not live together. The ethical code of the National Association of Real Estate Boards (NAREB) stated specifically that realtors should not introduce into a neighborhood "members of any race ... whose presence would clearly be detrimental to property values...." From its inception in 1934 until 1949, FHA regulations strongly suggested restrictive covenants in all federally-financed housing. When civil rights advocates began to systematically attack the covenants in the 1940s, they faced deep opposition in neighborhoods, government institutions and the courts.[6]

Urban Migration and the Legal Assault on Restrictive Covenants

At the same time, other trends were turning in favor of civil rights lawyers. Economic growth played a major role in this process. In the nation's largest urban areas, civil rights protest combined with worker shortages to open up new opportunities to trained and unskilled blacks.

---

they purchased their properties, the covenant would fail the horizontal privity requirement and therefore be unenforceable against subsequent purchasers. In addition to the questions about many agreements' compliance with the requirement of horizontal privity, there were frequently questions about whether subsequent purchasers had notice of the restrictions. Thirdly, those opposed to the covenants argued that the race of the occupants did not "touch and concern" the land. Courts, however, frequently ignored these requirements and enforced the agreements anyway.

[4] VOSE, *supra* note 2, at 5–13; HERMAN LONG & CHARLES S. JOHNSON, PEOPLE VS. PROPERTY: RACE RESTRICTIVE COVENANTS IN HOUSING 11 (1947).

[5] Corrigan v. Buckley, 271 U.S. 323, 330 (1926).

[6] National Association of Real Estate Boards, Code of Ethics 3 (1924).

As a result, income in black families increased significantly during the first half of the 1940s, along with their desire for decent housing. In the post-war years, black demands for shelter combined with upward mobility among whites to move racial boundaries in many cities. As white property owners looked to sell in areas that bordered black neighborhoods, they became increasingly willing to ignore restrictive covenants. Their white neighbors, however, often insisted on enforcing the agreements, and lawsuits were the result.

Restrictive covenants were of particular concern to the small but increasing number of professional blacks, who found themselves financially able to buy decent housing but prohibited from doing so. Myrdal had critiqued such agreements in *An American Dilemma*, arguing that "there exists a Negro upper and middle class who are searching for decent homes and who, if they were not shunned by the whites, would contribute to property values in a neighborhood rather than cause them to deteriorate." These families were often the "pioneers" in new neighborhoods, facing both physical violence and lawsuits when they entered.[7]

Because the economics in many neighborhoods favored black purchasers, attacks on restrictive covenants became a burgeoning industry for black lawyers in several cities, Chicago in particular. By one estimate, eighty percent of that city's housing was burdened by racially-restrictive agreements. By 1944, several Chicago attorneys were representing families that had been denied the right to purchase or occupy homes in several areas of the city. Most of the plaintiffs in these suits were home buyers, but one case involved black tenants evicted from a covenanted building. Since the restrictions affected many of their members, the Chicago branch of the NAACP led the fight against such agreements, publishing a pamphlet entitled "Restrictive Covenants: In a Democracy They Cost Too Much." The pamphlet argued that "race restrictive covenants undermine the foundation of our democracy," and told "the one and one-fourth billion people of color throughout the world that they are considered unworthy of an equal chance to live in the world." Because these agreements limited the availability of housing and increased its cost, blacks had paid $50,000,000 more for housing in the past ten years than they should have, NAACP leaders claimed.[8]

Civil rights activists in Chicago and elsewhere were joined by business leaders who worried that racial discrimination was preventing

---

[7] MYRDAL, *supra* note 1, at 625.

[8] Restrictive Covenants: In a Democracy They Cost Too Much; Cases in All Parts of City Being Fought in Chicago's Courts, NAACP Chicago Branch Bulleting, May 19, 1945, both in Papers of the National Association for the Advancement of Colored Persons ("NAACP Papers"), Part 5, Reel 21; *Covenant Suit Would Evict 1000 Families*, CHI. DEFENDER, Feb. 5, 1944.

their communities from growing. For example, The Metropolitan Housing Council of Chicago, an organization of white civic leaders, passed a resolution declaring that "covenants based on race, creed or color, which in practice prevent or interfere with the development of an adequate housing program for the City of Chicago, should be abolished," and the City Club of Chicago argued that "restrictive covenants are unethical because their existence denies the brotherhood of all men." A *Chicago Sun* editorial also declared support for a law banning covenants, calling them "unethical, undemocratic and uneconomic." Others, including the American Jewish Congress, the Illinois CIO and the Chicago Civil Liberties Union, joined the effort to oppose housing discrimination. Together, they formed a powerful coalition against restrictive covenants.[9]

Robert Weaver, Social Science, and Racial Liberalism

Activists and business leaders were joined by a growing group of social scientists who provided data and analysis to assist the attack on Jim Crow. Although a small number of African American scholars had been working on such issues for a long time, white scholars were spurred by Myrdal, who argued in *An American Dilemma* that "fact-finding and scientific theories of casual relations" would be "instrumental in planning controlled social change." Social scientists working with government, he claimed, could promote societal change through the creation of educational forums like race relations committees, which would bring "constant pressure . . . on race prejudice." The efforts of social scientists to amass and publicize the facts about the state of black Americans would convince white society to support needed reforms. This approach, subsequently titled "racial liberalism," would be the dominant approach to race relations throughout the rest of the twentieth century.[10]

Among the black social scientists leading this new effort was economist Robert C. Weaver. A PhD graduate of Harvard, Weaver had worked in several New Deal and war agencies. In 1945, he joined the newly created American Council on Race Relations (ACRR), a Chicago-based think tank supported by the Rosenwald Fund to support research in the area of racial equality. Working with ACRR Executive Director and University of Chicago sociologist Louis Wirth, Weaver devoted a great deal of attention to the battle against restrictive covenants. In several articles, he argued that covenants were not only wrong but ineffective. There was no evidence, he asserted, to support the allegation that the entrance of blacks into a neighborhood caused property values to de-

---

[9] Abstract of Hearings Proponents, House Judiciary Committee, May 28, 1945, NAACP Papers, Part 5, Reel 20.

[10] MYRDAL, *supra* note 1, at 19–20, 1022–23, 80; SOUTHERN, *supra* note 1, at 58–59; JACKSON, *supra* note 1, at 192–93, 198.

crease. While it was true that neighborhoods experiencing the arrival of large numbers of blacks in cities like Chicago also saw the deterioration of these neighborhoods, the causes of such decline were not racial, Weaver argued, but economic. Blacks were moving into areas that were already "blighted." Because of discrimination and low incomes, blacks were forced to "double-up," increasing the number of people in an area. This decreased the incentive for owners and managers to maintain their properties, beginning a cycle of decline. This process was inevitable, as long as blacks were limited in their housing options. Weaver's work was an early example of the directed use of social science research, an approach that NAACP lawyers would turn to frequently over the next decade.[11]

In addition to the problems they created for blacks, restrictive covenants gave "a false sense of security," because they had not and could not prevent the expansion of blacks into new areas, Weaver argued. The housing needs of blacks were severe, and the housing market could (and did) profit from exploiting these needs. At the same time, new developments in other areas of the city would provide new opportunities for white families, who would depart, leaving vacancies that would be filled by blacks. Despite the efforts of whites to keep blacks out, Weaver argued, restrictive covenants would fail. Using Chicago as an example, Weaver stated that blacks were moving into several areas on the southside and west of the central business district that were formerly restricted to whites.[12]

Instead of racially-restrictive covenants, which would not work, Weaver asserted, property values could be maintained by other mechanisms. To overcome the fears of white homeowners that blacks would lessen property values, Weaver championed residential restrictions based not on race but on occupancy and maintenance requirements. Property owners would agree that their homes would be used only for single-family residence, and they would meet community standards similar to today's homeowner's associations. Weaver argued that if residents entered into such agreements, they would provide protection against decline in property values. "This would afford an opportunity for the Negro who has the means and the urge to live in a desirable neighborhood," and it would "prevent, or at least lessen the exodus of all whites upon the entrance of a few Negroes," Weaver claimed.[13] Weaver's work on restrictive covenants sought to open up opportunities to the growing black middle class, enabling them to find decent housing in new areas of

---

[11] Robert C. Weaver, *Race Restrictive Housing Covenants*, 20 J. Land & Public Utility Econ., 183, 183–93 (1944).

[12] *Id*. at 185–88.

[13] *Id*. at 191–92.

the city. If this movement could be achieved without "panic selling" by whites, Chicago neighborhoods would prove that racial integration could work. Throughout the three years of the *Shelley* litigation, Weaver was an active participant in the case, providing research to civil rights attorneys at the NAACP and across the country.

The NAACP Battle Against Restrictive Covenants

While Weaver and others worked to improve the quality of social science research on racial matters, they assisted the legal attacks on racial discrimination. Unlike other civil rights initiatives that were directed from the New York offices of the NAACP, the attack on restrictive covenants began at the local level. The availability of middle class clients with the means to hire a private lawyer distinguished the fight against covenants from many other aspects of civil rights litigation.[14] By 1945, however, there were so many lawsuits attacking covenants across the country that Thurgood Marshall and his associates at the national NAACP office decided to take a larger role in shaping the strategy. Marshall's involvement raised concerns from several attorneys who worried that the national office would sacrifice their individual clients in pursuit of broader goals. However, in general, the civil rights attorneys worked together, sharing information and coordinating litigation strategies. Their goal was a decision by the United States Supreme Court declaring such agreements unconstitutional.[15]

In July of 1945, Marshall called a meeting of the NAACP National Legal Committee and asked more than fifty attorneys and consultants to come to Chicago to discuss the pending restrictive covenants cases. Recognizing that lawyers in many cities were attacking such agreements, he argued that "the best possible chance of success ... would result form a pooling of our legal resources."[16] Marshall hoped that the group would discuss the different approaches to attacking covenants and develop a common strategy that would culminate in a favorable Supreme Court opinion. The illustrious group of the nation's leading civil rights lawyers, which included William Hastie, Loren Miller, and Charles Hamilton Houston, met in Robert Weaver's office for two days. There they received reports from several attorneys handling cases, heard an analysis from Weaver of the economic and social impact of restrictive covenants, and debated the appropriate steps to get the issue in front of

---

[14] For an analysis of this approach, see Preston H. Smith, *The Quest for Racial Democracy: Black Civic Ideology and Housing Interests in Postwar Chicago*, 26 J. Urb. Hist., 131, 131–57 (2000).

[15] Vose, *supra* note 2, at 62.

[16] Letter from Thurgood Marshall to National Legal Committee, June 13, 1945, NAACP Papers, Part 5, Reel 20.

the court. After the meeting, Marshall announced that the NAACP was undertaking a new legal assault on restrictive covenants.[17]

In a memo to the participants shortly after the conference, Weaver argued that the financial and social aspects of restrictive covenants should be emphasized both in the legal attack and the public relations effort that would complement the court battles. "The most immediate effect of restrictive covenants is psychological in that they give legal sanction, and consequently, respectability to all other instruments for effecting residential segregation," he claimed. "In the whole network of devices and practices for exclusion, the race restrictive housing covenants have gained currency as a respectable and legitimate device. This is a fiction that must be dissipated by sociological and legal attacks."[18] Weaver advised the lawyers to emphasize the economic impact of covenants as well as their effect on the exacerbation of social problems in black neighborhoods.

During 1946 and 1947, civil rights attorneys pursued dozens of cases against restrictive covenants in states across the nation. Though they frequently shared information, the attorneys handling the disputes adopted their own strategies, a fact that disturbed Thurgood Marshall, who worried that the attorneys would create trial records that would make appellate success more difficult. Although all the attorneys agreed that the larger goal was a decision by the U.S. Supreme Court that invalidated racially restrictive covenants under the Constitution, many of them also wanted their case to be the one taken to the high court. This created both competition and friction among the group and frustrated Marshall's effort to manage litigation strategy. At the same time, the competition also probably improved the quality of the arguments and briefs the attorneys produced.

The Public Campaign Against Restrictive Covenants

While organizing the legal attack, civil rights activists also undertook a national campaign to raise public awareness about the problems caused by restrictive covenants which echoed many of the arguments that had been made in Chicago. In September of 1945, the ACRR published a pamphlet, written by Weaver, entitled "Hemmed In: ABC's of Race Restrictive Housing Covenants," that the group distributed widely around the country. "Of all the instruments which effect residential segregation, race restrictive covenants are the most dangerous,"

[17] Tentative Agenda for Conference on Restrictive Covenants; NAACP Legal Meeting Maps Drive at Two–Day Conference, July 12, 1945, both in NAACP Papers, Part 5, Reel 20; *Race Pacts Don't Pay, Group Told*, CHI. DAILY NEWS, July 10, 1945.

[18] Preliminary Notes on Coordination of Legal and Social Attacks on Race Restrictive Covenants, no date, NAACP Papers, Part 5, Reel 20.

because they give the appearance of respectability to segregation, the pamphlet argued. Covenants were "most prevalent among the middle and upper-income groups," and as a result of their use, "other groups resort to less formal but equally effective means of keeping minorities out. As long as the 'better people' in a community sign restrictions against certain groups and the courts enforce such agreements, other elements will 'protect' their neighborhoods against minorities too" it claimed.[19]

The pamphlet also explained in simple terms the effect of covenants on housing overcrowding and neighborhood decline. Echoing Weaver's earlier arguments, it claimed that covenants could not truly prevent the expansion of minorities, but they controlled the movements of blacks in ways that exacerbated segregation and helped increase racial animosity in areas where blacks did move. Reminding readers of the wartime calls for racial harmony and presaging the arguments for racial tolerance in the Cold War, the pamphlet criticized covenants for fueling racial misunderstanding. "As long as a group is relegated and confined to a physically undesirable area (as any overcrowded neighborhood inevitably becomes), its occupants are all lumped together in the minds of people." Adopting Myrdal's approach, the pamphlet argued that with segregation, "intergroup contact [diminishes], prejudiced attitudes grow stronger, and segregation gains increasing popular acceptance." At the same time, the pamphlet claimed, covenants and segregation increased animosity towards whites among African Americans.[20]

Over the next year, the ACRR distributed thousands of copies of the publication to race relations groups and other liberal organizations. Weaver and other scholars wrote about the struggle against covenants in popular magazines such as *Survey Graphic*, in the NAACP journal, the *Crisis*, and in academic publications including the *Annals of the American Academy of Political and Social Science*. In all of these essays, activists argued that race restrictive covenants were both undemocratic and unworkable.[21]

While the legal cases were winding through the courts and civil rights organizations were promoting public awareness, the attack on covenants received a major boost from President Truman's Committee on Civil Rights. Organized in 1946 in response to a wave of violence against African Americans, the group, led by the nation's business and

[19] Robert Weaver, Hemmed In: ABC's of Race Restrictive Housing Covenants, ACRR News Letter (Chicago, Ill.), 1945, at 3–8.

[20] *Id.* at 8–11.

[21] Robert C. Weaver, *Chicago: A City of Covenants*, THE CRISIS, Mar., 1946, at 75–78, 93; Robert C. Weaver, *Housing in a Democracy*, ANNALS AM. ACAD. POL. & SOC. SCI., Mar. 1946, at 95, 95–105.

civic leaders, held a series of hearings across the country to study American race relations. In 1947, the group released its report. Entitled "To Secure These Rights," it was the strongest denunciation of discrimination and prejudice in America ever sponsored by a government agency. African Americans, the report argued, had been systematically denied the four rights to which every American was entitled; safety and security, full citizenship, freedom of conscience and equality of opportunity. Because states and local government had failed to protect these rights, the report asserted, it was the federal government's responsibility to do so. The Committee recommended, among other things, the expansion of the civil rights section in the Justice Department and the creation of an office in the FBI to investigate and prosecute violations, the creation of a permanent Commission on Civil Rights, increased penalties for violations of civil rights, federal legislation against lynching, abolition of the poll tax and other restrictions on the vote, the end to discrimination and segregation in the military, the prohibition of restrictive covenants, and the creation of a permanent Fair Employment Practice Committee.[22]

Southern politicians and newspapers attacked the report, but it received a very positive response from northern business and political leaders and from civil rights activists. The *Pittsburgh Courier* called it a "courageous document" and compared it to the Magna Charta. NAACP executive secretary Walter White called it the "most uncompromising and specific pronouncement" ever issued by a government agency. Several organizations, including the NAACP, the American Jewish Congress, and the ACRR initiated campaigns to distribute the report to the public, and several newspapers serialized it or circulated it with their publications. Over the decade that followed, civil rights leaders referred frequently to the report when pressing claims for equal treatment.[23]

Shelley, Sipes, Hurd, and Uriculo

The public campaign against restrictive covenants was crucial to the success of the legal assault because the precedents were tilted against civil rights advocates. It was the President's Civil Rights Committee in particular, however, that focused attention to the battle against restrictive covenants at a particularly fortuitous moment. Just months before the release of the report, the U.S. Supreme Court agreed to consider four cases attacking the constitutionality of these agreements, *Shelley v. Kraemer, Sipes v. McGhee, Uriculo v. Hodge,* and *Hurd v. Hodge.* The

---

[22] PRESIDENT'S COMMITTEE ON CIVIL RIGHTS, TO SECURE THESE RIGHTS, (1947); DONALD MCCOY & RICHARD RUETTEN, QUEST AND RESPONSE: MINORITY RIGHTS AND THE TRUMAN ADMINISTRATION 82–92 (1973); SOUTHERN, *supra* note 1, at 113–15.

[23] MCCOY & RUETTEN, *supra* note 22, at 92; *Certain to Become Major Campaign Issue in 1948,* PITT. COURIER, November 8, 1947; *Washington Notebook,* PITT. COURIER, November 8, 1947.

Shelley case arose out of a Missouri dispute between J.D. and Ethel Shelley and members of the Marcus Avenue Improvement Association. In 1945, the Shelleys, a black couple, signed an agreement to purchase a house at 4600 Labadie Avenue in St. Louis from Louis and Fern Kraemer. The home was subject to an agreement, created in 1911, that barred the use of the property by "any person not of the Caucasian race." The original agreement had been signed by thirty of the thirty property owners in the area, but there were five African American homeowners in the area when the covenant was created.[24]

Although the Shelleys and the Kraemers denied knowledge of the covenant, several other homeowners brought suit, demanding that their agreement be rescinded. At trial, the Shelleys, represented by attorney George Vaughn, attacked both the validity of the covenant and the policy behind restrictive covenants. Vaughn argued that the agreement violated several aspects of covenant law, particularly the requirement of "horizontal privity," and he succeeded in convincing a local judge that the restriction was invalid. The Missouri Supreme Court, however, reversed the decision and issued an injunction ordering the Shelleys to vacate the premises. In 1947, the Shelleys appealed to the U.S. Supreme Court.[25]

The Michigan case, *Sipes v. McGhee*, also commenced in 1945. White Detroit property owners brought the case against Orsel and Minnie McGhee to oust them from the house they had bought from Benjamin and Anna Sipes at 4626 Seebaldt Avenue. The plaintiffs argued that a restrictive covenant signed by neighboring property owners limited occupancy to "Caucasians," and they asked a district court to issue an injunction. Like parties in other suits, the McGhees made a wide variety of allegations, contesting the fact that they were "Negro," arguing that the covenant had not been properly created, and attacking the constitutionality of such agreements as well as the policy behind them. The trial court, however, rejected all of these arguments and awarded an injunction to the plaintiffs. The Michigan Supreme Court upheld the decision and the McGhees appealed.[26]

At the same time attorneys across the nation were attacking restrictive covenants, Charles Hamilton Houston was working on several cases in the District of Columbia. One of them involved James Hurd, who in 1944 purchased a house at 116 Bryant Street in the North Capitol area. Hurd had purchased the house from Raphael Uriculo, a white realtor who had been involved in the transfer of many homes in areas with restrictive covenants from whites to blacks. Because of the great demand

---

[24] Vose, *supra* note 2, at 109–13.

[25] *Id.* at 109–21, 83; Shelley v. Kraemer, 334 U.S. 1 (1948).

[26] Vose, *supra* note 2, at 125–36.

among well-to-do blacks for decent housing, and despite the Washington Real Estate Board's termination of his membership for violating their code of ethics, Uriculo had done quite well financially, and he joined the suit to protect his business. Both Hurd and Uriculo were sued by Frederic and Lena Hodge, white residents of the area, and Houston agreed to represent both defendants. At trial, Hodge, testified that she would prefer an "untidy white person to a Negro, no matter how educated or cultured." Houston attacked the validity of the covenant, argued that Hurd was in fact "American Indian," introduced testimony arguing that racial characteristics were impossible to prove, and presented studies (prepared by Weaver and Howard sociologist E. Franklin Frazier) showing the negative impact of restrictive covenants on the housing opportunities of black D.C. residents.[27]

The evidence was not enough to convince the district judge, who upheld the covenants and declared the transfers void. Houston appealed, and the U.S. Court of Appeals affirmed the decisions in *Hurd v. Hodge* and *Uriculo v. Hodge* by a vote of two to one, arguing that the court had consistently approved such agreements for over twenty-five years. Judge Harry Edgerton dissented from the opinion. Edgerton, who had also dissented from a 1945 decision, *Mays v. Burgess*, upholding a restrictive covenant, relied heavily on the sociological and economic literature presented by Houston, and he cited *An American Dilemma* and Weaver's articles in the footnotes. "Negroes have a constitutional right to buy and use" property, he argued. Judicial enforcement of restrictive covenants, he claimed, violated the Civil Rights Act of 1866, because the government was taking action that infringed upon the rights of a racial minority. He further claimed that restrictive covenants were bad policy because they increased racial animosities. The judge was alone in his view at the time, but he would soon be joined by other jurists.[28]

In June of 1947, the Supreme Court agreed to hear arguments in the *Shelley* and *Sipes* cases, and in October, it granted certiorari in the *Hurd* and *Uricolo* cases. Because most of the existing law was against them, Marshall, Houston and the other attorneys agreed that they would have to base their arguments on policy—restrictive covenants had a negative impact on society and therefore should not be favored. The attack, argued Justice Department attorney Phineas Indritz, who aided Houston in preparing his briefs, "must be supported by a full sociological presentation. Legal arguments, standing alone, may find a less fertile

[27] Hurd v. Hodge, 334 U.S. 24, 27 (1948); VOSE, *supra* note 2, at 74–95; GENNA RAE MCNEIL, GROUNDWORK: CHARLES HAMILTON HOUSTON AND THE STRUGGLE FOR CIVIL RIGHTS 178–79 (1983).

[28] Hurd v. Hodge, 162 F.2d 233, 238, 243 (D.C. Cir. 1947); VOSE, *supra* note 2, at 95–99; SOUTHERN, *supra* note 1, at 132–33; MCNEIL, *supra* note 27, at 178–79.

field for acceptance in this controversy which has so frequently been dominated by unspoken emotional preconceptions and misconceptions."[29]

To aid the attorneys, Weaver and Wirth agreed to coordinate the production of a memorandum on the "economic and social aspects of race restrictive covenants" that would also describe the existing literature on the topic. They were assisted by Charles S. Johnson and Herman Long, Fisk University sociologists who had also written on the topic.[30] Although the participation of the social scientists in a Supreme Court case was not novel, the extent of their involvement was significant and provided an early experiment in the socio-legal analysis that would prove crucial to civil rights cases over the next two decades (most famously in *Brown v. Board of Education*). According to historian Clement Vose, it was "the first time that such a substantial amount of factual data was presented to the Supreme Court in civil rights cases."[31] Although aspects of the research appeared in several of the briefs filed with the court, Houston made the research the centerpiece of his argument. The economic and social analysis written by Weaver and Wirth took up fully one-third of Houston's 150–page submission. The introduction to their section stated that covenants had "drastically curtailed the ability of Negroes to secure adequate housing," were "a major contributor to the enormous overcrowding" that blacks endured, and were a direct cause of increases in "disease, death, crime, immorality, juvenile delinquency, racial tensions and economic exploitation." Furthermore, the brief claimed, there was no evidence that the entrance of blacks into an area resulted in a decline in property values. Relying in large part on Weaver's research and providing a comprehensive assessment of research in the area, the brief laid out in detail the economic and social consequences of restrictive covenants.[32]

With the policy analysis as the foundation of their arguments, civil rights lawyers attacked judicial enforcement of restrictive covenants. In their briefs and at oral argument, the petitioners in the state cases claimed that enforcement of restrictive covenants violated the Fourteenth Amendment and federal law. They also pointed to the negative

---

[29] Minutes of Meeting N.A.A.C.P. Lawyers and Consultants on Methods of Attacking Restrictive Covenants, September 6, 1947; Letter from Phineas Indritz to Charles Abrams, August 14, 1947, both in NAACP Papers, Part 5, Reel 22.

[30] Letter from Louis Wirth to Walter White, April 15, 1947, NAACP Papers, Part 5, Reel 20; Memorandum of Conference with Charles Houston from Marian Wynn Perry, September 11, 1947, NAACP Papers, Part 5, Reel 22; VOSE, *supra* note 2, at 159–62.

[31] VOSE, *supra* note 2, at 163.

[32] Consolidated Brief for Plaintiffs at 40, 73, Hurd v. Hodge, 334 U.S. 24 (1947) ("Consolidated Brief for Plaintiffs"). On the use of sociological analysis in the NAACP legal assault on Jim Crow, see MARK TUSHNET, MAKING CIVIL RIGHTS LAW: THURGOOD MARSHALL AND THE SUPREME COURT, 1936–1961 (1994).

consequences of restrictive covenants in forcing African Americans to live in overcrowded areas of St. Louis and Detroit. The *Sipes* brief ended by calling the case "a test as to whether we will have a united nation or a country divided into areas and ghettoes solely on racial or religious lines."[33]

At oral argument Houston, who presented the *Hurd* and *Uricolo* cases, claimed that the enforcement of restrictive covenants violated federal law and the due process clause of the Fifth Amendment to the U.S. Constitution. In addition, Houston claimed, the case had significant international ramifications, because restrictive covenants were an example of the failure of the United States to live up to the promises of equality under the law. These obstacles to racial mobility created "a divisive, caste society" that was "a direct danger to our national unity," Houston claimed, and they were morally wrong.[34]

The attorneys defending the enforcement of restrictive covenants were confident with the precedents behind them, and they presented briefs that were much shorter than those of the petitioners. The attorneys argued that the restrictive covenants were allowed under existing law in every state, and they claimed that private agreements were necessary to protect the property rights of the owners. The appellees were joined by several homeowners associations and the National Association of Real Estate Boards, which filed briefs in support of the decisions upholding covenants.[35]

The increase in national attention to civil rights issues brought about by the Truman Civil Rights Committee resulted in unprecedented support for the attack on restrictive covenants. More than twenty organizations, including the American Civil Liberties Union, the American Jewish Committee, the CIO and the National Bar Association, filed amicus briefs during the fall of 1947 asking the court to repudiate the enforcement of restrictive covenants. As further (albeit limited) evidence of the changing tone of the nation's racial debate, these groups were joined by the federal government. Just weeks after the President's Civil Rights Committee released its report, the Justice Department agreed to file a brief supporting the petitioners. In it, Solicitor General Philip Perlman argued that restrictive covenants "cannot be reconciled with the spirit of mutual tolerance and respect for the dignity and rights of the individual which give vitality to our democratic way of life."[36]

---

[33] VOSE, *supra* note 2, at 185–86.

[34] MCNEIL, *supra* note 27, at 181; VOSE, *supra* note 2, at 184–90. Consolidated Brief for Plaintiffs, *supra* note 32, at 90.

[35] VOSE, *supra* note 2, at 197–99.

[36] *Id.* at 163–64, 191–97; SOUTHERN, *supra* note 1, at 134–35; MCNEIL, *supra* note 27, at 181–82.

Shelley and "State Action"

Although the weight of submissions opposing restrictive covenants greatly surpassed those in favor, the outcome of the case was far from certain. The prevalence of such agreements was starkly revealed when three Supreme Court justices (Stanley Reed, Wiley Rutledge and Robert Jackson) all had to recuse themselves, because they owned property that was subject to restrictive covenants. The remaining six justices, however, voted unanimously in favor of the petitioners, marking a major victory for civil rights. Acknowledging that restrictive covenants themselves could not be "regarded as a violation of any rights guaranteed to petitioners by the Fourteenth Amendment," the court declared, in *Shelley v. Kraemer*, that judicial enforcement of such agreements constituted "state action" in violation of the United States Constitution.[37]

The role of the state in enforcing the covenants was crucial to the outcome of the case. In 1883, the Court had ruled, in the *Civil Rights Cases*, that racial discrimination by private parties did not violate the Fourteenth Amendment. This decision, which invalidated large parts of the federal civil rights laws passed during Reconstruction, removed from judicial oversight a significant portion of the discrimination that burdened African Americans. For example, discrimination in theaters, hotels, and restaurants was considered (until the passage of the Civil Rights Act of 1964) "private action" not subject to legal attack. Many proponents of restrictive covenants argued that they were private arrangements not subject to the Fourteenth Amendment. However, the Court had held in prior cases that when the government acted, it must do so in a non-discriminatory manner.[38] Applying these principles to the restrictive covenant cases, the Court declared, since there were willing buyers and sellers, it was "clear that but for the active intervention of the state courts ... petitioners would have been free to occupy the properties in question without restraint." Because it amounted to state action in the promotion of racial discrimination, judicial enforcement of such agreements was illegal.[39]

It is important to understand what the Court did not hold. It did not say that restrictive covenants, in and of themselves, were illegal. The opinion only declared that it was unconstitutional for courts or other government actors to enforce them. Such covenants continued in widespread use for several decades, and they severely limited housing opportunities for African Americans and other minorities. The *Shelley* ruling helped home seekers when there was a willing white seller, but it had no

---

[37] Shelley v. Kraemer, 334 U.S. 1 (1948).

[38] *See, e.g.*, Strauder v. West Virginia, 100 U.S. 303 (1880).

[39] Shelley v. Kraemer, 334 U.S. at 19.

impact on those sellers who did not want to violate the racial restrictions that bound their property and therefore refused to enter into agreements with blacks.

In a brief opinion, the court also held, unanimously, in *Hurd v. Hodge*, that the Civil Rights Act of 1866 prohibited enforcement of restrictive covenants in the District of Columbia. Neither opinion cited to the voluminous social science literature produced by Weaver and his colleagues and used in many of the briefs. The judges relied on the argument that judicial enforcement of restrictive covenants constituted government action in violation of the law. But there was little question from the participants and analysts of the cases that the sociological arguments played a crucial role in the outcome. The underlying basis for the conclusion that the state could not enforce restrictive covenants was a policy evaluation of the efficacy of such agreements. Restrictive covenants were, as the empirical data showed, a major problem for African Americans. The constitution forbade government support for activities that resulted in racial discrimination. Therefore, state enforcement of such agreements was unconstitutional.[40]

Civil rights groups responded to the decision with jubilation. "Live Anywhere" proclaimed the headline of the *Pittsburgh Courier*. "The ruling by the court gives thousands of prospective homebuyers throughout the United States new courage and hope in the American form of government," an NAACP release proclaimed. The *Chicago Defender,* in an editorial entitled "Let Democracy Flourish," declared that the decision had "ushered in a new era of racial relationships in Chicago and the nation." The *New Republic* declared the decision "a reaffirmation of the basic principle that the law can't be used as a weapon to deprive Americans, regardless of their color, creed or social condition, of equality of opportunity." At the same time, many civil rights leaders realized that the opinion was not going to have an immediate effect on the lives of most people. Loren Miller stated that it would be "folly to expect an overnight reversal of attitudes," and Walter White reminded blacks that real estate boards, neighborhood associations and other private groups remained strong enemies.[41]

Restrictive Covenants
and the Long Struggle for Civil Rights

Like many other decisions in the civil rights area, the Supreme Court opinions, rather than resolving a complex racial issue, opened up a

---

[40] Hurd v. Hodge, 334 U.S. 24, 34 (1948); *Fights Realty Covenants*, N.Y. TIMES, Dec. 15, 1947; *Clark Condemns Race Property Ban*, N.Y. TIMES, Dec. 6, 1947.

[41] NAACP Release, May 3, 1948, NAACP Papers, Part 5, Reel 22; *Live Anywhere*, PITT. COURIER, May 8, 1948; *Let Democracy Flourish*, CHI. DEFENDER, May 8, 1948; VOSE, *supra* note 2, at 212–14.

discussion that continues today. Several legal scholars critiqued the Court's approach, arguing that the justices extended the "state action" framework further than was appropriate. While the court's legal reasoning may have been radical, the actual impact of the decision was much less so. *Shelley*'s explicit condoning of restrictive covenants ensured their continuation. Even the federal government's implementation of the ruling was painfully slow. In the aftermath of the *Shelley* decision, civil rights advocates believed that a window of opportunity had opened to push federal officials, particularly those at the Federal Housing Agency, toward equal treatment. However, although small changes did occur in the years after *Shelley*, for the most part federal officials continued to sanction and support housing discrimination in suburban housing, public housing and the urban renewal program. The decisions made by federal housing officials in these years, the beginning of the suburban boom, exacerbated the racial segregation and placed additional obstacles to the fair housing laws later enacted.[42]

At the same time, witnessing the declining effectiveness of legal maneuvers to maintain racial barriers, some communities resorted to more violent responses to integration. In Chicago, despite the efforts of government and private organizations to stem the conflicts, there were dozens of attacks by whites on black newcomers in the late 1940s. Such violent responses were the norm in many communities for the next two decades. These incidents, like those across the country, tempered the victory in *Shelley*. Changing the law was one thing. Changing society was another.[43]

Shelley, the violent reaction of many white neighborhoods, and the government's tepid response, however, spurred greater activism in the area of housing discrimination, resulting in the creation of what today is known as the "fair housing" movement. Led by, among others, future HUD Secretary Robert Weaver, lawyer and housing activist Charles Abrams, and future New York Judge Hortense Gable, advocates argued that housing discrimination was bad law and bad policy. Unable to secure federal statutory or constitutional law against covenants and other forms of discrimination, activists focused their efforts on states and localities and built fair housing law brick by brick, beginning with laws preventing discrimination in public housing and working to expand the scope of fair housing to the private market.

---

[42] Arnold Hirsch, *Choosing Segregation: Federal Housing Policy Between* Shelley *and* Brown, *in* FROM TENEMENTS TO TAYLOR HOMES 206, 206–26 (John F. Bauman et al. eds., 2000).

[43] On racial violence in changing neighborhoods, see STEPHEN GRANT MEYER, AS LONG AS THE DON'T MOVE NEXT DOOR: SEGREGATION AND RACIAL CONFLICT IN AMERICAN NEIGHBORHOODS (2000).

By the early 1960s, fair housing advocates had made significant progress in winning the ideological debate between advocates for racial restrictions, who argued that property owners should have the right to refuse to sell if they chose, and minorities who demanded equal treatment. During his 1960 campaign, candidate John F. Kennedy stated that he would erase federal housing discrimination "with the stroke of a pen," by signing an Executive Order if elected. While Kennedy delayed after being elected and issued only a limited directive, by the early 1960s those who maintained that housing discrimination was legally permissible were on the defensive. States and cities across the country witnessed grassroots movements against housing discrimination during the 1960s, and these efforts culminated in the passage of the Fair Housing Act in 1968. That same year, in *Jones v. Alfred H. Mayer Co.*, the United States Supreme Court relying on the Civil Rights Act of 1866, declared that restrictive covenants violated federal law.[44]

Though racial segregation remains a persistent fact of American life, the *Shelley* case contributed greatly to the advancement of civil rights encouraging the efforts of activists fighting racial discrimination. The litigation strategy pursued by the lawyers in the battle against restrictive covenants also served as a model for other efforts in the areas of education and employment discrimination.

---

[44] Jones v. Alfred Mayer Co., 392 U.S. 409 (1968).

2

Risa L. Goluboff*

Brown v. Board of Education and The Lost Promise of Civil Rights

On May 17, 1954, Chief Justice Earl Warren shrugged on his long, black robe and took his place at the center of the Supreme Court dais. Appointed just seven months earlier by Republican Dwight D. Eisenhower, Warren was about to disappoint his president, incite a considerable portion of the nation to violence, and validate the claims of a racial minority who had worked hard and waited long to hear what he had to say. In *Brown v. Board of Education* and the cases from South Carolina, Virginia, and Delaware the Court had consolidated with it, Warren announced for a unanimous Court that "[s]eparate educational facilities are inherently unequal." As a result, he concluded, the African American children who attended such facilities had been "deprived of the equal protection of the laws guaranteed by the Fourteenth Amendment."[1]

It was a momentous day in the nation's capital. With banner headlines, newspapers announced the end of segregated education and, with it, the end of an era. The new era *Brown* initiated was one of upheaval and change, though not always in predictable directions. The Court's decision in *Brown* led to a modicum of desegregation of public schools in the South, especially in border states that had already begun moving slowly toward desegregation before 1954. *Brown* inspired hope among African Americans who had long resisted Jim Crow. It simultaneously radicalized southern whites to resist (sometimes violently) the

* This chapter draws on and portions are reprinted with permission from THE LOST PROMISE OF CIVIL RIGHTS, RISA L. GOLUBOFF. Copyright © 2007 Harvard University Press, Cambridge, Massachusetts. She thanks Rich Schragger and Myriam Gilles.

[1] 347 U.S. 483, 494–495 (1954).

changes the Supreme Court's decision set in motion. And it galvanized Congress to pass the first national civil rights legislation since 1875.[2]

The era *Brown* ended was not only the era of judicially legitimated segregation, however. It was also an era in which African Americans and their lawyers had experimented with a variety of legal challenges to Jim Crow, only a small portion of which the lawyers in the National Association for the Advancement of Colored People (NAACP) presented to the Supreme Court in *Brown*. The NAACP's victory in *Brown* thus changed not only the legitimacy of segregated education but also the overall scope of civil rights lawyering and the constitutional imagination.

In order to appreciate the magnitude of this transformation, it is necessary to step back and attempt to see the world of civil rights from the perspective of the pre-*Brown* era. Looking back from *Brown* and its aftermath, legal scholars and historians have often charted a path of civil rights that led directly to *Brown*, in which the form of civil rights *Brown* embraced and projected was natural and inevitable. The usual story about *Brown* has thus frequently assumed that civil rights always took as its centerpiece a challenge to the psychological injuries caused by legally segregated education—so-called stigmatic harms—under the equal protection clause of the Fourteenth Amendment.[3]

Looking forward from the years before *Brown*, by contrast, reveals the interstices and contingencies of *Brown*. Because legal doctrine was deeply unsettled at the time, and because the seventy-five-year-old racial and economic caste system civil rights lawyers sought to challenge was so intricate, lawyers in the 1940s pursued a diverse set of civil rights cases. They challenged economic inequalities as well as stigmatic harms, challenged the private components of Jim Crow as well as the public ones, and used a variety of constitutional, statutory, and common law resources to do so. There was neither a single essence of Jim Crow's harm nor a single legal basis for redressing it.

As lawyers in the NAACP clarified their litigation strategy in the years before *Brown*, they focused on certain doctrinal opportunities rather than others. Specifically, the economic harms and related rights of the 1940s disappeared from the case. Thus, contrary to the conventional wisdom, the decision to attack formal legal segregation in edu-

---

[2] *See, e.g.*, Editorial, *Equal Education for All*, Wash. Post, May 19, 1954, at 14. *See also* Michael J. Klarman, From Jim Crow to Civil Rights: The Supreme Court and the Struggle for Racial Equality 344–363 (2004).

[3] *See, e.g.*, Richard Kluger, Simple Justice: The History of Brown v. Board of Education and Black America's Struggle for Equality (1977); Mark V. Tushnet, The NAACP's Legal Strategy Against Segregated Education, 1925–1950 (1987); Mark V. Tushnet, Making Civil Rights Law: Thurgood Marshall and the Supreme Court, 1936–1961 (1994); Peter H. Irons, Jim Crow's Children (2002).

cation under the equal protection clause was just that—a conscious choice by historically situated actors to follow one strand of potential civil rights rather than others. Viewing it as such reveals not only the major success *Brown* achieved but also the elements of Jim Crow it left very much intact.

* * *

The story of *Brown* begins with the rise of the racial caste system the case was meant to dismantle. From the vantage point of the post-*Brown* era, Jim Crow has come to refer to the legal segregation of African Americans. But such a definition is partial and inadequate. A more complete description must look to the roots of Jim Crow in the aftermath of slavery. For many southern whites, the abolition of slavery following the Civil War had spawned two related problems: a race problem and a labor problem. How, they asked themselves, would they prevent the newly freed African Americans from contaminating the white race and debasing white politics? And how would they find a replacement for the cheap labor black slaves had previously provided and on which the southern economy was largely based?

The answer to both questions was the complex of laws and customs that arose in the late nineteenth century and eventually came to be called Jim Crow. When southern states managed through both violence and legal chicanery to nullify the vote blacks had so recently won, they made it possible to inscribe Jim Crow into legal and political structures for generations. When railroads decided to segregate their railroad cars and local school boards decided to allocate fewer tax dollars to black schools than to white ones, they helped create Jim Crow. When white planters preferred black to white farm hands and tenants because they could get more work out of black workers for less pay, they drew on and reinforced Jim Crow. When unions excluded black workers and companies refused to hire them, they perpetuated Jim Crow. When the Ku Klux Klan, often with the acquiescence and participation of local law enforcement, lynched black men and women, they enforced Jim Crow. Jim Crow existed because every day, in ways momentous and quotidian, governments, private institutions, and millions of individuals made decisions about hiring, firing, consuming, recreating, governing, educating, and serving that kept blacks out, down, and under.[4]

---

[4] In viewing Jim Crow as both a racial and an economic system, I draw on ROBERT RODGERS KORSTAD, CIVIL RIGHTS UNIONISM: TOBACCO WORKERS AND THE STRUGGLE FOR DEMOCRACY IN THE MID-TWENTIETH-CENTURY SOUTH (2003); ERIC ARNESEN, BROTHERHOODS OF COLOR: BLACK RAILROAD WORKERS AND THE STRUGGLE FOR EQUALITY 101 (2001); Thomas J. Sugrue, *Affirmative Action from Below: Civil Rights, the Building Trades, and the Politics of Racial Equality in the Urban North, 1945–1969*, 91 J. AM. HIST. 145 (2004).

Outside the South, African Americans could usually vote, and social isolation and terror were less ubiquitous. But Jim Crow as a system of economic exploitation, if not complete segregation and political exclusion, was very much in evidence across the country during the latter part of the nineteenth century and the first half of the twentieth. For black workers trying to make a living, Jim Crow North and South meant job announcements addressed specifically to white or "colored" workers. It meant whole swaths of industry, whole sectors of the workplace were off limits. It meant inadequate schooling, inaccessible labor unions, and unavailable government benefits. Black workers usually performed the worst work for the lowest pay. They could not eat in lunchrooms or use bathrooms on site. They worked in segregated gangs and were forced to join segregated unions or found themselves excluded from unions altogether. They had limited, and usually segregated, access to tolerable housing and other services.

Jim Crow, then, understood from the point of view of poor and working African Americans in the pre-*Brown* era, comprised a system of both racial oppression and economic exploitation. It was not simply that Jim Crow legally prevented those who could afford to eat at restaurants or stay at hotels from doing so. It was also that Jim Crow—maintained by both legal and extralegal force and coercion—structured the entire economic, political, and social world in which African Americans worked and lived.

* * *

Those who hoped to question the constitutionality of this multifaceted system faced quite a challenge. On paper, the task did not look that hard. After all, in the wake of the Civil War, the nation had ratified three new amendments to the United States Constitution, all intended to safeguard African American rights. The Thirteenth Amendment prohibited slavery and involuntary servitude. The Fourteenth Amendment guaranteed due process of law and the equal protection of the laws. And the Fifteenth Amendment protected the voting rights of African American men.

In the late nineteenth century, however, just as Jim Crow was gaining ground, the Supreme Court largely undermined the power of these amendments to protect African Americans. In two cases in particular, the Court gutted the Fourteenth Amendment's equal protection clause. In the 1883 *Civil Rights Cases*, the Court concluded that the amendment only protected against rights violations committed by governments, not those committed by private actors. And in the 1896 case of *Plessy v. Ferguson*, it upheld a state law requiring equal but separate accommodations on railroads. From then on, it would be difficult to challenge the extra-legal (often economic) harms of Jim Crow, and the best one could hope for regarding the state-mandated aspects of the system was that separate would really be equal.[5]

At the same time the Court largely forsook the rights of African Americans, in cases like *Lochner v. New York* it began to interpret the due process clauses of the Fifth and Fourteenth Amendments to protect the rights of all individuals to make and enforce contracts, the right to property, and the right to pursue one's livelihood and obtain the fruits of one's labor. African Americans' enjoyment of contract and property rights had been central to Reconstruction-era ideas of civil rights, but during the *Lochner* era, the Court largely divorced the due-process-based rights it would protect from those of African Americans.[6]

Even as the rights of African Americans continued to languish in the courts during the Depression decade of the 1930s, the Court began to dethrone the right to contract. It upheld New Deal and other legislative interference in the economy that it had previously viewed as violations of due process rights. In the aftermath of this constitutional revolution, legal professionals disagreed about what civil rights were, where in the Constitution courts could find authority to protect them, who exactly should provide that protection, and how they should do so.[7]

One particular category of rights did seem poised to serve as a replacement for *Lochner* rights in the late 1930s, but it was not the rights of African Americans. The political concerns of the Depression made workers' collective rights to organize into unions, bargain, and strike appear paramount. These rights were also a crucial component of the larger set of rights to economic security—to minimum subsistence, unemployment insurance, old age assistance, housing, and education— that the New Deal aspired to provide. No single doctrinal approach to civil rights was yet entrenched, but the collective rights of workers appeared the most likely to replace the *Lochner*ian right to contract within dominant legal discourse.

With the onset of World War II, however, black civil rights gained greater salience, both in mainstream political discourse and among legal professionals. The mobilizing war economy drew African Americans out of the South into northern and western regions where they could vote. As they turned increasingly to the Democratic Party, their support became critical to its success. In unions, the military, organizations like

---

[5] 109 U.S. 3 (1883); 163 U.S. 537 (1896).

[6] 198 U.S. 45 (1905). *See* ERIC FONER, FREE SOIL, FREE LABOR, FREE MEN: THE IDEOLOGY OF THE REPUBLICAN PARTY BEFORE THE CIVIL WAR 11–51 (1970); Civil Rights Act of 1866, ch. 31, 14 Stat. 27 (1866). For the argument that African Americans benefited from the Court's protection of contract and property rights, see DAVID BERNSTEIN, ONLY ONE PLACE OF REDRESS (2001).

[7] *See, e.g.*, BARRY CUSHMAN, RETHINKING THE NEW DEAL COURT (1998).

the NAACP, and outspoken black newspapers, African Americans pro-tested American segregation, discrimination, and inequality. Even those who lacked such organizational support protested on a more individual level—on streetcars in the South, in relationships with employers, and by calling on the federal government to vindicate their rights.

Black activists protested most vociferously about—and saw the most success with—civil rights issues that combined claims to racial equality with still-robust claims of New Deal labor and economic rights. In particular, the attempts of black workers to build on the labor and economic rights of the New Deal represented the most politically promising civil rights issues of the 1940s. Even as the Cold War chilled in the late 1940s and early 1950s, the economic claims of African Americans remained a key civil rights issue in national politics.

* * *

Within this changing legal and political environment, the question for lawyers was how to construct a new civil rights law with the materials at hand. As the conventional wisdom would have it, that process was an arduous one only because lawyers had to convince courts to accept their arguments. On this conventional account, the lawyers knew their goal (the destruction of state-mandated segregation, especially in education) and they knew their constitutional argument (that such segregation violated the equal protection clause of the Fourteenth Amendment). In other words, the story goes, *Plessy* was the obvious and abiding target of their efforts.

In reality, two of the most significant legal actors in the civil rights arena pursued cases that reflected considerable heterogeneity in the goals of civil rights, the role of the government in redressing civil rights violations, and the constitutional bases for bringing challenges to Jim Crow. The lawyers in the Civil Rights Section (CRS) of the Department of Justice (DOJ) and the NAACP viewed themselves as essentially and fundamentally constructing a new legal and constitutional framework for American civil rights in the 1940s. Despite that shared mission, the lawyers' disparate strategies, and the implications of those strategies for the civil rights that eventually emerged, suggest an implicit confrontation between (at least) two contending views. When the CRS lawyers used the Thirteenth Amendment and advocated on behalf of African American agricultural and domestic workers, and the NAACP pursued the cases of black industrial workers under both the equal protection clause and the due process clause, a diversity of approaches to that new civil rights, rather than a singularly of purpose, was the order of the day.

As a threshold matter, civil rights lawyers in the 1940s challenged just about every aspect of Jim Crow. They brought cases attacking police brutality, lynching, and voting discrimination, as well as segregation in education, transportation, and housing. The emblematic civil rights claims of the time, however, were the economic complaints of black workers rather than complaints about segregated education. Significantly, black support for desegregated primary education was fairly weak before *Brown*, and white opposition to such desegregation passionate and unyielding. In contrast, African Americans felt more ardently (and whites less so) about black economic advancement. Moreover, the claims of black workers drew on the prominence of labor and economic rights in general. Indeed, during WWII, Thurgood Marshall identified employment discrimination as one of the two most significant problems facing African Americans. (The other was the right to vote.) "When those problems are solved," he predicted, "other questions will settle themselves."[8]

In part because of the centrality of workers and their labor-related claims to pre-*Brown* civil rights cases, lawyers sought to redress a diversity of injuries under Jim Crow. The industrial workers who complained to the NAACP described the stigmatic harm of formal segregation—the degradations of exclusion, the failure of dignity that resulted from inhumane treatment. But they more often emphasized the economic harms that segregation entailed: less work, worse work, inadequate salaries, and economic insecurity and lack of advancement. The NAACP's labor cases had attempted to redress both parts of the workers' claims. Although the NAACP lawyers never approved of segregation, they nonetheless celebrated when their litigation efforts produced more and better jobs without achieving actual desegregation.

The Civil Rights Section's Thirteenth Amendment practice focused even more directly on material harms. The agricultural and domestic workers who came to the attention of the federal government complained about harms to their dignity. But for the most part their material needs were more urgent. They worked "long, hard hours" for little or no pay; they lacked adequate food, shelter, or clothing; and they lacked the ability to leave such conditions. The first task of the CRS, then, was to free these workers from their servitude, to open up labor markets and provide government protection.[9]

In part because of this focus on the material inequalities African American workers faced, the lawyers in the CRS and the NAACP

[8] *See, e.g.,* GUNNAR MYRDAL, AN AMERICAN DILEMMA: THE NEGRO PROBLEM AND MODERN DEMOCRACY 61 (1944); *America on Guard*, KSFO (radio), Nov. 27, 1943, transcript, 9–10, 10, *in Papers of the NAACP*, microfilm, pt. 13C, rl. 1:55–64, 63–64 (August Meier ed., 1982) (hereafter cited as *NAACP Papers*); Thurgood Marshall to Noah W. Griffin, May 9, 1946, *in NAACP Papers*, pt. 13C, rl. 1:492–493, 492.

[9] Affidavit of Elizabeth Coker, Jan. 30, 1947, *in NAACP Papers*, pt. 13C, rl. 12:390–391, 391.

attempted to challenge both the public and the private components of
Jim Crow. They brought cases against governmental actors as well as
against the private individuals and entities that prevented black workers
from attaining economic freedom and advancement. In particular, the
complaints farmworkers presented to the Civil Rights Section highlighted how difficult it was to disaggregate private from public harm. When a
planter apprehended an "escaped" worker, brought him before a court,
obtained a conviction, brought him back to work on his plantation, and
kept him there through violence and threats of imprisonment, the line
between public power and private—between the state's contributions to
Jim Crow and the individual's—blurred to the point of extinction.
Because the Thirteenth Amendment prohibited slavery and involuntary
servitude wholesale, and not only against government action, that
amendment was an ideal constitutional resource for attacking the entirety of Jim Crow's public and private apparatus. The CRS's Thirteenth
Amendment practice thus epitomized the "extension of civil rights," as
President Truman put it, from "protection of the people *against* the
Government [to] protection of the people *by* the Government."[10]

Responsibility for the problems that plagued black industrial workers also lay with both public and private actors. Moreover, over the
course of the 1940s, courts took steps to undermine the state action
requirement of the Fourteenth Amendment. Building on and expanding
these precedents, the NAACP lawyers challenged discrimination by
federal and state governments in job training, hiring, firing, and promotion, as well the decisions of private employers to hire African
Americans largely for the lowest paid, most grueling work. And they
took labor unions to task for excluding, segregating, and discriminating
against African American workers. For these lawyers, the state action
requirement of the *Civil Rights Cases* was as great an obstacle to racial
equality as the separate-but-equal doctrine imposed by *Plessy*.

Just as *Plessy*'s state-mandated segregation was not the sole target
of 1940s civil rights cases, the equal protection clause that *Plessy* had
interpreted was not the sole constitutional battleground. The CRS, for
example, often avoided the equal protection clause altogether, and for
both political and doctrinal reasons, avoided challenging *Plessy* directly.
Politically, attacking *Plessy* and the segregation it legitimated would
have alienated powerful southern elements of Roosevelt's Democratic
coalition. Doctrinally, the lawyers chose instead to expand upon favorable precedents, like Thirteenth Amendment cases prohibiting peonage
and involuntary servitude. When farmworkers wrote the federal govern-

---

[10] Harry S. Truman, Address before the National Association for the Advancement of
Colored People (June 29, 1947), *in* Public Papers of the Presidents of the United States:
Harry S. Truman, 1947 311–313, 311 (1963), *quoted in* President's Committee on Civil Rights,
To Secure These Rights: The Report of the President's Committee on Civil Rights 99 (1947).

ment that they were "only asking for [their] rights" under the Constitution not to work at a "low wage unfair and inhuman treatment," it was the Thirteenth Amendment rather than the Fourteenth that could answer their prayers for relief.[11]

Moreover, even within the NAACP's legal department during the 1940s, the equal protection clause had not reigned alone. To be sure, the lawyers launched equal protection claims on behalf of workers as well as students. But the workers who complained to the NAACP had wanted economic advancement as much as racial nondiscrimination. As a result, the NAACP lawyers drew on and reconfigured for the post-New Deal era the due process clauses of the Fifth and Fourteenth Amendments in order to argue for the rights of black workers to work. As important as the equal protection clause was in many of the NAACP's 1940s cases (especially in education), the due process clause figured as prominently as the equal protection clause in its labor cases.

By the late 1940s, however, when the NAACP's lawyers embarked on the direct attack on segregation that would eventually lead to victory in *Brown*, they largely rejected this multiplicity of approaches to challenging Jim Crow. The lawyers eschewed labor cases, the due process clause, private defendants, and material inequality in favor of a frontal attack on state-mandated educational segregation. They eventually came to regard as the essence of Jim Crow the stigma of governmental classifications, not the material inequality black workers experienced as a result of the interdependent public and private Jim Crow complex.

* * *

When the Supreme Court decided *Brown* in 1954, then, it vindicated the NAACP's decision in 1949 and 1950 to follow one particular strand of pre-*Brown* civil rights—the attack on *Plessy v. Ferguson* in the context of public education. The Court concluded that attending legally segregated schools deprived African American schoolchildren of educational benefits by making them feel inferior to whites and that "[a]ny language in *Plessy v. Ferguson* contrary to this finding is rejected." The NAACP lawyers had succeeded in dethroning *Plessy* and fundamentally undermining segregation.[12]

Their victory, however, was partial in many ways. Consider the constitutional basis for the decision in *Brown*. As the NAACP lawyers constructed their legal theories on the road to *Brown*, they came to understand *Plessy* as the lynchpin of Jim Crow. Because *Plessy* had legitimated segregation in the face of an equal protection challenge,

---

[11] Col. Elton D. Wright VI to U.S. Dept. of Justice, Nov. 1943, file 50–72–5, RG 60, National Archives (hereafter cited as DOJ Files).

[12] 347 U.S. 483, at 494–95.

Brown had to delegitimate it on the same basis. The equal protection clause "precludes a state from imposing distinctions or classifications based on race and color alone," the NAACP accordingly argued. Without much fanfare, the Court embraced the NAACP's equal protection arguments. Indeed, the Court went out of its way to clarify that its decision was based on the equal protection clause alone. "This disposition makes unnecessary any discussion whether such segregation also violates the Due Process Clause of the Fourteenth Amendment." This dominance of equal protection had not been foreordained. Because civil rights lawyers in the 1940s had not targeted *Plessy* exclusively, they had not viewed the equal protection clause as the only constitutional basis for their arguments.[13]

Just as the *Brown* litigation and opinion filtered out some of the core constitutional arguments of the 1940s, so too they painted only a partial picture of the harms of Jim Crow. Once again, the focus on *Plessy* was partly responsible. More than a half-century before the school segregation litigation, the *Plessy* Court had concluded that if "the enforced separation of the two races stamps the colored race with a badge of inferiority," it was only because "the colored race chooses to put that construction upon it." As the lawyers embarked on their attack on *Plessy*, they felt they had to prove the contrary. In order to do so, the lawyers had to isolate the harm of state-mandated segregation from the larger milieu of private and public discrimination and inequality that pervaded Jim Crow America. Contrary to *Plessy*, state racial classifications alone, they argued, caused African Americans intrinsic harm.[14]

Worried that the Court would not accept a mere assertion that such classifications violated the Constitution, the NAACP looked for a way to prove how these state rules stigmatized African Americans. Drawing on a growing body of social science data on race and psychology, the NAACP introduced evidence and testimony in the lower courts about how school segregation psychologically damaged African American children—that is, stigmatized them as inferior. "[U]nconstitutional inequality inheres in the retardation of intellectual development and distortion of personality which Negro children suffer as a result of enforced isolation in school," the NAACP argued.[15]

---

[13] Brief for Appellants, at 5, Brown v. Board of Educ., 347 U.S. 483 (1954) (No. 8), *in* 49 Landmark Briefs and Arguments of the Supreme Court of the United States: Constitutional Law 23–42, 31 (Philip B. Kurland & Gerhard Casper eds., 1975); 347 U.S. at 495.

[14] 163 U.S. 537, 551 (1896). *See* Brief for Appellants at 5, *Brown*, 347 U.S. 483 (No. 8), *in* 49 Landmark Briefs, *supra* note 12, at 23–42, 31.

[15] Brief for Appellants at 5, *Brown*, 347 U.S. 483 (No. 8), *in* 49 Landmark Briefs, *supra* note 12, at 23–42, 31; Appendix to Appellants' Briefs, at i, 4, *Brown*, 347 U.S. 483 (1954) (Nos. 8, 101, 191), *in Id.* at 41–66, 42, 46. *See* Daryl Michael Scott, Contempt and Pity:

Taking its cue from the NAACP, the Court set to one side the continuing material inequalities in the segregated school systems under attack. It cited "findings below that the Negro and white schools involved have been equalized, or are being equalized, with respect to ... 'tangible' factors." The Court then explicitly embraced the NAACP's stigma argument as to "intangible" factors. To separate black children "from others of similar age and qualifications solely because of their race generates a feeling of inferiority as to their status in the community that may affect their hearts and minds in a way unlikely ever to be undone," the Court concluded.[16]

Enshrined in constitutional law, then, was *Brown*'s image of a Jim Crow that had as its central harm the psychological injury of inferiority. The difference between that harm and the harms highlighted in the 1940s labor cases could not have been more striking. When the NAACP pressed, and the *Brown* Court accepted, stigmatic harm as the essence of Jim Crow, the case eclipsed the deep and abiding material inequalities that characterized the nation's caste system for most African Americans.[17]

The NAACP further marginalized material injury in *Brown* by emphasizing the specific harms of government-imposed segregation. The NAACP had essentially decided to attack *Plessy* without simultaneously trying to undermine the state action requirement of the 1883 *Civil Rights Cases*. That decision privileged the place of governmental action in the maintenance of Jim Crow. By challenging only *Plessy*, and therefore only state action, the NAACP parsed the public from the private aspects of Jim Crow. Once the NAACP demonstrated that the challenged public school segregation was in each instance enforced by law—an uncontroversial fact on its face—it met its burden of proving state action.

And yet the NAACP and the Court both treated state action as something more than simply a technical requirement the plaintiffs had to meet: they treated it as a major part of the harm of Jim Crow. Neither the NAACP nor its experts denied the force of privately sanctioned segregation, but they emphasized that the perceived legitimacy of the

---

SOCIAL POLICY AND THE IMAGE OF THE DAMAGED BLACK PSYCHE, 1880–1996 71–91, 119–136 (1997); Rebecca Lyn de Schweinitz, "If They Could Change the World": Children, Childhood, and African–American Civil Rights Politics 130–194 (2004) (unpublished PhD dissertation, University of Virginia); ELLEN HERMAN, THE ROMANCE OF AMERICAN PSYCHOLOGY: POLITICAL CULTURE IN THE AGE OF EXPERTS 174–207 (1995).

[16] 347 U.S. at 492, 494, 495 n.11.

[17] Affidavit of Elizabeth Coker, Jan. 30, 1947, *in NAACP Papers*, pt. 13C, rl. 12:390–391, 391; C. B. McCullar to Roger Baldwin, May 19, 1941, *in NAACP Papers*, pt. 13C, rl. 12:775–776, 775.

law enhanced Jim Crow's harm. The NAACP's social science experts denied that the case concerned "such segregation as arises from the free movements of individuals which are neither enforced nor supported by official bodies." And the Solicitor General of the United States—which submitted an amicus brief largely agreeing with the NAACP—emphasized that "[t]he cases at bar do not involve isolated acts of racial discrimination by private individuals or groups."[18]

In turn, the Supreme Court treated state action as not only a jurisdictional requirement but also a significant component of the harm itself. The Court quoted the Kansas court in *Brown* as finding that "the impact [of segregation] is greater when it has the sanction of the law; for the policy of separating the races is usually interpreted as denoting the inferiority of the negro group." The Court did not rule out the possibility that the private aspects of Jim Crow might be constitutionally problematic. But it emphasized the sanction of government as a critical part of the harm of segregation.[19]

This emphasis on state-derived harm represented yet another partial reflection of the civil rights practices that preceded *Brown*. The NAACP's choice to abide the public/private line was something of a departure from both the CRS's and the NAACP's own approach to the state action question in the 1940s. Whereas the attacks of the lawyers in the 1940s targeted both the private and the public aspects of racial and economic subordination, the Court's iconic construction of Jim Crow in *Brown* privileged the harms inflicted specifically by the state.

The NAACP's litigation choices similarly transformed the role of education in *Brown*, elevating it from a background condition of the litigation into an important substantive component of the case. The NAACP needed to convince the Court that educational segregation—rather than the many other indignities and inequalities African American children endured—was the cause of the inferiority African American children felt. It also hoped to find a way for the Court to interpret the Fourteenth Amendment to prohibit segregated education despite historical evidence that the framers of the Fourteenth Amendment countenanced the practice. NAACP lawyers accordingly waxed eloquent about the "basic function of the public school" as the instruction of "each succeeding generation in the fundamental traditions of our democracy." Moreover, the NAACP relied on the idea that interracial contact in schools was critical to counteracting the societal pressures toward racism

---

[18] Brief for Appellants at 9, *Brown*, 347 U.S. 483 (No. 8), *in* 49 LANDMARK BRIEFS, *supra* note 12, at 23–42, 35; Appendix to Appellants' Briefs at 2, 8, 9, *Brown*, 347 U.S. 483 (Nos. 8, 101, 191), *in Id.* at 41–66, 44, 50, 51; Brief for United States at 3, *Brown*, 347 U.S. 483 (Nos. 8, 101, 191, 413, 448), *in Id.* at 113–147, 118.

[19] 347 U.S. at 494 (quoting the lower court) (internal quotation marks omitted).

that undermined democracy. It emphasized how " 'education' compre-
hends the entire process of developing and training the mental, physical
and moral powers and capabilities of human beings."[20]

The Court embraced this privileged role of education. Education was
"the very foundation of good citizenship," it was "a principal instrument
in awakening the child to cultural values ... and in helping him adjust
normally to his environment." The Court described education as so
distinctive that when it overruled *Plessy* in *Brown*, it did so only "in the
field of public education." With education set up as the paradigmatic site
for the reproduction of Jim Crow and the crucial battleground for a new
civil rights, the victims of Jim Crow became grade-school children, and
the salient harms were to their psychological well-being and their
capacity for citizenship. As the *New Republic* editorialized just after
Brown, "Above the [political] tumult will remain the children themselves."[21]

From the perspective of pre-*Brown* civil rights practice, the focus on
schools and schoolchildren is striking, as the labor-market context had
marked many of the prominent cases of the pre-*Brown* era. *Brown* thus
constructed a partial and particular image of Jim Crow—as a problem of
state-mandated segregation in public education, causing psychological
harms. While many of the children who would benefit from school
desegregation were poor and isolated, the NAACP ensured as a matter of
litigation strategy that it was their psychological rather than their
material well-being that concerned the Court in *Brown*. The case thus
divorced the seventy-five-year-old caste system from its economic roots,
from its material inequalities, from the farmworkers who complained
about their immobility and the industrial workers who complained about
their inability to make a living.

* * *

Brown became the iconic civil rights case of the modern era. As legal
scholars spent considerable effort analyzing, justifying, and systematiz-
ing the Court's decision, the image of Jim Crow it projected and the legal
doctrine it embraced captured the collective legal imagination. Over the
decade that followed *Brown*, subsequent cases, the rise of the civil rights
movement, and legislative developments all contributed to this transformation of constitutional civil rights. To some extent, these developments

---

[20] Brief for Appellants at 27, 28, *Brown*, 347 U.S. 483 (Nos. 1, 2, 4, 10), *in* 49 LANDMARK
BRIEFS, *supra* note 12, at 481–748, 540, 541; Brief for Appellants at 9, *Brown*, 347 U.S. 483
(No. 8), *in Id.* at 23–42, 35. *See also* Brief for United States at 8, *Brown*, 347 U.S. 483 (Nos.
8, 101, 191, 413, 448), *in Id.* at 113–147, 123. *See* de Schweinitz, *supra* note 14, at 130–194;
SCOTT, *supra* note 14, at 85–86, 125.

[21] 347 U.S. at 492–493, 493–495; Editorial, *The Court Has Made an Historic Decision*,
NEW REPUBLIC, May 24, 1954, at 3, *quoted in* SCOTT, *supra* note 14, at 136.

reinvigorated particular aspects of pre-*Brown* civil rights. The pivotal civil rights protest of 1963 was called a March for Jobs and Freedom. The Johnson administration's War on Poverty tried to attack economic deprivation in part out of a recognition of the continuing connection between racial and economic inequality. And Title VII of the 1964 Civil Rights Act (and later amendments) legislatively prohibited discrimination in the private labor market and labor unions as well as among state actors themselves.

Even so, these developments often reinforced, rather than undermined, the image of Jim Crow and racial harm that *Brown* depicted. Media representations of the 1963 March on Washington largely forsook the protest's economic emphasis for Martin Luther King Jr.'s invocation of formal color-blindness—in which people would "not be judged by the color of their skin but by the content of their character." The War on Poverty took as its mission not the redress of economic inequality for its own sake but rather as a cause of the psychological alienation that underlay rising racial violence across the nation. And Title VII prohibited "discrimination on the basis of race" in the same terms as it prohibited discrimination in education and public accommodations. The law addressed work-related inequality as simply an ordinary manifestation of the general problem of race discrimination. Title VII, like *Brown* itself, submerged the substantive right to work that had been a hallmark of the pre-*Brown* years for the antidiscrimination paradigm that was a hallmark of the post-*Brown* era.[22]

Moreover, these and other developments remained largely separate from constitutional law itself. Title VII was not constitutionally mandated. Despite transitory judicial flirtations with the state action requirement, the *Civil Rights Cases* remained good constitutional precedent. And attempts to translate legislative and social movement momentum for protection of the poor into constitutional guarantees ultimately failed. Within the realm of constitutionally protected civil rights, *Brown*'s equal protection clause, with its state action requirement and concern for formal rather than material equality, remained dominant.

As legal scholars increasingly converged on a general framework for making sense of the constitutional law of civil rights, then, that framework was predominantly the one *Brown* had set into motion in 1954.

---

[22] Martin Luther King, Jr., I Have a Dream, Speech at the Lincoln Memorial (August 28, 1963); Civil Rights Act of 1964, tit. VII, § 703(b). *See* Sidney M. Milkis, *Lyndon Johnson, the Great Society, and the "Twilight" of the Modern Presidency, in* THE GREAT SOCIETY AND THE HIGH TIDE OF LIBERALISM 1–50 (Sidney M. Milkis & Jerome M. Mileur eds., 2005). On Title VII as transformative of American society, see NANCY MACLEAN, FREEDOM IS NOT ENOUGH: THE OPENING OF THE AMERICAN WORKPLACE (2006). *See generally* Jacquelyn Dowd Hall, *The Long Civil Rights Movement and the Political Uses of the Past*, 91 J. AM. HIST. 1233 (2005).

This is apparent in changes to succeeding editions of civil rights and constitutional law casebooks and treatises. Before and just after *Brown*, treatises and casebooks reflected considerable variety in both the subjects they included within the field of civil rights and the way they analyzed those subjects. Legal scholars treated "civil rights" as encompassing issues like involuntary servitude and labor rights as much as racial segregation; they saw rights as falling into categories like "the security of the person" as much as "discrimination"; and they described the vindication of civil rights as an affirmative responsibility of government as much as the responsibility of private litigants. By the 1960s, treatise and casebook authors eliminated sections on the security of the person; they condensed or eliminated discussions of involuntary servitude and the Thirteenth Amendment; and they eliminated chapters on freedom of labor altogether. Work-related civil rights were largely reduced to the question of job discrimination under the equal protection clause, akin to discrimination in other arenas.[23]

As scholars winnowed out the varieties of pre-*Brown* civil rights, they converged on a race-based, privately-litigated, equal protection-oriented civil rights framework that *Brown* had inaugurated. Indeed, they reconstructed a pedigree for *Brown* that made that framework seem more timeless than it really was. Rooting *Brown* in the 1938 case of *United States v. Carolene Products*, scholars suggested that courts had long before determined to treat race cases differently from those involving economic regulation. The canonization of *Carolene Products* doctrinally separated economics from race and justified judicial interference with the latter but not the former. It consequently interred any linkage civil rights lawyers had been able to make between the economic and formal legal aspects of Jim Crow in the pre-*Brown* era.[24]

The link to *Carolene Products* made it all too easy to assume that before *Brown*, as afterwards, civil rights doctrine primarily addressed questions of racial classification. In fact, neither lawyers, judges, nor scholars had viewed *Carolene Products* as determining the contours of civil rights law before its vindication in *Brown*. It was not until the post-Brown years privileged a race-focused equal protection clause, and contrasted stringent judicial review of government actions affecting racial minorities with those affecting the economy, that race and labor truly diverged in constitutional law. It was not until then that constitutionally-grounded civil rights became squarely rights against the government, in contrast to both rights against private power and rights protected by

---

[23] For a more extensive discussion of this process of doctrinal change, see GOLUBOFF, *supra* note *, at 263–268.

[24] *See* Louis H. Pollak, *Racial Discrimination and Judicial Integrity: A Reply to Professor Wechsler*, 108 U. PA. L. REV. 1 (1959); 304 U.S. 144, 152 n.4 (1938).

the government. It was not until then that it became clear how partial the victory in *Brown* was and how much of Jim Crow remained intact in the face of the new civil rights *Brown* had helped construct.

* * *

These developments were still largely immanent and unformed in the days just after the Supreme Court decided *Brown* in May of 1954. *Brown* represented the culmination of years of hard work by the NAACP lawyers and a tremendous victory for both those lawyers and African Americans generally. The constitutional energy it unleashed served as the driving force for a major revolution in civil rights doctrine. Absent from that new energy, however, was the legacy of the labor-related civil rights practices that preceded *Brown*: the African–American worker, the rights of labor more broadly understood, the challenge to Jim Crow's economic underpinnings, and the use of constitutional texts other than the equal protection clause—like the Thirteenth Amendment and the due process clause—as foundational resources for promoting civil rights.

At least in part because of the decisions of lawyers in the NAACP and elsewhere, our imagination of the civil rights plaintiff, the civil rights complaint, and the scope of constitutional civil rights protections is significantly different today. We take for granted, fifty years after *Brown*, that the crux of legally cognizable racism in the United States is the psychological, stigmatic, and symbolic injury of state-sanctioned racial classification.

That abstracted notion of harm might well have looked odd from the perspective of the poor and the working-class African Americans who complained to the CRS and the NAACP about the problems they endured living and working in Jim Crow America. Although workers would, and did, benefit from the decision in *Brown* and those that followed, those benefits did not reach all of the harms black workers faced under Jim Crow. Even after both legislative and doctrinal developments after *Brown* went some distance toward treating work as an appropriate site for government intervention and civil rights advancement, the constitutional framework largely remained the one created in *Brown*. To be sure, the *Brown* decision did not by itself cause the narrowing of constitutional discourse. Rather, that narrowing is a product of how lawyers, constitutional theorists, historians, and laypersons think about *Brown*. Without recognizing both the formal and the informal, the legal and the customary, the public and the private aspects of racial inequality, the constitutional law *Brown* inaugurated has had difficulty effectively undermining the entirety of the harms most black Americans endured under Jim Crow.

3

Myriam E. Gilles*

Police, Race and Crime in 1950s Chicago: *Monroe v. Pape* as Legal Noir

Writ large, *Monroe v. Pape* is equal parts Richard Wright and Raymond Chandler. Or maybe, *To Kill a Mockingbird* meets *Dirty Harry*. A hard-boiled hero cop runs headlong into the wall dividing the post-Reconstruction century from the Warren Court; the Great Migration from the Civil Rights Movement. At the dawn of the 1960s, Chief of Detectives Frank Pape—famously known to Chicago beat writers as the "Toughest Cop In America"—goes from protector against civil unrest to violator of civil rights.

The casting is perfect. Frank Pape was the archetypal old-school cop, squinting out from under his fedora and parading pinstriped mobsters onto the front pages of the *Daily Tribune*. Pape and his band of detectives were heroes in their own time: celebrities invited them to swanky parties and hard-working Chicagoans lined up to buy them drinks in corner taverns. The image was rough-but-basically-straight: sons of immigrants with thick hands planted firmly on the lid of a cauldron that was always in danger of boiling over into criminal chaos and social discord.

The city of Chicago likewise hails straight from central casting. During the half-century that preceded *Monroe v. Pape*, the city played host to some of the most infamous criminal enterprises the world has ever known, as well as several full-blown race riots and innumerable near-conflagrations. The first waves of the Great Migration filled its

* Many thanks to Gary Friedman, Risa Goluboff, Melanie Leslie and Rich Schragger; to Algeria S. Aljure and Joshua Andrix; and to the Cardozo library staff for providing tremendous assistance in tracking down research materials.

South Side ghettoes, and the later waves flushed its black denizens out into the historically Polish and Irish Westside—a sure recipe for trouble.

And the story behind *Monroe v. Pape* is very much a period piece; the product of a very specific moment in American history. Mid–1950s marches on Little Rock, Montgomery and Selma trained the attention of the world on Jim Crow laws and the quest for basic equality. But as the decade drew to an end, sophisticated civil rights advocates and lawyers shifted their focus to America's northern cities and the discriminatory treatment of blacks at the hands of urban police. It was becoming clear to many Americans that the Frank Papes of the world were not *everybody's* heroes, and that the law and order for which they were lionized imposed radically disparate burdens, and conferred disparate benefits, on black and white city-dwellers.

And so, with all of these elements in place, the stage was set for *Monroe v. Pape*.

BLACKS AND POLICE IN
EARLY 20TH CENTURY CHICAGO

In 1890, there were roughly fifteen thousand blacks living in Chicago, mostly in a discrete South Side community, and mostly working in low-paying domestic and service jobs. During this period in Chicago, historians tell us, there was little unrest or racial discord: "Negroes were viewed neither as a threat to the city's well-being nor as an integral part of the city's social structure."[1]

This relative indifference towards race began to fade at the dawn of the twentieth century, as the migration of blacks from the south went from a trickle to a mass movement. Between 1890 and 1915, the black population of Chicago grew to over 50,000; between 1916 and 1920, the number rose to nearly 110,000; and by 1930, it reached 234,000. All of these migrants arrived seeking better opportunities: the outbreak of World War I had "stopped the flow of European immigrants," while simultaneously creating a need for manpower in Chicago's war industries.[2] But while recently-arrived blacks initially found work, the demand for unskilled labor eventually slowed, with no corresponding reduction in the flow of migrants from the South.[3]

---

[1] ALLAN H. SPEAR, BLACK CHICAGO: THE MAKING OF A NEGRO GHETTO, 1980–1920, at 11, 7 (1967).

[2] ST. CLAIR DRAKE & HORACE R. CAYTON, BLACK METROPOLIS: A STUDY OF NEGRO LIFE IN A NORTHERN CITY 8 tbl.1 (1993 ed.).

[3] KEVIN BOYLE, ARC OF JUSTICE: A SAGE OF RACE, CIVIL RIGHTS AND MURDER IN THE JAZZ AGE 9 (2004) ("When the migration northward began during the war, blacks had been able to find

White Chicagoans grew anxious of the growing black population: "as the black belt grew, Negroes began competing for jobs and homes and exercised an often decisive influence in politics," in ways that threatened white Chicagoans, "especially the Irish and Poles who lived west of the black belt and the old stock middle-class families who lived to the south and east." These groups responded by attempting to tighten the color bar in housing, education and employment; failing that, they resorted to violence. Even well-to-do Chicagoans worried that the continuing influx of blacks would result in "epidemics, crime and chronic unemployment."[4]

Chicago police officers did their part to uphold the color line, keeping blacks out of "white" parks and other recreational spots, and turning a blind eye to acts of violence aimed at maintaining strictly segregated neighborhoods. Between 1917 and 1921, "there were fifty-eight racially-inspired bombings in Chicago, [leaving] two persons dead, several more injured and property valued at over $100,000 destroyed. Most of the bombings took place in disputed residential areas and were directed at the homes of Negroes." Yet police provided "scant protection for families that had been threatened" with violence for moving into white or mixed neighborhoods, and they failed to investigate or make arrests.[5]

Chicago police were also widely suspected of protecting whites who terrorized and assaulted blacks. In particular, a notorious gang of Irish youths, Ragen's Colts, were said to be "relatives of a number of the policemen of the Stock Yards Station and, as a result, their depredations seldom occasioned an arrest." During the summer of 1919, the Colts—who would later become the muscle for the Capone outfit—regularly attacked black teens in Washington Park, Fuller Park, and Armour Square. The gang was allegedly responsible for over a dozen brutal attacks and two murders of blacks in the months leading up to July 1919.[6]

In that blisteringly hot summer month, a young black boy named Eugene Williams accidentally waded into the white section of the Twenty-ninth Street beach and was killed by an angry white mob. The police assigned to patrol the beach area did nothing; by some accounts, they

a range of factory jobs. The opportunities shrank in the early 1920's, as many employers decided that all but the most menial and dangerous work should be reserved for whites.").

[4] SPEAR, *supra* note 1, at 201–02 (*citing Chi. Trib.*, Mar. 5, 1917).

[5] SPEAR, *supra* note 1, at 211.

[6] *See* WILLIAM M. TUTTLE, JR., RACE RIOT: CHICAGO IN THE RED SUMMER OF 1919, at 237 (1996); *see also* SPEAR, *supra* note 1, at 206 (noting that Ragan's Colts "was sponsored by an alderman and reputedly enjoyed police protection"); *id.* at 213.

even participated in the murder. Within hours, all of Chicago was gripped by mob violence and it quickly became "clear that the police were unable to handle the situation [because] not only were their forces insufficient, but many policemen sided with the white rioters and fired indiscriminately into Negro crowds."[7] Finally, after six days of bloodshed, leaving thirty-eight people dead, five hundred injured, and millions of dollars worth of property destroyed, the Illinois state militia restored an unstable order.[8] Six months later, the State's Attorney presented the grand jury with seventeen indictments resulting from the riot, all of them involving black men.[9]

The Chicago Commission Report on Race Relations later cited police conduct as a contributing factor in the escalation of racial tensions that led to the violent outbreak.[10] Indeed, as cities throughout the nation erupted in racial violence during the "Red Summer" of 1919, police brutality and indifference towards blacks were often implicated.[11]

The Depression saw a period of relative quiescence in black migration and racial tensions in Chicago.[12] But the industrial upswing of the post-war period brought with it another massive wave of migration: from 1940 to 1960, Chicago's black population grew by nearly half a million, with the attendant "overflowing of [the] black population from established areas of residence" in the Black Belt to mixed and all-white

---

[7] SPEAR, *supra* note 1, at 215; *see also* RICHARD C. LINDBERG, TO SERVE AND COLLECT: CHICAGO POLITICS AND POLICE CORRUPTION FROM THE LAGER BEER RIOT TO THE SUMMERDALE SCANDAL 153 (1991) (asserting that "the predominantly white police force was obviously in sympathy with the rioters, who desired nothing less than the complete destruction of the black neighborhoods").

[8] CHICAGO COMMISSION ON RACE RELATIONS, THE NEGRO IN CHICAGO: A STUDY OF RACE RELATIONS AND A RACE RIOT 1–50 (1922) [hereinafter THE NEGRO IN CHICAGO]. On the instability of the racial tensions, *see* Boyle, *supra* note 3, at 99 ("On Chicago's bloody racial frontier, whites bombed eight separate properties bought by Negroes in the first three months of 1920.").

[9] *See, e.g.,* LINDBERG, *supra* note 7, at 154 (describing the grand jury as "shocked and surprised" that the State's Attorney had decided not to bring charges against the white mobs involved in the riot).

[10] THE NEGRO IN CHICAGO, *supra* note 8, at 24–32.

[11] *See, e.g.,* BOYLE, *supra* note 3, at 96–97 (describing the role of police in the 1919 Washington, D.C., riots); ROBERT V. HAYNES, A NIGHT OF VIOLENCE: THE HOUSTON RIOT OF 1917 (1976); RANDALL KENNEDY, RACE CRIME AND THE LAW 114 (1991) (stating that in Washington, D.C., the police "gave the impression both to Negroes and to white men that they would be the allies of the white men"); Robin D.G. Kelley, *"Slanging Rocks . . . Palestinian Style,"* *in* POLICE BRUTALITY 21, 31 (Jill Nelson ed. 2000) (describing race riots during the summer of 1919 in Elaine, Arkansas, Longview, Texas, Omaha, Nebraska, and Knoxville, Tennessee).

[12] *See, e.g.,* LINDBERG, *supra* note 7, at 154 ("[C]lowed by a growing belief that the police were unwilling to protect them from the white gangs, Chicago's blacks retreated behind a wall of stony silence and compliance to the system.").

neighborhoods. Ethnic violence again followed: "the late 1940s became an era analogous to that of 1917–21, when one racially motivated bombing or arson occurred every twenty days."[13]

Once again, the police were at the center of the escalating racial crisis during the second "Red Summer" of 1943, as altercations between police and black residents led to deadly riots in several major cities.[14] In Harlem, a massive riot broke out when word spread that police had shot and killed a black serviceman.[15] Days later, "it looked as if the war had come home: 6 people lay dead, 550 had been arrested, and 1,450 stores had been damaged or burned to the ground."[16] In Detroit, over one hundred people were killed and the city was nearly burned to the ground amidst allegations that police officers allowed white mobs to shoot blacks without repercussion.[17] Thurgood Marshall, reporting on police abuses for the NAACP, described the scene in Detroit as "resembling part of a battlefield."[18]

In Chicago, "half-forgotten memories of the Great Migration and the Race Riot [of 1919] and its aftermath were revived among both Negroes and whites. The Negro was once more becoming a 'problem' and racial conflict seemed to loom in the offing." The city was so concerned about a possible repeat of the 1919 riot that the mayor established a Committee on Race Relations to quell any conflict. The committee "appealed to the police officials to lay plans for quickly squelching the first signs of a riot [and] exacted a pledge that if a riot should occur, white policemen would refrain from giving assistance, active or passive, to the whites." Nevertheless, when a "sixteen-year-old colored boy was killed by an over-zealous white policeman, the inciting incident seemed at hand." But somehow, Chicago was spared massive rioting in 1943, as the summer passed with only scattered incidents of violence; the "anticipated trouble did not materialize, but the fear remain[ed]."[19]

---

[13] Arnold Hirsch, Making the Second Ghetto: Race and Housing in Chicago, 1940–1960, at 4–5, 41 (1983).

[14] Kelley, *supra* note 11, at 34 (describing the incidents between police and black residents that led to major urban race riots during the summer of 1943).

[15] *Id.*

[16] The Complete Report of Mayor LaGuardia's Commission on the Harlem Riot of March 19, 1935, at 114 (1969) (noting that "the police practice aggressions and brutalities upon the Harlem citizens" in part "because they are Negroes").

[17] Kelley, *supra* note 11, at 34.

[18] *Id.* at 35; *see also* Kennedy, *supra* note 11, at 114 (quoting Marshall as saying that Detroit police used brutal force against blacks: "night sticks, revolvers, riot guns, submachine guns, and deer guns... Negroes killed by police—17").

[19] Drake & Cayton, *supra* note 2, at 91–93, 12; *see also* Hirsch, *supra* note 13, at 43 (describing the extraordinary precautions taken by city officials to forestall a riot: "Even

As the 1950s progressed, Chicago remained a city marred by deep and unresolved racial tensions that were most strongly symbolized by the relationship between its police officers and minority residents.

* * *

And so, against this backdrop, we may do well to pause and ask: how might Chicagoans in 1958 expect their police to react if a young, attractive white woman—living in a West Side neighborhood not a mile from the color line—were to claim that "two young Negroes" entered her home and shot her husband to death for $185?

Well, maybe the answer depends on the cops.

FRANK PAPE: THE EARLY YEARS

Frank Pape was born in 1909 to German immigrant parents living and working in Bucktown, a poor neighborhood in Chicago. His father died when he was nine, so young Frank felt an early responsibility to care for his mother and sister, Leona. Pape worked odd jobs for years, and eventually dropped out of high school in his junior year to work as a sheet-metal journeyman. But then the Depression hit, and Pape was out of work.[20]

Frank decided to take the policeman's exam, but failed at his first try because he only weighed one hundred and forty-seven pounds, while the department minimum was one hundred and fifty. His Uncle Charley told young Frank to "drink a lot of water and eat a lot of bananas," so he followed the old man's advice, reapplied under the name Francis Pape, and made it through. On March 25, 1933, Francis Pape took the oath to serve and protect as a member of the Chicago Police Department, becoming a rookie in the Albany Park District.[21]

The 1930s was quite a time to be a Chicago Police officer: "Chicago remained a place of larger-than-life cops and robbers. Those were the days when policeman would set a trap for a suspected police killer, cut him down in a hail of bullets and pose for newspaper pictures afterward."[22] The grainy black-and-white, top-of-the-fold photographs gave

---

before the Detroit fires were extinguished, the Army's Sixth Service Command requested the shipment of 12,000 tear gas and smoke grenades and 10,000 twelve-gauge shotgun shells 'for use in the event of disorders in Chicago.' "); *id.* (noting that police sought to avoid a riot by implementing "a program of 'unexpressed, expedient segregation,' " in which officers "encourage[d] members of both races to 'avoid known areas of conflict,' " and black police officers were "routinely assigned to handle 'Negro trouble' and those incidents that displayed 'provocative racial qualities' ") (internal citations omitted).

[20] CHARLES F. ADAMSON, THE TOUGHEST COP IN AMERICA 27–34 (2001).

[21] *Id.*

[22] Douglas Martin, *Frank Pape, Celebrated Chicago Police Detective, Dies at 91*, N.Y. TIMES, Mar. 12, 2000

Chicagoans the sense that their police force was in control: "they supported the police in the performance of their duty and damn well demanded results when the criminal element got the upper hand."[23]

The popular picture of the triumphant lawman wasn't entirely accurate: Chicago in 1930s was in the midst of "a ten-year orgy of murder and mayhem unprecedented in U.S. cities," with its violent crime rate at all-time high. The city constantly "teetered on the edge of a criminal abyss; larceny was its soul."[24] Police tried to stem the wave of violence—"there were chases and gunfights and fistfights"—but cops were often outnumbered and unprepared for the growing complexity of the city's infamous criminal syndicates.[25]

When Frank Pape joined the department, there was a great deal of status attached to being a police officer. Pape and his partners "wore fedoras and natty suits and carried Tommy guns on raids."[26] Early on, Pape earned a reputation as an aggressive, hard-nosed cop who "backed away from no one and was a natural leader." He was said to have an "uncanny ability to recognize somebody or something that didn't look right, that looked out of place, or suspicious."[27] He "established an identity by never carrying his gun in a holster; instead, he kept it in his front pants pocket, which his wife had reinforced by sewing in a canvas lining."[28] The gun itself, a .38 caliber "Police Positive" with a bone handle, became another Pape signature.

Pape rose quickly through the ranks to become a lieutenant in the elite Robbery detail, and later, Chief of Detectives. He and his partners, Morrie Friedman, Rudy Friedl and John Moss, together secured over eight hundred convictions, sent five men to the electric chair, and fought in twenty-three gun battles over a thirty-year period.[29] Pape and his crew were said to have "helped tame Chicago ... a brutal and savage sprawling metropolis." He "went up against the worst gunmen of his time and headed a robbery unit whose cases were front page media headlines." Nine "criminals who roamed Chicago's mean streets and who had the misfortune to tangle with this no-nonsense cop became

---

[23] ADAMSON, *supra* note 20, at 2.

[24] LINDBERG, *supra* note 7, at 156.

[25] ADAMSON, *supra* note 20, at 47.

[26] James Janega, *Frank Pape: Chicago's 'Toughest Cop' Never Took Lip*, TORONTO GLOBE & MAIL, Mar. 8, 2000, at R8.

[27] ADAMSON, *supra* note 20, at 5, 43.

[28] Martin, *supra* note 22.

[29] Janega, *supra* note 26.

residents of the county morgue for their troubles."[30] Pape's exploits were said to be the inspiration for the 1950s television show, "M Squad," which featured Lieutenant Frank Ballinger as the head of an elite detective squad in Chicago and launched Lee Marvin's career.[31] And of course, there were the constant rumors that Pape was a wise guy— connected to the mob—which he staunchly denied or refused to discuss.[32]

One fateful afternoon, Pape and his gang noticed a car full of hoodlums "casing" a bank. Realizing they were being watched, the thieves abandoned their car and scattered in different directions. Pape's partner, Morrie Friedman gave chase and closed in on one of the perpetrators. Friedman "always made it a practice of firing a few warning shots over a fleeing criminal's head," and did so on this occasion. But this time "the criminal, one Lyman Stanton Heiman, shot Friedman through the stomach before he could return fire. Heiman, a two-bit gunman out of Detroit who had a string of grocery store robberies to his name, was instantly killed in the crossfire. Whether it was Pape, Friedman or Rudy Friedl who fired the fatal shot, no one can be sure." Pape ran over to his fallen partner and held Friedman in his arms as he slowly bled to death. After that day, Pape famously declared that he would "never use his gun to fire warning shots, only to kill."[33]

But Frank Pape is barely remembered for any of this. All the local fame he achieved from his hundreds of arrests, shoot outs and medals of honor—the whole real-life action hero side of Frank Pape—has inevitably faded for all but a handful of older Chicagoans. Instead, Pape's name is indelibly associated with a federal civil rights case, *Monroe v. Pape,* that began with the murder of a white insurance agent named Peter Saisi.

THE SAISI AFFAIR

On the night of October 27, 1958, thirty-year-old Peter Saisi, an agent at Western and Southern Life Insurance Company, arrived at his home at 530 N. St. Louis Avenue on the West Side of Chicago. Saisi had had a long day at work and had then met his best friend, Sam Coniglio, for post-work cocktails before heading home.[34] Saisi spent some time

---

[30] John J. Flood & Jim McGough, *A Legendary Chicago Police Officer "Francois,"* available at http://www.ipsn.org/pape.html.

[31] *Id.*

[32] *Id.* (describing allegations by Ovid Demaris, author of "Captive City," implying that Pape was connected to the Chicago Outfit; and by Chuck Giancana whose memoir implies that Pape's unit "only went after the same guys that are givin' us (the Chicago Outfit) trouble").

[33] Martin, *supra* note 22; Flood & McGough, *supra* note 30.

[34] ADAMSON, *supra* note 20, at 171.

with his wife, Mary, and looked in on their three sleeping children before heading down to his basement office to do some work. Minutes later, a shot rang out, leaving Peter Saisi lying on the floor, dead of a single gunshot wound to the head.

Chief of Detectives Frank Pape went personally to the scene of the crime, along with his core group of detectives. The distraught widow, Mary Saisi, a "demure, 120–pound brunette," told the detectives that at about 9:30 p.m., she had heard her husband speaking with someone down in the basement. When she went down to investigate, she saw two "young Negroes" confronting her husband. One of them told her "Go upstairs and nothing will happen to your husband."[35] But as she neared the top of the stairs, she heard the deadly shot. Mrs. Saisi also told police that she believed the two men—one armed with a pistol and one with a knife—had probably fled through a rear door. An inventory of the basement office revealed that the $185 Peter Saisi had collected from his customers that day was missing, as well as a number of shirts from the closet.

Fifty officers were immediately dispatched to search the neighborhood for the two suspects; the search lasted all night and into Tuesday morning with no luck. Meanwhile, Pape and his squad began to discover some discrepancies in Mary Saisi's account of that deadly night. First, the detectives could not "determine how [the] two gunmen [had] entered" or fled the Saisi home:[36] the doors and windows in the basement office were locked from the inside, and there was no sign of forced entry. Second, if the motive for the murder was burglary, the thieves left behind more than they took: detectives found Peter Saisi's cash-filled wallet, wrist watch and other valuables within feet of his dead body. Third, detectives interviewed family members and learned that Mary Saisi's brother had gone down to the Saisi's basement at approximately 9:30 p.m. on the night of the murder to pick up a drum set he stored in their closet—exactly the time Mary said she had gone downstairs to investigate the strange voices—but he had not seen his brother-in-law or anyone else.[37]

To try to nail down this discrepancy in the timeline, the detectives interviewed Peter Saisi's friend, Sam Coniglio, about their boys night out. Coniglio confirmed that he and Peter had met up at a restaurant located at Armitage and California Avenues at approximately 8:00 p.m., and left just after 9:30; Coniglio also told police that Peter had believed "his wife [was] running around on him." By this point, Pape was

[35] 50 Policemen Hunt Slayers of Father, CHI. DAILY TRIB., Oct. 28, 1958, at 2.

[36] Cops Baffled by Slaying of Holdup Victim, CHI. DAILY TRIB., Nov. 26, 1958, at 5.

[37] ADAMSON, supra note 20, at 168–70.

beginning to doubt Mary's story about the events of that night; plus, there was just that gut-feeling of the seasoned detective: "[s]ince when does a stick-up man let someone leave his presence during the commission of a crime?"[38]

Mary Saisi may have sensed the detective's increasing skepticism. She immediately agreed to come down to the station house on Tuesday, the day after the murder, to look through mugshots. "She studied several pictures, making it look like she was struggling with an identification of the suspect she had seen on the stairs, but would shake her head and continue. Then she came to a photograph, studied it for a moment, then told the attending Detective, 'This is the man.' "[39]

The man she identified was James Monroe, a black father of six living just two-and-half miles away from the Saisi home, south of Garfield Park. The detectives were relieved: Monroe "fit the description [Saisi] had given the crime scene Detectives" (he was black) and had a criminal record for burglary and auto theft. Pape decided that his team would raid Monroe's apartment "in order to have the opportunity to look for the shirts that were allegedly taken from the Saisi home."[40] And so, without first securing a search or arrest warrant, Pape led twelve officers out at 5:45 a.m. to a large, four-story apartment building at 1424 S. Trumbull Avenue.

The Monroe apartment was located in the basement near the back of the building. All was quiet on the street and in the building at that early hour, but Pape nevertheless stationed officers at the front and sides of the building, as he and two other detectives went to the back door of the Monroe apartment. What happened next was in dispute.

Frank Pape described it as a "very routine arrest." By his account, he and the detectives were let into the apartment by a young child, who led them directly to his sleeping father, James Monroe. Monroe was quietly awakened, and easily agreed to go down to the stationhouse. According to Pape, the only momentary problem occurred as Monroe was being led out of the apartment for further questioning: two of his older boys "started swearing at us and one of them made a move toward me. I shoved him back to where he was standing and that was the end of his aggressiveness." And even then, Pape insisted he did not find it "necessary to handcuff [Monroe] in front of his children," but instead led him quietly out of the apartment into the waiting squad car.[41]

---

[38] *Id.* at 170–71.

[39] *Id.* at 170.

[40] *Id.* at 171.

[41] *Id.* at 172–73.

James Monroe and his lawyers described the incident quite differently in their civil rights complaint, filed six months later:

> In the early morning of October 29, 1958, Mr. and Mrs. James Monroe and their six children were at home in their Chicago apartment, asleep in their beds. At 5:45 A.M., Deputy Chief of Detectives Pape and twelve other policemen broke and entered through the front and rear doors of the Monroe dwelling. Chief Pape and two others entered the bedroom of Mr. and Mrs. Monroe. They shined flashlights into the faces of the sleeping couple, pointed their pistols and ordered James Monroe out of his bed. Chief Pape cursed Mr. Monroe and threatened to shoot him if he didn't move fast. Mr. Monroe was naked. He left the bedroom at gunpoint. He was forced to stand in the center of his living room naked. Another officer ordered Mrs. Monroe out of bed. She refused, explaining that she was naked. The officer dragged her out and pushed her into the living room. Chief Pape was questioning Mr. Monroe. He kept calling him 'nigger' and 'black boy,' and hit him in the belly with his flashlight several times. Meanwhile, the six children were being herded into the living room. One detective kicked four–year–old James Monroe, Jr., who fell to the floor and began to cry. Later, Chief Pape struck Robert Stevens, knocked him down and pushed a third child, Houston, to the floor on top of Robert.
>
> Mrs. Monroe's daughter Jacqueline started for the back door. She wanted to reach a telephone, call a family friend and get help. An officer stepped between Jacqueline and the door, pushed her down and prevented her from leaving. The police searched every room. They ransacked the closets, throwing all the family's clothing on the floor. They opened and dumped all the drawers in the various pieces of furniture. They ripped open all the mattresses. Mr. Monroe was then allowed to dress. His hands were chained together and he was escorted outside. The police had no warrant for the search or the arrest.[42]

The following day, Mary Saisi was brought down to the stationhouse to pick Monroe out of a lineup. She fainted twice while looking at the seven black men behind one-way glass, but was ultimately unable to identify her husband's killer.[43] As a result, James Monroe was released.[44]

---

[42] *See* Brief for Petitioners, Monroe v. Pape, 365 U.S. 167 (1961) (No. 39), 1960 WL 63600 (internal references omitted).

[43] *Holdup Slaying Inquest Delayed for Killer Hunt*, CHI. DAILY TRIB., Oct. 30, 1958, at 2.

[44] Monroe v. Pape, 365 U.S. 167, 169 (1961) (reciting the complaint's allegations that Monroe had been detained on "open" charges "for 10 hours, while he was interrogated about a two-day-old murder, that he was not taken before a magistrate, though one was

The discrepancies in Saisi's story and whispers of her infidelity made Pape and the other detectives increasingly suspicious, and they started asking around about Mary Saisi.

Finally, a month after the murder, the detectives caught a break and located Mary's rumored boyfriend, Richard Lansing. Lansing immediately confessed to murdering Peter Saisi, provided police with the murder weapon, and implicated Mary as a co-conspirator for providing him $45 to purchase the .25 caliber revolver and for planning the entire thing in order to collect on her husband's $25,000 life insurance policy.[45] Lansing pled guilty to the murder and received a life sentence,[46] then testified against Mary Saisi. On March 2, 1960, Mary Saisi was found guilty and sentenced to sixty years at the Dwight Women's Prison in central Illinois.[47]

THE *MONROE V. PAPE* LITIGATION

Weeks after the police arrested and charged Richard Lansing with Peter Saisi's murder, James Monroe and his family were contacted by Donald Page Moore of the Illinois branch of the ACLU. Moore was a prominent civil rights attorney who had successfully defended dozens of black suspects in criminal cases by challenging confessions and other evidence obtained by overzealous and often brutal police tactics.[48] It is not clear how Moore or the ACLU found Monroe, whose arrest was never reported in all of the ubiquitous news coverage surrounding the "Saisi love triangle case." But Moore would likely have suspected that Mary Saisi's initial identification of "two young Negroes" necessarily

---

accessible, that he was not permitted to call his family or attorney, that he was subsequently released without criminal charges being preferred against him").

[45] *Admits Triangle Slaying*, CHI. DAILY TRIB., Nov. 30, 1958, at 1.

[46] *Killer Names Mrs. Saisi in Murder Plot*, CHI. DAILY TRIB., Feb. 25, 1960, at 1.

[47] *Saisi's Widow Found Guilty; Gets 60 Years*, CHI. DAILY TRIB., Mar. 2, 1960, at B7; *see also* People v. Saisi, 24 Ill. 2d 274 (1962).

[48] Moore had most famously represented Paul Crump, a twenty-two-year-old black man who was taken into custody by Chicago police officers in 1953 based on suspicion that he had been involved in a botched hold-up that resulted in the murder of a security guard. Crump was held for several days, released, and then rearrested; during these intermittent interrogations, Crump repeatedly asked to speak with a lawyer, but was denied. Finally, after a particularly rough twenty-two-hour interrogation session, Crump confessed to the crime. He was later sentenced and put to death, but his treatment by the police is credited with bringing public attention to abusive interrogation practices. *People ex rel. Crump v. Sain*, 264 F. 2d 424 (7th Cir. 1959); *see also Reck v. Pate*, 367 U.S. 433 (1961) (Moore represented a nineteen-year-old, mentally-handicapped black youth who was arrested, interrogated and brutalized by the Chicago police for four days before confessing to a murder he later said he did not commit.).

resulted in a number of black men being arrested and interrogated on the West Side of Chicago in the days following the murder.

On March 2, 1959, Moore filed an action in the Northern District of Illinois seeking $200,000 in damages against Frank Pape and the twelve detectives who participated in the raid, as well the City of Chicago, under 42 U.S.C. § 1983.[49] The complaint detailed the events of October 29, 1958, and claimed that, in illegally entering and searching the Monroe home and seizing James Monroe, the police officers had violated the Monroes' rights under the 14th amendment. On June 2, District Judge Julius Hoffman (who would later preside over the trial of the Chicago Seven) quickly dismissed the complaint, finding that § 1983 did not provide a cause of action against state officers who engaged in a search that violated state law. In other words, § 1983's "under color of" language required a finding that the official was authorized by state law or custom to do what he did; here, the policemen, in breaking into the Monroe home, "violated the Constitution and laws of Illinois" rather than acted under authority of those laws. On November 23, 1959, the Seventh Circuit affirmed, suggesting that Monroe seek relief in the state courts. Moore filed for Supreme Court review.[50]

The Justices granted certiorari in March 1960 and heard oral arguments on November 8, 1960. On February 20, 1961, the Court, in an opinion by Justice William O. Douglas (over a solitary dissent by Justice Felix Frankfurter on the issue of whether the city of Chicago was a "person" within the meaning of § 1983), reversed the lower courts and found that the federal civil rights statutes indeed provided a remedy to the Monroes. Justice Douglas began by reviewing the historical foundations of the Reconstruction-era legislation, enacted by the 42nd Congress largely in response to the failure of local law enforcement to curb incidents of racial violence.[51] Douglas then famously concluded that the "legislation was passed to afford a federal right in federal courts because, by reason of prejudice, passion, neglect, intolerance or otherwise, state laws might not be enforced and the claims of citizens to the enjoyment of rights, privileges and immunities guaranteed by the Fourteenth amendment might be denied by the state agencies."[52] As such, the Monroes had a valid § 1983 claim against Frank Pape and his detective squad, who

---

[49] Complaint, Monroe v. Pape, No. 59–C–329.

[50] 272 F.2d 365 (7th Cir. 1959).

[51] 365 U.S. at 175–76 ("While one main scourge of the evil—perhaps the leading one— was the Ku Klux Klan, the remedy created was not a remedy against it or its members, but against those who representing a State in some capacity were *unable* or *unwilling* to enforce a state law.")

[52] 365 U.S. at 180.

were "clothed with the authority of state law," and whose actions were therefore taken "under color of" state law.

The justices remanded the case for trial, which started on November 5, 1962, before District Judge James B. Parsons, who presided over an all-white jury of nine women and three men. Claims against eight of the officers were dismissed during the course of the trial.[53] Finally, on December 4, 1962, the jury returned a verdict finding Frank Pape and the remaining four detectives liable for violating the civil rights of James Monroe and his family, and awarding $13,000 in damages.[54] Judge Parsons denied the defendants' motions to vacate the jury award and for a new trial, but did reduce the damages to $8,000.[55] Pape did not appeal the ruling; he quickly paid the judgment and refused to be interviewed on the subject. His co-defendants, however, were vocal in criticizing the Supreme Court's decision and the subsequent jury verdict as "a travesty on justice, a severe blow to law enforcement, and a step backwards."[56]

Frank Pape was not entirely silent about this case. In its November 1961 report on race relations entitled *Justice*, the United States Commission on Civil Rights devoted a section to "police brutality and related private violence."[57] That section contained a description of the facts underlying *Monroe v. Pape* and a discussion of the Supreme Court's recent opinion, allegedly based primarily on interviews with James Monroe, his lawyer, Donald Moore, as well as the pleadings filed in the case.[58] In particular, the Commission's report stated that "Pape and the other Detectives went to the Monroe house ostensibly to investigate a murder."[59]

A week later, on March 24, 1961, *Time* magazine reported on the publication under the caption "Civil Rights": "*Justice* carries a chilling text about police brutality in both the South and the North—and it stands as a grave indictment, since its facts were carefully investigated by field agents and it was signed by all six of the noted educators who

[53] *Pape Suit Jury Is Out in Civil Rights Case*, CHI. DAILY TRIB., Dec. 4, 1962, at 6.

[54] *Order Pape, 4 Others to Pay $13,000*, CHI. DAILY TRIB., Dec. 5, 1962.

[55] *Refuses New Trial to Pape, 4 Other Cops*, CHI. DAILY TRIB., Dec. 13, 1962, at 14.

[56] *Id.*

[57] U.S. COMM'N ON CIVIL RIGHTS REPORT, BOOK V: JUSTICE 20–21 (1961).

[58] ADAMSON, *supra* note 20, at 193 (complaining that neither Frank nor any of the detectives that were there that night were interviewed for the Report)

[59] U.S. COMM'N ON CIVIL RIGHTS, *supra* note 57, at 20–21; *see also* Adamson, *supra* note 20, at 193 ("There was no 'ostensibly' about it. When Frank went to the Monroe house to take him into custody, it was because his photograph had been identified by Mary Saisi as the killer of her husband. He didn't go there to 'ostensibly' do anything; he went there to arrest Monroe, as he should have.").

comprise the commission."[60] The article then described the *Monroe* incident, quoting at length from the complaint (as did this author, above). The article concluded that, while "[t]he officers were not punished" for their actions, "Monroe has carried a suit to the Supreme Court [and] is still seeking a civil judgment."

Frank Pape sued *Time* for libel, asserting that the article had failed to clearly indicate that the charges it described were made by James Monroe rather than the Commission itself. At the defamation trial, Pape called eight of the policemen who had participated in the Monroe raid to testify on his behalf: all swore that nothing resembling the events described in the *Time* article had occurred that night. Pape's case went all the way up to the Supreme Court, where he lost once again: the Court found the magazine article privileged and the publishers without malice or intent to falsify.[61]

FRANK PAPE: THE LATER YEARS

It is a testament to the changing ethos of the 1960s that the *Monroe* affair badly damaged Pape's reputation with the brass. This was especially true of superintendent O.W. Wilson, the former dean of criminology at the University of California, who had been hired by Mayor Richard Daley in 1960 to modernize the Chicago Police Department. Perceiving the political pressure, Pape decided in March 1961 to take a leave of absence from the department to run security at Arlington Park Racetrack.[62] During his four year absence, Pape was approached to run for Cook County Sheriff, to head the state police and to interview for police superintendent.[63] But he refused these opportunities because, as he later told a reporter, "I didn't want to become a political football being kicked from one goal post to another."[64]

---

[60] *Dawdling on the Corner*, TIME, Nov. 24, 1961, available at http://www.time.com/time/magazine/article/0,9171,828835,00.html.

[61] Time, Inc. v. Pape, 401 U.S. 279 (1971); *see also Judge Dismisses Police Capt. Frank Pape's Libel Suit*, N.Y. TIMES, Jan. 1, 1979, at 24.

[62] *Pape to Take Tracks Job This Week*, CHI. TRIB., Apr. 9, 1961, at A12; *see also* ADAMSON, *supra* note 23, at 189–90 (suggesting that Wilson and his cronies were afraid of Pape because he had "the ear of the Mayor and the press," so they pushed him to take a leave to save the Department further embarrassment.)

[63] *See* ADAMSON, *supra* note 20, at 186–87. When Pape interviewed for Police Commissioner, he was forced to submit to a psychological exam, which "was not Pape's shining hour, as [the psychological evaluators reported] that he 'lacked the qualities of a competent administrator.' " *Id.*

[64] Anne Keegan, *Toughest Cop in Town: The Legendary Frank Pape Has Been Retired for 22 Years, But the Force is Still With Him*, CHICAGO TRIBUNE, Feb. 9, 1994, at 1.

Still, Pape could not stay away from the job he loved. He returned to the police force in 1965—a return that was loudly criticized by local civil rights groups[65]—and found a much changed department.[66] Police procedures had been updated, motorized patrol had overtaken foot patrol and officers wore brass nametags. The Department even had an official motto, "We Serve and Protect."

But much was the same: the racially charged climate of the City of Chicago had only intensified in the 1960s, as black Chicagoans "broke the relative calm by raising their voices and taking to the streets to protest racial inequalities."[67] In August 1965, a fire truck allegedly driven by a drunken white fireman swerved and killed a black girl on the West Side, leading to four nights of rioting in which seventy-seven blacks were injured in fights with the police.[68] In July 1966, Martin Luther King, Jr. visited Chicago to meet with Mayor Daley, touching off three days of rioting that caused King to comment that "the people of Mississippi ought to come to Chicago to learn how to hate." After King was assassinated in April 1968, rioting broke out in cities all over America, but Chicago saw some of the worst: the National Guard was called in and Daley infamously ordered police "to shoot to maim or cripple" any rioter and "shoot to kill" any arsonist.

Nor was the essential culture of the Chicago police force altered. In April 1968, over six thousand people gathered in the Civic Center to protest the Vietnam War, and the police broke up the rally with clubs and batons. This set the stage for the infamous Democratic National Convention in the summer of 1968, when anti-war protesters repeatedly clashed with police. As *Time* magazine later reported, "[w]ith billy clubs, tear gas and Mace, the blue-shirted, blue-helmeted cops violated the civil rights of countless innocent citizens and contravened every accepted code of professional police."[69]

In 1970, the Walker Report to the National Commission on the Causes and Prevention of Violence pointed to the Chicago police as the source of the violence, and recommended massive changes: "many policemen charged with preserving law and order in the nation's second

---

[65] *2 Groups Rap Pape's Return as Policeman*, CHI. TRIB., Apr. 21, 1965, at C10.

[66] *Capt. Pape Returns to Duty with Police*, CHI. TRIB., May 4, 1965, at B10.

[67] JAMES R. RALPH, JR., NORTHERN PROTEST: MARTIN LUTHER KING, JR., CHICAGO, AND THE CIVIL RIGHTS MOVEMENT 13 (1993).

[68] ROGER BILES, RICHARD J. DALEY: POLITICS, RACE, AND THE GOVERNING OF CHICAGO 113 (1995). The Watts riot in Los Angeles also occurred in mid-August 1965, but resulted in thirty-one deaths and hundreds of injuries.

[69] *Chicago Examined: Anatomy of a "Police Riot,"* TIME, Dec. 6, 1968, available at http://www.time.com/time/magazine/article/0,9171,844633-1,00.html.

largest city at a crucial moment in history responded . . . with frequently unrestrained and indiscriminate violence."[70] The Kerner Commission on Civil Disorders, appointed by President Lyndon B. Johnson to study the cause of the urban rebellions of the 1960s, also reported that police were central to comprehending and resolving racial hostilities: "in practically every city that has experienced racial disruption since the summer of 1964, abrasive relationships between police and Negroes and other minority groups have been a major source of grievance, tension and, ultimately disorder." According to that report, "[p]olice misconduct—whether described as brutality, harassment, verbal abuse, or discourtesy. . . contributes directly to the risk of civil disorder [and] is inconsistent with the basic responsibility of a police force in a democracy."[71]

Pape, meanwhile, was made commander of the Englewood District, a gang-ridden, racially-polarized section of the city. He later described an incident in which he heard rumors of a gang war in his district, so he "went around to the places all these punks hung out and I said, 'I hear you are going to have a gang war. Fine. I'll be there with five of my guys with baseball bats, and you all better bring a lot of cars, because when we get done with you there won't be enough ambulances to take you to the hospital.'"[72] As official Pape hagiography would have it, "there was no gang war that day."[73]

But it seems doubtful such old-school tactics were really very effective at the dawn of the 1970s, and Pape did not last long in Englewood. He was transferred around a few times until he finally retired from the Chicago Police Department in 1972 as a captain, having served for nearly thirty-nine years. Fifteen hundred people attended his retirement dinner, including Mayor Daley, and the toasts alone reportedly lasted over three hours.[74]

Towards the end of his life, Frank Pape was bitter about the changes he saw around him. He told the *Chicago Tribune* in 1994 that "he wouldn't join the police department nowadays because the methods had changed so much." He believed that police officers were no longer respected for the work they did and longed for the "good old days":

> Criminals respect one thing—that you have more muscle than
> they have. When you've got that, they listen. The police force is

---

[70] THE WALKER REPORT TO THE NATIONAL COMMISSION ON THE CAUSES AND PREVENTION OF VIOLENCE, VIOLENCE IN CHICAGO: RIGHTS IN CONFLICT vi–vii (1968).

[71] REPORT OF THE NATIONAL ADVISORY COMMISSION ON CIVIL DISORDERS 299 (1968).

[72] ADAMSON, *supra* note 20, at 165.

[73] *Id.*

[74] *Id.* at 200.

our peacetime army, but they are getting no support anymore from John Q. Public. Today, every move a policeman makes is scrutinized by the public, more so than the criminal. Hell, they are investigated within the department, from without the department and by anyone else who wants to take a crack at them. These men have mortgages. They have children like everyone else. They have not been divested of their conscience because they are policemen. But because of the scrutiny, because the public wants to talk about crime but not do anything about it like we did in my day, these policemen are retreating from crime rather than going forward and confronting it. They are doing this because their jobs are in jeopardy. It hurts me to see this. It takes guts to fight crime, but it takes everyone to have guts. Policemen today have lost the support of the people, and because of that the people have lost control of their country. Damn shame, really.[75]

On March 5, 2000, Frank Pape died of a heart attack in his home in Park Ridge at the age of 91.[76]

The Effect of *Monroe*
On Police Brutality Claims

It is understandable if Frank Pape and his squad of detectives felt largely above the law in 1958. Surely, the defendants and their attorneys must have been utterly stunned to find that the actions alleged in *Monroe* could lead to federal civil liability. Of course, that is the entire reason why *Monroe* is a seminal case in civil rights courses.

Less clear is how much has changed in the intervening half-century. Police officers have come to understand that assaultive and racially denigrating behavior can expose them to liability in the federal courts. And the federal courts probably remain, by and large, less prone to pro-police biases than the local court systems in which the officers ply their trade on a daily basis. But the deterrent force of federal civil liability presents an open question.

On the one hand, the issues of racially tinged police misconduct and brutality have only become more visible since "explod[ing] onto the nation's consciousness—and into the streets of Los Angeles—with the home video depicting the vicious beating of Rodney King by four police officers."[77] In New York, a series of high-profile incidents have likewise

---

[75] Keegan, *supra* note 64.

[76] Obituaries, Chi. Trib., Mar. 12, 2000.

[77] Myriam Gilles, *Breaking the Code of Silence: Rediscovering "Custom" in Section 1983 Municipal Liability*, 80 B.U. L. Rev. 17, 18 (2000).

brought the issue of police brutality into sharp focus, making household names of victims like Abner Louima and Amadou Diallo. And indeed, U.S. cities of all sizes continue to have their own experiences with police victimization of members of minority populations.

On the other hand, my intuition—informed more by anecdote than empiricism—is that police abuse *has* proven responsive to the threat of civil rights liability. In particular, I think, the everyday brand of abuse has abated in significant measure: the heavy-handed policing of old-school cops giving vent to old-school prejudices, secure in the knowledge that the victim is certain to take his beat-down and remain silent, as he has nothing to gain by coming forward. It is difficult to imagine being Frank Pape—policing like Frank Pape—in a world where multi-million dollar civil rights settlements have as much mythological pull as hard-boiled Chicago lawmen once did.

As with Pape himself, it is the myth that matters.

4

Sheryll Cashin*

Hadnott v. Amos: Unleashing the Second Reconstruction

On July 29, 1969, nine days after man landed on the moon, four years after enactment of the Voting Rights Act, and a century after Reconstruction, black Americans gained political control of Greene County, Alabama—one of the nation's poorest corners, located near the Mississippi border in the state's Black Belt.[1] The Greene County special election was the first election ordered by the Supreme Court as a consequence of the Voting Rights Act and the first time since Reconstruction that blacks, voting *en masse*, were the dominant political actors in an election, albeit a local one. It was also the first time that a predominantly black, independent political party, the upstart National Democratic Party of Alabama (NDPA), rather than the radical Republican Party, led the black rural poor to electoral success. *Hadnott v. Amos* is the little known case that enabled this political party to field a statewide slate of candidates—a first for a black-led third party—and transform Wallace-dominated politics in the "keystone state of massive resistance." The case is significant not for the substance of the legal issues resolved by the Court but the second Reconstruction it helped unleash. In Alabama, NDPA became a training ground for political

---

* This essay includes excerpts from my book, The Agitator's Daughter: A Memoir of a Family (forthcoming, PublicAffairs). In writing the essay, I chose to dispense with footnote citation methods typical of legal scholarship. The bibliography following the essay lists sources that I relied upon in writing this work.

[1] The Black Belt had been the greatest source of black political power in the Deep South a century before. The plantation economy that reigned in these dark-soiled, agriculturally rich counties necessarily concentrated large populations of slave labor among a small, white planter elite. When Reconstruction transformed former slaves into voters by the thousands, suppression became the only route to white political dominance. And, after the fall of Reconstruction, for nearly a century suppression had worked.

engagement for the first wave of newly registered black voters propelled into full citizenship by the Voting Rights Act. It was the most pronounced example in the south of the re-emergence of black political strength—one that inspired similar mobilization of black voters in other Deep South states and marked the beginning of racial realignments in American politics. Through its challenges for recognition at the 1968 and 1972 Democratic national conventions, NDPA forced liberalization of party rules on delegate selection, opening the way for a more inclusive state and national Democratic Party.[2] As the Democratic Party became a meaningful home to most southern black voters, the racial narrative under-girding southern and American politics would be transformed indelibly, even as modern racial schisms of an increasingly diverse electorate continue. This is the story of the beginnings of that second Reconstruction.

The Historical Context

"White supremacy" had been a mainstay of Alabama politics since Reconstruction. Before 1966, upon entering the voting booth in Alabama elections, a voter would find candidates for the Alabama Democratic Party (ADP) listed under the party's emblem, a white rooster. The rooster crowed under a banner that read "White Supremacy," with "for the Right" ruffled below its feet.[3]

The ADP's white supremacy strategy was a direct response to the biracial coalitions that had formed during Reconstruction, 100 years earlier. The interracial alliances among newly emancipated Negroes, recently arrived northern "carpetbaggers" and moderate southern "scalawags" that animated successful radical Republican politics in other southern states during Reconstruction was slow in coming and short-lived in

---

[2] As the author of this "civil rights" story, I must disclose that I am not unbiased in its telling. My father, Dr. John L. Cashin, Jr., was the founder of NDPA. I grew up licking NDPA envelopes, attending NDPA meetings, and watching my parents' activism in the social and political movements that dominated the South in the 1960s and '70s. A measure of the political transformation that occurred in Alabama, in no small part as a result of NDPA, is that by the time I entered a voting booth for the first time in March, 1980, as an eighteen year old, I voted for Jimmy Carter in that Democratic presidential primary and for myself as a convention delegate pledged to Carter. By then the Alabama Democratic Party was actively recruiting women and minorities to serve as delegates and to play a leadership role in the party. When they approached my father to run for delegate he demurred, instead suggesting that his daughter, the next generation, take up the mantle. I garnered enough votes to attend the Democratic National Convention of 1980 as an alternate delegate, and have been a close observer of national and southern politics ever since.

[3] It was at the urging of the same instigators that would found NDPA a year later that the Alabama Democratic Party finally replaced its long-held official slogan with "Democrats for the Right." Such "reform" was not enough, however, to stop black insurgents from forming an independent party.

Alabama. In 1868 a majority of Alabama voters, most of whom were black, ratified a progressive state constitution guaranteeing universal male suffrage. The state's first Reconstruction legislature convened the same year. It included twenty-seven proud colored men. With the help of Negro votes, this legislature made some valiant strides toward a vision of human equality. In 1869 it adopted a system of free, albeit segregated, public education and ratified the 15th Amendment.

By 1874, however, this brief interlude of inclusive, interracial politics had come to an end. Racial battle lines had been drawn, or redrawn. Four years before, in 1870, the ADP had adopted the slogan of "white supremacy." Alabama Republicans responded to the white supremacy movement by relegating blacks to the lowest positions in their party and suppressing their demands for participation in government. In the fall elections of 1874, Democrats would succeed in retaking control of all branches of state government, using every legal and extra-legal method at their disposal. A month after the election one black Republican expressed his dismay in a letter to President Grant and Congress:

> [F]or three or four months past, especially, our lives and the lives of nearly all Republicans in this state have had no protection ... hundreds of the active and earnest Republicans of this state ... have been assassinated and many of our race were shot down and killed at the polls on the 3rd day of November last only because they chose to exercise their right to vote.

The Ku Klux Klan, the Knights of the White Camelia and other secret societies had, by then, become the terrorist wing of the Democratic Party. Between the terror inflicted by these groups and the machinations of Democratic politicians, resistance to black participation in politics and lawmaking was systemic, organized and concrete. Nevertheless, in Montgomery my great-grandfather, Herschel V. Cashin, was among the colored candidates elected to the legislature in 1874 as a radical Republican. Even in that blood-soaked election, Negro candidates succeeded in Black Belt counties in which the sheer numbers of black voters overwhelmed any armed insurgents. There were 80,000 registered black voters in Alabama and many of these former bondsmen were determined to exercise the signature right of citizenship, even at the risk of death or loss of livelihood. Still, Reconstruction died.

With the Hayes–Tilden Compromise of January 1877, the weary Republican Congress agreed to remove federal troops from the last of the occupied southern states in exchange for Democrats accepting Rutherford Hayes as the electoral winner in the disputed presidential election of 1876. Through violence, fraud, economic reprisals and gerrymandering, Alabama Democrats tightened their hold on power. After 1878 the Negro lawmaker all but disappeared from the Alabama legislature.

By 1900, with the collapse of the Populist Party in 1898, and a Republican camp badly weakened by multiple fissures, Democrats were completely dominant. Following the lead of Mississippi, South Carolina and other southern states, in January 1901 the party leaders issued a call for a state constitutional convention, with the chief aim of forever removing the Negro from political life in the state of Alabama. One hundred fifty-five white men, most of whom were Democrats, were sent to the constitutional convention to decide the fate of black and poor white voters. The President of the Convention, John B. Knox, was pointed in his opening keynote address as to the task at hand, "to establish white supremacy in this State . . . by law." He canvassed some of the race-neutral innovations that had been deployed in other southern states to elude the 15th Amendment, arguing that such provisions were justified "in law and morals" because of the purported intellectual and moral inferiority of the Negro.

The Convention delegates produced a proposed constitution that deployed several subterfuges to disenfranchise black voters, chief among them poll taxes and literacy tests.[4] The document was ratified in November 1901, in a tightly contested state election in which the margin of victory was provided by Negroes in the Black Belt who "voted" overwhelmingly to disenfranchise themselves. The effect of the new constitution on black voting strength was devastatingly swift. In 1900, according to the *Alabama Official and Statistical Register*, there were 181,315 eligible black voters in Alabama. By January of 1903, only 2980 blacks were registered in the entire state.

This history left an indelible imprint in on my family. As a young boy growing up in the Depression and the era of Jim Crow, my father, Dr. John L. Cashin, Jr., would hear the family elders—his father, aunts and uncles—refer with derision and humor to the Alabama Constitution of 1901 as the "Cashin Castration Constitution." The elders spoke with pride about my great-grandfather H.V. Cashin's exploits during Reconstruction. He was one of 700 blacks who served in legislatures of the former Confederacy in the late 19th century. H.V. Cashin's six children

---

[4] Institutionalizing white supremacy was not the only obsession of the constitution's drafters. In the previous decade elite planters and industrialists had weathered a brief, interracial insurgency of poor white and black farmers working through the Populist Party. The 1901 Constitution was designed to prevent such uprisings for all time. Crafted as a detailed legal code rather than a generalist document, it maintained the status quo—a low tax state that placed the burden of raising revenue for public improvements and education on local communities—by greatly restricting local communities' powers. As a consequence, a locality seeking to do anything remotely progressive would have to seek approval of the state legislature. The stratagem succeeded, resulting a century later in the world's longest, most-amended constitution and a state with the lightest tax burden by far in the south—one where large farmers and timber interests especially contribute little to government coffers.

developed a family lore and hero worship about their father that they passed on to the next generation.[5]

Dad grew up with an unusual sense of personal obligation to "finish Grandpa Herschel's work." This great stream of history—the fact that blacks wielded power commensurate to their numbers and that 19th century Alabama boasted three (three!) black Congressman—imbued my father with a sense of the promise of "Africanus Alabamus," one of many colorful phrases he coined to describe the people he loved dearly. Grandpa Herschel's trajectory became fused in my father's mind with the successes of Reconstruction, and fueled his determination a century later, in founding NDPA, to return Negroes in the Black Belt to their rightful place in American democracy.

The Founding of NDPA

Being sentimental and perhaps superstitious, my father planned to file the paperwork for the NDPA charter on December 15, 1967, my sixth birthday. He had two main objectives. First, liberals in the state had grown disgusted with the hegemony of segregationist, Wallace-oriented politics. In four of the five previous presidential elections a voter could not support the national Democratic Party candidate for president because the ADP was beholden to its "Dixiecrat" elements. In 1964, for example, in Alabama it was impossible to vote to support the re-election of President Lyndon B. Johnson because the "white rooster" party offered a slate of un-pledged presidential electors. White liberals within the party attempted solve this problem, and perhaps to pre-empt the founding of NDPA, by forming the Alabama Independent Democrat Party (AIDP) which was created for the sole purpose of allowing citizens in the state to vote for a slate of electors formally pledged to the national Democratic presidential nominee.[6] But the AIDP had no intention of fielding candidates for state or local office, and therefore it could not solve the second problem that blacks and progressive whites perceived with the state of Alabama: disempowerment and disenfranchisement of the state's black voters.

After the passage of the Voting Rights Act, as federal registrars descended upon the state and indigenous and exogenous voting rights

---

[5] Not all of the lore was true; Grandpa Herschel was not the "chief architect" of Reconstruction in the state, as my father believed. But he did serve in the legislature and in 1878 was an early, rare example of a colored man admitted to the Alabama Bar. His work on behalf of public education, as a lawyer, and as Receiver of Public Monies—a federal patronage appointment that put him in charge of distributing public lands in north Alabama under the Homestead Act—loomed large in the family history.

[6] AIDP filed its charter shortly before NDPA, causing Dad to delay the founding of the party by a few weeks. But in his memories NDPA was always referred to as my birthday gift.

workers labored diligently to expand the franchise, the ranks of registered black Alabamians swelled to hundreds of thousands.[7] Many of
these new voters were semi-literate, desperately poor residents of the
Black Belt, where local Democratic operatives tended to be white political and economic elites who were uncooperative and obstructionist when
local black leaders attempted to organize black voters and field black
candidates. Most Black Belt counties were ruled literally and figuratively
by a small number of white families who derived economic might from
timber, soybeans or whatever the dominant use of land was in a given
county. Through black voter empowerment, the founders of NDPA
hoped to break the yoke of rural feudalism in the state.

But they were not the first to try. The Reverend William McKinley
Branch, a schoolteacher and Baptist preacher, had founded the Greene
County Civic Organization in 1965, which had been working doggedly to
register blacks to vote. Elsewhere in the Black Belt, Stokely Carmichael
and other members of the Student Non–Violent Coordinating Committee
(SNCC) had founded the Lowndes County Freedom Organization
(LCFO), an independent political party which fielded a roster of candidates in November 1966, in an attempt to rally blacks to register to vote
and break the hold of the white political and economic elites on this
overwhelmingly black and poor county in central Alabama. Carmichael
had coined the mantra "black power" a few months before and would
soon take SNCC in a direction of militant, separatist activism, especially
in the realm of grassroots electoral politics.[8] But no LCFO candidates
succeeded in the 1966 election, leaving many local blacks to believe the
election had been stolen though fraud and intimidation by the "white
rooster" Democrats.[9]

---

[7] Many voter registration workers hailed from the Southern Regional Council, the
Southern Christian Leadership Conference (SCLC), or the Student Non–Violent Coordinating Committee (SNCC), the two latter groups having been seminal in the mobilization of
the sit-in movement throughout the south.

[8] This new direction for SNCC included an explicit rejection of its integrationist origins
and explicit embrace of black nationalism; in 1967 Carmichael presented his intellectual
argument for such separatist tactics in *Black Power: The Politics of Liberation*, which he
co-authored with Charles Hamilton. Although the LCFO may have been borne of this
nationalist ideology, the founders of NDPA were explicitly integrationist, even as they
harbored a healthy respect for the competence of blacks to lead themselves out of political
bondage.

[9] The LCFO became known as the "Black Panther Party," because, pursuant to
Alabama election law, political parties were required to choose an emblem to appear on
ballots. The militant leaders in Lowndes chose a black panther as its symbol. The LCFO
should not be confused with the Black Panther Party for Self Defense, which was founded
in October 1966 in Oakland, California by Huey P. Newton and Bobby Seale.

Several blacks throughout the Black Belt had attempted to integrate the ADP by seeking to run for office in 1966. A young Reverend Thomas Gilmore, a cousin to the older Branch, was one of them. He lost his bid to become Sheriff of Greene County in the Democratic primary. He tried again in the fall of 1966 as a candidate on the Greene County Freedom Party ticket, a local independent party Branch and others founded that year on the heels of LCFO's example. But the probate judge left his name off the ballot, presaging the battle NDPA would have to fight a few years later.[10] Not surprisingly, Gilmore, Branch and others were highly receptive when they heard about efforts to organize a statewide independent political party.

The founders of the AIDP had chosen the national Democrats' symbol, the donkey, for its ballot emblem, leaving NDPA in a quandary as to what mascot would be its standard bearer. When Dad and Orzell Billingsley,[11] NDPA's general counsel, filed the party's charter, constitution and proposed party emblem with Mabel Amos, the Secretary of State, they too had initially chosen the donkey, which Amos rejected, citing its use by another party. Dad then opted for the bald eagle. Such symbols were of particular importance in the Black Belt. The clarion call of NDPA became, "Mark your X under the Eagle." Voting the straight NDPA ticket in this manner provided an easy way for illiterate black voters to identify and select progressive black and white candidates for state and local office, while also voting for presidential electors pledged to the national Democratic party's presidential nominee.[12]

The LCFO became the base of organization for NDPA in Lowndes County. Several black candidates would be elected to local positions in Lowndes in 1968 and 1970 on the NDPA ticket.

[10] NDPA's other, more famous precursor, the Mississippi Freedom Democratic Party (MFDP), also did not succeed in fielding its own candidates on any state-sanctioned electoral ballot. Organized mainly by black Mississippians with the assistance of SNCC, and spurned from participating in the Mississippi Democratic Party's primaries, the MFDP held its own election to select delegates to attend the 1964 Democratic National Convention in Atlantic City, none of whom were formally seated. The MFDP garnered fame with Fannie Lou Hamer's passionate, televised oratory declaiming the exclusion of black Democrats loyal to the national party in favor of the white segregationist Mississippi delegation that had been seated at the convention. "Is this America?" she intoned, looking directly into the cameras. The national party, trying desperately not to lose its traditional base of white southern support to Republican presidential candidate Barry Goldwater, offered a compromise of two honorary seats to the MFDP, which its leaders refused.

[11] Orzell Billingsley was a close family friend and an unsung civil rights lawyer-hero in Alabama. Among his many acts of altruism, he provided counsel to Dr. Martin Luther King during the Montgomery Bus Boycott of 1955, helped incorporate over twenty majority black local governments in Alabama, and successfully challenged all-white juries in the case of *Billingsley v. Clayton*, 359 F.2d 13 (5th Cir. 1966).

[12] Two years later, Secretary Amos authorized two other parties to use the eagle emblem. When NDPA lawyers challenged this in federal court, she testified that the

Under Alabama election law, a political party could nominate its candidates for the general election either by a primary ballot or by a nominating caucus. NDPA chose the latter course. On May 7, 1968, primary-election day in the state, scores of blacks and liberal whites met at courthouses and churches throughout the state to nominate candidates for local office and delegates to the state NDPA convention. At the state convention held on July 20 in Birmingham, the NDPA delegates, mostly residents of the Black Belt—black people of modest means but great pride—nominated a slate of presidential electors and delegates to the now infamous Democratic National Convention in Chicago. They also selected a bi-racial slate of candidates for state and local races, among them Reverend Branch was nominated to run for Congress from his district. Unique among state political parties of the time, the NDPA delegates also debated and developed a party platform that was adopted at the convention. Harkening back to the radical politics of the late nineteenth-century Populists, the NDPA platform called for, *inter alia*, abolition of tax advantages given to industrial interests, a progressive restructuring of the tax system, a guarantee of the right to collective bargaining for farm workers, balancing the racial composition of juries, abolition of capital punishment and equal educational opportunities in completely integrated public school systems. It also weighed in on issues of environmental protection, abolishing the draft, encouraging U.N.-led efforts to stop nuclear and weapons proliferation, and halting the Vietnam War.[13]

One platform plank anticipated the court battle that would come: the NDPA delegates called for a repeal of the 1967 "Garrett Law," which required that any potential candidate for public office file a declaration of intent to run by March 1st—a full eight months before Election Day. The law was clearly aimed at the formation of new political parties, and if valid, the Garrett Law would keep NDPA ballots off the ballot in the fall elections.[14]

---

illiteracy of blacks and the difficulty of voting without clearly identifiable symbols had not occurred to her. The court blocked her action, enabling the NDPA eagle to fly solo in the November 1970 elections.

[13] NDPA was unique not only in committing to an explicit platform but also in creating a party newspaper, *The Eagle Eye*, which was circulated monthly throughout the state. The platform was reprinted on the back of every issue—a repeated, passionate call to purpose.

[14] The Garrett Act represented a new type of tool for obfuscation of black political engagement in the post-civil rights movement south. A similar provision deployed by the Mississippi legislature changed the time for filing a petition as an independent candidate from forty days before the *general* election to sixty days before the *primary* election. That provision was struck down by the Supreme Court in *Whitley v. Williams*, 393 U.S. 544 (1969), as a violation of the Voting Rights Act "pre-clearance" provision. Likely because Alabama election law otherwise made the formation and seeking of ballot position for

The Fight for Legitimacy

My father's vocation was dentistry but his avocation and passion was black political emancipation in Alabama. In 1968, when he and my mother left Alabama to attend the Democratic National Convention in Chicago I was aware of the tragedies convulsing the country. Dr. King had been assassinated in April, Robert Kennedy in June. The Vietnam War continued, seared in my memory mostly as war correspondents on television with echoes of gunfire and tanks rolling in the background. Even at six years old, I knew that "burn baby burn" had something to do with riots going on in black urban neighborhoods across the country. I would also experience the violent upheavals in the streets outside the Chicago convention through television, watching with my babysitter and hoping that my parents would not have to inhale tear gas. But I was oblivious to what was going on before the Credentials Committee at the convention.

The AIDP was now in direct competition with NDPA for official recognition by the national Democratic Party. The founders of AIDP offered two arguments against seating NDPA delegates. First they claimed that in Madison County, in northern Alabama where we lived, NDPA had not held a nominating meeting as required on primary election day, rendering NDPA out of compliance with nomination rules. In fact, NDPA had met, but simply had moved the meeting from the halls of the local courthouse to its coffee shop, for the convenience of attendees. Second, and more substantively, the AIDP lawyers argued, in effect, that NDPA was too liberal to represent the interests of Alabamians and that it was therefore a separate party from the Democratic Party. The Credentials Committee denied NDPA's challenge and, in effect, agreed to seat the AIDP. It imposed a loyalty requirement on Alabama delegates, most of whom harbored allegiances to George Wallace; all those who refused to sign a document disclaiming any disloyalty to the national party were replaced by AIDP delegates.

NDPA did not relent, taking the credentials fight to the convention floor. Willie Brown, who would later become the venerable Speaker of the California legislature, and the seasoned Mississippi Freedom Democratic Party (MFDP) veteran, Fannie Lou Hamer,[15] spoke to the conven-

independent third parties a relatively straightforward procedural endeavor, in enacting the Garrett Act, the Alabama legislature similarly sought to inhibit such parties' effectiveness.

[15] As described above in footnote 10, Ms. Hamer made her national debut at the 1964 DNC in Atlantic City with her powerful advocacy for credentials for the Mississippi Freedom Democratic Party of which she was Vice Chair. A daughter of Mississippi sharecroppers, she was the first in her town to answer SNCC's call to seek to register to vote, and paid for it with an arrest, threats and the loss of her job and residence as a sharecropper. She became a field secretary for SNCC and courageously endured death

tion delegates on behalf of NDPA. While their passionate eloquence roused the convention hall, it was not enough to garner victory. On the proposition of whether to replace the Alabama delegation with NDPA delegates, NDPA lost the roll call vote: 1605 against, 833 for.

The fight would continue back home in Alabama, only much more was at stake. In early September, Secretary of State Mabel Amos, citing a state attorney general's opinion, announced that NDPA had not complied with the Garrett Act and therefore NDPA candidates would not appear on any November ballot. In each county the probate judge had authority to certify local candidates and prepare the ballots that would be presented to voters in that county on election day. Several probate judges echoed Amos' charges. Amos also invoked the affidavits filed by AIDP lawyers in Chicago, claiming that NDPA had not held required mass meetings and caucuses on primary-election day.

Dad was ready for a fight, as he had been on many prior occasions. He and my mother were among the leaders of the sit-in movement in Huntsville, Alabama in 1962, in which public accommodations were successfully integrated well before passage of the Civil Rights Act of 1964.[16] And he had been a chief strategist behind the desegregation of the University of Alabama in Huntsville, where we lived. In these prior skirmishes he had relied successfully on the good work of Charles Morgan, Jr., a white liberal attorney from Birmingham who garnered fame, or infamy, for calling the white middle-class establishment to account for its complicity in the dynamics that led to the church bombing that killed four little girls. Morgan had been forced to leave Birmingham in a hurry after his speech to the Young Men's Business Club in which he said, "Who threw the bomb? . . . We all did it. Every last one of us is condemned for that crime." Morgan had become head of the ACLU's legal offices in Atlanta and had led the charge for NDPA before the Credentials Committee in Chicago, along with Orzell Billingsley.[17] Together Morgan and Billingsley filed *Hadnott v. Amos* in federal court in Montgomery on September 13, 1968.

---

threats and a severe beating for her work as an ardent, uncompromising local and national leader for voting rights.

[16] The turning point in this movement occurred when two women were arrested at a lunch counter under unusual circumstances. One, my mother, Joan Carpenter Cashin, was holding her four-month-old baby, Sheryll Denise, and the other, Martha Hereford, was eight months pregnant. These two doctors' wives spent two days in jail, although I was handed off to my grandmother. The publicity broke a months-long stalemate; city leaders finally appointed a committee to negotiate the terms of desegregation, which occurred peacefully in July 1962.

[17] Morgan was also lead counsel in the seminal case of *Reynolds v. Sims*, 377 U.S. 533 (1964), in which the Supreme Court issued its "one man—one vote" edict. That case, coupled with the Voting Rights Act, provided a necessary foundation on which NDPA was

The lead plaintiff, Mrs. Sally Mae Hadnott was Alabama's answer to Fannie Lou Hamer. A resident of Prattville, Alabama, and candidate for Autauga County Commissioner on the NDPA ticket, she was an ample, brown-skinned mother of eight with prodigious leadership skills and a homespun activist demeanor. She had founded the Autauga chapter of the NAACP and added a room to her home so that blacks had a means for organizing and a place to meet. Legend had it that she was personally responsible for registering hundreds of blacks to vote. Morgan and Billingsley thought her deserving of top billing in the case, but they also thought her surname "Hadnott" appropriately resonated the "have not" condition of NDPA's grass roots constituents.

After the suit was filed against her, Secretary Amos added the charge that NDPA had not complied with Alabama's Corrupt Practices Act, alleging that the NDPA candidates had failed to provide her with names of persons designated to manage their campaign finances. The NDPA leadership found this claim laughable as most of their candidates had no such finances. Three days after filing suit, Morgan sought a temporary injunction, arguing before a three-judge panel[18] the imperative of allowing NDPA candidates to be listed on absentee ballots while the case was pending. He invoked the ironic situation of George Wallace, who had been battling obstructions in his attempt to be listed as an independent candidate for president on the November ballot in the other forty-nine states. In the interests of promoting rather than constraining democracy, Justice Potter Stewart had ordered that Wallace's name be listed on ballots while his case against Ohio election officials, who invoked the tardiness of Wallace's filings, was pending. The federal panel in Montgomery must have concluded that what was fair for Wallace in Ohio was fair for NDPA in Alabama: the judges issued a temporary injunction requiring NDPA candidates be certified on any printed ballot pending the outcome of the case, which meant that no absentee ballots would be printed until the court issued a decision. The District Court, however, did not agree with NDPA on the merits. On the substantive challenges Morgan raised, the panel ruled two to one against NDPA, accepting the state's affidavit evidence suggesting non-compliance with

---

able to build a grass roots political movement in the Black Belt. Because of the *Reynolds* case, election districts in the state were now apportioned solely by population rather than skewed to favor the interests of the rural landed gentry. As one NDPA worker in Greene County eloquently put it during the special election of July 1969, "on election day my shoes will be the same size as the man who owns the bank!"

[18] At the time federal law, 28 U.S.C.A. § 2281, which has since been repealed, provided that an interlocutory or permanent injunction restraining the enforcement of a State statute on grounds of unconstitutionality could not be granted unless the application had been heard and determined by a three-judge district court.

the corrupt practices law and concluding that it and other election laws were valid both facially and as applied to NDPA.

Judge Frank Johnson dissented. He was emerging as a dependable judicial voice favoring civil rights and this case was no exception. He reasoned that the application of the corrupt practices and Garrett laws to NDPA constituted an equal protection violation under the U.S. Constitution. On the belated application of the corrupt practices law to NDPA candidates he stated: "The best of laws ... can be invoked in an unworthy manner." Here, he observed the law had been "invoked strictly as an afterthought." Worse, Johnson noted, this was the first time in recent memory that state officials had enforced the law. In previous cases of disqualification for failure to comply with the statute, it was invoked by opposing candidates or by concerned voters.

> Alabama State officials having adopted a consistent practice of relying on party and public policing and enforcement of this Act, it is not tolerable for this Court to allow these officials to make their first foray in the enforcement direction against a small, new, and almost surely impecunious group of candidates seeking to form a new party in Alabama. This is particularly true when the defendant officials who are taking such action are candidates for presidential electors on the ballot of an opposing party. Whether or not a formal conflict of interest, this circumstance, when conjoined with those above, justifies the inference that the Corrupt Practices Act, fair on its face, has been applied and administered by public authority with an evil eye and an unequal hand, so as practically to make unjust and illegal discriminations between persons in similar circumstances.

Regarding the Garrett Act's March 1 deadline for declarations of intent to run in primary and/or general elections, Johnson invoked the reasoning employed by the Southern District of Ohio on behalf of George Wallace: " 'to the extent that these laws prevent the qualification of political parties and their candidates for ballot position,' " they do not "satisfy the tests of 'necessity,' 'equality,' and 'reasonableness.' "

The District Court decision was issued on a Friday, October 11. With the general election looming, NDPA lawyers prepared an emergency appeal to Supreme Court Justice Hugo Black, a former U.S. Senator from Alabama, who, having been an active Democrat and briefly a Klansman, would have had a certain familiarity with the ways of Alabama politics.[19] After an heroic weekend of work, NDPA's jurisdictional statement was filed the following Monday morning. Justice Black

---

[19] Justice Black happened to be the justice at the Supreme Court assigned to receive emergency appeals from the then-Fifth Circuit in which Alabama was located.

recused himself from the case because his sister-in-law, Virginia Durr, was one of NDPA's nominees for presidential elector.[20]

The Supreme Court reinstated the temporary relief granted by the lower court, placed the case on its summary calendar, and heard oral argument on Friday, October 18. Morgan argued for NDPA and emphasized the complicated nature of Alabama ballots. Even the exceptionally literate Justices had difficulty understanding the eight columns of candidates and parties that comprised Alabama's proposed general election ballot.[21] Without the straight NDPA ticket, less literate souls who were inclined to support the national Democratic presidential ticket would have to first choose the slate of presidential electors offered by AIDP, as opposed to the Wallace-pledged electors offered by ADP's "white rooster" party. Then, because AIDP offered only a slate of presidential electors, blacks would have to go in search of state and local candidates offered by other political parties. Again, the offerings of the rooster party were not likely to be representative of the interests and concerns of the state's black voters. Six justices were sufficiently persuaded of the efficacy of NDPA's claims to issue an order the very next day, continuing the temporary relief pending their final decision. All of NDPA's candidates were required to appear on the November ballot. A slate of presidential electors pledged to the Humphrey–Muskie presidential ticket and eighty-nine candidates for state and local offices now had sixteen days to campaign.

The First Election

NDPA launched into action. With its shoestring budget, the party relied heavily on the altruism of well-known civil rights figures and the indigenous leadership of Black Belt counties. Sample ballots with the slogan "Mark your X under the Eagle" were passed out at mass meetings in the black churches that had provided the base of grass roots mobilization throughout the civil rights movement. On the airways of

---

[20] A privileged white southerner who became a civil rights and political activist, Durr and her husband Clifford were seasoned veterans of progressive causes, including posting bail for Rosa Parks when she was arrested for refusing to give up her seat on a Montgomery bus in 1955. They were active supporters of the sit-in movement and they opened their home to Freedom Riders who came south as citizen enforcers of the Supreme Court's edict barring discrimination in interstate transportation.

[21] "How many electors are there in Alabama?" a justice asked.

"Ten electors," Morgan replied.

"There are only eight in column one," a justice responded.

"No, sir, there are ten in this column, column three, and column seven, and also column five, which is the Republican party. If an illiterate person walks in, he can flip this lever here and then he would have to wander all across the ballot to find whoever he wants," Morgan offered.

black radio stations, Julian Bond, Corretta Scott King, and Ralph Abernathy offered urgent appeals to "Vote the Eagle Party."

It was a valiant effort that produced some clear victories. Nationally, Richard Nixon won the presidency even as George Wallace swept him at the polls in Alabama. Despite Wallace's and hence the ADP's dominance, seventeen of NDPA's local candidates won. Not surprisingly, all of these successes were in Black Belt Counties: Etowah, Marengo, and Sumter.[22] Overnight, whether she was ready for it or not, Alabama could now boast the most black elected officials of any southern state. And, because NDPA candidates came in second in most of the other races, the party was now entitled to appoint its own poll workers to participate during the next election. A funny thing happened in Greene County, however.

At 8:15 a.m. on Election Day, November 5, Dad's phone rang. It was Rev. Gilmore, the Greene County NDPA Chairman. "Doc, our candidates are not on the ballot!," Gilmore said. At Dad's direction, Gilmore checked the ballots at every polling place and NDPA candidates were not on any ballot anywhere in the county. Incensed, Dad placed a person to person call to the Greene County Probate Judge Herndon:

"This is the NDPA State Chairman and my Greene County Chairman tells me that our candidates are not on the ballot," Dad said.

"That's right, they sure aren't." Herdon responded.

"But the U.S. Supreme Court ordered them on the ballot," Dad exclaimed.

"Well, I've got a copy of that court order too, and in my opinion they are not legally qualified." Herndon replied.

"Man, what did you say your name was?" Dad challenged.

"My name is Judge James Dennis Herndon, that's who, the Probate Judge of Greene County, Alabama and you can do any damn thing you think you are big enough to do!" the judge shouted in outrage.

And with the uppity, even arrogant, assurance my father had managed to carry with him all of his life, despite growing up as a negro under Jim Crow, he replied firmly, "My name is Dr. John Cashin, Jr., Chairman of the National Democratic Party of Alabama, and I intend to do exactly that." Dad hung up, and after a few moments of shocked disbelief, called his lawyers. NDPA was headed back to the Supreme Court.

The Greene County Special Election

On November 15, ten days after the general election, Morgan and Billingsley filed a motion to hold Herndon in contempt, to declare elected

---

[22] In Marengo County, for example, NDPA elected five justices of the peace, three constables and the chairman of the board of education.

the seventeen NDPA candidates who won in other counties, and to order an unprecedented special election in Greene County.[23] The United States Solicitor General, former Harvard Law Dean Erwin Griswold, while tepid on the contempt claim, filed a brief strongly supporting NDPA's other claims. Meanwhile, the Justice Department succeeded in obtaining an injunction from the district court in Montgomery, preventing the ADP "rooster" candidates in the tainted election in Greene County, most of whom were incumbents, from beginning new terms of office.

The oral argument occurred on an icy winter morning, the day after President Nixon's inauguration. Alabama's lawyers were resolute in their defense of the application of the Garrett law to the NDPA candidates. And Herndon's lawyer attempted to evade contempt for his client by claiming that the probate judge simply had not heard about the Supreme Court's order in *Hadnott v. Amos*. It was a dubious assertion, one Morgan assaulted during oral argument by underscoring the affidavit evidence he had collected. The six black NDPA candidates, four who sought seats on the county commission and two on the school board, had thought it mighty strange that none of their white opponents bothered to campaign during election season.[24] In a county where black voters now outnumbered white ones by two to one, they must have had some reason to be utterly sanguine about the outcome.

In depositions, the ADP candidates all feigned ignorance about the Supreme Court order requiring ballot position for NDPA. "They all subscribe to newspapers, but nobody seems to have read them," Morgan argued. "They have all got television sets and they have got two television stations that they receive clearly .... And they never campaigned for office." Morgan concluded that their decision not to campaign had to be deliberate and coordinated. He could hear them all saying to Herndon, "Leave those names off the ballot!," Morgan exclaimed to the Court.

During rebuttal Justice Marshall interrupted Morgan, "So your only precedent is the dissenting opinion [below]?" As Morgan attempted to respond, Justice Marshall cut him off with a smile: "Judge Johnson is a

---

[23] Specifically they filed a motion before the Supreme Court to show cause why Herndon should not be held in contempt and why the election results in Greene County should not be set aside and new ones held.

[24] The four candidates for the five-member County Commission were Vassie B. Knott, Harry C. Means, Levi Morrow Sr., and Frenchie Burton. By law, the probate judge, Dennis Herndon, served as chair of the Commission. The two candidates for the five-member school board, on which one black incumbent already served, were Robert Hines and J.A. Posey. Because NDPA candidates for statewide office and presidential electors did appear on the ballot, and votes cast for the "straight" NDPA ticket outnumbered those cast for the ADP, it was clear to the Court that these local candidates would have won had they appeared on the ballot.

good judge." It was an apt harbinger of the opinion to come. Like Judge Johnson, Justice Douglas, writing for a majority of six, also found that the disparate application of the Corrupt Practices Law to impecunious black candidates ran afoul of the U.S. Constitution, only he invoked the First and Fifteenth Amendments rather than the Fourteenth Amendment's equal protection guarantee.[25] And the application of the Garrett law to the NDPA candidates constituted a violation of the Voting Rights Act's section 5 pre-clearance provision. Thus the Court overturned the District Court, instructed that the seventeen candidates elected in Sumter and Marengo counties be treated as "duly elected," and ordered a new election for Greene County, which state and local officials were required to schedule "promptly."

As for Herndon, Justices Douglas and Harlan believed there was "probable cause to conclude that Judge Herndon knowingly and purposefully evaded our order." With such evidence, they would have tried him before the Supreme Court itself. Instead, a majority of their colleagues left it to the District Court to initiate such proceedings. Throughout the civil rights movement, no public official, much less a judge, had been held in contempt of a federal court's desegregation order. By early 1971, Herndon's brand of southern defiance of the imperatives of civil rights would be met with a conviction for civil and criminal contempt. With the Greene County special election scheduled for Tuesday, July 29, the six NDPA candidates returned to campaigning and Dad called in as many favors he could of his friends in civil rights and political circles. As usual, he dug into his own pocket to help finance the campaign, and called on others for donations.[26] Once again civil rights veterans like Ralph Abernathy and Hosea Williams of the Southern Christian Leadership Conference (SCLC) descended on Greene County and the methods of the movement continued. In mass meetings at black churches, oratory and song were brought to bear to urge ordinary folk to get to the polls on election day and take up their place in history.

On the eve of the election, the First Baptist Church was filled to overflowing. The faithful and curious endured 100–degree heat for over four hours as speaker after speaker sought to inspire the masses. "We

---

[25] Specifically he invoked the Fifteenth Amendment "right of people regardless of their race, color, or previous condition of servitude to cast their votes effectively" and the First Amendment right "to band together for the advancement of political beliefs." Justices Stewart and White dissented in part and Justice Black took no part in the case.

[26] In his usual colorful vernacular, Dad said this of his altruism in an interview in 1972: "I made a pretty good killing in the stock market in 1966–67. So I have spent, hell, $150,000 keeping this thing [NDPA] going. That's the reason NDPA is alive; because an honest son-of-a-bitch like John Cashin said, 'People are more important than money; let's keep the damn thing alive.' "

can change the course of history!!" shouted Hosea Williams. Referring to the rough percentages of black and white populations of the county he continued. "It is not God's will that 85 black people be dominated by 15 white people. The Eagle party will prove that Martin Luther King's dream can come true!"

The day of the election whites in the county seemed either apprehensive or resigned. Blacks, dressed in their Sunday best, flocked to the polls, many giddy with the freedom of voting for the first time. They walked with pride. Or they rode to the polls in frantically organized car pools set up the night before. NDPA volunteers and SCLC workers from across the state drove and cajoled whomever they could find. Dad reserved the most recalcitrant cases for himself. He often told me the story of a woman, a septuagenarian, who refused to leave her house to vote. She lay in her bed, complaining of a toothache and whining about how nothing would change in a county where whites had run everything since time out of memory. Dad physically picked her up and carried her to his car and then to the polls. She entered the polling place in his arms, in disbelief that she would be allowed to vote. She came out the voting booth with her head high, walking on her two feet as if they had been renewed in some way. For the rest of the day she told Dad where to go and went with him into house after house, corralling voters and souls with the zeal of an apostle for her new religion of democracy.

"The victors of the Greene County Special Election appear at the county courthouse for their inauguration along with Rev. Ralph Abernathy (center) and their spouses."

Despite a two-to-one registration advantage and a heavy turnout, NDPA won the election by a surprisingly narrow margin of only about 200, suggesting that there were efforts to suppress or steal votes. Yet with federal observers swarming the county and the black electorate energized and organized, honest voters prevailed. With a clean sweep in the election, blacks gained a controlling majority on the county commission and school board. Black political aspirants throughout the state and the south were electrified by the possibilities. As Ralph Abernathy put it at the inauguration celebration, "This is the first time since Reconstruction that blacks have taken over a county in the Deep South or in America. We are going to replicate this throughout the Black Belt!" Dennis Herndon offered a different perspective to a reporter for the *New York Times*, "It was a black day for Eutaw," the county seat, he said dejectedly.

"Dr. John L. Cashin, Jr., founder and chairman of NDPA on the occasion of the 20th anniversary of the Greene County special election."

The 1970 Election

If NDPA hoped to replicate the Greene County example elsewhere, many whites were determined to preserve the status quo. The seventeen counties of the Black Belt became a fresh battleground in 1970. NDPA again ran a slate of statewide candidates and Dad ran for Governor against George Wallace, not with any illusion of winning but as the spokesperson for voting the "straight NDPA ticket." By then Dad had acquired a four-seat airplane, which he piloted himself in countless forays across the Black Belt. Often he took his family with him. At seemingly every church in the Black Belt, I watched Daddy give the same speech, and I never got tired of it. Always he entreated the faithful to mark their "X" under the eagle. He told them that the "X" was the Greek letter *chi*, the symbol of Jesus Christ. They could bear *His* cross in the voting booth. He would quote his hero, and later mine, Frederick Douglass, my favorite part:

> Those who profess to favor freedom and yet depreciate agitation are men who want crops without plowing up the ground, they want rain without thunder and lightning. They want the ocean without the awful roar of its many waters. This struggle may be a moral one, or it may be a physical one, and it may be both moral and physical, but it must be a struggle. Power concedes nothing without a demand. It never did and it never will. Find out just what any people will quietly submit to and you have found out the exact measure of injustice and wrong which will be imposed upon them.

The grassroots folk always liked what Dad had to say. As an affluent dentist he was not of them. And he was from north Alabama, which may as well have been Chicago. Yet they knew he had tied his fate to theirs and they appreciated the hell he was giving the white establishment.

But white political and economic elites in the Black Belt did not intend to give up their "way of life" without a fight. The chief obstacle NDPA faced in recruiting black candidates and registering voters was a well-cultivated fear of economic or physical retaliation. It was not uncommon for an announced NDPA candidate to be threatened with death or loss of employment.[27] On Election Day, college students who had been recruited by NDPA to serve as poll watchers observed repeated acts of voter intimidation and fraud.[28] The U.S. Commission on Civil

---

[27] In Lowndes County, for example, black sharecroppers who had worked for generations on large white-owned plantations lost their jobs and homes if they attempted to register to vote or participate in politics. A local NDPA leader in Sumter County was beaten when he attempted to observe ballot counting. In Greene County, NDPA candidates were told they would never live to take office if they won the election.

[28] A black Harvard student described a hostile atmosphere at a polling place in Hale County that was designed to discourage blacks from voting and elicit disqualifying mistakes: "Black people were constantly insulted and made to feel stupid. ... On the other hand white people who made mistakes were informed of the correct way to vote." An NYU student assigned to Greene County reported, "White people brought their maids and cooks in early in the morning and voted for them." A student assigned to Wilcox county reported that the probate judge "required anyone who needed assistance in voting to vote orally, only after hearing all 135 names read off" and forbade poll workers from indicating which

Rights found that white voter registration in many rural counties far exceeded 100 percent of the eligible white voting population. Against these odds, NDPA outpolled the ADP in four counties in the 1970 election.[29]

In Greene County, despite death threats, Reverend Branch became the probate judge, replacing Dennis Herndon in the most powerful office in the county,[30] and Thomas Gilmore became the county sheriff.[31] Although Wallace won by a landslide and NDPA did not fair well outside the Black Belt, suddenly it was possible to drive from the Georgia to Mississippi borders in the state and pass through mostly counties with black sheriffs, probate judges, school board members and county commissioners. The impoverished black electorate now had black representatives in official positions that had a greater impact on their daily lives than the American presidency. By assuming local roles of considerable authority, black officeholders ensured a pronounced decline in the political and economic exploitation endured by the black masses in these communities. Rural feudalism and white supremacy politics backed by threats of economic and physical reprisal were being replaced with robust competition for the hearts and minds of the entire electorate. Through NDPA, grass roots activists in the Black Belt also learned firsthand the mechanics of political organizing and party politics.[32] And, for the first time since Reconstruction, two blacks returned to the Alabama legislature, one elected on the NDPA ticket and the other elected under the ADP.[33]

---

names were on the NDPA ticket. A Radcliffe student observed that in Perry County: "They made sure all the white folks put their ballots in the correct box and they just smiled as they permitted Black folks to place their ballots in the wrong box. . . . All the ballots in the [wrong] box . . . were disqualified."

[29] While Dad and NDPA carried Bullock, Greene, Lowndes, and Macon counties, NDPA local leaders moved to filed suit in federal court, alleging vote fraud and challenging the results in Sumter, Perry and Hale counties. They were unsuccessful.

[30] In addition to chairing the County Commission and overseeing the preparation of ballots for elections, the probate judge controlled the issuing of deeds, land transfers, eviction notices, wills and mortgages. Decades later, for his long and faithful public service, Judge Branch was honored with the naming of the new William McKinley Branch Courthouse in Eutaw.

[31] Gilmore defeated "Big Bill" Lee, the longtime white incumbent who had once physically whipped him for demanding the arrest of a deputy who had struck a black schoolgirl. Once in office Gilmore garnered fame as a "movement sheriff" who wielded such moral authority in the county that he never had to carry a gun.

[32] At the county level, many of NDPA's leaders were veterans of the civil rights movement. Most notably, E.D. Nixon, widely recognized as the man who launched the Montgomery Bus Boycott and a former head of the Montgomery County chapters of the NAACP and the Pullman Porters union, was an influential force for the Montgomery County NDPA chapter.

[33] Thomas Reed was elected to the legislature on the NDPA ticket while renowned civil rights attorney Fred Gray was elected on the ADP ticket. By 1976, the number of blacks

Racial Transformations

By its very existence, NDPA helped hasten an attitude of inclusion on the part of the ADP. Having always included whites as candidates, workers and organizers, albeit as a pronounced minority, NDPA offered a model for coalition politics in the state.[34] Its formal challenges for recognition at the 1968 and 1972 Democratic National Conventions put pressure on ADP to recruit blacks and liberalize its rules for participation in party activities and delegations. It was inevitable, then, that NDPA's successes would lead to its own obsolescence. As newly elected blacks turned to the realities of *governing*, the need to seek state and federal funds administered by Democratic Party regulars underscored the advantages of working within the mainstream. And, in the face of a newly organized black voting bloc, the ADP was increasingly inclined to cultivate black leaders and followers.[35] In the interim, NDPA was a source of inspiration and debate for black political aspirants in other states. After the 1970 elections, Alabama boasted 107 black elected officials, substantially more than any other southern state, raising the question whether blacks should form independent parties elsewhere.[36]

---

serving in the legislature had risen to sixteen. Today thirty-four African Americans serve in that body, eight in the senate and twenty-six in the house, matching the numbers of their ancestors during Reconstruction.

[34] NDPA's proposed delegations to the Democratic National Conventions in 1968 and 1972, for example, were half black, half white, half female and half male, the exact kind of inclusive goals the national party would encourage and the ADP would ultimately adopt.

Among the whites who were NDPA stalwarts were Bill Edwards, a minimally paid idealist who served as the party's Executive Director from 1970–74 and occupied the guest bedroom in our home for several years, and Myrna Copeland, a party Vice–Chair and close family friend. The Unitarian Church in Huntsville, which my family attended, and the American Friends Service Committee were also a source of many white party volunteers.

[35] In 1970, six blacks won office on the ADP ticket, marking the beginning of that party's ascension as a stronghold of black political engagement. NDPA elected more blacks to office (17) in the 1968 general election than in 1970 (12), although many party leaders felt the 1970 results were tainted by voting rights violations. NDPA would continue to make inroads in the 1972 elections, however, when 34 of its candidates won local offices mostly in the western rural Alabama counties that had become NDPA strongholds: Greene, Monroe, Perry, Hale and Sumter. NDPA would win fewer offices in the 1974 and 1976 election cycles. In 1976, the party closed its state headquarters in Huntsville.

[36] In reality such an independent course was only viable in states with black belt counties that boasted majority black populations. In South Carolina, where blacks constituted a majority in 16 of 46 counties, the United Citizens Party (UCP) was formed in September 1970 in an effort to dismantle systemic exclusion in that state's politics. Its founder, a thirty-year old black attorney named John Harper declared to *Ebony Magazine*

Yet a necessary impetus for such third parties was rigid exclusion of blacks from regular Democratic Party operations. In states like Georgia, where Democrats had never been as systemically segregationist as in Alabama, and now in Alabama where the regular party was beginning to reform, third parties were much less viable.

In the 1970s George Wallace himself would moderate on race. Likewise, throughout the south, the Democratic Party would transform from pro-segregation to pro-civil rights. As the "white supremacy" politics of southern Democrats was replaced by an orientation toward inclusion, the Republican Party emerged in the south through a rather intentional strategy of cultivating disaffected whites with race-coded issues like affirmative action, busing, crime, and welfare. Fortunately overt race-coded appeals have less resonance today. Yet the racial schisms of the past persist in a southern electorate that remains divided between white voters who lean heavily Republican and communities of color that lean Democratic. The second Reconstruction has wrought dramatic improvements in black political representation, yet we have not yet transcended a dominant narrative of racial cleavage in southern politics. Instead, southern politics is shaped by a tight racial architecture. Republicans dominate in districts with few blacks and Democrats win in districts with black populations above thirty percent—a situation exacerbated by racial and partisan gerrymandering designed to increase both the numbers of minority elected officials and "safe" Republican districts. This pronounced racial structure dramatically influences how and whether a politician can assemble a winning coalition. In geographically and ideologically stratified districts, white Republicans can espouse a robust conservatism designed to attract substantial white majorities and black Democrats can be equally robust liberals. The racial architecture of southern politics does not leave much room for moderation and it certainly does not encourage cross-racial competition for votes or a discourse of racial empathy. Worse it greatly inhibits the possibilities for enacting progressive policies designed to expand opportunity for the middle, working and impoverished classes of whatever color.[37]

My hope as a progressive, a southerner, and an African American is that in the coming decades the interracial alliances that I was exposed to as a young child, the ideal NDPA strove for despite being a predominately black vehicle, will become the norm in American politics. This possibil-

---

that he was "greatly inspired and encouraged" by NDPA and the Mississippi Freedom Democrats. In November 1970 the UCP ran a limited slate of candidates, three of whom were elected to the state house of representatives.

[37] For example, repeated efforts in Alabama to reform the unwieldy state constitution and introduce much needed progressivity and tax relief for the poor into the state tax code have been stymied, I would argue, by a long history of race-tinged politics that encourages working-class whites to vote against their economic interests.

ity will be enhanced, I believe, as the numbers of Latino and other racial minority voters grow and both parties must compete vigorously for a diverse electorate. As with the radical Republicans during Reconstruction, the civil rights movement, and NDPA's electoral victories, progressives can achieve majorities for dramatic change by building positive alliances across boundaries of difference.

Bibliography

AUDREY BORENSTEIN, CHIMES OF CHANGE AND HOURS: VIEWS OF OLDER WOMEN IN TWENTIETH CENTURY AMERICA 177–78 (1983) (featuring an interview with Sallie Mae Hadnott).

SHERYLL CASHIN, THE AGITATOR'S DAUGHTER: A MEMOIR OF A FAMILY (forthcoming).

Sheryll D. Cashin, *Democracy, Race & Multiculturalism in the 21st Century: Will the Voting Rights Act Ever Be Obsolete?*, 22 WASH. U. J. LAW & POL'Y 71 (2006).

Dr. John L. Cashin, Jr., *Unrecognized Heroics in Alabama: the Hadnott v. Amos Story, Part I*, SPEAKIN' OUT NEWS, Page 5, May 29–June 4, 1991.

Dr. John L. Cashin, Jr., *Unrecognized Heroics II: Sallie Hadnott / Fannie Lou Hamer*, SPEAKIN' OUT NEWS, Page 5, June 5–11, 1991.

Dr. John L. Cashin, Jr., *Unrecognized Heroics III: The Greene County Special Election*, SPEAKIN' OUT NEWS, Page 5, June 12–18, 1991.

Carlyle C. Douglas, *Black Politics in the New South: Emerging black-dominated third party movements may prove more effective than Dixie versions of 'liberal' coalition*, EBONY MAGAZINE, January 1971, p. 27.

W.E.B. DuBOIS, BLACK RECONSTRUCTION (1935).

ERIC FONER, RECONTRUCTION: AMERICA'S UNFINISHED REVOLUTION, 1863–1877 (2002).

HARDY T. FRYE, BLACK PARTIES AND POLITICAL POWER: A CASE STUDY (1980).

Greene County, Ala.: Change Comes to Courthouse, TIME, Feb. 1, 1971, available at http://www.time.com/time/magazine/article/0,9171, 909744–1,00.html.

CHARLES MORGAN, JR., ONE MAN, ONE VOICE (1979).

CHARLES MORGAN, JR., A TIME TO SPEAK (1964).

Wesley R. Swift, *The National Democratic Party of Alabama: The First Year*, Aug. 25, 1984, unpublished paper on file with the author.

Martin Waldron, *Six Negroes Win Alabama Offices*, N.Y. TIMES, July 30, 1969, p.1.

Hanes Walton, Jr., Black Republicans: The Politics of the Black and Tans (1941).

Hanes Walton, Jr. & William H. Boone, *Black Political Parties: A Demographic Analysis*, Journal of Black Studies, Vol. 5, No. 1 (Sep., 1974), pp. 86–95.

Hadnott v. Amos, 394 U.S. 358 (1969).

Hadnott v. Amos, 295 F. Supp. 1003 (M.D. Ala. 1968).

The Greene County Special Election, Pacifica Radio documentary, 1969, on file in the Hardy T. Frye Oral History Collection, Auburn University Library.

Interview with Dr. John L. Cashin Jr., February 1–3, 2006.

Interview with Myrna Copeland, March 12, 2006.

Interview with Bill Edwards, January 7, 2006.

Interview with Dr. Hardy Frye, February 27, 2006 and February 1, 2007.

Interview with Rev. Thomas Gilmore, February 14, 2006.

Interview with Rev. William Branch, February 13, 2006.

5

Richard Schragger[*]

San Antonio v. Rodriguez and the Legal Geography of School Finance Reform

It is easy to forget that important Supreme Court cases involve people; it is even easier to forget that they are rooted in particular places. Every case begins somewhere, and *San Antonio v. Rodriguez* is no exception. The case began its journey through the legal system on July 30, 1968. On that summer day, Arthur Gochman, a lawyer representing Demetrio Rodriguez and a handful of other parents of Texas school children, filed a complaint in the United States District Court in San Antonio, Texas, asserting that Texas's system for funding primary education was unconstitutional. Although Gochman sought a legal ruling that would apply across the state and the nation, the legal case he filed was firmly grounded in the soil of south Texas and in the history and geography of San Antonio, where the case would begin and eventually end.

San Antonio was an appropriate setting for a lawsuit that aspired to bring about a revolution in constitutional law. The city, home of the Alamo, had been an important actor in two dramatic revolutions, first the Mexican and then the Texan wars for independence. Indeed, the *Rodriguez* case was both a product and reflection of the long history of territorial struggle in borderland Texas, as it pitted poor school districts against rich ones, Hispanics against Anglos, rural against urban. Two geographic and jurisdictional places—both nominally part of the city of San Antonio, but conceptually distinct from it—became the surrogates for that contest. On the West Side, populated predominantly by poor Hispanics, was the Edgewood Independent School District, which spent

* Special thanks to Jim Ryan, George Rutherglen and Risa Goluboff for comments on earlier drafts, and to Judge J. Harvie Wilkinson III for a very informative discussion. Joe Esmont provided excellent research assistance.

less money per pupil than any school district in the county. And on the North Side was the almost exclusively white, wealthy Alamo Heights Independent School District, which spent more money per pupil than any school district in the county. Though only five miles apart, Edgewood and Alamo Heights would come to represent the racial geography of San Antonio and all of south Texas. And they would come to define the terms of the battle over school finance throughout the state for years to come.

How those places—Edgewood and Alamo Heights—came to be, and what legal conclusions could be drawn from their existence was the question posed to the Supreme Court in the *Rodriguez* case. The plaintiffs, who came from Edgewood, complained that they could not raise enough money through local taxation to provide their children an adequate education—a right, they argued, guaranteed to them by the United States Constitution. But the plaintiffs' legal argument was predominantly comparative: they argued that the Texas system of financing public schools was constitutionally offensive because it permitted the residents of Alamo Heights to spend significantly more on the education of their children than the residents of Edgewood ever could. That disparity, the plaintiffs argued, violated the Equal Protection Clause of the United States Constitution: It resulted from a system of education finance that treated poor people differently from rich ones and Hispanics differently from Anglos.

I.

San Antonio is the archetypal borderland city; its history is characterized by disputes over territory—both literal and metaphorical. Founded to help Christianize Indians along the border of New Spain, the mission San Antonio de Padua became the official capital of Spanish Texas in 1772. The settlement was always racially mixed, with Indians, Spanish immigrants to Mexico, Canary Islanders and increasing numbers of Anglos making up a polyglot frontier population. When Mexico gained its independence from Spain in 1821, San Antonio was the largest settlement in Bexar, one of four districts in Mexican Texas. The famous Battle of the Alamo occurred in 1836, the same year Texas gained its independence from Mexico, and Bexar county was officially organized as a Texas county, with San Antonio as its county seat.[1]

After independence, the Republic of Texas granted San Antonio a municipal charter. The city's first aldermen all had Spanish surnames, though the first mayor was John W. Smith, an Anglo. During the 1837 elections, forty-nine of the fifty candidates for municipal office were of

---

[1] *See* CHRISTOPHER LONG, *Bexar County*, in THE HANDBOOK OF TEXAS ONLINE, http://www. tsha.utexas.edu/handbook/online/articles/BB/hcb7.html (last accessed July 17, 2006).

Spanish–Mexican descent. But by 1845, the year that Texas joined the
United States as the twenty-eighth state, Anglo immigrants had arrived
in significant numbers. In 1847, only five candidates for municipal office
were non-Anglo and the new immigrants had "squeezed [Hispanics]
from their dominant position on the board of aldermen."[2]

San Antonio continued to add population throughout the antebellum
period. And though the foundations of a mercantile (and predominantly
Anglo) elite had been established before 1865, it was the coming of the
railroads that solidified both the city's stature and the elites' status.[3] By
1910, San Antonio had become the chief urban center in Texas with over
96,000 residents. And Anglos had become its dominant ethnic group,
becoming numerically what it had been politically since the mid–1800s.
Moreover, the city's socio-ethnic geography was in many ways set.[4] As
Peter Irons has observed, "Wealth looks down on poverty in most cities,
and despite its modest hills, San Antonio is no exception."[5] The bankers,
doctors, and lawyers—all predominantly Anglo—lived in the wooded hills
of San Antonio's North Side, which included the appropriately named
Alamo Heights. The small black community was concentrated on the
East Side. To the West and South, in low lying areas, lived poor and
working class Hispanics. The area known as Edgewood—on the western
edge of the city, near the woods—was in the heart of the "Mexican
Quarter," which developed after the influx of Mexican refugees from the
Mexican Civil War in the early 1900s. By 1940, three-fourths of the city's
Hispanic population lived there.[6]

That the (relatively) high ground was taken by the rich was no
accident; until the late–1970's the West Side Barrio was afflicted with
flash flooding caused by South Texas's torrential rains. The flooding
would turn the West Side's unpaved roads into mud and result in the
occasional fatality—there were reports of children killed as they walked
to school.[7] And though there was no formal segregation ordinance in San
Antonio, racially restrictive covenants kept blacks and Hispanics from

---

[2] JOHN A. BOOTH & DAVID R. JOHNSON, *Power and Progress in San Antonio Politics, 1836–1970, in* THE POLITICS OF SAN ANTONIO 3, 6, (John Booth et. al. eds. 1983).

[3] LONG, *supra* note 1; *see also* BOOTH & JOHNSON, *supra* note 2, at 6–7.

[4] *See* T.R. FEHRENBACH, *San Antonio, in* THE HANDBOOK OF TEXAS ONLINE, http://www.tsha.utexas.edu/handbook/online/articles/SS/hds2.html (last accessed July 17, 2006).

[5] PETER IRONS, THE COURAGE OF THEIR CONVICTIONS 287 (1988) [hereinafter IRONS, COURAGE].

[6] *See* Daniel D. Arreola, *The Mexican American Cultural Capital,* 77 GEOGRAPHICAL REV. 17, 25–26 (1987); EDGEWOOD INDEPENDENT SCHOOL DISTRICT, *History of EISD,* available at http://www.eisd.net/history.htm (last accessed July 17, 2006).

[7] *See* MARY BETH ROGERS, COLD ANGER 110–113 (1990); PETER SKERRY, MEXICAN AMERICANS, THE AMBIVALENT MINORITY 177–178 (1993).

purchasing housing in the northern part of the city. The first public housing, built in the 1930s, was also explicitly segregated; the Hispanic project was sited on the West Side and the black projects were sited on the East Side.[8]

The region's informal racial geography, established by the early 1900s, was formalized with jurisdictional boundaries, which multiplied in the twentieth century. In 1922, San Antonio sought to annex Alamo Heights, which was one of a number of silk-stocking northern suburbs. The Heights countered by incorporating as an independent municipality. In 1939, two other wealthy northern suburbs, Terrell Hills and Olmos Park, also resisted annexation by incorporating. Efforts by San Antonio to annex these communities failed again in 1945, and they remained independent municipalities as the city developed around them.[9]

School district boundaries also tracked the city's ethnic geography, although those lines took more time to solidify. In the nineteenth century, education in frontier towns like San Antonio was virtually non-existent, as it was in most southern cities. Though Texas cited the failure of Mexico to provide schools as a central reason for independence, the Republic of Texas provided little in the way of financial support for public schools. And though the first Texas state constitution contained an Article requiring "the legislature ... to make suitable provisions for the support and maintenance of public schools," the money set aside for education was appropriated to the Confederate war effort. In the 1880s, the state authorized communities within urban municipalities to subdivide into "independent school districts," empowered to levy taxes for school funding. The state also allowed counties—the unit of government for unincorporated and most often rural areas—to divide their territory into "common school districts," which initially had no independent taxing authority.[10]

In 1919, the Edgewood Common School District was created. Four years later, citizens in what would become the South San Antonio Independent School District petitioned the county to separate from

---

[8] RICHARD A. GAMBITTA ET AL., *The Politics of Unequal Educational Opportunity, in* BOOTH & JOHNSON, *supra* note 2, at 142; Robert Goldberg, *Racial Change on the Southern Periphery*, 49 J. S. HIST. 349, 351 (1983); Christopher Ramos, *The Educational Legacy of Racially Restrictive* Covenants, 4 SCHOLAR 149, 158, n.48 (2001).

[9] MINNIE B. CAMERON, *Alamo Heights, Texas, in* THE HANDBOOK OF TEXAS ONLINE, http://www.tsha.utexas.edu/handbook/online/articles/AA/hfa2.html (last accessed July 19, 2006); CITY OF TERRELL HILLS, *History of Terrell Hills*, available at http://www.terrell-hills.com/Articles/History.html (last accessed July 19, 2006); SAN ANTONIO PUBLIC LIBRARY, *San Antonio: A Chronology*, http://www.sanantonio.gov/library/texana/sachronology.asp?res=1680 & ver=true.

[10] *See* GAMBITTA, *supra* note 8, at 133–40.

Edgewood, taking with them a great deal of taxable property.[11] In 1923, the Alamo Heights Independent School District was created in parallel with the new city of Alamo Heights. The district eventually came largely to encompass the wealthy suburbs of Terrell Hills and Olmos Park along with parts of northern San Antonio.

In 1947, Bexar County had forty-nine separate school districts and embarked on a program to consolidate them. Alamo Heights, the richest of the districts, refused to join a consolidated city district, but three other districts joined the San Antonio Independent School District ("ISD"). In 1950, Edgewood received permission to switch from a common school district to an independent school district, which increased its taxing authority under state law. Nevertheless, between 1950 and 1960, Edgewood made three attempts to consolidate with the San Antonio ISD. Each petition was denied. As one commentator observed, "Edgewood simply had too poor a tax base to adequately support education and the San Antonio ISD had no desire to acquire responsibility for such a burden."[12] After Edgewood's third petition attempt, the state legislature blocked the petition route for school district consolidation by giving a veto to affected school boards.[13]

By 1960, then, Edgewood and Alamo Heights were long established both as geographical places and legal jurisdictions. The Heights, its own municipality, was literally not part of San Antonio, nor was the Alamo Heights Independent School District a part of the San Antonio school system. Its residents, however, were among the region's most influential figures. Edgewood, while nominally part of San Antonio, was not part of its school system. And its residents, though numerically large, were not politically salient.

Over the next ten years, as the population of Hispanics in San Antonio grew, Edgewood was responsible for educating approximately 20,000 children per year, in a district where the median family income was $4,686. Alamo Heights educated 5,000 children per year, in a district where median family income was $8,001.[14] And because Edgewood and Alamo Heights contained vastly different amounts of property wealth, the money each district could raise through the local property tax was markedly different. In 1970, Edgewood had $5,429 per student worth of taxable property; Alamo Heights had $45,095 per student. Thus, even though Edgewood parents taxed themselves at the highest rate in the city, property taxes only provided $26 for each student. State funding

[11] Id. at 142.

[12] Id. at 145.

[13] Id. at 142–147.

[14] *San Antonio Indep. Sch. Dist. v. Rodriguez*, 411 U.S. 1, 12–13 (1973).

contributed another $222 and federal funding another $108, for a total of $356 per student.

By contrast, Alamo Heights had the lowest tax rate in the city and raised $333 per student in local funds alone. The state contributed another $225 per student and federal monies contributed $26, for a total of $594 per student. This pattern was repeated throughout the state: in the 162 poorest districts in Texas, a $20,000 home was taxed $130 a year in school taxes, while in the 203 richest districts, a $20,000 home was only taxed $46 a year in school taxes. Nevertheless, the richest districts outspent the poorest districts almost two-to-one.[15]

II.

When Demetrio Rodriguez helped organize a protest over Edgewood school conditions in 1968, he faced this geographic and fiscal reality. Rodriguez was a "born Texan," as were his father and grandfather; his mother was from Mexico. He had gone to school in San Antonio since he was six, when his father, a migrant farm worker, sent him to live with his uncle in the city. After he served in the Pacific in World War II, he returned to San Antonio and worked at Kelly Air Force Base, one of five major military bases in the city. In 1957 he moved into Edgewood. In 1968, three of his four sons attended Edgewood Elementary School.[16]

Rodriguez joined the Edgewood District Concerned Parents Association. The Association was worried about plans to build a tax-exempt public housing project that would add additional school-age children into the district without adding more taxable property. The parents were also angry at what they perceived to be financial mismanagement by the Edgewood school board and its superintendent, Dr. Jose Cardenas. Edgewood was severely cash-strapped and the district's twenty-five schools were crumbling; there was a real possibility that the district would have to move to half-day sessions for its 22,000 students because of a lack of funds.[17] The parents' association thought that "money was being stolen from them"—that "somebody was taking kickbacks."[18]

The Concerned Parents Association was a small-scale operation. Nevertheless, it was part of a larger Hispanic rights movement that was beginning in the late 1960s, much of it based in southwest Texas. To be sure, there had already been a tradition of Hispanic political and legal organizing before the 1960s. Older, middle-class organizations like the

---

[15] Id. at 14.

[16] IRONS, COURAGE, *supra* note 5, at 296.

[17] GAMBITTA, *supra* note 8, at 147.

[18] Tom Edwards, *Lawyer Helped Make History But Regrets Supreme Court Opinion*, AP NEWSWIRE, July 31, 1998 (quoting Arthur Gochman).

League of United Latin American Citizens (founded in 1929) and the American GI Forum (founded in 1948) were still robust; Demetrio Rodriguez was a member of both.[19] In the late 1960s and early 1970s, however, Hispanic grassroots political organizing exploded. A number of these organizations were based in San Antonio, including the Raza Unida Party, the Southwest Voter Registration Education Project, and PADRES, the national caucus of Latino Priests. San Antonio was the original headquarters of the Mexican American Legal Defense and Education Fund ("MALDEF"), founded in 1968 by a local attorney with a grant from the Ford Foundation. And, in the early 1970s, Ernesto Cortes and poor south and westside San Antonians founded Communities Organized for Public Service ("COPS"). COPS would become one of the most influential political organizations in San Antonio and all of south Texas, successfully agitating for sidewalks, storm sewers, paved roads, parks, and housing for poor west and southside neighborhoods.[20]

When the Edgewood parents confronted the Edgewood school system, however, the south and westsides' political energy was largely untapped. Poor Hispanics were mostly kept out of city governance. And though San Antonio had become "a Mexican city" demographically by the late 1960s,[21] it was also a badly unequal one, with poorer communities lacking the basic municipal services that richer areas took for granted. The Edgewood District Concerned Parents Association was responding to this relative privation. When the school district superintendent would not meet with them, the parents staged a number of public protests and in May 1968, 400 students walked out of Edgewood High School. These protests attracted the attention of Willie Valesquez, the founder of the Southwest Voter Project, who introduced the parents to Arthur Gochman.[22]

Gochman was a thirty-seven-year-old attorney who had marched with Velasquez and joined in the sit-ins that led to San Antonio becoming the first southern city voluntarily to desegregate its lunch counters in 1960.[23] His family had roots in San Antonio. His father Max began selling tires in the city in 1938 and then shifted to military surplus; in the 1950s Max opened a number of Academy Super Surplus stores in Austin. Arthur, a graduate of the University of Texas Law School, would

---

[19] PETER IRONS, *Demetrio Rodriguez*, *in* 100 AMERICANS MAKING CONSTITUTIONAL HISTORY 174 (Melvin Urofsky ed. 2004) [herinafter IRONS, *Rodriguez*].

[20] *See generally* ROGERS, *supra* note 7 (describing the development of COPS).

[21] ROBERT BRISCHETTO ET AL., *Conflict and Change in the Political Culture of San Antonio in the 1970s*, *in* BOOTH & JOHNSON, *supra* note 2, at 75.

[22] IRONS, *Rodriguez*, *supra* note 19, at 174.

[23] Edwards, *supra* note 18.

join his father's business in 1973 and turn the company into one of the largest sporting goods retailers in the south. In 1968, however, he was practicing law with a small firm in San Antonio that was well-known for its civil rights work.

The "problem's not your superintendent," Gochman told the Edgewood parents. "Your problem," he explained, "is the way the state finances your schools." Texas's structure of property-tax financed local school districts meant that districts with little property wealth and lots of students, like Edgewood, simply could not afford to provide more than a rudimentary primary and secondary education. Gochman had read Judge J. Skelly Wright's 1967 decision in *Hobson v. Hansen*, which held that Washington, D.C.'s system of neighborhood schools and educational tracking unconstitutionally perpetuated socio-economic and racial segregation.[24] Based on that case, Gochman suggested filing a class action lawsuit against the San Antonio Independent School District, six other city school districts, the Bexar County School Trustees, and the state of Texas. The complaint would seek a declaration that the means by which Texas funded its schools—through local property taxes—was unconstitutional.[25]

Gochman chose Demetrio Rodriguez as the lead plaintiff (in part because his Hispanic surname would highlight the racial aspects of the case). Rodriguez signed on right away and spent the next few weeks seeking out additional plaintiffs. Some parents were wary of joining the complaint. When the lawsuit was reported in the media, Rodriguez was criticized. As he later told an interviewer: "A lot of Anglo guys used to argue with me; they didn't like it. They thought I was a Communist. I told them, I'm no more Communist than you are. I'm using the judicial system and I don't care what you say. I told them, You know why I'm doing this. Because I've been the victim of discrimination."[26]

Despite the criticism, five other parents joined Demetrio and his wife Helen as plaintiffs. Their complaint alleged that the Texas school finance system violated the Equal Protection Clause because it discriminated against racial minorities. The complaint also asserted two novel claims: first, that wealth (independent of race) was an unconstitutional basis on which to discriminate, and second, that education was a fundamental right. Gochman argued that these two propositions taken together required the courts to subject the Texas finance system to the strictest constitutional review.

---

[24] Paul Sracic, San Antonio v. Rodriguez and the Pursuit of Equal Education 19–24 (2006).

[25] Irons, Courage, *supra* note 5, at 284–285, 298.

[26] Irons, Courage, *supra* note 5, at 299.

III.

The federal court that heard *Rodriguez v. San Antonio* received the case in 1968 but took over three years to render a final decision. For over a year the parties battled over procedural issues. The court then postponed the trial so that the Texas legislature could consider pending school reform legislation. The legislators came and went from Austin without enacting any new legislation, however, and the long-delayed trial finally got under way without it.

The contours of the case were relatively simple. Primary and secondary schools in Texas were funded primarily from the local property tax, with some additional funds being provided by the state. Because school districts had differing amounts of property wealth per student ($5,429 versus $45,095 in the case of Edgewood and Alamo Heights, respectively), the amount of money school districts could raise with any given tax effort differed dramatically.[27] Edgewood residents would have to tax themselves at exorbitant rates even to approach the amounts generated by Alamo Heights. And even if it was practical to do so, Edgewood could not duplicate Alamo Heights's effort because state laws limited the maximum tax rate. Gochman called six experts to testify about this state of affairs, including Edgewood Superintendent Dr. Jose Cardenas, Dr. Joel Berke of Syracuse University, a well-known expert on school finance, and two professors from Trinity University.[28] The state did not contest the plaintiffs' core factual allegation, however. All the parties agreed that the Texas system resulted in significant differences in education spending across districts—the only question was whether those differences violated the Constitution.

The legal theory of the case was grounded in the Equal Protection Clause of the Fourteenth Amendment, which prevents a state from "deny[ing] to any person within its jurisdiction the equal protection of the laws." That clause was the obvious place to start for civil rights lawyers beginning to challenge state school finance systems in the late 1960s. For the fifteen years following *Brown v. Board of Education*, decided in 1954, civil rights lawyers had focused on desegregating (mostly southern) schools. But desegregation had moved slowly, especially in the south, and even where integration was successful, the poor—whether black or white—continued to attend poor schools. The NAACP's theory that resources would follow integration—that "green would follow white"—was a disappointment. Moreover, integration—which had never been popular—was losing the little momentum it had. Whites resisted forced remedies like busing while blacks wanted more control over their own schools.

---

[27] *Rodriguez*, 411 U.S. at 14.

[28] Irons, Courage, *supra* note 5, at 285–286.

Thus, in 1969, when law professors John Coons, Stephen Sugarman and William Clune published an influential law review article describing a legal theory for challenging state school finance systems, civil rights advocates were primed.[29] A year later, the same authors published a book entitled *Private Wealth and Public Education*, laying out the road map for a U.S. Supreme Court challenge. They dedicated it "To nine old friends of the children."[30] The equal protection theory advocated by the authors was already being applied in *Serrano v. Priest*, a challenge to the California school system that was making its way through the state court system.[31] In 1971, the California Supreme Court would declare California's system in violation of state equal protection guarantees.

Gochman had not originally relied on *Serrano*, which had yet to be decided when he filed the Edgewood parents' complaint in 1968. But the district court panel found *Serrano's* reasoning quite persuasive. In December 1971, more than three years after the Edgewood parents had filed their lawsuit, the district court found unanimously that Texas's system of education finance violated the Equal Protection Clause. Relying in part on *Serrano*, the court held that the state funding system discriminated on the basis of wealth because it permitted rich districts to provide a higher quality education at a lower tax cost. There was no compelling state interest for such a system; indeed, there was not, the district court concluded, even a "reasonable basis" for it. The court gave Texas two years to adopt reforms that would ensure that the "educational opportunities afforded to ... the children of the state of Texas, are not a function of wealth other than the wealth of the state as a whole."[32]

IV.

The district court's decision was a powerful vindication for the Edgewood parents, but it was only a temporary victory. Because the case came from a three-judge district court, the Supreme Court was required by statute to decide the case. Argument was set for the beginning of the next Term, October 1972.

The Court had changed dramatically since Gochman had filed his complaint almost four years earlier. Nixon had won the 1968 election in part by arguing against the activism of the Warren Court. The Republican's "Southern Strategy" made explicit appeals to whites' racial fears,

---

[29] John Coons et al., *Educational Opportunity: A Workable Constitutional Test for State Financial Structures*, 57 CAL. L. REV. 307 (1969).

[30] JOHN COONS ET AL., PRIVATE WEALTH AND PUBLIC EDUCATION (1970).

[31] Serrano v. Priest, 5 Cal. 3d 584, 487 P.2d 1241 (Cal. 1971).

[32] Rodriguez v. San Antonio Indep. Sch. Dist., 337 F.Supp. 280, 286 (W.D. Tex. 1971), *rev'd*, 411 U.S. 1 (1973).

capitalizing on suburbanites' opposition to forced busing and linking the Democratic Party to the radical movements of the late 1960s. Those movements—feminist, civil rights, anti-corporate, anti-war—led the "establishment" and Richard Nixon's "silent majority" to believe that it was under siege. Between 1969 and 1971, three of the Court's most liberal Justices had resigned and been replaced by Nixon appointees: Chief Justice Earl Warren was replaced by Warren Burger, Abe Fortas by Harry Blackmun, and Hugo Black by Lewis Powell. Further, the moderately conservative John Harlan was replaced by the distinctly conservative William Rehnquist. Nixon's new justices were decidedly more hostile to the social movements of the time than were their predecessors on the Court.

The Texas Attorney General hired Charles Allen Wright, a University of Texas law professor and well-known expert on federal courts, to represent Texas. Wright and Gochman appeared before the Supreme Court on October 12, 1972. As the petitioner, Texas argued first. The effort to equalize spending across districts would, Wright asserted in his opening statement, "seriously inhibit, if not destroy altogether, the possibilities of local variety, experimentation, and independence." Wright also challenged two of the plaintiffs' key factual assumptions: first, that money produces better educational outcomes, and second, that poor people normally live in property-poor school districts. Wright pointed out that poor people often live near industrial plants or commercial districts that generate lots of property tax revenue. He also asserted that the correlation of race and poor districts was overstated. Though Edgewood was primarily Hispanic, that fact was "happenstance"; there was no necessary connection between property-poor districts and racial minorities.[33]

Gochman, arguing on behalf of the Edgewood parents, contested each of Wright's claims, pointing to evidence showing that there was indeed a correlation between poor families and poor districts. The justices pushed him to consider the inter-state aspects of the case. Wouldn't equal protection require the equalization of school funding across states as well as within them? Gochman argued that the Fourteenth Amendment applies to states, and that once a state provides a service it must provide it on equal terms. This led to questions about the relative value of education services. What distinguishes education from other basic needs, like police protection, fire protection or public health facilities? Gochman argued that education is unique in that it is the foundation for the basic citizenship rights contained in the Constitution, making it possible to exercise First Amendment and voting rights. He

---

[33] Audio of Arguments available at: The Oyez Project, Oyez: San Antonio Independent School Dis. v. Rodriguez, 411 U.S. 1 (1973), available at: http://www.oyez.org/oyez/resource/case/343/ (last accessed July 20, 2006).

further contested Wright's claim that local control would be protected by upholding Texas's system. Local control is "the one thing that the Texas system does not have ... because those that tax at the highest rates have the lowest expenditures per pupil and those that tax at the lowest rates have the highest expenditures per pupil. There is just the reverse of local control."

The oral argument revealed a closely divided Supreme Court—and one in a period of significant transition. In a number of cases in the 1960s, the Warren Court had closely scrutinized state laws that placed particular burdens on the poor in the exercise of their rights. The Court had seemed poised to treat poverty as a suspect class for equal protection purposes and perhaps even adopt a constitutional rule requiring that the government affirmatively provide the poor with a minimum level of basic social goods. With the arrival of the Nixon justices, however, the Court moved quickly to limit the import of the Warren Court's poverty cases. On one side of the debate were those who believed that the Constitution provided, at least implicitly, for a robust set of positive economic and social rights. On the other side were those who believed that the Constitution was a charter of negative liberties and who feared the "quagmire" that would result if the judiciary attempted to mandate the provision of food, housing, education, or other basic services. *Rodriguez* became the focal point in this debate.

The justices discussed *Rodriguez* on October 17 during their regularly scheduled conference. They expressed their opinions in order of seniority, with the Chief Justice speaking first. Burger voted to reverse the district court, arguing that an affirmance would undermine state and local government. Justice Douglas, the longest serving justice on the Court, voted to affirm, arguing that while it may be impossible to equalize educational outcomes, it was possible at least to equalize the money received. Justice Brennan also voted to affirm. "Few cases trouble me more," he said, arguing that the Texas scheme did not even have a rational basis—the least rigorous standard applied by the Court in assessing the constitutionality of legislation. Justice Stewart disagreed with Brennan and Douglas, arguing that the "equal protection clause does not require egalitarianism" and that "rich" and "poor" (terms of relative wealth) were not identifiable classes amenable to equal protection analysis. But both Justices White and Marshall voted to affirm. With the six most senior justices having voted, the count was four-to-two in favor of affirmance.

All of the most recently appointed justices voted to reverse, however. Justice Blackmun, appointed in 1970, commented that he would have preferred letting the lower courts wrestle with the issue more, but agreed that the Texas system provided an adequate basic education. Justice Powell, appointed less than a year earlier, also voted to reverse, arguing that education is not a fundamental right. He also worried that high property wealth/high taxing jurisdictions would lose funds under a state equalization system. Justice Rehnquist, the Court's most junior justice, also voted to reverse.[34]

The final count was 5–4 with the four Nixon appointees joining Justice Stewart in reversing the three-judge district court. The remaining Warren Court Justices—Marshall, White, Brennan, and Douglas—were in dissent. Gochman later lamented that he would have won 6–3 had the case been heard in 1968—he was probably correct that the delays in the district court had cost him the case.[35]

V.

Justice Lewis Powell was given the assignment to draft the opinion for the Court. It was, for him, a very personal case. Before joining the Court, Powell—a native of Richmond, Virginia—had been a prominent attorney in one of the leading law firms in the south. He had been a member of the Richmond School Board for eleven years and the Virginia State Board of Education for eight years, serving as chairman of the former and president of the latter. As the only justice with direct experience in school governance, he was the natural author of the majority opinion.

Powell was solidly within Nixon's "silent majority"—he believed that the radical movements of the 1960s were a threat to the established order. In a confidential memorandum addressed to the United States Chamber of Commerce written a few months before he was nominated to the Court, he warned that the "American economic system is under broad attack" by "liberal" and "far left" groups. The Chamber of Commerce should assume a "more vigorous role in the political arena," advised Powell, and should not "neglect[] opportunity in the Courts." "Under our constitutional system," Powell wrote, "especially with an activist-minded Supreme Court, the judiciary may be the most important instrument for social, economic, and political change."[36]

Powell's memorandum was prescient. As a justice, Powell now had the opportunity to remake the Warren Court: *Rodriguez* would be the doorstop to the Warren Court's poverty precedents. In notes he made

---

[34] *See* Harry A. Blackmun, Untitled Conference Notes, in the Papers of Justice Harry A. Blackmun, Box 161 Folder 4; William O. Douglas, Conference October 17, 1972, in the Papers of Justice William O. Douglas, Box 1575; Lewis F. Powell, Conference Notes (71–1332), in the Papers of Justice Lewis F. Powell, Series 10.6, Box 8 of the Sct. Cases / Box 153 of the Powell Papers, Docket #71–1332.

[35] Edwards, *supra* note 18.

[36] Lewis F. Powell, Memorandum of September 29th, 1972 to Conference, in the Papers of Justice Thurgood Marshall, Container 95, Folder 7 (circulating memo to justices after public criticism).

before oral argument, Powell took a dim view of the district court's opinion, which he thought "slavishly" followed "*Serrano v. Priest*, which in turn adopted almost literally the 'activist scholarship' theory of Professors Coons and Sugarman in their book...."[37] In light of his "own twenty years experience in public education," Powell was skeptical of "facile new theories."[38] His clerk, Larry Hammond, was more sympathetic and wrote a highly personal bench memorandum advocating affirmance. Hammond related that his family had lived in one of the poorest Texas school districts. While he was "fortunate enough" to be sent to high school in the wealthier El Paso School District, his three siblings each attended the local district high school and received a "plainly deficient" education. Hammond also defended the Coons, Clune, and Sugarman book, recommending to Powell that he read it.[39]

Powell's views, however, were set by his experience in Virginia after *Brown*, when the state was in the throes of "massive resistance," the southern campaign to resist desegregation that followed the Court's ruling. As his leading biographer has observed, Powell was among the "hard-line moderates," or "middle-grounders," more interested in improving the quality of the schools than in keeping blacks out of them.[40] Nevertheless, Powell had stated quite clearly that he was not in favor of compulsory integration. He wrote an amicus brief opposing busing, and between 1951 and 1959 (when Powell was school board chairman) "school segregation in Richmond remained virtually complete."[41] Desegregation was, for Powell, an "unwelcome social change forced upon us by the law," and he "found it diplomatically sound not to do any more than absolutely required" to comply with *Brown*.[42]

Powell's racial conservatism took the rhetorical form of local control. Though he was an advocate for education—Powell lobbied for increased state and federal aid and helped add a clause to the Virginia Constitution that made education a constitutional responsibility—he was deeply skeptical of federal regulation.[43] The local school board, he wrote, is a

---

[37] Lewis F. Powell, Memorandum of August 30th, 1972 to J. Harvie Wilkinson, III, in the Papers of Justice Lewis F. Powell, container *supra* note 34.

[38] Lewis F. Powell, Memorandum of August 31, 1972 from Lewis F. Powell to Mr. Larry A. Hammond, in container *supra* note 34.

[39] Larry Hammond, Bench Memo (1972), in the Papers of Justice Lewis F. Powell, container *supra* note 34.

[40] JOHN C. JEFFRIES, JUSTICE LEWIS POWELL 169 (2001).

[41] Id. at 141.

[42] Id. at 172.

[43] *See* Lewis F. Powell, Memorandum of October 12, 1972 at p. 2, in the Papers of Justice Lewis F. Powell, container *supra* note 34.

"unique American institution . . . that played a vital role in the development of the public school system." "Local government has played a fundamental role in making our system work, in preventing the bigness even of state government from overwhelming the citizen. . . ."[44] He worried that the "ultimate effect" of the Edgewood plaintiffs' theory would be "national control of education."[45] That would be abhorrent, Powell argued: "I have in mind the irresistible impulse of politicians to manipulate public education for their own power and ideology—e.g., Hitler, Mussolini and all communist dictators."[46] "In an era that has witnessed a consistent trend toward centralization of the functions of government," he wrote in *Rodriguez*, "local sharing of responsibility for public education has survived."[47]

Powell also rejected the plaintiffs' arguments that wealth constituted a suspect class and that education was a fundamental right. "In a free enterprise society," he observed in his notes, "we could hardly hold that wealth is *suspect*. This is communist doctrine but is not even accepted (except in a limited sense) in socialist countries." And though Powell observed in his opinion that education "is perhaps the most important function of state and local governments,"[48] he concluded that "it is not the province of this Court to create substantive constitutional rights in the name of guaranteeing equal protection of the laws."[49]

The dissenting justices challenged the majority's opinion across the board. They saw *Rodriguez* as a dramatic step backwards. The Court had held that the Equal Protection Clause was not an independent guarantee of basic, non-specified constitutional rights. The Warren Court's line of fundamental rights/equal protection cases, which had implied that equal treatment might require the government to affirmatively provide certain social goods to everyone on an equal basis, had been truncated. Moreover, the opinion was authored by Lewis Powell, a white southerner who had been on the wrong side of the most important civil rights struggle of the century. Justice Thurgood Marshall—the architect of *Brown*—was particularly incensed; he would become increasingly disillusioned through the 1970s as the Court seemed to move further and further away from the vision of equality it had so boldly articulated in 1954.

---

[44] Id. at 4.

[45] Lewis F. Powell, Memorandum of October 9, 1972, at page 3, in the Papers of Justice Lewis F. Powell, container *supra* note 34.

[46] Id. at 4.

[47] *Rodriguez*, 411 U.S. at 49.

[48] Id. at 29, 30.

[49] Id. at 33.

As the other justice most familiar with southern schools, Marshall thought that Justice Powell's claim that money did not matter to educational quality was "absurd[]." If money does not matter to educational outcomes, why are the rich districts so eager to keep the existing system?[50] He further challenged Powell's claim that because the state had not classified the population according to some spurious criteria and because education was not specifically protected by the Constitution, the Texas system only needed to be rational.

For Marshall, schoolchildren living in property poor districts were properly considered a class for equal protection purposes. Those children (whether rich or poor) were discriminated against by the misfortune of living on the wrong side of a particular school district line. And that discrimination had to be accounted for by the state because education is such an important and vital interest. For equal protection purposes, Marshall further argued, a "minimum" education is not enough. "The Equal Protection Clause," wrote Marshall, "is not addressed to the minimal sufficiency but rather to the unjustifiable inequalities of state action. It mandates nothing less than that 'all persons similarly circumstanced shall be treated alike.' "[51]

The dissenters had the better of the argument. First, the majority's rationale of local control made little sense. As Marshall pointed out, the state already controlled much that went on in the Texas public schools, including many details of school administration. And any remaining "local control" meant very little to a district forced to cut essential programs because of a lack of resources. The Texas system, as Justice White observed in a separate dissenting opinion, provided a "meaningful option to Alamo Heights ... but almost none to Edgewood."[52] "No matter how desirous [Edgewood] parents are of supporting their schools with greater revenues, it is impossible to do so through the use of the real estate property tax."[53] Local control was a shibboleth behind which rich districts could protect their own privilege.

Second, the majority's deep aversion to "discovering" a "new" fundamental right to equal education seemed specious. Education had been a special province of the Court since *Brown*; its particular importance had been well-articulated in the pre-*Brown* separate-but-equal cases, as well as in the post-*Brown* integration cases. Moreover, in *Roe v. Wade*, handed down only two months before *Rodriguez*, the Court had extended the constitutional right of privacy—a right nowhere mentioned

---

[50] Id. at 82. (Marshall, J., dissenting).

[51] Id. at 89.

[52] Id. at 64. (White, J., dissenting).

[53] Id. at 64–65.

in the Constitution—to include a woman's right to terminate her pregnancy.[54] *Roe* was relatively uncontroversial on the Court at the time; it was decided 7–2, with Powell joining Blackmun's majority and Stewart concurring in judgment. Thus, the majority's insistence in *Rodriguez* that the Court stick close to the constitutional text and not "create" new rights seemed to be an excuse for avoiding a decision with significant redistributive implications rather than a reflection of a genuine concern for avoiding judicial activism. In the early 1970s, extending the right of privacy to abortion was less radical than extending the equality principle to poor people.

That the Court's decision fell short did not mean, however, that the dissenters had solved all the difficult conceptual problems raised by the case. The dissenting opinions elided the distinction between the rights of places and the rights of people. But those rights might be at odds: Edgewood's right to decide how much to spend on education was not necessarily compatible with the schoolchildren's right to an equal education. Even if Texas created a system by which every school district had equal amounts of property wealth or generated the same amount of tax revenue for any given tax effort (so-called "district power equalization"), school districts could still exercise different choices about how much to spend on education. What would happen if an anti-tax district decided to spend very little on education? If a neighboring district with an education-friendly electorate chose to spend more per pupil, would the children of the low-tax district have a claim that they were being treated unequally? If Texas schoolchildren had a fundamental right to an equal education, why would district choice solve the inequalities that would arise from different local majoritarian preferences?

The equal protection problems invited by a place-based equalization system led Justice Powell to believe that the plaintiffs' equal protection arguments would lead inevitably to state—if not national—fiscal centralization. And it allowed Texas to argue that the plaintiffs were not seeking to protect Texas schoolchildren by vindicating a right to education. Rather, as Charles Wright argued, the plaintiffs were seeking to protect the rights of district taxpayers to have a meaningful vote on education expenditures unrestrained by local property wealth. The former claim might have had some constitutional traction, but the latter claim certainly did not: local taxpayers had no constitutional right to vote on education expenditures at all, let alone a right to a tax system that generated equal revenues for any given tax effort.

A place-based right—the right of Edgewood to have a chance to spend as much on education as Alamo Heights—was constitutionally incoherent. Unless the legal jurisdiction of Edgewood perfectly aligned

---

[54] 410 U.S. 113 (1973).

with an invidiously-defined group of individuals, the fact that Edgewood taxpayers were treated differently from Alamo Heights taxpayers was not relevant for constitutional purposes. The Texas tax system discriminated against property-poor places. But places do not have constitutional status. As Harvard law professor Frank Michelman wrote in a prescient (and now famous) 1969 *Harvard Law Review* article: "Wealth as a classifying trait is invidious; place is not."[55]

VI.

The conceptual distinction between places and people bedeviled both the majority and the dissent. They certainly eluded most lay readers, who tended to see the case in more black and white terms. On March 21, 1973, the Court convened to hand down the *Rodriguez* opinion. Powell read a summary from the bench. Justice Blackmun had predicted that the decision would not be popular.[56] The National Education Association railed against the decision as a rejection of "the idea of equal educational opportunity." Senator Edmund Muskie responded by calling for the federal government to get more involved in education, especially in reforming "arbitrary and inexpert" state property tax assessors, which he blamed for some of the inequality.[57]

Despite Blackmun's premonition, the major papers rallied behind the Court. The *Wall Street Journal* argued that the Supreme Court "could hardly have chosen a better case" to limit its involvement in social matters. The *Journal* counseled that only local communities, which are better able to take into account local peculiarities, can effectively bring about the "subtle and elusive" social justice the dissent sought.[58] The *Chicago Tribune* lamented the condition of poor schools, but observed that the Court had kept "Big Brother" from "push[ing] us all into a uniform mold in the name of guaranteeing equality."[59] The *Washington Post* expressed fear that a contrary decision would have taken equality too seriously, and drained funds from cities that needed more money per pupil because of their large at-risk populations.[60] The

---

[55] Frank Michelman, *On Protecting the Poor Through the Fourteenth Amendment*, 83 HARV. L. REV. 7, 52 (1969).

[56] Blackmun, Monograph re: No. 71-1332 San Antonio Independent School District v. Rodriguez, (Oct. 11, 1972), at 7, in the Papers of Justice Harry A. Blackmun, Box 161, Folder 4.

[57] Edmund Muskie, *Editorial: Sen. Muskie on Schools*, WASH. POST, March 28, 1973, at A27.

[58] Op–Ed, *What the Courts Can't Do*, WALL ST. J., March 23, 1973, at 10.

[59] *Local School Taxes are Legal*, CHI. TRIB., March 22, 1973, at 16.

[60] William Greider, *Novel Theory of School Spending Cashiered By Court*, WASH. POST, Mar 22, 1973, at A16; Op–Ed, *The Schools and Equality*, WASH. POST, Mar. 22, 1973, at A26.

New York Times also "sympathize[ed] with the Court's school ruling" while arguing that the Nixon administration and states must fix the system, which it saw as chaotic and unjust.[61]

In contrast, the *Forward Times*, a black weekly newspaper in Houston, was "appalled" at the decision, which it claimed "[r]eopened the 'Separate and Unequal' [t]rap." It argued that elite whites deliberately used white flight and secession from city districts to keep blacks poor. "We have seen dramatically what has happened when the court has left things to the discretion of the states," the paper noted, invoking white violence and resistance to civil rights. "We are not so naïve not to recognize what the Nixon-stacked court is doing."[62] One irate attorney wrote to Powell to complain that he had authored an opinion "exceeded in meanness of spirit only by the Dred Scott decision." Even so, Powell would consider *Rodriguez* "one of his favorite children" and "one of the most important [opinions] I have written."[63]

The problem of place-based inequality did not go away after the Court's decision, however. Nor, despite the Court's increasingly hostile stance toward education reform, did the case put an end to legal efforts at achieving educational parity. In 1974, in *Milliken v. Bradley*, the Burger Court held 5–4 that the federal courts did not have the authority to order a school desegregation plan that included school districts outside the city of Detroit.[64] The case effectively insulated the suburbs from desegregation efforts and judicially affirmed the Republicans' no-busing policy. Combined with *Rodriguez*, *Milliken* sounded the death knell for the pursuit of education finance reform mandated by the federal Constitution. The cases also encouraged civil rights lawyers, who had already begun to pursue cases in the state courts before *Rodriguez*, to direct their attention fully to the states. Twenty-six state supreme courts would eventually side with the civil rights lawyers.

Texas turned out to be one of those states. Following *Rodriguez*, and in part because of it, the Texas legislature finally turned its attention to fixing what many admitted was a broken educational finance system. In 1975, the legislature adopted an "equalization" bill, which increased state aid across the board and introduced a state equalization aid component to assist poorer districts. Another equalization bill was

----

[61] Evan Jenkins, *Court's School Ruling Gives States Breathing Spell on Taxes and Reformers a Setback*, N.Y. Times, March 22, 1973, at 33; Op–Ed, *Last Chance for Fairness*, N.Y. Times, Mar 26, 1973, at 38.

[62] *Reopens Separate and Unequal Trap*, Forward Times (Houston), March 31, 1973, at 11A.

[63] Lewis F. Powell, Letter to J. Harvie Wilkinson, in the Papers of Justice Lewis F. Powell, container *supra* note 34.

[64] 418 U.S. 717 (1974).

adopted in 1977 and again in 1984. While all the bills increased state financing, none of them significantly remedied the huge fiscal disparities between Texas school districts.

In 1987, Demetrio Rodriguez joined a new lawsuit, this time initiated by MALDEF. In *Edgewood Ind. School District v. Kirby*,[65] a coalition of parents, children, and sixty-eight school districts filed suit against the Texas Commissioner of Education alleging that the state's system of school finance discriminated by race and poverty in violation of the Equal Rights and Due Course of Law provisions of the Texas Constitution. The plaintiffs further claimed that the state finance system violated the Texas Constitution's education provision which provided that "it shall be the duty of the Legislature of the State to establish and make suitable provision for the support and maintenance of an efficient system of public free schools."[66] This time around, the Texas Supreme Court found unanimously for the plaintiffs on the basis of this "efficient public schools" clause. The Court observed that property-poor districts were "trapped in a cycle of poverty from which there is no opportunity to free themselves," and held that "there must be a direct and close correlation between a district's tax effort and the educational resources available to it."[67] As did the district court in *Rodriguez*, the Court gave the state legislature time to fix the system.

Edgewood v. Kirby (which would be known as *Edgewood I*) began in earnest what would arguably become the country's longest-running effort at school finance reform. After two failed legislative sessions, the legislature eventually adopted a school reform bill, which the Governor promptly vetoed. After the district court ordered the schools shut down, the state legislature responded with Senate Bill I. That bill was unanimously struck down in *Edgewood II* for failing to remedy the defects held unconstitutional in the first case.[68] This pattern—the state legislature adopting legislation and the courts striking it down—would be repeated over the next twenty years: *Edgewood II* was followed by *Edgewood III*, *Edgewood IV*, *West Orange I*, and, most recently, *West Orange II*.

The *Edgewood/West Orange* saga began with poor districts suing for more funding; it ended with rich districts suing to challenge any limitation on their ability to raise funds beyond state-imposed caps. The first problem was that the legislature was not willing to redraw district lines or otherwise significantly disturb the prerogatives of the wealthy dis-

---

[65] 777 S.W.2d 391 (Tex. 1989).

[66] Vernon's Ann. Tex. Const. Art. VII § 1 (2006).

[67] 777 S.W.2d at 393, 397.

[68] Edgewood Indep. Sch. Dist. v. Kirby, 804 S.W.2d 491 (Tex. 1991).

tricts. The second problem was that the state constitution forbade the state legislature itself from imposing any kind of property tax, which the Texas courts read to prevent the state from unduly limiting local discretion in setting local tax rates. This provision limited the ability of the state legislature to redistribute local property tax monies. The Texas Supreme Court was thus both the impetus for redistribution and a leading obstacle. For every step forward, the legislature or the Court or both would take two steps back. As Mark Yudof—a Texas Law School professor and one of the Edgewood parents' original lawyers—observed, "School finance reform is like a Russian novel; it's long, tedious, and everybody dies in the end."[69]

The political trajectory of school finance reform reflected the changes in the political complexion of the state as a whole. From the time of *Rodriguez* (decided in 1973) to *West Orange II* (decided in 2006), the Texas legislature changed from Democratic hands to Republican ones, and the Texas Supreme Court—an elected body—changed from 6 Democrats and 3 Republicans to 9 Republicans. By *Edgewood IV*, the Texas Court's initial equity theory had been replaced by a modified adequacy theory: the Court held that once school funding reaches an adequate level, the state is relieved of its burden to ensure that similar tax rates raise similar funds. Nevertheless, the Court still held that the Texas system was "minimally acceptable only when viewed through the prism of history. Surely Texas can and must do better."[70] By *West Orange II*, the Court was concerned with those rich districts that were forced by political realities to tax near the state maximum property tax, a violation of the Texas constitution's ban on state-imposed property taxes. In the state legislature, opposition to redistribution made amending the constitution impossible.

Nevertheless, school funding did improve, albeit slowly. In 1967–68, Alamo Heights outspent Edgewood $594 to $356 per pupil. In 1989, when the Supreme Court of Texas decided *Edgewood I*, the wealthiest districts still spent $19,333 per student while the poorest spent $2,112. When *Edgewood IV* came down in 1995, the state equalized the funding for eighty-five percent of the students at any given tax rate, with the richest schools outpacing the poorest by only $600.

In San Antonio, the politics of race and place also changed between *Rodriguez* and the *West Orange* cases. The change began in the mid–1970s, when Hispanics began to exercise real influence in city politics. Working through Catholic parishes, Communities Organized for Public Service successfully pressed for greater equity in city services and for

---

[69] Mark Yudof, *School Finance Reform in Texas*, 28 HARVARD J. ON LEGIS. 499, 499 (1991).

[70] Edgewood Indep. Sch. Dist. v. Meno, 917 S.W.2d 717, 726 (Tex. 1995).

capital improvements in the west and south-side barrios. Their influence
was dramatically enhanced after the Justice Department pressured the
city to remedy the dilution of the Mexican–American vote. In response,
the city switched from an at-large council electoral system to a district-
based one.[71] In 1975, there was one African–American, one Hispanic, and
six Anglos on the city council; in 1977, there was one African–American,
four Hispanics, and five Anglos. At around the same time, the Good
Government League, which had exercised power in the city for years,
began to unravel as the business elites split between central city and
northside interests. Henry Cisneros, originally a GGL candidate who
joined the city council in 1975, became modern San Antonio's first
Hispanic mayor (and the first Hispanic mayor of any major American
city) in 1981. He would go on to serve four two-year terms.

Edgewood would eventually convince the city to provide sewers and
other basic public services.[72] And one group of Hispanic schoolchildren
would eventually get a win in the U.S. Supreme Court. In the 1982 case
of *Plyler v. Doe*,[73] MALDEF challenged a Texas law that authorized local
school districts to deny enrollment to school-aged children of undocu-
mented aliens. Justice Brennan, writing for a 5–4 majority, declared the
law unconstitutional as a violation of the Equal Protection Clause.
Justice Powell, the author of *Rodriguez*, joined him. Justice Burger,
writing in dissent, observed that in *Rodriguez*, "Justice Powell ... [had]
expressly rejected the proposition that state laws dealing with public
education are subject to special scrutiny under the Equal Protection
Clause."[74] Powell appeared to disagree: "A legislative classification that
threatens the creation of an underclass of future citizens and residents,"
Powell wrote in a separate opinion, "cannot be reconciled with one of the
fundamental purposes of the Fourteenth Amendment."[75]

VII.

In June of 2006, a Texas state court dissolved the most recent
injunction ordering the state to repair its school financing system. The
Republican Governor, Rick Perry, signed a plan that shifts more responsibility for school funding to the state. Business interests and the League
of United Latin American Citizens endorsed the plan because it reduces

---

[71] Mexican American Legal Defense Fund, *President Tallman's Statement Regarding the Reauthorization of the Temporary Provisions of the Voting Rights Act*, Oct. 18, 2005.

[72] Rogers, *supra* note 7, 110–113.

[73] 457 U.S. 202 (1982).

[74] Id. at 247 (Burger, C.J., dissenting).

[75] Id. at 239 (Powell, J., concurring).

the state's reliance on the local property tax.[76] But the plan is controversial, as are all things related to schools in Texas. Critics, such as State Comptroller Carole Keeton Strayhorn, proclaim that the system "replaces Robin Hood with Robbin' Everybody."[77] She claims sixty percent of districts would receive no funding increases, while rich districts—she specifically cited Alamo Heights—would receive large boosts.

Nevertheless, over thirty years after *Rodriguez*, Edgewood's schools are now comparatively well-funded. Indeed, Edgewood now spends more money per pupil than Alamo Heights. In 2003–2004, state aid helped Edgewood outspend Alamo Heights $8,670 to $8,201, and both exceeded the statewide average of $7,784 per student.

But Edgewood test scores are still far below those in Alamo Heights. Concentrated poverty and segregation contribute to the poor showing of poor minorities in poor places. According to the 2000 census, Edgewood continues to be ninety-two percent Hispanic and twenty-five percent below the poverty line. Alamo Heights continues to be seventy-five percent Anglo and only four percent poor. The racial geography of the city, which is now majority Hispanic, remains similar to what it was over 100 years ago. The poor people still live on the Edge and the rich live in the Heights. Moreover, the suburbs of San Antonio have grown apace and whites have fled San Antonio, reproducing the racial geography of the city on a regional scale. Between 1960 and 1970, approximately 98,000 Hispanics settled in the city and 44,000 whites left.[78] The San Antonio Independent School District is seventy-five percent Hispanic, while the region's suburban districts are predominantly Anglo.

San Antonio is not exceptional. Across metropolitan areas, schools are highly segregated, and performance differences between inner-city schools and suburban schools are striking. In light of this metropolitan reality, civil rights lawyers, scholars, and courts have directed their attention away from seeking equal funding toward seeking adequate funding. They argue that state constitutional provisions that require public education explicitly or implicitly impose a minimum standard of quality that school districts with little taxable property or a high percentage of at-risk students cannot meet. And some scholars and

---

[76] Texans for Rick Perry, *Perry–Sharp Plan Wins Support of San Antonio Chamber, LULAC*, available at http://www.rickperry.org/news/display.php?id=255 (Apr. 21, 2006) (last accessed July 21, 2006).

[77] Janey Elliot and Clay Robison, *Comptroller Blasts Perry's School Finance Plan*, HOUS. CHRON., Apr. 20, 2004.

[78] San Antonio Planning Department, *Ethnic Composition of San Antonio & Bexar County* (2003).

courts have advocated integration as the only effective remedy for failing urban school systems.[79]

The shift toward adequacy reflects the realization that students in inner-city schools often cost more to educate than their counterparts in suburban schools. Inner-city students face hurdles associated with concentrated poverty that suburban students do not face. The shift also reflects a belief that reforms that depend on equalizing money across districts are more likely to fail politically and strategically. Indeed, local fiscal control has reemerged as an important consideration for some school finance reformers. A few scholars have argued that school finance litigation and reform has led to decreases in overall support for the public schools. Applying a more sophisticated version of Justice Powell's argument in favor of local control, these scholars argue that local funding, even with all its disparities, is superior because it gives local voters the incentive to invest in their schools.

This concern with the source of education funding is probably misplaced, however. Certainly in Texas state funding has led to increased spending on education generally and to dramatic increases in the poorest jurisdictions. The perceived failures of school finance reform are not attributable to centralized funding, but to a system that permits wealthier (and often white) parents to "buy" a better education for their children by purchasing a home in a good school district.

Thirty-five years ago, Coons, Clune and Sugarman suggested that the best solution for this kind of placed-based inequality was a family-based voucher system.[80] If Texas students could take their per pupil cost with them to any school, then parents might have a real choice about what kind of education their children would receive, regardless of where they happened to live. Moreover, school districts would have less incentive to resist consolidation or property wealth equalization because they would be unable to "choose" their students by manipulating district boundaries. A voucher system would also solve the equal protection problems generated by a district-equalization system, as Frank Michelman recognized in his 1969 article.

But a true voucher program—state or national or even regional—is and always has been a political non-starter. Suburban school districts, and the homeowners who live in them, do not want to uproot their local education systems. The result of forty years of school finance reform has thus been a patchwork of increased state and federal funding, charter school experiments, some voucher-like choice plans in limited areas,

---

[79] Sheff v. O'Neill, 678 A.2d 1267 (Conn. 1996).

[80] See JOHN COONS & STEPHEN SUGARMAN, FAMILY CHOICE IN EDUCATION: A MODEL STATE SYSTEM FOR VOUCHERS (1971).

and—most recently—massive federal intervention. The No Child Left Behind Act—promulgated by a Republican President and embraced by a Republican Congress—has brought about the regulatory centralization of education in ways well beyond what Justice Powell could ever have imagined.

Indeed, despite Justice Powell's spirited defense of local control in *Rodriguez*, the long term trajectory of education policy in the United States has been in the direction of increased centralization. The problems of the schools reflect the larger problems of concentrated poverty, racial division, and long-term residential socio-economic segregation. Local school boards have little ability to address those problems.

By reaffirming the already great social and political distance between Edgewood and Alamo Heights, the Court's decision in *Rodriguez* recognized constitutionally what was already well established geographically. But neither the original *Rodriguez* plaintiffs, the state of Texas, the Supreme Court, subsequent state courts, nor state legislatures have been able to mediate the tensions between local control and equal access, the rights of individual children and the rights of communities, or the relative wealth of places and the relative wealth of people. And, where it has been adopted, the silver bullet that was supposed to be education finance reform has not succeeded in solving the difficult problems that face the country's education system. Thus, despite the important legal reforms that have taken place over the last four decades, the students who attend schools in Alamo Heights and Edgewood are in about the same place as they were in 1968. The chances of a high school student from Edgewood attending college is under ten percent;[81] the chances of a high school student from Alamo Heights attending college is ninety-six percent.[82] Over fifty years after *Brown* and thirty-five years after *Rodriguez*, the legal geography of San Antonio remains roughly the same.

[81] Jeanne Russell, *High Hopes for College Often Redirected Low*, SAN ANTONIO EXPRESS-NEWS, May 21. 2006.

[82] Alamo Heights Independent School District, *Alamo Heights High School*, available at http://www.ahisd.net/campuses/ahhs/default.htm (last accessed October 31, 2006).

6

George Rutherglen*

Civil Rights in Private Schools: The Surprising Story of *Runyon v. McCrary*

Few decisions could have raised more controversial issues than *Runyon v. McCrary*,[1] which declared segregation in private schools to be illegal. It subordinated private choice to civil rights policy and extended federal law beyond the limitations of the state action doctrine. Yet few major civil rights decisions have been more anticlimactic. Where demonstrations and massive resistance greeted *Brown v. Board of Education*,[2] the decision in *Runyon* was grudgingly accepted even by those who profoundly disagreed with it. Resistance took the form of subtle evasion rather than public protest. As a matter of legal doctrine, *Runyon* was decided when the state action doctrine under the Fourteenth Amendment was still an object of active judicial and scholarly interest, yet the opinion in *Runyon* effortlessly avoided these thorny issues by the simple expedient of resting on statutory grounds. And in a poignant sequel, the two-year-old plaintiff, Michael McCrary, who first appeared in the newspaper coverage of the case as the child on the tricycle below, reappeared a few decades later as the defensive lineman hugging the owner of the Baltimore Ravens after they had won the Super Bowl. In the process, not only was he transformed, but his case was transformed from a technical

* I would like to thank my colleagues on the faculty at the University of Virginia School of Law, and particularly those in the law library, for their assistance with this article. Molly Mitchell provided indispensable research assistance, as did Walton Walker and Stephanie Wright.

[1] 427 U.S. 160 (1976).

[2] 347 U.S. 483 (1954).

matter of statutory interpretation into a symbol of national progress on civil rights.

The personal and political evolution in *Runyon v. McCrary* is not the only surprising development in the history of section 1981,[3] the statute that formed the basis for this case. Its roots extend all the way back to Reconstruction and the passage of the Civil Rights Act of 1866, the very first piece of civil rights legislation. And the implications of *Runyon* reach forward to the most recent civil rights act, the Civil Rights Act of 1991. Yet for all its distinguished lineage and its doctrinal consequences, *Runyon* exists primarily as a symbol—a valuable symbol but one with necessarily limited effects. It could not, in and of itself, greatly expand the enrollment of minority students in private schools, which has stagnated at a disproportionately low fraction of the enrollment of white students. The enrollment of African American students is particularly low, and more surprisingly still, has remained concentrated in a fraction of private schools. In this respect, *Runyon* reflects in microcosm the central paradox of civil rights law: having achieved formal equality of opportunity, how to get beyond it to actual equality of resources and results.

This paradox unfolds in *Runyon* in three stages: the immediate factual circumstances of the case and its place in the struggle over desegregation of public education; the doctrinal background and immedi-

---

[3] 42 U.S.C. § 1981 (2000).

ate effects of the decision; and its long-term consequences for private education. These three stages are recounted in the succeeding parts of this chapter, beginning with the case itself.

I. Civil Rights and Segregated Academies

Runyon was actually two cases consolidated for trial and appeal. One involved the future professional football player, Michael McCrary, and it all began when his mother, Sandra McCrary, called Bobbe's School, a private pre-school in northern Virginia, to inquire about her son's possible enrollment there. After discussion of programs and qualifications, she asked whether the school accepted African Americans and was told that it did not. Bobbe's School later disputed her account of this conversation, but the district court believed her account, which was corroborated by others who had made similar calls to Bobbe's School.[4] Having been told of the school's exclusionary policy, she never submitted a written application on Michael's behalf and eventually enrolled him in another nursery school, farther away and less convenient for the family.

As a specialist in equal employment matters with the Navy, Sandra McCrary was not content to drop her dispute with Bobbe's School.[5] Several friends advised her to apply anyway because she and her son were light enough to "pass" as white. As she said, however, at the time:

> There are a lot of people in the area who have been or will be faced with the same problem, ... but after a while you get battle weary; you get tired of fighting, and then there's always the problem of not getting involved, not wanting to go where you aren't wanted.[6]

Her determination persisted despite ongoing threats that she received in the course of the litigation.

She began her efforts to protest these segregationist policies by contacting her friends, Raymond and Margaret Gonzales, who had complained of a similar experience. Raymond Gonzales had called Bobbe's School about enrolling his son, Colin, and had been told that the school was all-white. The Gonzaleses were from Trinidad and were regarded as black and so dropped any further attempt to enroll Colin in Bobbe's School. They had previously attempted to enroll him in the Fairfax–Brewster School, where they had visited and made a written application for admission to the school's summer program with the

---

[4] Gonzales v. Fairfax–Brewster Sch., Inc., 363 F. Supp. 1200, 1202–03 (E.D. Va. 1973), *aff'd in part and rev'd in part*, 515 F.2d 1082 (4th Cir. 1975) (en banc), *aff'd*, 427 U.S. 160 (1976).

[5] Joint Appendix at 226–B to –C, Runyon v. McCrary, 427 U.S. 160, No. 75–62 (1976).

[6] Helen Dewar, *White Private Schools Sued*, WASH. POST, May 31, 1973, at G1.

intent of enrolling him in the first grade. Their application, however, was rejected without explanation and their check for the application fee was returned to them. When Raymond Gonzales called to seek an explanation, he was told, as he later testified, that the school was not integrated.

Lawsuits against both schools soon followed, alleging violations of section 1981 because the defendants had engaged in racial discrimination in refusing to enter into contracts for the schooling of Michael and Colin. In the words of the statute, which date back to the Civil Rights Act of 1866, the plaintiffs had been denied "the same right ... to make and enforce contracts, ... as is enjoyed by white citizens...." Both schools denied that they had engaged in racial discrimination and officials from both schools testified to this effect, denying the substance of the telephone conversations with Michael's and Colin's parents. This issue of credibility was resolved against the schools by the district court and the litigation proceeded on appeal on the pure question of law: whether section 1981 prohibited discrimination by private schools.

An intervenor on the defendant's side, the Southern Independent School Association (SISA), confronted this question directly, candidly admitting that "[a] substantial proportion of the schools represented by intervenor deny admission to applicants of the Negro race" and arguing bluntly for the advantages of segregated education.[7] For its pains in intervening in the lawsuit, SISA and its member schools became subject to the same injunction against discrimination as the other defendants.[8]

The basis for this remedy, as well as the damages awarded to the plaintiffs, was the defendants' violation of section 1981. As discussed more fully in Part II, this holding followed directly from then-recent decisions of the Supreme Court broadly interpreting section 1981 to prohibit discrimination by private parties, not just by the government. Since the statute literally applies to all forms of contracting, and since private schooling involves a contract, the district court easily concluded that the defendants violated the statute by refusing to enter into contracts with the plaintiffs on the basis of race. Constitutional arguments advanced by the defendants that the statute, so interpreted, infringed upon the right to privacy or to freedom of association were brushed aside, on the ground that the schools held themselves out to any white student who applied.[9] These conclusions of the district court all were affirmed on appeal, first to the Fourth Circuit and then to the

---

[7] Brief of Petitioner S. Indep. Sch. Ass'n at 4, 35–36, Runyon v. McCrary, 427 U.S. 160, No. 75–278 (1976).

[8] Joint Appendix, *supra* note 5, at 132, 141.

[9] *Gonzales*, 363 F. Supp. at 1204.

Supreme Court.[10] The defendants' arguments for reversal, however, were sufficient to provoke dissents at each level, as Part II also discusses in more detail.

These arguments derived from the social and legal context in which the defendant schools operated. *Runyon* did not involve isolated acts of discrimination, but schools that shared, even if equivocally, in exploiting white flight from integration of the surrounding public schools. This reaction to *Brown* preceded *Runyon* and persisted afterwards. It was first manifest in actions taken to subsidize private education by the states and localities undergoing desegregation. As whites moved from the public schools to private schools, government funds followed them to subsidize a new form of segregated education. These initiatives were strongest in the Deep South, and particularly in Mississippi, but they were also a feature of massive resistance in Virginia.[11] The Supreme Court put an end to such blatant attempts to reestablish segregation at public expense in *Norwood v. Harrison*.[12] Hence the emphasis of the defendants in *Runyon* was on the complete absence of public subsidies for their policies, whether discriminatory or not.[13]

Both Bobbe's School and the Fairfax–Brewster School were founded in the years immediately after *Brown*, in which opposition to integration took the form of "massive resistance," eventually causing some public schools in Virginia to close as soon as they became subject to desegregation orders. Bobbe's School was founded at the height of massive resistance in 1958 and the Fairfax–Brewster School a few years earlier in 1955. For all the record reveals, these schools might have been founded for reasons apart from the backlash against *Brown*, but it is doubtful. They gradually grew in enrollment during the era of desegregation, each teaching approximately 200 students in the late 1960s and early 1970s.[14] The willingness of both schools to agree to SISA's joinder as an intervening defendant[15] indicates that they had some sympathy with its position. This was, as noted earlier, an unequivocal defense of the right of private schools to discriminate on the basis of race, as a majority of SISA's members did.

---

[10] Gonzales v. Fairfax–Brewster Sch., Inc., 515 F.2d 1082, 1086–88 (4th Cir. 1975) (en banc), *aff'd*, 427 U.S. 160, 167–79 (1976). The district court's decision was reversed only on the award of attorney's fees to the plaintiffs. *Id.* at 1086–88, *aff'd*, 427 U.S. at 182–86.

[11] J. Harvie Wilkinson III, From *Brown* to *Bakke*: The Supreme Court and School Integration: 1954–1978 82, 98 (1979).

[12] 413 U.S. 455 (1973).

[13] Joint Appendix, *supra* note 5, at 121, 126; *Gonzales*, 363 F. Supp. at 1201.

[14] *Id.* at 1201–02.

[15] Joint Appendix, *supra* note 5, at 129.

If not full-fledged "segregation academies," Bobbe's School and the Fairfax–Brewster School were fellow travelers in the same movement. Both schools denied that they had discriminated, but not very convincingly, since they also admitted that they had never enrolled, or even received any other applications from, any African American students.[16] Of the two schools, Bobbe's had a more nuanced policy, taking the position that it was desegregated because it admitted students from Asia and the Middle East. As the school's superintendent testified, "We have just about all nationalities in the school."[17] Only African Americans were excluded.

The decision in *Runyon* might have been thought to foreclose all further efforts to provide a private alternative to public integration, but the opposition to *Brown* was too widespread and resourceful to be cured by a single decision. Even after white flight to suburban school districts became the dominant means of avoiding court-ordered desegregation, advocates of segregated private education persisted, using religious affiliation as a basis simultaneously for avoiding regulation and for obtaining the benefits of tax-exempt status. These efforts, too, were thwarted by the Supreme Court, which, in *Bob Jones University v. United States*,[18] upheld the denial of tax-exempt status to religious schools that explicitly discriminated on the basis of race. Yet even after this decision, doubts persisted about the extent to which the Internal Revenue Service (IRS) actively pursued its regulations denying tax-exempt status to such institutions.[19] The persistence of such litigation, almost a decade after the decision in *Runyon*, raises continuing doubts about the effectiveness of the decision. It is first necessary, however, to explore the doctrinal intricacies of the decision and its effect on civil rights law.

II. The Unsettled History of Section 1981

The plaintiffs asserted their claims under section 1981 and under Title II of the Civil Rights Act of 1964, which prohibits racial discrimination in public accommodations, such as hotels, restaurants, and movie theaters. The latter claim apparently was asserted in an effort to bolster the plaintiffs' request for attorney's fees, which were not then generally available under section 1981. Private schools, however, were not among the public accommodations covered by Title II,[20] and so the plaintiffs were forced to rely upon a statute passed almost a century earlier. That

---

[16] *Id.* at 61–62, 108, 112, 244, 266.

[17] *Id.* at 88–89, 259.

[18] 461 U.S. 574 (1983).

[19] Allen v. Wright, 468 U.S. 737 (1984) (denying standing to taxpayers on this issue).

[20] 42 U.S.C. §§ 2000a(b), 2000a–3(b) (2000).

statute has had a controversial and checkered history, from its enactment in 1866 through a series of re-enactments, interpretations, re-
interpretations, and amendments. Many of these figured in the opinions
handed down at various stages in *Runyon*.

The history of section 1981 follows the vicissitudes in our nation's
changing commitment to civil rights. The statute was originally enacted
to assure full legal capacity to the former slaves. Enacted under Congress's power to enforce the Thirteenth Amendment, the Civil Rights Act
of 1866 guaranteed "all persons born in the United States ... the same
right ... to make and enforce contracts, to sue, be parties, and give
evidence, to inherit, purchase, lease, sell, hold, and convey real and
personal property, and to full and equal benefit of all laws and proceedings for the security of person and property, as is enjoyed by white
citizens...."[21] The act's immediate aim was to invalidate the "Black
Codes," enacted or under consideration in several southern states, to
deny rights of full legal capacity to the newly freed slaves, who had been
emancipated by the Thirteenth Amendment itself. The act granted equal
citizenship in the realm of "civil rights," narrowly understood to comprise the rights of equality as a legal person, but not political rights, such
as the right to vote, which were later protected by the Fifteenth
Amendment. Nor did it embrace "social rights" which were thought to
be the last and most significant category of rights in the nineteenth
century, leading to full social equality among members of different races.
Even the strongest supports of racial equality refused to go that far.[22]

Nevertheless, doubts were raised about the constitutionality of the
1866 Act, even while it was being debated in Congress, on the ground
that it went beyond the power granted to Congress to enforce the
Thirteenth Amendment. Section 1 of that amendment abolished slavery
in all its forms, whether created by law or by private contract, a crucial
feature of the amendment that has figured prominently in subsequent
debates over the interpretation of section 1981. Almost alone among
constitutional rights, those granted by the Thirteenth Amendment are
not limited to "state action" (or action by the federal government). The
actual limits on the Thirteenth Amendment depend on what constitutes
the "badges and incidents of slavery" subject to congressional power
under section 2 of the amendment. The various rights listed in the 1866
Act were thought, by its supporters, to exemplify the minimum rights
necessary to participate in civil society, like the right "to sue, be parties,
and give evidence." Denying such rights was thought to be a mark of
inferiority that identified an individual as a former slave. To the act's
critics, however, these rights extended too far beyond the direct conse-

---

[21] Ch. 31, 14 Stat. 27 (1866).

[22] *See* Plessy v. Ferguson, 163 U.S. 537, 561 (1896) (Harlan, J., dissenting).

quences of slavery. Was, for instance, denial of the right to hold property a badge of slavery? At the time, aliens could not hold property, and in some states, married women could not either. Initiating a controversy that has ensued ever since, critics of the act argued that the newly freed slaves suffered few direct consequences of slavery after it had been abolished, while supporters of the act saw the consequences of slavery spreading throughout the legal system.

This debate over the constitutionality of the 1866 Act led Congress to take two steps that profoundly affected its subsequent development. First, Congress proposed and eventually obtained the ratification of the Fourteenth Amendment. Many of the provisions in section 1 of this amendment, including the Equal Protection Clause and the Privileges or Immunities Clause, were meant to protect the same rights as those enumerated in the 1866 Act. Second, after ratification of the Fourteenth Amendment, Congress re-enacted the central provisions of the 1866 Act in the Enforcement Act of 1870,[23] using its newly conferred powers under section 5 of the amendment to protect the rights granted by section 1. This step, taken to preserve the constitutionality of the 1866 Act, had the side effect of introducing questions about the act's scope, questions that eventually divided the Supreme Court in *Runyon*. The fundamental question was whether the 1866 Act covered private discrimination or only discrimination involving state action. The act would have the first, private interpretation, if it had the full reach of the Thirteenth Amendment, which prohibited all forms of slavery, public and private. It would have the second, public interpretation, if it reached only as far as the Fourteenth Amendment, which extends only to state action.

For over a century, the 1866 Act received the latter interpretation and was treated as if it protected virtually the same rights under the same conditions as the Fourteenth Amendment. All of that changed with the Supreme Court's decision in *Jones v. Alfred H. Mayer Co.*[24] That case concerned a companion statute to section 1981, section 1982, which was also derived from the 1866 Act. Where section 1981 protects the right "to make and enforce contracts," section 1982 protects the right "to inherit, purchase, lease, sell, hold, and convey real and personal property." The plaintiffs in *Jones* alleged that they were discriminatorily denied the right to purchase a home in a private development and asserted a claim under section 1982. The Supreme Court eventually upheld this claim, reasoning that the statute prohibited private as well as public discrimination because the Civil Rights Act of 1866 was directed against all the badges and incidents of slavery, not just those imposed by government. Before *Jones*, the act was thought to protect

---

[23] Ch. 114, 16 Stat. 140 (1870).

[24] 392 U.S. 409 (1968).

only the general capacity to hold property or to contract regardless of race, not the right to hold any particular piece of property or to enter into any particular contract free of discrimination. As Chief Judge Haynsworth pointed out in his opinion for the Fourth Circuit in *Runyon*,[25] section 1981 was thought to grant everyone the power to acquire property or to enter into a contract regardless of race, but not the power to force anyone to enter into a transaction with someone else. The Supreme Court justified its radical break from past interpretations of the 1866 Act in *Jones* by a renewed examination of the act's legislative history.

Whether the Court's renewed examination of the legislative record actually supports its conclusion has proven to be controversial. What had changed in *Jones*, more than the sources for the Court's decision in the legislative record, was the statutory context in which the 1866 Act was now situated. In the nineteenth century, the act was the first piece of civil rights legislation passed by Congress, followed by others that, at most, obliquely regulated private conduct, or in the case of the Civil Rights Act of 1875,[26] did so explicitly but were held unconstitutional for that reason.[27] By the middle of the twentieth century, the Civil Rights Act of 1964[28] had legitimized federal regulation of private discrimination. As a consequence, the extension of the 1866 Act to private discrimination in *Jones* was both much more acceptable and much less radical. The decision itself, on private discrimination in real estate sales, added only modestly to the prohibitions and remedies in fair housing legislation, notably the Civil Rights Act of 1968,[29] which was passed simultaneously with the Court's consideration of *Jones*.

A similar point can be made about the decision in *Runyon*. Recall that the plaintiffs also asserted claims under Title II of the Civil Rights Act of 1964, prohibiting discrimination in public accommodations. Private schools were not among the public accommodations covered by Title II, but the very existence of the statute, regulating businesses that held themselves out to the general public, justified the same form of regulation of private schools, like those in *Runyon*, which accepted applicants drawn from the same pool. Indeed, both sets of parents in *Runyon* learned about the schools from mailed advertisements or entries in the

[25] 515 F.2d at 1086.

[26] Ch. 114, 18 Stat. 335 (1875).

[27] For my previous account of these developments, see George Rutherglen, *The Improbable History of Section 1981: Clio Still Bemused and Confused*, 2003 SUP. CT. REV. 303, 317–22.

[28] Pub. L. No. 88–352, 78 Stat. 241 (1964).

[29] Pub. L. No. 90–284, 82 Stat. 73 (codified at 42 U.S.C. §§ 3601–91 (2000)).

Yellow Pages.[30] The schools advanced no defense that they were private in any sense other than that they were not public schools. Their argument that the constitutional right of free association allowed them to discriminate on the basis of race required more: either some kind of individual right to privacy or a right to engage in concerted political action, neither of which were at stake in this case.[31]

If sections 1981 and 1982 have served, after *Jones*, to fill the gaps in modern civil rights legislation, they have not laid to rest doubts about the basis for that decision. This was the fundamental issue in *Runyon* when it came to the Supreme Court. The majority's reasoning, like that of the lower courts, was straightforward: *Jones* interpreted section 1982, and the Civil Rights Act of 1866 from which it is derived, to prohibit private discrimination. Section 1981 is also derived from the 1866 Act, so it, too, prohibits private discrimination. Section 1981 covers discrimination in contracting. Admission to a private school involves contracting. Therefore, section 1981 prohibits private discrimination in admission to private schools. Neither the dissent in the Fourth Circuit nor the dissent in the Supreme Court took issue explicitly with the first, and most important, step in this argument, apparently conceding that it was foreclosed by *Jones*. Instead, they looked for other ways to limit the implications of that decision.

In the Fourth Circuit, Judge Russell dissented on the ground that attendance at a private school involved more than a contractual relationship, but one, like marriage, that involved a change of status.[32] This analogy, if plausible at all, depends upon an implicit appeal to a right to privacy that acts as a general limitation on the scope of government regulation. But as we have seen, Bobbe's School and the Fairfax-Brewster School were private only in a much more limited sense, a point emphasized by Justice Powell in his concurring opinion in the Supreme Court.[33] They were neither operated nor funded by the government. Even if they were private, they remained open to the general public and so involved no element of the constitutional right to privacy.[34]

Justice White took issue neither with this point nor with the majority's reaffirmation of *Jones*. Instead, he took issue with the second step in the majority's argument, denying that section 1981 is derived from the Civil Rights Act of 1866. Instead, he traced section 1981 back

---

[30] *Gonzales*, 363 F. Supp. at 1202–03.

[31] Brief of Petitioners at 11–13, Runyon v. McCrary, 427 U.S. 160, No. 75–306 (1976); Brief of Petitioner S. Indep. Sch. Ass'n, *supra* note 7, at 22–28, 30.

[32] 515 F.2d at 1095–96 (Russell, J., dissenting).

[33] 427 U.S. at 188 (Powell, J., concurring).

[34] *Id.* at 176–79.

only to the Enforcement Act of 1870, which involved the re-enactment of the 1866 Act using the powers newly conferred on Congress by section 5 of the Fourteenth Amendment.[35] For White, this made section 1981 a statute subject to the same state action requirement as the Fourteenth Amendment. Section 1982 was different according to the dissent, because as it was officially codified, it rested directly on the 1866 Act and so could be interpreted, as it was in *Jones*, to apply to private action, just like the Thirteenth Amendment. In the end, this distinction between section 1981 and section 1982 depended upon a marginal notation of the codifiers who compiled the Revised Statutes of 1874, a thin and unpersuasive basis for such a sharp distinction between two statutes with such a similar heritage.

Justice White's highly technical argument, if unconvincing on its own terms, is convincing for what it reveals about the history of section 1981. This history has been, from its inception, contentious and dependent as much on a general commitment to civil rights as on legal doctrine. Justices who, like Justice White in *Runyon*, were concerned about the extent of federal power to prohibit discrimination took a narrower view of the statute than justices who gave greater weight to the need to eliminate discrimination and its persistent effects. It was natural for Justice Stewart, the author of the majority opinion, to give decisive weight to the prior decision in *Jones*, since he was the author of that decision also. Yet more than simply the force of precedent or the preferences of a majority of justices were involved. As Justice Stevens recognized in his concurring opinion, the force of the decision in *Jones* was confirmed by the political developments that made it possible: the civil rights legislation that extended the principle against discrimination to private action.[36]

This principle was vindicated in *Runyon*, although with only modest remedies for the plaintiffs. They recovered damages, $2,500 for Colin Gonzales and $3,000 for the McCrary family, and an injunction against the defendants prohibiting future discrimination.[37] They were denied an award of attorney's fees because their claim under Title II of the Civil Rights Act of 1964, which would have supported an award of fees, had been dismissed by the district court and because such fees were not yet generally available in other civil rights actions.[38]

The precedential value of the decision was far more consequential, but mainly for what it did not do rather than for what it did. The

---

[35] *Id.* at 195–205 (White, J., dissenting).

[36] *Id.* at 191–92 (Stevens, J., concurring).

[37] Joint Appendix, *supra* note 5, at 142.

[38] *Runyon*, 427 U.S. at 182–86.

Supreme Court did not retreat from *Jones* or limit its application to section 1982. These conclusions were eventually confirmed by Congress, but not before the Supreme Court tried to limit the scope of section 1981 in other respects. The most serious challenge to the scope of section 1981 emerged from a decision involving a claim for racial harassment by an employee who already had a continuing contract with her employer. In *Patterson v. McLean Credit Union*,[39] the Court held that such claims fell outside the scope of section 1981 because they did not involve the right "to make and enforce contracts," but only the performance of a preexisting contract. The ruling however, could have been much more restrictive, since the Supreme Court asked for briefing on the question whether *Runyon* should be overruled.[40]

The Court refused to go so far in *Patterson*, but even so, this case was soon superseded by the Civil Rights Act of 1991, which amended section 1981 to make clear that it covered all aspects of contractual relations and applied to all contracts.[41] The first of these provisions rejected the decision in *Patterson* and the second codified the holding in *Runyon*. With this most recent piece of civil rights legislation Congress closed the circle by confirming a broad interpretation of its very first civil rights act. Whether the same progressive consequences could be translated from the realm of legal doctrine to social reality constitutes a different question, taken up in the next part of this chapter.

III. Personal Consequences and Social Effects

Both Michael McCrary and Colin Gonzales eventually went to schools that were already integrated instead of attending schools that did not want them in the first place. Their parents were hardly unique in making this decision. Minority families who can afford to send their children to private school have a choice about which private school to send them to. An integrated school is likely to be far more congenial to them and beneficial to their children than one that has integrated only under court order. The parents of Michael and Colin were unique only in taking on the burden of litigation. Many parents, unlike Sandra McCrary, would simply have accepted the fact of continuing discrimination, offensive and demeaning as it is, and looked elsewhere for education for their children.

The dynamics of litigation over public schools is quite different. Most parents who fought the battles over public school desegregation faced the stark choice between segregated education or litigation. Private schools were not a feasible option for most African Americans, and even

---

[39] 491 U.S. 164 (1989).

[40] *Id.* at 171–75.

[41] Pub. L. No. 102–166, § 101, 105 Stat. 1071, 1072 (1991) (codified at 42 U.S.C. § 1981(b), (c) (2000)).

for those who had this option, it depended on the variety of private schools in the area. More often, as with "segregation academies," this range of choice stood in the way of integration, offering another form of "white flight" from integrated public schools. This tendency was exaggerated by the distribution of income and wealth, which worked to the disadvantage of African Americans, preventing them from opting out of segregated public schools as much as whites did. As their alternatives to public education diminished, the commitment of African Americans to integration increased, as did the corresponding opposition of whites who favored continued segregation but could not afford to send their children to private school. The same incentives came into play even more strongly with respect to movement to the suburbs, where higher real estate values often reflected the higher quality of suburban schools. All parents, both black and white, who could not avoid urban public schools had a greater stake in what happened to them. Private schools were peripheral to the central disputes over desegregating these schools.

Runyon did not initiate a wave of litigation by African American parents seeking to have their children admitted to private segregated schools. A few cases in the immediate aftermath of the decision did raise claims of this kind.[42] Most of the litigation was indirect and some of it preceded Runyon by several years, like the decision in Norwood v. Harrison,[43] preventing the use of public funds to subsidize segregated private schools. The named plaintiffs in Norwood were students in public school and they limited their challenge to state support of segregated private schools, not the segregation of the schools themselves.[44] The plaintiffs' claim was that such support interfered with desegregation of the public schools, confirming the derivative status of litigation over private schools. Other cases, after Runyon, concerned the tax-exempt status of segregated private schools. The leading decision on this issue was Bob Jones University v. United States,[45] involving the denial of tax-exempt status to two private educational institutions. One of them, Bob Jones University, in fact, had abandoned its segregated admissions policy after Runyon was decided, but had instituted instead a policy against interracial dating.[46] The other, the Goldsboro Christian Schools, maintained a discriminatory admissions policy.[47] The Supreme Court upheld

---

[42] Brown v. Dade Christian Sch., 556 F.2d 310 (5th Cir. 1977); Riley v. Adirondack S. Sch. for Girls, 541 F.2d 1124 (5th Cir. 1976).

[43] 413 U.S. 455 (1973).

[44] Id. at 457–58.

[45] 461 U.S. 574 (1983).

[46] Id. at 580–81.

[47] Id. at 583. A few children with only one white parent were admitted under this policy. Id.

the rulings of the IRS denying tax-exempt status to these schools, but again, no African American student challenged the discriminatory policies of either school.

In fact, the absence of any interest in attending currently segregated schools came back to haunt the plaintiffs in yet another case in this series. In *Allen v. Wright*,[48] another group of parents alleged that the Internal Revenue Service had not done enough to enforce the revenue rulings upheld in *Bob Jones University*. Their claim, like that in *Norwood v. Harrison*, was that the lax enforcement of these regulations prevented effective desegregation of the public schools. They did not allege that their children (or any children of parents in the nationwide class that they represented) had sought or had been denied admission to any private school that continued to practice segregation. Partly for this reason, the Supreme Court denied standing to the plaintiffs, finding any connection between the alleged failures in enforcement and their own rights to be too attenuated to support standing. Wholly apart from whether this conclusion is entirely justifiable, it reveals how far civil rights groups had to go to mount a challenge to segregation in private schools. They could not readily find the plaintiffs most directly harmed by segregated private schools: children and their parents who sought admission to these schools.

Moreover, even if they had found these plaintiffs, the relief that they would have been able to obtain would have been limited to the particular schools involved. It would not have extended to systematic underenforcement of the rulings on tax-exempt status or, more generally, to attempts by private schools to comply with section 1981 only in form, but not in substance. Such schools could, for instance, use locations in segregated areas (with or without geographical restrictions on admissions) to depress minority attendance. Increased fees would have had the same effect on minority enrollment from low-income families. The wide range of responses open to private schools meant that a legal prohibition to end discrimination would not, by itself, produce widespread integration. The pressure to integrate had to be as much social as legal.

The fate of Bobbe's School offers a pointed illustration. The owners of the school were resolutely opposed to integration and had the school up for sale even before the Supreme Court handed down its decision. The school was sold immediately thereafter to new owners who supported integration and who promptly changed the named of the school to the Fairfax Academy in order to avoid the bad publicity generated by *Runyon*. The owners of the Fairfax–Brewster School were less opposed to integration, as evidenced perhaps by their willingness to admit Asian and Middle Eastern students, but they eventually sold their school to the

---

[48] 468 U.S. 737 (1984).

owners of the Fairfax Academy, who continue (to this day) to operate both schools and to pursue a consistent policy of integration. Segregation, it appears, could not hold out for long in the Washington metropolitan area. Northern Virginia, where these schools were located, might be more conservative than the District of Columbia itself, but the large presence of government workers, like Sandra McCrary, made it more liberal than the rest of the South. In order to remain competitive within this market for private education, private schools could not afford to be, or to be perceived as, segregationist.

It does not follow, of course, that these private schools, or private schools generally, are as integrated as the public schools, let alone that they conform to ambitious goals of racial balance according to the proportion of different races and ethnic groups in the general population. Any number of otherwise neutral prerequisites and requirements could work to depress the representation of minority groups in private education. Private schools, unlike public schools, need not be equally accessible to all. Against the background of free public education, relatively few minority families would find private schools to be a feasible and appealing option and there is little reason to expect that they would be representative of the general population.

The studies of integration in private schools bear this conclusion out. Explicit segregation virtually disappeared in the wake of *Bob Jones University*. Enforcement of the revenue ruling against tax-exempt status for segregated schools dropped off dramatically within a decade of that decision, and although some cases still are brought, the IRS investigates a different issue now than it did then. The principal question in all the recent cases is whether the private school seeking tax-exempt status has lived up to its official policy of accepting students regardless of race or color.[49] Schools that resolutely adhere to an explicit policy of segregation appear to be dwindling in number, at least if anecdotal evidence of the decline of "segregation academies" is to be believed.[50] Here, as elsewhere, Jim Crow has died.

The extent to which his spirit lives on, however, is another question. The recent IRS cases make tax-exempt status turn on whether the school has ever admitted members of a minority group. The "inexorable zero," as it has been called in employment discrimination cases, yields a compelling inference of discrimination, particularly when it is combined with circumstantial evidence, such as the establishment of a private school at the same time as a nearby public school was undergoing

---

[49] *See, e.g.*, Exemption Ruling, Bob Jones Elementary School, Inc. (Feb. 11, 2003); Advice Review (Oct. 28, 2003).

[50] *See Private White Academics Struggle in a Changing World*, BIRMINGHAM NEWS, Oct. 27, 2002.

desegregation.[51] In this respect, private schools are no better than public schools, and in some respects, are much worse.

These conclusions are documented in an important paper by Sean Reardon and John T. Yun that compiles and analyzes a wealth of statistics about enrollment in private schools over the last several decades of the twentieth century.[52] During this period, 10–12% of K–12 students were in private school, with a disproportionate number of these students being white.[53] Thus in 1997–98, almost 10% of students were enrolled in private school, but the enrollment rates for whites (and Asians) were about twice as high as the enrollment rates for African Americans and Latinos. Almost 12% of white students were in private school, but less than 6% of African American and Latino students. It follows that schools in the private sector have a higher proportion of whites than the public sector, a conclusion which is entirely predictable given the higher income and wealth of white families and the greater cost of private schools.[54]

What is less predictable is the higher level of de facto segregation among private schools. Within the private sector, students of different races and ethnicities are not distributed evenly among private schools, but are concentrated in schools that are either identifiably white (not counting Latinos) or minority (counting African Americans and Latinos). In 1997–98, 43.7% of black students attended private schools that were 90–100% non-white, while 34.3% of black students attended public schools with this degree of non-white enrollment.[55] The comparable figures for whites attending schools that are 90–100% white are 63.6% for whites in private schools and 46.9% for whites in public schools. Students in private schools are more likely to be exposed primarily to members of their own race than those in public schools.

Surprisingly, the most segregated private schools are Catholic, most of which are located outside the South. Only New Orleans among major southern cities has a high concentration of Catholic schools. Altogether, Catholic schools account for about half of the students enrolled in

---

[51] These cases rely primarily on Revenue Procedure 75–50, promulgated while *Bob Jones* was pending, which established a series of presumptions of continuing discrimination. A private school subject to these presumptions must submit evidence of present integration and nondiscrimination.

[52] Sean F. Reardon & John T. Yun, *Private School Racial Enrollments and Segregation* (Harv. Civ. Rts. Project, June 26, 2002), *available at* http://www.civilrightsproject.harvard.edu/research/deseg/Private_Schools.pdf.

[53] *Id.* at 15–16.

[54] *Id.* at 18.

[55] *Id.* at 34, 52.

private schools, with another quarter accounted for by schools with some
other religious affiliation. The religious schools generally are more
segregated (in the sense of concentration of students of the same race)
than secular schools, a pattern largely attributable to the smaller geographical area served by most religious schools.[56] Thus Catholic parochial
schools are generally limited to students within the parish, as the very
name of the schools implies. (Diocesan schools, mainly high schools, are
not so limited.) More than secular private schools, which tend to serve a
wider area, religious schools reflect patterns of residential segregation.[57]
These facts complicate any straightforward inference from racial imbalance to intentional discrimination. The Catholic Church took a strong
stand against segregation after *Brown*, and even before 1954, it began
the process of desegregating its own schools in the border states and
outside the South.[58] Half a century later, it is difficult to infer continued
discrimination from the number of African American students in its
schools.

Nevertheless, these figures do not absolve private schools of any
complicity in the resistance to desegregation. Enrollment in private
schools dramatically increased in the South, a region which historically
has had the fewest private schools in the country, as public school
districts came under desegregation decrees.[59] Mississippi represented the
most extreme example of this tendency, giving rise to cases like *Norwood
v. Harrison*, involving public subsidies to private schools, and prolonged
litigation over the tax-exempt status of segregated private schools.[60] That
effect has subsided in recent years, but only to be replaced by another
disturbing trend: increased attendance in private schools and increased
segregation in public school districts with a high proportion of African
American students. In a series of regression analyses of the one hundred
largest public school districts, Reardon and Yun reach the following
pessimistic conclusion: "Regardless of the variables we used as controls,
the strongest predictor of white private school enrollment rates in all our
models was the percentage of students living in the district who are
black."[61] Whether or not white parents were motivated by racial consid-

---

[56] *Id.* at 20–31.

[57] *Id.* at 38.

[58] MICHAEL J. KLARMAN, FROM JIM CROW TO CIVIL RIGHTS: THE SUPREME COURT AND THE
STRUGGLE FOR RACIAL EQUALITY 115, 186, 189, 291, 346 (2004).

[59] Reardon & Yun, *supra* note 52, at 42–44.

[60] Green v. Connally, 330 F.Supp. 1150 (D.D.C. 1971), *aff'd sub nom.* Coit v. Green,
404 U.S. 997 (1971). *See* Note, *The Judicial Role in Attacking Racial Discrimination in
Tax-Exempt Private Schools*, 93 HARV. L. REV. 378, 379 n.3 (1979); Virginia Davis Nordin &
William Lloyd Turner, *Commentary*, 35 WEST ED. L. REP. 329, 331–34 (1986).

[61] Reardon & Yun, *supra* note 52, at 43.

erations in deciding to send their children to private school, they have acted to perpetuate continuing de facto segregation.

Even the most stringent enforcement of section 1981 would not alter the racial imbalance in private schools. A prohibition against intentional discrimination, especially one enforced through private lawsuits, can only go so far to achieve integration. Even cutting off tax subsidies, as the IRS tries to do, results only in a modest progress towards full integration. The presumptions the IRS uses to test a private school's commitment to integration address only the most egregious forms of racial imbalance. Litigation to prevent discrimination cannot be expected to accomplish more. *Runyon* and *Bob Jones* forced private schools to abandon explicit segregation and forced continuing discrimination to take less visible forms, perhaps not apparent even to those who operate private schools or those who attend them. This is a considerable achievement, but one that still leaves much to be done.

As private schools become a more prominent alternative to public schools, through such programs as vouchers or creation of quasi-public charter schools, the unresolved issues of segregation in private education also become more pressing and conspicuous.[62] A private alternative to public education cannot be used as an excuse to permit continuing patterns of segregation. Yet the steps necessary to achieve genuine integration so far appear to be elusive.

The defendants in *Runyon* took the contrary position, stridently insisting on the right to free association as a license to engage in discrimination. This argument was easily rejected by the Court because the defendants held their schools open to members of the general public, with the sole exception of their racially exclusive policies. It is harder to reject the sense, which still remains prevalent today, that private decisions about discrimination should receive, if not complete immunity, less scrutiny than those involving public resources.[63] This invocation of the public-private distinction no doubt imposes some limits on the scope of section 1981, as the Supreme Court has conceded.[64] The statute cannot be interpreted to eliminate private choice in contracting, without defeating the very freedom of contract that it seeks to protect. Yet as private

---

[62] Erica Frankenberg & Chungmei Lee, *Charter Schools and Race: A Lost Opportunity for Integrated Education* (Harv. Civ. Rts. Project, July 2003), *available at* www.civilrights project.harvard.edu/research/deseg/Charter_Schools03.pdf (finding concentration of minority students in charter schools).

[63] Richard Epstein, FORBIDDEN GROUNDS: THE CASE AGAINST EMPLOYMENT DISCRIMINATION LAWS 141–43 (1992).

[64] Notably in *Runyon* itself which recognized the right of parents to send their children to schools that promoted a belief in segregation, so long as those schools did not practice it. 427 U.S. at 175–79.

schools move closer to the public sphere, they must accept the full force of the judgment rendered in *Runyon*: that they are subject to the same prohibition against discrimination that applies to the government as a matter of constitutional law.[65] Even if this judgment cannot always be fully enforced, it stands as a testament to our nation's commitment to civil rights.

Epilogue

Sandra McCrary organized the effort to bring the litigation to desegregate Bobbe's School and the Fairfax–Brewster School. Together with her husband, she brought suit on behalf of her son Michael and convinced Raymond and Margaret Gonzales to sue on behalf of their son Colin. This effort, despite the personal costs and threats of violence that accompanied it, led her to attend law school herself and become a lawyer. In a remarkable achievement, she also had the opportunity to argue for the vitality of the precedent that she had helped to create. When the Supreme Court asked for briefing on whether to overrule *Runyon* in *Patterson v. McLean Credit Co.*, she submitted an amicus brief on why *Runyon* was and should remain good law.

When her son went on to play in the Super Bowl, her efforts again became well publicized and widely celebrated. Within little more than two decades, racially exclusive private schools went from a matter of intense controversy to nearly universal condemnation. As a lawyer from the American Civil Liberties Union later observed, after Michael had become a well-known football player, "How on earth could that not have been decided until 1976?"[66] Major sporting events often serve as the occasion for reaffirming our commitment to integration, most often when one color barrier or another has fallen, as when Tiger Woods won the Masters Tournament at the previously segregated Augusta National Golf Course. An otherwise obscure statute, like section 1981, and a highly technical decision, like *Runyon*, seldom receive such attention. The acceptance and approval that both received, so long after the legal issues had been decided, confirms the wisdom of the justices who saw *Runyon* as posing the question whether to take a step forward or back in

---

[65] For a recent illustration of the coextensive scope of section 1981 and the Constitution, see Gratz v. Bollinger, 539 U.S. 244, 275–76 (2003) (holding that an affirmative action plan by public university violates both the Fourteenth Amendment and section 1981).

[66] Gary Lambrecht, *All Work, All Play*, BALTIMORE SUN, Aug. 5, 1997, at 4D (quoting Dwight Sullivan).

civil rights law. Having taken a step forward three decades ago, we now must search for the next steps to take today, even if the way forward remains less certain now than it appears, perhaps inevitably, to have been in the past.

7

Erwin Chemerinsky*

The Story of *City of Los Angeles v. Lyons*: Closing the Federal Courthouse Doors

Few cases have had a more devastating effect on civil rights litigation than the Supreme Court's decision in *City of Los Angeles v. Lyons*.[1] By a 5–4 margin, the Court held that a plaintiff lacks standing to seek an injunction unless he or she can demonstrate a likelihood of future injury. In other words, a person harmed by an illegal government action cannot sue for an injunction to halt the practice unless the individual can show that he or she is likely to be subjected to suffer the injury again.

A simple example illustrates the profound effects of this decision. Imagine a police department which has the humiliating and degrading practice of subjecting women to strip searches when brought to a jail for even minor offenses, such as traffic violations. A woman who suffered this indignity could not bring a lawsuit for an injunction because she would be unable to demonstrate that she was likely to be stopped, arrested, and stripped again in the future. Indeed, lower courts have dismissed challenges in exactly this situation.[2]

Government practices, such as in schools or prisons, that predictably will affect certain individuals still can be challenged in suits for injunc-

---

* I want to thank David Weiss for his excellent research assistance.

[1] 461 U.S. 95 (1983).

[2] *See, e.g.,* Jones v. Bowman, 664 F. Supp. 433 (N.D. Ind. 1987) (no standing to challenge strip searches of women performed by county jail); John Does 1–100 v. Boyd, 613 F. Supp. 1514 (D. Minn. 1985) (no standing to challenge strip searches of people brought to the city jail for minor offenses).

tive relief. By contrast, a government policy or practice that will harm people in the future, but with no way of knowing who will be hurt, cannot be stopped by the courts even in a suit brought by a person who has suffered from it in the past. The victim still may sue for damages, but there are many other obstacles to recovery of monetary relief in civil rights cases, including the inability to hold a city liable on a respondeat superior basis,[3] the immunities accorded to individual government officers,[4] and the small amount of damages available for violations of many constitutional rights.[5]

As a civil rights lawyer, I have been involved in countless discussions about possible litigation to stop illegal police and other government behavior that did not lead to lawsuits because of the inability to overcome the standing hurdle imposed by *City of Los Angeles v. Lyons*. It is a case that has closed the courthouse doors to many civil rights litigants seeking to halt unconstitutional government actions.

The underlying story of *City of Los Angeles v. Lyons* tells a great deal about policing and racism in big cities in the second half of the twentieth century. It also illustrates vastly different views about the role of the federal courts in American society.

The Los Angeles Police Department

Lyons could have arisen in countless cities across the country. Most cities, according to a survey at the time, trained their officers to use the chokehold as a way of subduing suspects.[6] Additionally, other departments engaged in abusive police practices, such as racial profiling, that might have led to suits for injunctive relief and the Supreme Court limiting standing.[7] Yet, it also hardly seems coincidental that the case arose from a police department with such a long and notorious history of

---

[3] Monell v. Department of Soc. Servs., 436 U.S. 658 (1978) (cities are liable only for their own policies and customs and not on a respondeat superior basis).

[4] All government officers sued for money damages have either absolute immunity or qualified immunity. Absolute immunity is accorded to judges performing in a judicial capacity, legislators in a legislative capacity, prosecutors in a prosecutorial capacity, police officers testifying as witnesses, and the President of the United States for acts done in office. All other government officers can be sued only if qualified immunity is overcome; that is, an officer is liable only if it is shown that the officer violated clearly established law that the reasonable officer should know. For a description of these immunities, *see* ERWIN CHEMERINSKY, FEDERAL JURISDICTION Ch. 8 (4th ed. 2003).

[5] *See* Memphis Cmty. Sch. Dist. v. Stachura, 477 U.S. 299 (1986) (damages cannot be based on the abstract value or the importance of constitutional rights).

[6] Petition for a Writ of Certiorari by the City of Los Angeles, City of Los Angeles v. Lyons, 1981 U.S. Briefs 1064; 1981 U.S. S. Ct. Briefs LEXIS 1411, at 11 n.7.

[7] *See, e.g.*, DAVID A. HARRIS, PROFILES IN INJUSTICE: WHY RACIAL PROFILING CANNOT WORK (2002) (describing racial profiling by police departments in the United States).

using excessive force. The events that gave rise to the case must be understood as the product of the Los Angeles Police Department ("LAPD") and its culture.

Every police department has a culture—the unwritten rules, mores, customs, codes, values, and outlooks—that creates the policing environment and style. The LAPD's organizational culture drives everything that happens within the Department, including its serial scandals. In 1991, following the beating of Rodney King, a commission, chaired by later Secretary of State Warren Christopher, began its report on page one by identifying the culture of the LAPD as a central problem to reform.[8] David Dotson, former Assistant Chief of the Los Angeles Police Department, wrote: "[A]t bottom, the problems at the Los Angeles Police Department's Rampart Division are cultural in nature, the result of an institutional mind-set first conceived in the 1950s."[9]

The prime driver of the LAPD culture is authoritarian control. Chief William Parker took over management of the department in the 1950s and instilled this philosophy, which included use of force to ensure control on the streets. As one commentator expressed: "Bill Parker who had taught his protégé Daryl Gates the essential philosophy of policing that Gates, Ed Davis, [both later Police Chiefs] the LAPD hierarchy—the entire department—would follow as if sent down by Moses from the Mount:.... Confront and command. Control the streets at all times. Always be aggressive.... And never, never, admit the department had done anything wrong."[10]

As I wrote in a report on the LAPD in 2000: "The LAPD's street patrolling culture is hard to miss. It can be summed up as a 'confront, command and arrest' or 'proactive' paramilitary style of policing. It relies on 'command presence.' Within the Department, the LAPD officers prize aggressive crime suppression that projects omnipresent intimidation and total command of the streets."[11] The Christopher Commission noted that the approach left citizens feeling that the LAPD was "unnecessarily aggressive and confrontational."[12] It is a department with a

---

[8] Indep. Comm'n on the L.A. Police Dep't, Report of the Independent Commission on the Los Angeles Police Department 1 (1991).

[9] David D. Dotson, *A Culture of War*, L.A. TIMES, Feb. 27, 2000, at M1.

[10] JOE DOMANICK, TO PROTECT AND TO SERVE: LAPD'S CENTURY OF WAR IN THE CITY OF DREAMS 12 (1994).

[11] My report is published as Erwin Chemerinsky, *An Independent Analysis of the Los Angeles Police Department's Board of Inquiry Report on the Rampart Scandal*, 34 LOY. L.A. L. REV. 545, 568 (2001).

[12] See Indep. Comm'n on the L.A. Police Dep't, Report of the Independent Commission on the Los Angeles Police Department xiv (1991).

culture that shields and lauds Dirty Harry and shuns Frank Serpico. It is thus hardly surprising that the suit about the ability to sue a city and a police department to stop aggressive practices would arise in Los Angeles.

In the spring of 2000, seventeen years after the Supreme Court's decision in *Lyons*, it was revealed that officers in the anti-gang unit in the Rampart precinct of the Los Angeles Police Department had been engaged in framing innocent people and lying in court to gain convictions. I was asked by the Los Angeles Police Protective League, the police union, to do an independent report on the Los Angeles Police Department and the Rampart scandal. Working with six other civil rights attorneys, I spent six months examining the LAPD, interviewing over seventy-five officers and countless current and former judges, prosecutors, and defense lawyers. I was convinced that the Rampart scandal, and the police use of the chokehold which was at issue in *Lyons*, was the result of the long-standing culture within the Department. Time and again, I heard officers express the need for ensuring control on the streets in a way that reminded me of how the chokehold came to be used in Los Angeles and why it was used against Adolph Lyons.

The Stop and the Choking of Adolph Lyons

On October 6, 1976, at approximately 2:00 a.m., Adolph Lyons, a twenty-four-year-old African–American man, was stopped by four Los Angeles police officers for driving with a burned out tail light.[13] The officers ordered Lyons out of his car and greeted him with drawn revolvers as he emerged from it.

Lyons was told to face his car and spread his legs. He did this and was then ordered to clasp his hands and put them on top of his head. He again complied. After one of the officers completed a pat down search, Lyons dropped his hands, but was ordered to place them back above his head. One of the officers grabbed Lyons' hands and slammed them onto his head. Lyons complained about the pain caused by the ring of keys he was holding in his hand. Apparently, he "mouthed off" to the officers.[14] Within five to ten seconds, the officer began to choke Lyons by applying a forearm against his throat. As Lyons struggled for air, the officer handcuffed him, but continued to apply the chokehold until he blacked

---

[13] The stop is described in detail in the Petitioner's brief in *City of Los Angeles v. Lyons*. Also, Justice Thurgood Marshall's dissent describes these facts. *See* 461 U.S. at 114–15.

[14] *See* Jerome H. Skolnick & James J. Fyfe, *Perspective on Law Enforcement; Chokehold Defenders Crying Wolf; It's a Red Herring to Say that the Chokehold Ban on Forced LAPD to Use Batons; Most Cops Think the Hold is More Deadly*, L. A. Times, May 6, 1993, at Part B, Page 7, Column 2 (Lyons "mouthed off in protest of a traffic ticket" to the officers.).

out. When Lyons regained consciousness, he was lying face down on the ground, choking, gasping for air, and spitting up blood and dirt. He had urinated and defecated. He was issued a traffic citation and released. He suffered an injured larynx as a result of being choked by the officer.

The chokehold was commonly used by Los Angeles police officers, as well as by other police departments across the country, to subdue suspects. Indeed, a survey in 1980 revealed that 90% of departments authorized the carotid hold and 53.33% authorized the bar arm hold.[15] Los Angeles Police Department policy manuals expressly authorized officers to use the chokehold as a way to subdue suspects.[16] Officers were trained in its use at the Police Academy.[17]

Control holds utilizing neck restraints are derived from the sport of judo. Specifically, the Los Angeles Police Department authorized the use of the modified carotid and carotid holds.[18] The modified carotid is designed to bring the subject to a sitting position where the carotid hold can generally be more easily applied. The carotid hold is designed to encourage the subject to submit to control, but, if necessary, to render the subject unconscious. The holds are applied when an officer is able to take a position behind the subject. The officer places one arm around the subject's neck, holding the wrist of that arm with his or her other hand. The officer's chest is brought flush against the subject's back. Pressure is applied on two sides of the neck by the lower forearm and the bicep muscle. In the carotid hold, the pressure is focused by the lower forearm and bicep muscle upon the carotid arteries located on each side of the neck.[19] The bar arm hold, which was less commonly used, involved an officer putting pressure on the front of the suspect's neck. It, too, reduces oxygen to the brain and can render a suspect unconscious.[20]

As the City of Los Angeles explained in its Petition for Certiorari, the carotid hold is capable of rendering the subject unconscious by diminishing the flow of oxygenated blood to the brain through constriction of the carotid arteries. When the brain is sufficiently deprived of oxygen, the subject becomes unconscious. Normally, unconsciousness will occur within eight to fourteen seconds.

---

[15] Petition for a Writ of Certiorari by the City of Los Angeles, City of Los Angeles v. Lyons, 1981 U.S. Briefs 1064; 1981 U.S. S. Ct. Briefs LEXIS 1411, at 11 n.7.

[16] Id. at 9–10.

[17] Id. at 16.

[18] Id. at 11.

[19] This description is from the Petition for Certiorari by the City of Los Angeles. Id. at 11.

[20] 461 U.S. at 98 n.1.

There is great danger to such chokeholds. At oral argument in the Supreme Court, the attorney for the City of Los Angeles, Fred Merkin, conceded that sixteen people had died in Los Angeles from use of the chokehold.[21] In fact, Lyons presented to the federal district court extensive testimony about the dangers when police use the chokehold. For example, one witness for the plaintiff, Dr. Alex Griswold, stated: "[P]ressure on both carotid sheaths also result in pressure, if inadvertent or unintended, on both vagus nerves ... [s]timulation of these nerves can activate reflexes ... that can result in immediate heart stoppage (cardiac arrest)."[22]

Lyons' brief to the Supreme Court quotes experts describing this: "[V]iolent struggle is 'very definitely' likely to ensue (Deposition of City's Medical Director, Thrift Hanks, M.D., A.378) with the victim seeking to 'flee or escape.' Deposition of City's expert Jarvis. A.385. The victim's face turns blue, becoming cyanotic (lacking oxygenated blood), and he goes into a spasmodic state of convulsions. Ex 44:55. The victim's eyes roll back and he will sometimes 'jerk' (Deposition of City's expert Speer, A.382), his body 'wriggles', his feet kick up and down and his arms move about wildly. Deposition of City's expert Sua, A.391–392."[23] Thus, the involuntary physical reaction for a person being choked is to struggle and that causes the police to choke harder until the individual is rendered unconscious. The person being choked will often urinate and defecate upon losing consciousness.

Justice Marshall, in his dissenting opinion, summarized this evidence: "Depending on the position of the officer's arm and the force applied, the victim's voluntary or involuntary reaction, and his state of health, an officer may inadvertently crush the victim's larynx, trachea, or thyroid. The result may be death caused by either cardiac arrest or asphyxiation."[24]

Lyons' brief to the Supreme Court included an appendix which described the deaths that had occurred in Los Angeles from police use of the chokehold.[25] Although the City tried to minimize the danger, in its brief it conceded a risk and stated: "The City does not deny that it is

---

[21] Transcript of Oral Argument, *City of Los Angeles v. Lyons*, 461 U.S. 95 (1981) (No. 81–1064); 1982 U.S. TRANS LEXIS at 5 (November 2, 1982).

[22] Declaration of Alex Griswold, M.D., A.365, 367, quoted in Brief for Respondent, City of Los Angeles v. Lyons, at 22.

[23] Id. at 23.

[24] 461 U.S. at 117 (Marshall, J., dissenting).

[25] Brief for Respondent, at 44.

possible to injure seriously or even kill someone using the control holds; they are not failsafe."[26]

Additionally, there was a racial dimension to the use of the chokehold by Los Angeles police officers. According to statistics presented to the Supreme Court, an African–American man was twenty times more likely to be subjected to a police chokehold than a white man.[27] Justice Marshall, in his dissent, noted that African–Americans also were much more likely to die from use of the chokehold. He wrote: "Although the City instructs its officers that use of a chokehold does not constitute deadly force, since 1975 no less than 16 persons have died following the use of a chokehold by an LAPD police officer. Twelve have been Negro males."[28] Justice Marshall noted: "Thus in a City where Negro males constitute 9% of the population, they have accounted for 75% of the deaths resulting from the use of chokeholds."[29]

When questioned about why a disproportionate number of victims of the chokehold had been African–American, then Los Angeles Police Chief Daryl Gates declared that it was because of physiological differences between black people and "normal people," stating that "veins or arteries of Blacks do not open up as fast as they do in normal people."[30]

The Long and Winding Road of the Litigation

Lyons filed his complaint on February 7, 1977, in the United States District Court for the Central District of California. The defendants were the City of Los Angeles and four of its police officers. The complaint contained seven counts alleging serious police misconduct. Lyons sought damages, an injunction, and declaratory relief.

The complaint maintained that the strangleholds violated the First Amendment (prior restraint on speech), the Fourth Amendment (unreasonable seizure of the person), the Eighth Amendment (cruel and unusual punishment), and the Fourteenth Amendment (due process). The first four counts of the complaint sought money damages, invoking 42 U.S.C. §§ 1983, 1985, and 1986. Counts five and six sought injunctive and declaratory relief, respectively, to restrain the City from authorizing the use of the stranglehold controls except where the victim reasonably appears to be threatening the immediate use of deadly force. Count seven requested a declaratory judgment concerning the constitutionality

---

[26] Brief for Petitioner, at 11.

[27] Brief for Respondent, at 30.

[28] 461 U.S. at 115–16 (Marshall, J., dissenting).

[29] Id. at 116 n.3.

[30] Quoted in Gregory Howard Williams, *Controlling the Use of Non–Deadly Force: Policy and Practice,* 10 HARV. BLACKLETTER J. 79 n.34 (1993).

of a local ordinance creating an alleged conflict of interest within the office of the city attorney. Lyons did not file the suit as a class action and did not request class certification.

The case was assigned to United States District Court Judge Robert Tagasuki. Judge Tagasuki, an appointee of President Jimmy Carter, was a Japanese–American who, at age twelve, had been interned with his family during World War II. Judge Tagasuki has spoken eloquently of the profound effect that had on him and his sense of justice and injustice.[31]

The City moved to dismiss the injunctive counts of Lyons' complaint and Judge Tagasuki granted this motion. The City argued that Lyons lacked standing to seek an injunction on the ground that he could not show that he was likely to be choked again in the future. The City relied heavily on the Supreme Court's decision in O'Shea v. Littleton, where the Court declared non-justiciable a suit contending that the defendants, a magistrate and a judge, discriminated against African–Americans in setting bail and imposing sentences.[32] The Court observed that none of the plaintiffs currently faced proceedings in the defendants' courtroom and hence "the threat of injury from the alleged course of attack is too remote to satisfy the case-or-controversy requirement."[33]

The City argued that the same was true of Lyons: it was too remote a chance that Lyons would suffer an injury to meet Article III's standing requirements. Presaging what would later be the holding of the case in the Supreme Court, Judge Tagasuki accepted this argument and ruled that "there was no standing because there was insufficient showing that the police were likely to do this to the plaintiff again."[34]

The United States Court of Appeals for the Ninth Circuit reversed. The opinion was written by Judge Elbert Tuttle, from the United States Court of Appeals for the Fifth Circuit, sitting by designation. Judge Tuttle, then a senior judge, was a liberal Republican from Georgia. Judge Tuttle had been chief judge of the United States Court of Appeals for the Fifth Circuit during the 1950s and 1960s, when that court became known for a series of decisions crucial in advancing the civil rights of African–Americans.

---

[31] Speech by Robert Tagasuki accepting an award at the Criminal Courts Bar Association, March 2001. I should disclose that I have known, been friends with, and worked with Judge Tagasuki for over 15 years. He is one of the kindest and most decent people that I have ever met.

[32] 414 U.S. 488 (1974).

[33] Id. at 489.

[34] Lyons v. City of Los Angeles, 615 F.2d 1243, 1246 (9th Cir. 1980) (describing Judge Tagasuki's reasons for dismissing the case).

The Ninth Circuit, in reversing Judge Tagasuki, explained: "But in this case, the threat of future injury to not only Lyons, but to every citizen in the area is much more immediate. To be subject to these strangleholds, a citizen need only be stopped for a minor traffic violation while driving an automobile, as shown by the alleged facts in this case. The use of these strangleholds is accepted police practice, even in non life-threatening situations."[35] The court responded directly to the City's argument that the chances of injury for any individual were small. The court explained: "It is not farfetched to suggest that especially in a city like Los Angeles, where many motorists drive long distances daily, the chances of being stopped by a policeman for an alleged motor vehicle violation are fairly good.... [This case] therefore meet[s] the constitutional requirements of 'case' or 'controversy.' "[36]

In eloquent language, the Ninth Circuit spoke of the need to ensure that the government could be stopped when its officers were breaking the law. The court concluded its opinion by declaring: "The strangleholds challenged here may be illegal or they may not be. But as long as we refuse to allow anyone to attack their constitutionality here, we tell the citizen that there is no guardian of his constitutional rights. That is a principle that has no foundation either in the Constitution or in our beliefs about what a government ought to be."[37] Indeed, this was the crucial underlying issue in the case: how important is it for the federal courts to be available to enjoin unconstitutional government action?

The City sought certiorari in the United States Supreme Court, but review was denied.[38] Interestingly, Justice White dissented from the denial of certiorari and was joined by Justices Rehnquist and Powell. A few years later, when the case made its way back to the Supreme Court, Justice White wrote the opinion in favor of the City and it was joined by both Justices Rehnquist and Powell.

The case was then remanded to Judge Tagasuki for further proceedings. On remand, Lyons' lawyers requested a preliminary injunction. After being presented with detailed evidence of the LAPD's use of the chokehold and its dangers, Judge Tagasuki concluded that the use of the chokehold violated the due process rights of suspects when it was used where there was not a threat to the officers' safety. He issued a preliminary injunction forbidding police officers to use carotid artery or bar arm holds under circumstances that do not threaten death or serious

[35] Id. at 1246.

[36] Id. at 1246–47.

[37] Id. at 1250.

[38] 449 U.S. 934 (1980).

bodily harm to the officer.[39] The terms of the injunction are important and provided:

> IT IS ORDERED that defendants are hereby enjoined from the use of both the carotid artery and bar arm holds under circumstances which do not threaten death or serious bodily harm.

> IT IS FURTHER ORDERED that this injunction is effective ... and shall continue in force until this Court approves a training program presented to it. Such program shall consist of a detailed written training manual, prepared by qualified individuals, in addition to appropriate, practical training sessions for the members of the Los Angeles Police Department.

> IT IS FURTHER ORDERED that defendant City of Los Angeles establish a requirement, forthwith, that all applications of the use of the holds in question, even under the conditions permitted by this Order, to wit, the death or serious bodily harm situation, be reported in writing to said defendant within forty-eight hours after the use of such holds.[40]

Judge Tagasuki did not ban all use of the chokehold. Rather, he ruled that the practice should be employed only when there was a serious risk to the officer's safety and that there should be training in and monitoring of its use.

The United States Court of Appeals for the Ninth Circuit, in a very short opinion, affirmed.[41] The Ninth Circuit noted that under well-established law, it could overturn a preliminary injunction only if it was convinced that there was an abuse of discretion by the district court. The Ninth Circuit concluded that there was no abuse of discretion in this case:

> All the trial judge has done, so far, is to tell the city that its police officers may not apply life threatening strangleholds to persons stopped in routine police work unless the application of such force is necessary to prevent serious bodily harm to an officer. This relatively innocuous interference by the judiciary with police practice can hardly be characterized as an abuse of discretion when the record reveals that nine suspects who have been stopped by the police and who have been subdued by the use of carotid and bar arm control holds have subsequently died,

---

[39] See Appendix to Petition for Writ of Certiorari.

[40] Quoted in City of Los Angeles v. Lyons, 453 U.S. 1308 (Rehnquist, J., in chambers).

[41] Lyons v. City of Los Angeles, 656 F.2d 417 (9th Cir. 1981).

allegedly of the injuries sustained in the application of these holds.[42]

The City sought a stay of the injunction from then-Justice William Rehnquist, pending the Supreme Court's consideration of its second petition for a writ of certiorari. Justice Rehnquist granted the stay and noted that certiorari was likely.[43] He noted that when the case had come before the Court earlier, there had been three votes in favor of granting certiorari. He wrote: "[T]here is a substantial likelihood that an additional Member of this Court would now join Justice White's dissent from denial of certiorari in Lyons I, thereby resulting in a grant if the city, as it proposes to do, files a timely petition for certiorari."[44] Justice Rehnquist concluded that there was "sufficient doubt about the correctness of the basic holding of the Court of Appeals with respect to standing on the part of respondent" to warrant the stay.[45] On February 22, 1982, the Supreme Court then granted certiorari.[46]

Meanwhile, the City of Los Angeles was forced to confront its policy with regard to the chokehold. The deaths of additional individuals and concerns over the disproportionate impact on African–Americans had fueled a public controversy that included hearings in the City Council and before the Los Angeles Police Commission.[47] The Board of Police Commissioners then imposed a six-month moratorium on the more commonly used technique, the carotid holds, allowing their use only under circumstances when "deadly force is authorized."[48] Chief of Police Daryl Gates, days earlier, had prohibited use of the less frequently employed and more dangerous bar arm technique.[49]

---

[42] Id. at 418.

[43] 453 U.S. 1308 (1981) (Rehnquist, J., in chambers).

[44] Id. at 1310–1311.

[45] Id. at 1311.

[46] 455 U.S. 937 (1982).

[47] Memorandum Suggesting a Question of Mootness and Other Issues, filed by the City of Los Angeles in the United States Supreme Court in City of Los Angeles v. Lyons. The City describes this in its brief: "Following the most recent of these deaths (of James Mincey, Jr. on April 5, 1982), the LAPD's use of the control holds became a major civic controversy. Numerous public hearings were conducted by a committee of the Los Angeles City Council and by the City's Board of Police Commissioners. The City's Chief of Police made a number of pronouncements and issued a number of statements on the matter. One issue in this controversy was whether the control holds were being applied in a manner discriminating against Blacks. In sum, a spirited, vigorous, and at times emotional public debate ensued during the months of April and May of this year." Id. at 5.

[48] Partial transcript of Board of Police Commissioners proceedings of May 12, 1982, at 10.

[49] Memorandum Suggesting a Question of Mootness, at 5.

The City filed a brief on June 2, 1982, informing the Supreme Court of this change in policy. Lyons' lawyers then moved to have the case dismissed as certiorari having been improvidently granted on the ground that the case was moot since the City had changed its policy with regard to the use of the chokehold.[50] But the City maintained that that the case was not moot because it could return to its earlier policy at any time, the injunction remained in place, and Lyons' standing to seek the injunction remained an open question.[51] The City concluded its brief by stating: "If the City should find in the next few months that the welfare of suspects and officers requires that its present policy be abandoned or modified, the City must have the flexibility to make necessary changes without first having to obtain court approval."[52]

These briefs reflect interesting strategic choices by the attorneys. If the City had moved to dismiss its petition for certiorari, this request certainly would have been granted even though the case had been briefed and oral argument had been scheduled.[53] Likewise, if the City and Lyons had agreed to this request, the Court would have been forced to dismiss the case. But the City, which lost below, wanted Supreme Court review, while Lyons, who had prevailed, wanted the Court to dismiss the case. In large part, this reflected the fact that the Ninth Circuit's decision would remain intact if the Supreme Court dismissed the case. The City wanted to have that precedent overturned because it feared that such precedent could be the basis for other suits against it for other practices in the future. Lyons' attorney, by contrast, was content with that victory and did not want to risk reversal in the high Court.

The Court took no explicit action on the motion to dismiss the case, but instead proceeded with briefing and oral argument in the case. At oral argument, Lyons' lawyer, Michael Mitchell, aggressively argued that the case should be dismissed as moot because the City had changed its policy.[54] The attorney for the City, Fred Merkin, a long-time lawyer in the City Attorney's office, disagreed, but admitted that it was uncertain what policy would be adopted by the City after the six-month moratori-

---

[50] City of Los Angeles v. Lyons, Respondents' Brief, at 1–2.

[51] Opposition to Dismiss Writ of Certiorari as Improvidently Granted, City of Los Angeles v. Lyons, filed June 5, 1982.

[52] Id. at 11.

[53] In fact, this is exactly what occurred in *Medical Board of California v. Hason*, 538 U.S. 958 (2003). After the petition for certiorari was granted, the case was briefed, and oral argument was set, the petitioner moved to dismiss its petition for a writ of certiorari. The Supreme Court, over the objections of the respondent, dismissed the petition.

[54] Transcript of Oral Argument at 27, *Lyons*, 461 U.S. 95 (No. 81–1064); 1982 U.S. TRANS LEXIS 27 (November 2, 1982).

um restricting the use of chokeholds expired. There was the following exchange between Merkin and Justice Blackmun:

QUESTION: Let me ask another question. There's been a six-month moratorium?

MR. MERKIN: Yes.

QUESTION: It expires in ten days.

MR. MERKIN: That's right.

QUESTION: What's the city going to do then?

MR. MERKIN: I don't know, and I don't know that the city knows.

QUESTION: You're representing them. You don't know?

MR. MERKIN: I don't know, and part of the reason for that is that the city submits that this is the kind of thing that is subject to reasonable debate, indeed there's a debate going on, not just within city government but to some extent nationwide; and that these decisions, especially in this particular situation, are such that there may be tentative decisions such as we have already now from the city of Los Angeles, that are subject to change and modification.[55]

The Decision

The Supreme Court, in a 5–4 decision, ruled that Lyons did not have standing to seek injunctive relief. Justice White wrote the opinion for the Court, which was joined by Chief Justice Burger and Justices Powell, Rehnquist, and O'Connor. Justice Marshall wrote a dissenting opinion, which was joined by Justices Brennan, Blackmun, and Stevens. The Court thus divided along ideological lines, with the five most conservative Justices ruling in favor of the City and against Lyons. The case reflected a deep, underlying ideological divide over the importance of federal courts being available to remedy civil rights violations.

Justice White's majority opinion began by agreeing with the City that the case was not moot because it had not permanently changed its policy.[56] The City, at any time, could return to its prior practice of authorizing the chokehold as a method of subduing suspects.

The Court then proceeded to dismiss the case on another justiciability ground: that Lyons lacked standing to seek an injunction to challenge the City policy of using chokeholds to subdue suspects when there was no threat to the officers' safety. The Court said that "Lyons' standing to seek the injunction requested depended on whether he was likely to

---

[55] Id. at 5–6.

[56] 461 U.S. at 110.

suffer future injury from the use of the chokeholds by police officers."[57] In other words, Lyons could not sue for an injunction unless he could demonstrate that it was likely that he personally would be choked again by Los Angeles police officers. The Court declared:

> That Lyons may have been illegally choked by the police on October 6, 1976, while presumably affording Lyons standing to claim damages against the individual officers and perhaps against the City, does nothing to establish a real and immediate threat that he would again be stopped for a traffic violation, or for any other offense, by an officer or officers who would illegally choke him into unconsciousness without any provocation or resistance on his part.[58]

Lyons had argued that even if he could not show that he was likely to be choked again in the future, he still suffered an injury as long as the LAPD authorized use of chokeholds in that he had great fear of it happening again. He knew that any time he was driving in Los Angeles, he could be stopped by police for a minor traffic infraction and be choked again. The Court expressly rejected this as a sufficient basis for injury:

> The reasonableness of Lyons' fear is dependent upon the likelihood of a recurrence of the allegedly unlawful conduct. It is the reality of the threat of repeated injury that is relevant to the standing inquiry, not the plaintiff's subjective apprehensions. The emotional consequences of a prior act simply are not a sufficient basis for an injunction absent a real and immediate threat of future injury by the defendant.[59]

The Court concluded that "[a]bsent a sufficient likelihood that he will again be wronged in a similar way, Lyons is no more entitled to an injunction than any other citizen of Los Angeles; and a federal court may not entertain a claim by any or all citizens who no more than assert that certain practices of law enforcement officers are unconstitutional."[60] The Court said that state courts may allow injunctions in such circumstances, "but it is not the role of a federal court" to hear such a case or provide relief.[61]

Justice Thurgood Marshall wrote a strong dissent joined by three other Justices. For the dissenters, like the Ninth Circuit earlier, the primary concern was that denying Lyons standing would mean that no

---

[57] Id. at 105.

[58] Id.

[59] Id. at 109.

[60] *Id.* at 111.

[61] Id.

one ever would have standing to seek an injunction to stop an illegal government practice. Justice Marshall began his dissent by declaring: "Since no one can show that he will be choked in the future, no one—not even a person who, like Lyons, has almost been choked to death—has standing to challenge the continuation of the policy. The City is free to continue the policy indefinitely as long as it is willing to pay damages for the injuries and deaths that result."[62]

The dissent especially criticized the majority opinion's requiring that standing be analyzed separately for claims for injunctive relief in cases where there also were requests for money damages. Justice White's majority opinion did not dispute that Lyons had standing to seek monetary relief. The dissent said that it was unprecedented in such circumstances to deny standing for a claim for an injunction.[63] Justice Marshall wrote: "We have never required more than that a plaintiff have standing to litigate a claim. Whether he will be entitled to obtain particular forms of relief should he prevail has never been understood to be an issue of standing. In determining whether a plaintiff has standing, we have always focused on his personal stake in the outcome of the controversy, not on the issues sought to be litigated."[64]

For the dissent, the key was that the effect of the Lyons decision would be closing the federal courthouse doors to challenges to unconstitutional policies where it could not be known who would be hurt by them in the future. Justice Marshall concluded his dissent by stating:

> The Court's decision removes an entire class of constitutional violations from the equitable powers of a federal court. It immunizes from prospective equitable relief any policy that authorizes persistent deprivations of constitutional rights as long as no individual can establish with substantial certainty that he will be injured, or injured again, in the future. Under the view expressed by the majority today, if the police adopt a policy of 'shoot to kill,' or a policy of shooting one out of ten suspects, the federal courts will be powerless to enjoin its continuation. The federal judicial power is now limited to levying a toll for such a systematic constitutional violation.[65]

The Aftermath in Los Angeles

Having prevailed in the United States Supreme Court, the City of Los Angeles nonetheless decided to continue its ban on the chokehold.

---

[62] Id. at 113 (Marshall, J., dissenting).

[63] Id. at 123.

[64] Id. at 127.

[65] Id. at 137.

The Board of Police Commissioners made permanent the prohibition on the use of the chokehold except where necessary to protect the officers' safety.

But the controversy over the Lyons decision flared again, in dramatic fashion, less than a decade after the Supreme Court's decision. In 1991, a suspect in an altercation with several police officers was severely beaten. A person nearby captured on videotape the beating of Rodney King. The beating lasted seven minutes and involved four police officers; twenty-one other officers watched.[66] The officers themselves acknowledged the beating in a computer exchange among themselves after it occurred:

> Sgt. Stacey Koon: "You just had a big-time use of force . . . Tazed and beat the suspect of CHP pursuit big time."
>
> Headquarters: "Oh well . . . I'm sure the lizard didn't deserve it . . . ha-ha."
>
> From officers Laurence Powell and Timothy Wind's patrol car: "Oops."
>
> Another unit responds: "Oops what?"
>
> From Powell and Wind: "I haven't beaten anyone this bad in a long time."[67]

The horrifying image of the beating was repeatedly broadcast on national and local television stations. The four officers were prosecuted in California state court, but acquitted by a jury in April 1992. The day the acquittal was announced, devastating riots erupted across Los Angeles. A year later, the four officers were prosecuted in federal court and two were convicted.

Interestingly, both sides of the debate over police reform see a direct link between the Rodney King beating and the Supreme Court's decision in *City of Los Angeles v. Lyons.* Critics of the decision saw Lyons as delivering a clear message to officers that they were free to use excessive force. David Rudovsky, a civil rights attorney and a professor at the University of Pennsylvania Law School, spoke of this connection: "[Lyons sent] a fairly direct message. You don't have to worry because the courts are not going to do a lot—we'll find some technical reason. The tipoff that the message has been received is that the L.A. police brag about it."[68]

---

[66] Darlene Ricker, *Does Society Condone Police Brutality in Exchange for Getting Criminals off the Streets?*,77 A.B.A.J. 45 (July 1991).

[67] Id.

[68] Id.

At the same time, the officers who beat Rodney King said that the Lyons litigation was responsible for their actions for another, very different reason: denying the officers the ability to use the chokehold meant that they had to resort to physical force to subdue King.[69] They said that if only the chokehold had been available, they would not have needed to beat King into submission.

Implications

Ultimately, the dispute in *Lyons* was over the proper role of the federal courts. For the majority, the power of the federal courts is narrowly circumscribed by Article III and exists to remedy specific injuries suffered by particular individuals. For the majority, Lyons was not entitled to sue for an injunction because he could not show that he personally would benefit from it in the future. The majority expressed no concern over the fact that this meant that no one could sue for an injunction. That was simply the consequence of having a judiciary limited to deciding "cases and controversies" and meant that remedies had to be obtained from the political branches of government.

In this way, the decision in *Lyons* must be seen as one of many cases during this time in which the Supreme Court limited standing to sue in civil rights cases.[70]

By contrast, the dissent saw the essential role of the federal court as upholding the Constitution. For the dissent, a person injured by an unconstitutional government practice had a sufficient personal stake to seek an injunction, even if there was no way to know whether he or she would be injured again in the future. The dissent was deeply troubled that unconstitutional government policies which inevitably would cause injuries could be challenged by no one.

In the more than two decades since the decision in *Lyons*, the Supreme Court and lower courts have repeatedly dismissed suits for injunctive relief based on a lack of standing when the plaintiff cannot demonstrate a likelihood of future injury. For example, in *Lujan v. Defenders of Wildlife*, the Supreme Court considered a challenge to a revision of a federal regulation that provided that the Endangered

---

[69] Jerome H. Skolnick and James J. Fyfe, *Perspective on Law Enforcement; Chokehold Defenders Crying Wolf; It's a Red Herring to Say that the Chokehold Ban on Forced LAPD to Use Batons; Most Cops Think the Hold is More Deadly*, L.A. TIMES, May 6, 1993, at Part B, Page 7, Column 2.

[70] *See, e.g.,* Allen v. Wright, 468 U.S. 737 (1984) (plaintiffs lacked standing to challenge federal government's grant of tax benefits to private schools that engaged in racial discrimination); Warth v. Seldin, 422 U.S. 490 (1975) (plaintiffs lacked standing to challenge exclusionary zoning practices); O'Shea v. Littleton, 414 U.S. 488 (1974) (plaintiffs lacked standing to challenge discriminatory practices in setting bail and imposing sentences).

Species Act does not apply to United States government activities outside the United States or the high seas.[71] The plaintiffs claimed that the failure to comply with the Act "with respect to certain funded activities abroad increases the rate of extinction of endangered and threatened species."[72]

The Court expressly applied *Lyons* and held that the plaintiffs lacked standing because they could not show a sufficient likelihood that they would be injured in the future by a destruction of the endangered species abroad. Two of the plaintiffs had submitted detailed affidavits describing their trips abroad and their viewing of endangered animals such as the Nile crocodile, the elephant, and the leopard. The Court said that the fact that the women had visited the areas in the past "proves nothing," and their desire to return in the future—"some day"—is insufficient for standing "without any description of concrete plans or indeed any specification of when the some day will be."[73] Justice Blackmun wrote a vehement dissent and lamented that the requirement that a plaintiff have specific plans to return to a foreign country created only a silly formality that a plaintiff must purchase a plane ticket in order to sue.[74]

Lower courts, too, repeatedly have dismissed suits for injunctions based on *Lyons*. For example, lower federal courts have dismissed the following for lack of standing: requests for injunctions to regulate the use of the chemical mace by police; challenges to a state practice of paying police officers a bonus if their arrest led to a conviction; and attempts to halt strip searches conducted at county jails of those arrested for minor crimes.[75] Additionally, lower courts consistently have ap-

---

[71] 504 U.S. 555 (1992).

[72] Id. at 562 (citations omitted).

[73] Id. at 564; *see also* Steel Co. v. Citizens for a Better Env't, 523 U.S. 83 (1998) (relying on *Lujan* to deny standing to plaintiffs who sought relief for past violations of a federal law, but did not seek compensation for themselves, and did not allege that the company was likely to violate the statute in the future).

[74] Id. at 592 (Blackmun, J., dissenting). For a thorough criticism of *Lujan, see* Cass Sunstein, *What's Standing After Lujan: Of Citizen Suits, "Injuries," and Article III*, 91 MICH. L. REV. 163 (1992).

[75] Curtis v. City of New Haven, 726 F.2d 65 (2d Cir. 1984) (no standing to challenge police use of mace); Brown v. Edwards, 721 F.2d 1442 (5th Cir. 1984) (no standing to challenge state policy awarding money to constables for each arrest they made that led to a conviction); Jones v. Bowman, 664 F. Supp. 433 (N.D. Ind. 1987) (no standing to challenge strip searches of women performed by county jail); John Does 1–100 v. Boyd, 613 F. Supp. 1514 (D. Minn. 1985) (no standing to challenge strip searches of people brought to the city jail for minor offenses).

plied *Lyons* to prevent standing in suits seeking declaratory judgments where standing for injunctive relief would be unavailable.[76]

Conclusion

When the police stopped Adolph Lyons in the early morning hours on October 6, 1976, they could not possibly have imagined that their actions would result in a lawsuit culminating in a Supreme Court decision that would change the law across the country. Perhaps that is one of the great lessons of *City of Los Angeles v. Lyons*—how major precedents are less likely to come from well planned test cases than from a routine traffic stop for a burned out tail light.

---

[76] *See, e.g.*, Fair Employment Council of Greater Wash., Inc. v. BMC Mktg. Corp., 28 F.3d 1268 (D.C. Cir. 1994) (suit for injunctive and declaratory relief to halt discriminatory placement practices dismissed based on *Lyons*); Knox v. McGinnis, 998 F.2d 1405 (7th Cir. 1993) (prisoner's suit to stop prison officials from using "black box" restraining device dismissed based on *Lyons*); Alabama Freethought Assoc. v. Moore, 893 F. Supp. 1522 (N.D. Ala. 1995) (dismissed based on *Lyons* request for injunctive and declaratory relief to halt judge from causing prayers to be uttered in the jury room and the placement of the Ten Commandments in the courtroom).

8

William N. Eskridge, Jr.*

The Crime Against Nature on Trial, *Bowers v. Hardwick,* 1986

Michael Hardwick was an all-American boy. He was born in Miami, Florida on February 23, 1954. His parents, Billy Dale (Rick) and Kathleen (Kitty) Hardwick, already had three children (Patrick, Alice, and Susan). A veteran of World War II, the hard-edged Rick made a good living as a fireman and builder; he was both playful and emotionally unavailable to his children. Kitty, on the other hand, was deeply devoted to her children. Soon after Michael was born, the family moved into a large three-bedroom house in southwest Miami, right off Miller Road and Eighty–Seventh Avenue. There were six or seven mango trees in the yard, and from a young age, Michael would climb the trees, thump the fruit to determine which were ripe, and toss them down. He and his sister Susan sometimes piled the ripe mangoes onto their little red wagon to try to sell to their neighbors.[1]

Michael was sensitive and deeply empathetic. "Even as a child, he was very compassionate, very caring, very tuned into people's feelings," his sister Susan recalls. One of his mother's friends told her, "Your son looks just like how Christ must have looked," referring to Michael's golden hair that cascaded down his head like an angelic waterfall. Yet

---

* John A. Garver Professor of Jurisprudence, Yale Law School. I am indebted to the family of Michael Hardwick for their helpful cooperation in the construction of this chapter. An expanded account of the story of Bowers v. Hardwick will be a chapter in my forthcoming book, tentatively entitled "Dishonorable Passions": A History of the Crime Against Nature in America (Viking, forthcoming 2008).

[1] Interview with Kathleen Blalock Hardwick (Michael's Mother), in Archer, Florida (March 2005); Telephone Interview with Kathleen Blalock Hardwick (March 20, 2004); Telephone Interview with Susan Browning Chriss (Michael's sister) (Oct. 6, 2006).

**"Santa and the Hardwick children: Michael,
Susan, Alice, and Patrick"Michael's**

teenage years were a time of uncertainty and searching. When he was
twenty-one, Michael fell in love with a man and, subsequently, came out
as gay to his mother and sister, who were sympathetic. As it turned out,

this all-American family produced a straight son (Patrick), a lesbian daughter (Alice), a straight daughter (Susan), and a gay son (Michael). Kitty quips, "God gave me four kids—one of each."[2]

In 1981—the same year Kitty's gay son moved to Atlanta and started to work as a bartender at The Cove, one of the city's twenty-four gay bars and discos—Michael Bowers became Attorney General of Georgia. Born in a farmhouse in Jackson County in 1944, Bowers was a smart and ambitious young man, graduating from West Point and, after distinguished service in the Air Force, earning a law degree from the University of Georgia. He then joined the staff of Attorney General Arthur Bolton, where he impressed the Attorney General so much that Bolton urged Bowers' appointment as his successor.[3]

The two Michaels had much in common: Bowers and Hardwick were both handsome blue-eyed young men of the New South, well-mannered, family-oriented sons of the civil rights and sexual revolutions. But it was the one way in which they were dissimilar—sexual orientation—that would bring Bowers and Hardwick together as adversaries in one of the most socially significant legal dramas of the last century.

It all started on the morning of August 3, 1982.

Michael Hardwick's Lawsuit Against Michael Bowers
The Arrest of Michael Hardwick

After World War II, Atlanta re-invented itself as the "city too busy to hate." It was the first large southern city to integrate its police force (1948), its buses (1959), and its schools (1961). In the 1960s, however, whites fled the inner city for still-segregated suburbs, and Atlanta became the city "too busy moving to hate." A new minority—homosexuals—replaced people of color as the objects of *open* public discrimination and, for many, bitter private hatred. Homosexuals became the "new niggers," as civil rights activist Bayard Rustin put it.[4]

A particularly deplorable form of discrimination against gays was police violence. Around Piedmont Park, Ansley Park (Hardwick's neighborhood), and other cruising areas, police would hassle suspected homo-

---

[2] Telephone Interview with Susan Browning Chriss (Jan. 2004) (first quotation in text); Telephone Interview with Kathleen Blalock Hardwick (March 20, 2004) (second quotation); Interview with Robert Hardwick Weston (Michael Hardwick's nephew), in New York City (West Village) (Jan. 22, 2004).

[3] Interview with Michael Bowers, in Atlanta, Georgia (Buckhead) (Jan. 4, 2004).

[4] KEVIN M. KRUSE, WHITE FLIGHT: ATLANTA AND THE MAKING OF MODERN CONSERVATISM (2005) 19–41; Bayard Rustin, *The New Niggers Are Gays, in* TIME ON TWO CROSSES: THE COLLECTED WRITINGS OF BAYARD RUSTIN 275 (Devon W. Carbado & Donald Weise eds., 2003) (quotation in text); B. Newman, *What's Cookin' in Atlanta, Southern Style,* ADVOCATE, Jan. 22, 1981, at 20–21.

sexuals, slap them around, and book them for activities that were either lawful or, at worst, minor infractions of park rules. "[O]ne officer [said], we're going to get those (deleted) queers out of Piedmont Park yet." Another citizen reported that when he attended a symphony in the park the previous summer, straight couples were making love underneath blankets. "If it had been a gay couple as opposed to a heterosexual couple they would have been arrested."[5]

There was "rage in the community towards the police," because undercover vice cops were wasting their time entrapping gay men into making sexual advances, while robberies, murders, and anti-gay violence were epidemic in the city. Police Chief George Napper assured gay citizens that, while the department did not target them, "[s]ome of the activities engaged in by gays are against the law." But "[t]o do it out of wedlock or with any style is also against the law," was the response. "It's not like the folks are out mugging or stealing things." To confront these abusive police practices, a Lesbian/Gay Rights Chapter of the Georgia ACLU formed in April 1981.[6]

Michael Hardwick spent the night of July 4, 1982, designing and installing a lighting display at The Cove. When he emerged from the bar early the next morning, he tossed a beer into the trash can next to the front door. Witnessing this act outside of a known homosexual hangout, Officer Keith Torick bounded from his police car and handed Hardwick a citation for drinking in public. Denying that he had even taken a swig outside the bar, Hardwick felt the officer "was just busting my chops because he knew I was gay." Gay Atlantans had often complained to Chief Napper, "if I come out of Numbers, the Armory or other [gay bars] with a drink in my hand, I will be arrested on the spot. If this were to occur at the corner of Peachtree and Pharr Road," an upscale straight bar venue, "where I've crossed six lanes of traffic, nothing would be said." Although subject to a stream of citizen complaints for rudeness and roughness, the feisty twenty-three year old Torick did not consider himself a gay-basher. He had homosexual friends and worked as a security guard at the Bulldog Lounge, another gay bar. Short, wiry, and darkly handsome, with a cute little mustache, Torick, a married man, could have passed as gay.[7]

---

[5] Lesbian/Gay Rights Chapter Meeting [with Commissioner Brown and Chief Napper], Sept. 22, 1981, in Atlanta Historical Center, Kenan Research Center, Atlanta, Georgia, Manuscript Series 773, on Lesbians, Gay Men, Bisexuals, and Transgendered People in Atlanta, Series II, Subseries 6, Box 1, Folder 5 (quotations in text); Police/Community Action Agreement, Nov. 3, 1981 (Commissioner Brown's proposed new policies to reduce police harassment of gays).

[6] Lesbian/Gay Rights Chapter Meeting, supra note 5 (quotations in text).

[7] Art Harris, *The Unintended Battle of Michael Hardwick*, WASH. POST, Aug. 21, 1986, at C4 (recounting Hardwick's and Torick's conflicting accounts of the citation); Telephone

Hardwick missed his court date for responding to the charge because Torick had written the wrong date at the top of the citation. Immediately, Torick obtained a warrant for Hardwick's arrest. Subsequently, Hardwick went to court, paid a $50 fine, and thought he had settled the matter. Three weeks later, when he returned to his home, three burly men were waiting for him. "[T]hey proceeded to beat the hell out of me. Tore all the cartilage out of my nose, kicked me in the face, cracked about six of my ribs. I passed out." When he regained consciousness, he crawled up the stairs and into his bedroom, where his mother (visiting from Florida) found him and took him to the hospital. Hardwick and his family believed that the assailants were friends of Officer Torick.[8]

On August 3, 1982, shortly after the assault, Torick showed up, at about 9:00 a.m., to arrest Hardwick. (At this point, the warrant had been invalid for three weeks.) Later claiming the front door was ajar, Torick entered the apartment and asked for Michael Hardwick. A friend who had been sleeping on the living room couch groggily pointed the officer to the bedroom. According to Hardwick: "Officer Torick then came into my bedroom. The door was cracked, and the door opened up and I looked up and there was nobody there. I just blew it off as the wind and went back to what I was involved in, which was mutual oral sex," with a male friend visiting from North Carolina to apply for a teaching job. "About thirty-five seconds went by and I heard another noise and I looked up, and this officer is standing in my bedroom. . . . Michael Hardwick, you are under arrest. I said, for what? What are you doing in my bedroom?" According to Torick: The school teacher begged, "Please don't tell my wife. . . . I'll lose my teaching job." And Hardwick "rant[ed] and rav[ed] about how I had no right to be in his house, how he'd have my job. . . . I would never have made the case if he hadn't had an attitude problem."[9]

While the uppity homosexual and the petrified school teacher dressed themselves, Torick searched the room and confiscated a small amount of marijuana. Handcuffing the suspects together, the officer drove them downtown to be booked for violating the state sodomy law—a fact Torick broadcast to everyone in the station. "They should find what they're looking for here," snickered a jailer.[10]

Interview with Kathy Wilde (Feb. 13, 2004) (The Cove); Lesbian/Gay Rights Chapter Meeting, supra note 5 (citizen complaint, quoted in text).

[8] PETER IRONS, THE COURAGE OF THEIR CONVICTIONS 394–95 (1988); Telephone Interview with Kathleen Blalock Hardwick (March 20, 2004).

[9] IRONS, supra note 8, at 395–96 (Hardwick's account of his arrest); Harris, supra note 7, at C4 (accounts by both Hardwick and Torick).

[10] IRONS, supra note 8, at 395; Harris, supra note 7, at C4.

Although consensual sodomy was technically a crime in more than half of the United States, more than ninety percent of the reported sodomy cases in the 1970s involved forcible sodomy or intercourse with minors; the remaining ten percent involved public activities. That the rare case of an arrest for private consensual sodomy should involve homosexual conduct was no surprise, however. While sodomy laws had originally been aimed at coercive or public anal intercourse, the twentieth century had seen illegal sodomy gradually become *homosexualized*. By 1945, most adult Americans (including most married persons) had engaged in oral sex; many found it enjoyable but were ambivalent. Not wanting to embrace sex purely for pleasure, most rationalized oral sex as a warm-up, at least potentially, for the main event, penile-vaginal intercourse that theoretically could be justified as a productive and not solely hedonic activity. This thin rationalization, and the sexual anxiety it reflected, left homosexual activities uniquely immoral: because they could not be linked with procreation or marriage, oral sex between two men was nothing but sex-for-pleasure, which was at best shallow and at worst abomination under most moral systems. Americans vested the "homosexual" not only with all the moral opprobrium they supposed God required of them and the unnatural relations that brought doom to Sodom, but also with the anxiety about uncertain gender roles and expanded sexual repertoires in our dynamic society. Americans terrified of a morality without limits and a society without form drew new lines: the homosexual became the repository for anxieties about sexual practices, gender role nonconformity, and the decline of marriage.[11]

The Tables Turn: Michael Hardwick versus Michael Bowers

The ACLU offered to represent Hardwick and make his a test case, challenging the constitutionality of consensual sodomy laws in general. The lawyers warned Michael and his mother that, if convicted of sodomy, the law required a sentence of *at least* one year in prison, and perhaps as many as twenty! After pondering the matter for a few days, Hardwick, the laid-back party boy, "realized that if there was anything I could do, even if it was just laying the foundation to change this horrendous law, that I would feel pretty bad about myself if I just walked away from it." So he agreed to ACLU representation and pleaded guilty to the minor marijuana charge. District Attorney Louis Slaton then dismissed the sodomy charge. Given the expired warrant, citizen complaints against

---

[11] An estimated ninety percent of the men born between 1948 and 1952, and more than eighty percent of those born between 1944 and 1948, had enjoyed oral sex in their lifetimes. EDWARD O. LAUMANN ET AL., THE SOCIAL ORGANIZATION OF SEXUALITY: SEXUAL PRACTICES IN THE UNITED STATES 103–04 (1994) (National Opinion Research Center Study); WILLIAM N. ESKRIDGE, JR., GAYLAW: CHALLENGING THE APARTHEID OF THE CLOSET 328–37, app. A1 (1999) (listing each state's history of regulating consensual sodomy); id. at 375, app. C2 (listing reported sodomy cases).

Torick, and his questionable entry into the apartment, Slaton feared embarrassing publicity and a blot on his record. (While serving as Fulton County D.A. from 1965 to 1996, Slaton won praise for his professionalism and early integration of his office to include blacks and women.)[12]

But on Valentine's Day, 1983, after the criminal charges were dropped, ACLU attorneys John Sweet and Kathy Wilde filed a complaint in federal district court against Bowers, Slaton, and Napper. Plaintiffs were Hardwick, a "practicing homosexual, who regularly engages in private homosexual acts and will do so in the future," and a married couple (John and Mary Doe) who desired to commit similar acts within their home. The complaint asked the court to declare the Georgia sodomy law unconstitutional as a violation of both the Due Process Clause's right of privacy and the First Amendment's rights of free expression and association.[13]

Meanwhile, Hardwick's arrest had generated considerable discussion among gay rights lawyers elsewhere. Founded in 1972, Lambda Legal Defense and Education Fund was the oldest gay rights organization in the country and had cooperated with the ACLU in challenging consensual sodomy laws during the 1970s. When Abby Rubenfeld became Lambda's Legal Director in January 1983, she was determined to finish the job her Lambda predecessors (Bill Thom, Cary Boggan, Margot Karle, and Roslyn Richter) had started—the full-on and coordinated legal assault against the states' sodomy laws. Soon after the federal district court dismissed Hardwick's complaint in April 1983, Rubenfeld hosted a meeting of gay rights lawyers. There was a consensus at that meeting that sodomy law reform should be a priority for their social movement, because "sodomy laws are the bedrock of legal discrimination against gay men and lesbians."[14]

ACLU attorney Kathy Wilde's appellate brief on Hardwick's behalf primarily relied on the right of sexual privacy that the Supreme Court had recognized in *Griswold v. Connecticut* (1965), which invalidated a state law barring the use of contraceptives. Although *Griswold* involved

---

[12] IRONS, supra note 8, 395–96 (quotations in text); Interview with Kathleen Blalock Hardwick (Michael's Mother), in Archer, Florida (March 2005); Telephone Interview with Susan Browning Chriss (Michael's sister) (Oct. 6, 2006); Ga. Code Ann. 16-6-2 (1984) (sodomy law, which covered oral sex, and penalty of "imprisonment for not less than one nor more than 20 years").

[13] Complaint, Hardwick et al. v. Bowers et al., (U.S. District Court for the Northern District of Georgia) (Civil Action No. C83–0273A) (filed Feb. 14, 1983), reprinted in Joint Appendix at 2–7, Bowers v. Hardwick, 478 U.S. 186 (1986) (No. 85–140).

[14] Lambda Update, Feb. 1984, at 3 (quotation in text); Telephone Interview with Abby Rubenfeld (Feb. 13, 2004); Interview with the Honorable Rosalyn Richter, in New York City (Chelsea) (Sept. 2004); ELLEN ANN ANDERSEN, OUT OF THE CLOSETS & INTO THE COURTS 40–42, 84–86 (2005).

a married couple, the Court in *Eisenstadt v. Baird* (1973) struck down a law denying contraceptives only to unmarried persons. "If the right of privacy means anything, it is the right of the *individual*, married or single, to be free from unwarranted governmental intrusion into matters so fundamentally affecting a person as the decision whether to bear or beget a child." In *Stanley v. Georgia* (1969), the Court had invalidated the arrest of a man viewing illegal pornography within his own home; resting upon the First and Fourth Amendments as well as the privacy right, the Court warned the state against intrusions into the home. In a Lambda amicus brief supporting Hardwick, Rubenfeld made an anti-discrimination argument: to the extent the Georgia sodomy law was applied solely against gay people, it denied gays the equal protection of the laws.[15]

Representing the state and local officials, Michael Hobbs of the Attorney General's Office argued that the lower federal courts were bound by the Supreme Court's summary affirmance of a judgment upholding Virginia's consensual sodomy law in *Doe v. Commonwealth's Attorney* (1976). Wilde responded that the Supreme Court had not explained the basis for its *Doe* affirmance. And because Doe had not actually been arrested, the Court may simply have believed the challenger lacked standing. In an opinion written by Judge Frank Johnson, the famous anti-segregation judge, the Eleventh Circuit sided with Wilde, finding that *Doe* was not dispositive and that *Eisenstadt* and *Stanley* established a right of privacy protecting Hardwick's personal life against Georgia's intrusion. The Court also found that Hardwick (who had actually been arrested) had standing to sue, but the married couple did not (the state maintained it would not arrest a married couple for consensual sodomy). The Court remanded the case for trial to determine whether Georgia could demonstrate a *compelling* state interest which could only be satisfied by invading Hardwick's *fundamental* privacy right. No one thought the state could make such a showing.[16]

The Supreme Court Appeal: Michael Bowers versus Michael Hardwick

Hobbs filed the state's petition for Supreme Court review on July 25, 1985. In the Court's Conference on October 11, 1985, Justice Byron

---

[15] Griswold v. Connecticut, 381 U.S. 479, 482–85 (1965); Eisenstadt v. Baird, 405 U.S. 438, 445 (1972) (quotation in text); Brief of Plaintiffs–Appellants, Hardwick v. Bowers, 760 F.2d 1202 (11th Cir. 1985) (No. 83–8378); Brief of Joint Amicus Curiae Lambda Legal Defense & Education Fund, Inc. and National Gay Rights Advocates in Support of Plaintiffs–Appellants, Hardwick v. Bowers, 760 F.2d 1202 (11th Cir. 1985) (No. 83–8378).

[16] Hardwick v. Bowers, 760 F.2d 1202 (11th Cir. 1985); see id. at 1206–07 (standing), 1207–10 (Doe), 1210–13 (privacy violation). Arguing that the appeal was governed by Doe, Judge Phyllis Kravitch dissented. Id. at 1213–16.

White advanced an excellent reason to take the case—it conflicted with
Baker v. Wade (1985), a Fifth Circuit decision upholding the Texas
Homosexual Conduct Law against privacy and equal protection claims.
As White emphasized, state as well as federal judges had ruled every
which way on the constitutionality of consensual sodomy laws. *Doe* had
resolved nothing, and the Court should settle the matter for good.
Justice William Rehnquist agreed; he and White were the only dissenters
from the Court's decision in *Roe v. Wade* (1973), where the Court had
extended the privacy right to protect a woman's right to choose to have
an abortion. Chief Justice Warren Burger suggested he would vote for
certiorari if three other Justices did so ("join three"). But with four
votes required to take review, the Conference of October 11 denied the
petition.[17]

Surprisingly, another vote to take Bowers's appeal came the next
day, from pro-privacy Justice William Brennan. Thinking strategically,
Brennan concluded that the odds of striking down consensual sodomy
laws would not improve with time. President Reagan had just won a
landslide re-election, and new conservatives would surely join the Court
in Reagan's second term. Believing that there was a chance of striking
down such laws with the current membership, Brennan voted for immediate review in a second Conference on October 18. Sensing Brennan's
strategy, Justice Thurgood Marshall also changed his vote, making four
(two conservatives and two liberals), with the Chief a probable fifth. On
October 23, after law clerks and colleagues had persuaded Brennan that
it was unlikely he could secure five votes to strike down the Georgia
sodomy law on privacy grounds, he withdrew his vote for review. But the
next day, Burger then changed his "join three" to a firm vote to grant.
Four was the magic number. On November 4, the Court announced that
it was granting review in *Bowers v. Hardwick*.[18]

---

[17] Justice White's dissent from denial of certiorari can be found in the Papers of
Justice Lewis A. Powell, Jr., Washington & Lee University Library, Lexington, Virginia,
Supreme Court Files, O.T. 1985, Bowers v. Hardwick, Docket No. 85–140. The Texas case
was Baker v. Wade, 769 F.2d 289 (5th Cir. 1985) (en banc), rev'g, 553 F. Supp. 1121 (N.D.
Tex. 1982).

[18] The tally sheets for the certiorari votes in Bowers v. Hardwick are in the Papers of
Justice William J. Brennan (special permission), Library of Congress, Madison Building,
Washington, D.C., Manuscript Collection, Box I: 693, Folder 4 [hereinafter Brennan
Papers], and Papers of Justice Harry A. Blackmun, Library of Congress, Madison Building,
Washington, D.C., Manuscript Collection, Box 702, Folder 8 [hereinafter Blackmun Pa-
pers]. Memoranda among the Justices can be found in Blackmun Papers, Box 451, Folder
7, and Powell Papers, Supreme Court Cases, Bowers v. Hardwick, Docket No. 85–140
[hereinafter Powell Papers, Bowers v. Hardwick File]. Details of Justice Brennan's strategy
come from Interview with Professor Larry Kramer, in New York City (West Village) (Oct.
1993). (Kramer clerked for Brennan during the 1985 Term; the documents support his
account.) The memoranda from Brennan and Burger changing their votes are in the
Blackmun Papers, Box 451, Folder 7.

The Supreme Court Decides *Bowers v. Hardwick*
The Challengers' Strategy

The Supreme Court briefs were as much cultural artifacts as legal documents. Representing Bowers, Hobbs framed the issue as whether Americans had a fundamental right to engage in "homosexual sodomy," an activity most citizens considered disgusting. Representing Hardwick, at the request of Wilde and the ACLU, Harvard Professor Laurence Tribe sought to focus the Justices' attention away from homosexuality and on "intimate sexual conduct in the privacy of the home." This characterization would allow Hardwick's conduct to fit within the holdings of *Eisenstadt* (unmarried people have a right to contraceptives) and *Stanley* (obscene materials can be viewed within the home).[19]

But Hobbs pointed out that the Court's privacy cases only protected activities relating to marriage, decisions whether to bear children, and child-rearing—*family*-based activities with no relevance to homosexuals. Tribe responded that this characterization did not explain *Stanley*: the narrowest principle covering both *Stanley* and *Eisenstadt* is that the state cannot tell consenting adults how to comport their sex lives within the home. To which Hobbs responded that states have constitutional discretion to create a moral framework, grounded in values held dear by the community, for family law. The Court had just ruled that the state can prosecute consenting adults for the sale or consumption of obscene materials that appealed to "abnormal sexual appetites," which the Justices contrasted with a "good, old-fashioned, healthy interest in sex." The epitome of old-fashioned, healthy sex is procreative activities within marriage, and surely the antithesis of such socially productive sex is a one-night stand that could never produce children.[20]

Hobbs marred an otherwise well-crafted argument by asserting that Georgia could reasonably believe that homosexuality not only "epitomizes moral delinquency," but also leads to other "deviate practices such as sado-masochism, group orgies, or transvestism, to name only a few"; is usually practiced in public parks, with adolescents, and is typically

---

[19] Brief of Petitioner at 2–4, 18–34, Bowers v. Hardwick, 478 U.S. 186 (1986) (No. 85–140) (repeated emphasis on "homosexual sodomy" and "rights of homosexuals"); Brief for Respondent at 7–19, *Bowers,* supra (emphasis on "intimate sexual conduct" in the "home"); see Laurence H. Tribe, *The Fundamental Right That Dare Not Speak Its Name,* 117 HARV. L. REV. 1893, 1951–52 (2004) ("[T]he only hope of [Hardwick's] prevailing was to shift the Court's gaze from [homosexual] applications of the statute to application to couples of all sorts."). According to the Roper Center for Public Opinion Research, Americans in September 1985 believed that homosexuality is "basically wrong" by a two-to-one margin (62–31%).

[20] Compare Brief for Petitioner, supra note 19, at 19–20, 31–34 (Hobbs's argument), with Brief for Respondent, supra note 19, at 9–16 (Tribe's argument). See Brockett v. Spokane Arcades, Inc., 472 U.S. 491, 499 (1985) (quotation in text).

accompanied by violence; and is pervasively linked to the transmission of
AIDS. These allegations rested upon largely false stereotypes. The American Public Health Association filed an amicus brief rejecting most of
Hobbs's claims as factually erroneous, and arguing that sodomy laws
undermine public health goals by inflicting psychological harm upon gay
people, discouraging safer sex education, and impeding medical efforts to
track people infected with HIV. Also, the incidence of public sex, affairs
with teenagers, and AIDS among *lesbians* was substantially less than
rates for gay men, straight men, and even straight women. To include
lesbians in Georgia's sodomy law, and in Hobbs' parade of "deviate
practices" was deeply misleading.[21]

Oral Argument: Privacy Triumphant

At oral argument on March 31, 1986, the soft-spoken Hobbs immediately conceded that Georgia's sodomy law could not constitutionally be
applied to married couples. This concession was potentially troubling,
because *Eisenstadt* had invalidated a contraception law that discriminated against unmarried couples. If he had been asked about the
inconsistency, Hobbs would have responded that *Eisenstadt* was only
about *heterosexual* activities, which could result in productive pregnancies, while this case was about *homosexual* sodomy, which was socially as
well as biologically sterile. The major theme of his argument was that
making homosexual sodomy a crime was essential to the long-standing
and important program of encouraging Georgia residents to marry and
form healthy families. Justice Stevens wondered: If Hardwick was guilty
of violating this very important public policy, why did Lewis Slaton
refuse to prosecute a case handed to him "on a silver platter"? Hobbs
had no idea. Earlier, he told the Court that the last consensual sodomy
prosecution he could name occurred in the 1930s. The case involved two
women, whose conviction was overturned on appeal.[22]

---

[21] Compare Brief for Petitioner, supra note 19, at 36–37 (degraded practices allegedly
associated with homosexuality, including AIDS), with Brief of Amici Curiae American
Psychological Association and American Public Health Association at 19–30, Bowers v.
Hardwick, 478 U.S. 186 (1986) (No. 85–140) (refuting associations of homosexuality with
degraded practices and arguing that sodomy laws retard medical efforts to research HIV
and slow down the AIDS epidemic).

[22] My discussion of the oral argument in Bowers v. Hardwick is based upon the audio
tape of the argument and the transcript in 164 Landmark Briefs and Arguments of the
Supreme Court of the United States: Constitutional Law 633–57 (Philip B. Kurland &
Gerhard Caspar eds., 1987) (Bowers v. Hardwick); see also Thompson v. Aldredge, 187 Ga.
467 (1939), where the Georgia Supreme Court ruled that oral sex between two women was
not sodomy covered by the criminal law. 6 Landmark Briefs and Arguments of the
Supreme Court of the United States: Constitutional Law 535, 537–38 (Philip B. Kurland &
Gerhard Casper eds., 1975).

As they had with Hobbs, the Justices immediately got to the point in Tribe's half-hour argument. In his honeyed Virginia whisper, Justice Powell asked what *limiting principle* there would be on a right of privacy that included sodomy. Tribe answered that the right would not necessarily apply outside the home. What about incest within the home, asked Powell and Burger. And adultery and polygamy within the home, chimed in Rehnquist. So where *do* you draw the line, wondered O'Connor. Tribe shifted to another limiting principle: the privacy right should not extend to physical intimacies that are harmful. Polygamy and incest could be regulated, because they harm wives and daughters. Hardwick's intimacy with another consenting adult harmed no one, and the fact it was in the home, a person's refuge, made it doubly immune from state nosiness. What is the *legal* basis for this conclusion, Powell gently inquired. Dodging the question, Tribe suggested that the common law, case-by-case approach would develop appropriate lines. If a line has to be drawn, Hardwick's case—where a police officer serving an expired warrant walks into a man's bedroom and arrests him for engaging in the most private and most intimate behavior—was a good place to draw it.[23]

After the argument, several dozen lawyers joined Tribe and his client for a triumphant lunch at the American Café on Massachusetts Avenue, several blocks from the Court. The mood was ebullient; everyone felt that Tribe had persuaded Justice Powell, and perhaps even Justice O'Connor. After the meal, Hardwick wandered off to see the city with Evan Wolfson, who had worked on Lambda's amicus brief. When Tribe asked where the client was, Rubenfeld quipped, "Michael is off exercising his constitutional rights." Wolfson and Hardwick spent a romantic afternoon holding hands and smooching at the Tidal Basin, but no crime against nature was committed. In the District, consensual sodomy could still bring you ten years in prison.[24]

Conference: Fighting for the Soul of Lewis Powell

Tribe's oral advocacy had less effect than his allies thought. Powell agreed with Tribe that applying sodomy laws to private activities between consenting adults was ridiculous, but he felt that Tribe lacked a defensible *constitutional* basis for striking down the statute. Having joined *Roe v. Wade* (1973), Powell believed the Due Process Clause limits the state's ability to deprive people of fundamental liberties, but *Roe* had also taught the Justice that substantive due process required a firm

---

[23] Transcript of Oral Argument, Bowers v. Hardwick, 478 U.S. 186 (1986) (No. 85–140); Poe v. Ullman, 367 U.S. 497, 553 (1961) (Harlan, J., dissenting) (privacy right does not protect "[a]dultery, homosexuality and the like").

[24] Telephone Interview with Abby Rubenfeld (Feb. 13, 2004); Interview with Evan Wolfson, New York City (Chelsea) (Jan. 13, 2004); D.C. Code § 22–502 (1981) (oral and anal sex felonious in the District).

limiting principle—and Tribe had not provided him with one. Powell found "repellant" Tribe's emphasis on the *home*, "one of the most beautiful words in the English language. It usually connotes family, husband and wife, and children," not one-night stands. Tribe was reading too much into *Stanley*, which the Court had never expanded beyond its narrow facts, home possession of smutty movies. If the Court read *Stanley* broadly, Powell feared opening the courts to challenges for drug use and other illicit activities. This would limit the states' ability to maintain or work toward the creation of decent communities. Tribe did not assuage Powell's doubts by his second limiting principle, that the privacy right does not protect activities that are non-consensual or harm third parties. Did drug use within the home then have constitutional protection? Incest? When Tribe compared Hardwick's activities to "normal" marital intimacy, Powell felt an "emotional recoil from an argument that seemed to place homosexual sodomy on a par with the sexual intimacy between man and wife."[25]

Whatever doubts Powell harbored were fanned by Michael Mosman, the law clerk who worked on the Hardwick case. The darkly handsome Mosman was a devout Mormon, married with three children. In his memorandum, Mosman argued that the privacy right had to be limited to those activities which American history and tradition suggested was off-limits to state regulation. "Homosexual sodomy" had no protection within our traditions. "Personal sexual freedom is a newcomer among our national values, and may well be . . . a temporary national mood that fades. This may be reflected in the fact that in the 1970s twenty states decriminalized homosexual sodomy, while in the 1980s only two states have done so."[26] Powell felt the memo did not reflect a subtle understanding of the issue and sought out the views of his other law clerks. One was Cabell Chinnis, his liberal law clerk. "I don't believe I've ever met a homosexual," Powell confided. "Certainly you have, but you just don't know that they are," responded Chinnis, who was gay. As the clerk

---

[25] Telephone Interview with Professor William J. Stuntz (Feb. 15, 2005) (general analysis in text); Memorandum from Justice Lewis Powell to Mike Mossman, March 31, 1986, in Powell Papers, Bowers v. Hardwick File, at 6 (first quotation in text); JOHN C. JEFFRIES, JR., JUSTICE LEWIS F. POWELL, JR. 515 (1994) (second quotation). In Zablocki v. Redhail, 434 U.S. 374 (1978), Powell refused to join an opinion articulating a right to marry, for he saw no limiting principle and feared such a right might lead to same-sex marriage. Id. at 399.

[26] Memorandum from Michael Mosman to Justice Lewis Powell, March 29, 1986, 11–12 (quotation in text), Powell Papers, Bowers v. Hardwick File. Mosman followed up his argument with another post-oral argument memorandum assailing Tribe for "condescendingly" (Powell wrote "yes!" in the margin) "dismiss[ing] the state's interest in legislating some moral principle" and for offering no limiting concept for his own moral theory. Memorandum from Mike Mosman to Justice Lewis Powell, March 31, 1986, Powell Papers, Bowers v. Hardwick File.

later told Powell's biographer, "[h]e couldn't understand the idea of sexual attraction between two men. It just had no content for him."[27]

The barely closeted Chinnis (few of his classmates at the Yale Law School doubted his sexual orientation) wondered whether he should have come out to the Justice. After all, many of Powell's law clerks had been gay or lesbian—including several early clerks who remained close to the Justice and recent clerks Paul Smith (1980 Term), Mary Becker (1981 Term), David Charny (1983 Term), Dan Ortiz (1984 Term), as well as himself (1985 Term). Sally Smith, Powell's long-time secretary, was an unmarried woman whom many of the clerks believed to be a lesbian. Powell was not a homophobe "but he was almost hysterically uninterested in anyone's private sexual activities." Not wanting to make his beloved boss uncomfortable, Chinnis did not come out but did make a passionate speech: "The right to love the person of my choice would be far more important to me than the right to vote in elections." Powell blandly responded, "That may be, but that doesn't mean it's in the Constitution."[28]

Powell next turned to another law clerk, Bill Stuntz, to develop a constitutional basis for overturning the Georgia law that was narrower than Tribe's privacy theory. An evangelical southern Christian, also married with children, Stuntz accepted the importance of family and moral values in public discourse. But, unlike Powell, Stuntz knew gay people and could understand how they could form meaningful relationships that society should not be demonizing. Stuntz came up with a theory grounded on the Eighth Amendment, which bars government from imposing "cruel and unusual punishments." Even if the state could constitutionally adopt laws discouraging extra-marital or homosexual activities, it could not make private activities between consenting adults a serious crime, with *mandatory* jail time (one year in prison), as Georgia had done. This theory had case support. In 1962, the Court had ruled that the state could not criminalize the *status* of being a drug addict, and in 1968 five Justices had opined that the state could not arrest an alcoholic for becoming drunk in his own home.[29]

---

[27] JEFFRIES, supra note 25, at 521.

[28] Id. at 522. In a presentation to my reading group in Washington, D.C., Dean Jeffries opined that Chinnis would probably not have "changed Powell's mind" if he had come out, but that the conversation would have been different.

[29] Telephone Interview with Professor William J. Stuntz (Feb. 15, 2005); Memorandum from Bill Stuntz to Justice Lewis Powell, re: Robinson/Powell Argument in Bowers v. Hardwick (no date), Powell Papers, Bowers v. Hardwick File (one of the Stuntz memoes); Robinson v. California, 370 U.S. 660 (1962), and Powell v. Texas, 392 U.S. 514 (1968) (statements of four dissenting Justices and of Justice White, who concurred only in the judgment).

On April 2, 1986, the Justices discussed *Bowers v. Hardwick* at Conference. Introducing the case, Warren Burger insisted the issue was a claimed right to engage in "homosexual sodomy," which had been regulated for 500 years by Anglo–American law. "Our society has values that should be protected. Teachings of history and custom frown on and sanction its prohibition." Reverse the Eleventh Circuit, demanded the Chief Justice, emphatically. Speaking next, William Brennan quietly countered that "this is not a case about homosexuality but is a case of privacy by consenting adults," and also a case about government intrusion into the home. There is surely a fundamental right here—but even if there were not, Hobbs had advanced no public-regarding reason for making this conduct a crime. Even under lenient "rational basis" scrutiny, there has got to be a neutral *reason* apart from anti-homosexual prejudice. Send the case back to trial on that issue. Affirm the Eleventh Circuit.[30]

Agreeing with the Chief Justice, but without his emotionalism, Byron White felt there was no reason not to defer to legislative judgments on such a delicate moral issue—especially recent judgments (Georgia's law was updated in 1968) in accord with those of half the other states. Emphasizing *Stanley* and the context of the home, Thurgood Marshall and Harry Blackmun concurred with Brennan. Both Justices knew gay people, including gay couples, and felt there were parallels between racism and homophobia. Blackmun, in particular, viewed White's deferential stance as a challenge to the ongoing validity of *Roe*, a precedent that Blackmun guarded with the ferocity of a tigress protecting her cub.[31]

With the votes three-to-two for affirming, Lewis Powell spoke up. "I have mixed emotions." Certainly, "sodomy in the home should be decriminalized," and Georgia had not enforced the law against consenting adults for fifty years. Unwilling (like White and Burger) to understand any connection with family, Powell compared homosexuality to "drug addiction." The homosexual is addicted to sodomy the way others are addicted to drugs. The Court had held in *Robinson v. California* (1962) that sending someone to jail because he was a drug addict violated the Eighth Amendment. "If [we] accept [the] allegation that only acts of sodomy can satisfy this fellow [Hardwick], isn't that pertinent?" Powell

---

[30] The Chief Justice's remarks are taken from Brennan Papers, Box I:693, Folder 4; Blackmun Papers, Box 451, Folder 9; Powell Papers, Bowers v. Hardwick File. Brennan's remarks are taken from the Blackmun Papers and the Powell Papers.

[31] David D. Meyer, *Justice White and the Right of Privacy: A Model of Realism and Restraint*, 52 Cath. U. L. Rev. 915 (2003); David A.J. Richards, The Case for Gay Rights: From Bowers to Lawrence and Beyond 83–85, 193 n.25 (2005) (personal account of Blackmun's acquaintance with gay couples).

was willing to affirm on the basis of this Eighth Amendment analysis. Blackmun silently groaned, "Can this [rationale] possibly hold?"[32]

William Rehnquist responded that Powell's position was the "most extreme" of all. Because the state never prosecuted, much less imprisoned Hardwick, *Robinson* could not resolve his case. Reverse. John Paul Stevens stunned his colleagues as much as Powell did: "I have a bias," against homosexuality, "but we have to live with this," namely, the presence of gay people in public culture. The American Psychological Association told the Justices that homosexuality is not a mental illness; homophobia, in fact, is the problem the state needs to address. Why should homosexuals be treated differently from other Americans? Georgia told the Court it could not constitutionally apply its sodomy statute to married couples, and *Eisenstadt* then suggested it could not be applied to unmarried straight couples either. If the sodomy statute cannot be applied to married or unmarried straight couples, what *reason* supports its application to homosexuals? "Only prejudice supports the distinction," Stevens concluded. "This is a liberty case for me, and for homosexuals as well." Just as *Roe* protected women's freedom of sexual choice, so homosexuals have a constitutional freedom to make sexual choices in their lives.[33]

Although Stevens made five votes to affirm, Sandra Day O'Connor's vote was hardly irrelevant in light of Powell's odd rationale. Speaking without the emotion of her male colleagues, she expressed a reluctance to limit state morals regulation based upon the unbounded privacy right. Opining that substantive due process required guidance from the nation's legal history and traditions, she found it notable that "this prohibition [was in place] in 1787 and when the Fourteenth Amendment was adopted." She labeled Powell's Eighth Amendment compromise "a real risk and dangerous" for the Court's reputation. Reverse.[34]

After Conference, Burger sent Powell a personal letter objecting to the Eighth Amendment theory. The Chief Justice noted that none of the parties or amici had briefed the matter; the Court is less likely to be on solid ground when it decides issues without full briefing (a point that Brennan had made in *Doe*, where the Chief Justice was willing to dismiss rights for gays without briefing on the merits). He rejected Powell's conclusion that sodomy laws are *status* crimes. "Hardwick merely wishes to seek his own form of sexual gratification," no different

---

[32] Brennan Papers, Box I:693, Folder 4; Blackmun Papers, Box 451, Folder 9.

[33] Brennan Papers, Box I:693, Folder 4; Blackmun Papers, Box 451, Folder 9. In Blackmun's notes, Stevens suggested that the Court should simply declare the Georgia law unconstitutional, rather than remand to the lower courts for a trial on the state's justifications.

[34] Brennan Papers, Box I:693, Folder 4; Blackmun Papers, Box 451, Folder 9.

in kind than the gratification others seek through "incest, drug use, gambling, exhibitionism, prostitution, rape." In closing, Burger reminded Powell that April 13, 1986, would mark Burger's thirtieth year on the federal bench. "This case presents for me the most far-reaching issue of those 30 years," the suggestion being that Powell should reconsider his position out of respect for the long service. Powell circled this language and wrote "Incredible statement!" Yet despite much "nonsense," Burger's letter deepened Powell's misgivings about his ability to make the Eighth Amendment theory work. In a memorandum to the Court on April 8, Powell reaffirmed his view that "in some cases it would violate the Eighth Amendment to imprison a person for a private act of homosexual sodomy," but not in Hardwick's case. Because he did not accept Tribe's privacy arguments, Powell's "bottom line" in *Bowers* was to reverse.[35]

The next day the Chief Justice assigned the opinion to White, who asked a law clerk to draft an opinion. Laboring to craft a relatively mild law-like opinion, the clerk failed to meet the Chambers' "nine-day rule" for drafting opinions—and the impatient Justice dashed off his own draft after the nine days were up. After less than a week of effort, White circulated it to the Court on April 21. Rehnquist and Burger joined it immediately; O'Connor joined after seeing the dissenting opinions in June. Initially, Powell indicated he would join only the result and would write a separate opinion, thereby depriving White of a majority. Lobbied hard by Mosman and unable to craft a suitable concurring rationale, Powell ultimately joined White's opinion.[36]

The Decision and Reactions

Delivered on June 30, 1986, the last day of the 1985 Term, Justice White's opinion for the Court in *Bowers v. Hardwick* was brusque, simple, and historical. The Court's previous privacy precedents were limited to personal decisions involving marriage, procreation, and child-rearing. To *add* a protection for "homosexual sodomy" as a fundamental right would require a showing that this liberty is deeply rooted in this Nation's history and tradition. Hardwick's attorneys had not made such a showing, nor could they, because proscriptions against "consensual sodomy" have "ancient roots." Sodomy had been a capital crime in England and its colonies since King Henry VIII's statute of 1533.

---

[35] Letter from Chief Justice Warren E. Burger to Justice Lewis F. Powell, Jr., April 3, 1986, Powell Papers, Bowers v. Hardwick File (quotations in text, including Powell's annotations); Lewis F. Powell, Jr., Memorandum to the Conference, re 85–140 Bowers v. Hardwick, April 8, 1986, Blackmun Papers, Box 451, Folder 7 (quoted in text).

[36] Memorandum from Justice Lewis F. Powell, Jr. to Mike Mosman, May 21, 1986, Powell Papers, Bowers v. Hardwick File; Memorandum from Mike Mosman to Justice Lewis Powell, June 12, 1986, Powell Papers, Bowers v. Hardwick File.

According to White, it was a crime in all thirteen states when they ratified the Bill of Rights in 1791, and in all but five of the thirty-seven states when the Fourteenth Amendment was added in 1868. "Against this background, to claim that a right to engage in such conduct is deeply rooted in this Nation's history and traditions ... is, at best, facetious." So the Eleventh Circuit was wrong to hold that Hardwick enjoyed a fundamental right to engage in homosexual sodomy. Hence, the law would be constitutional if it rested upon a "rational basis," the lenient constitutional default test. In one concluding paragraph, White ruled that Georgia was within its constitutional discretion to criminalize sodomy to reflect "majority sentiments about the morality of homosexuality."[37]

Chief Justice Burger wrote a concurring opinion elaborating on White's historical discussion. Blackstone, the English commentator every American lawyer would have known at Independence, described "the infamous *crime against nature*" as an offense of "deeper malignity than rape." Sodomy was punishable by death in almost all states until well into the nineteenth century. "To hold that the act of homosexual sodomy is somehow protected as a fundamental right would be to cast aside millennia of moral teaching."[38] Also concurring, Justice Powell wrote: "I cannot say that conduct condemned for hundreds of years has now become a fundamental right." A prison term for acts of consensual sodomy within the home would be subject to Eighth Amendment questions, but Hardwick's case did not present that issue.[39]

Joined by Justices Brennan, Marshall, and Stevens, Justice Blackmun filed a dissenting opinion which closely followed Hardwick's brief. The case was no more about a fundamental right to homosexual sodomy than *Stanley* had been about a right to watch obscene movies. The statute made no such distinction; indeed, the state had expanded the law in 1968 to make sure it included heterosexual as well as homosexual cunnilingus (oral sex upon a woman). Hardwick was only asking for the same right to be left alone that the state conceded to married couples and *Eisenstadt* assured unmarried straight couples. The Court's sexual privacy precedents guaranteed his freedom to make *decisions* regarding intimate relations, and its privacy-of-the-home precedents guaranteed his freedom against state intrusion into certain *places*. "[T]he right of an

---

[37] Bowers v. Hardwick, 478 U.S. 186, 192 (1986), quoting Moore v. City of East Cleveland, 431 U.S. 494, 503 (1977) (plurality opinion of Powell, J.). The other quotations in text are from Bowers, 478 U.S. at 192, 194, 196. White's opinion distinguished Stanley as involving only First and Fourth Amendment rights, and not relevant to a general privacy right. Id. at 195–96.

[38] Bowers, 478 U.S. at 196–97 (Burger, C.J., concurring).

[39] Id. at 197–98 (Powell, J., concurring); id. at 198 n.2 (quotation in text).

individual to conduct intimate relationships in the intimacy of his or her own home seems to me to be the heart of the Constitution's protection of privacy." Even if Hardwick had no fundamental right, however, Blackmun argued that anti-homosexual "sentiments" could not provide the rational basis the Constitution requires for *any* statute, especially criminal laws. Certainly, the sectarian justifications emphasized by the state could not be a *neutral* reason that can justify "invading the houses, hearts, and minds of citizens who choose to live their lives differently."[40]

Justice Stevens wrote a separate dissenting opinion. The Court was right to say that sodomy was long condemned by Anglo–American law— but the damnable conduct was *always* understood to apply to men and women, men or women with beasts, as well as men and men. The crime against nature could be committed by married men with their wives. *Griswold* barred Georgia from prosecuting sodomy between married partners, as Hobbs conceded. *Eisenstadt* questioned the state's ability to criminalize sodomy by unmarried heterosexuals. In light of these limits, could the state apply its broad statute *only* against homosexuals? Under the Constitution, there must be "something more substantial than a habitual dislike for, or ignorance about, the disfavored group." That the state itself cannot name a prosecution, even against homosexuals, for consensual sodomy since the 1930s suggested there was no such interest.[41]

Reaction to the Supreme Court's Decision

Michael Hardwick learned that he had lost when television reporters called him. He was devastated. When he read the opinions, he was astounded that the Supreme Court would dismiss his human rights claims as, "at best, facetious," because King Henry VIII (an adulterer who ran through six wives and murdered a couple of them) viewed his conduct as unnatural. He was angered by Burger's reference to Blackstone's view that the crime against nature is worse than rape. The chief moral lesson of the majority opinions, suggested by their obsession with "homosexual sodomy," seemed to be that the Constitution authorized homophobia and anti-gay discrimination.[42]

The night after the Court's judgment was announced, thousands filled the streets of San Francisco in spontaneous demonstrations protesting gay people's apparent exclusion from constitutional citizenship.

---

[40] Id. at 199–214 (Blackmun, J., dissenting); id. at 208 (first quotation in text); id. at 213 (second quotation).

[41] Id. at 214–20 (Stevens, J., dissenting); id. at 219 (quotation in text).

[42] Telephone Interview with Kathy Wilde (Feb. 13, 2004) Interview with Robert Hardwick Weston (Michael Hardwick's nephew), in New York City (West Village) (Jan. 22, 2004).

Smaller demonstrations occurred in New York and Washington, D.C. Hundreds of homosexuals and their friends wrote personal letters to the Justices, in numbers greater than any other case outside the abortion context. Arthur Wirth, the President of Parents and Friends of Lesbians and Gays, wrote Justice White: "If you knew our gay children personally I know that you would reject as wrong the idea that they are to be treated as pariahs, because that was the custom of the past. It is true that our children have been called faggots because some Christians chose to burn them as kindling. I find it hard to believe that you consider that sufficient grounds for declaring them outlaws today." Steven Cantor of Athens, Georgia wrote Powell, asking him to reconsider his vote, because the Court's ruling will "encourage hateful, bigoted, and ignorant people to pursue [anti-gay] policies that have already destroyed—or at least terrified or harassed—many innocent people." Barbara Shor, a married woman, called her best friend and burst into tears after she read the *New York Times* account of the decision. "All I can think to say to you is that, after my child, you are the person I love most in the world. And my best friend, who is gay, said, 'Thank you. It helps. I just wish you'd tell that to Justice White.' And so I have," in a letter she mailed the next day.[43]

Father Robert Nugent, a Catholic theologian, wrote Blackmun praising his recognition that gay as well as straight people need protection for their expressions of sexuality and intimacy. "I regret that the Court's obsession with same-sex behavior has blinded them to the larger issues of human sexual interaction and intimacy which are distorted by such a narrow focus based on popular prejudices and even, at times, misreading of religious doctrines." Reverend Kenneth Bastin, an evangelical Baptist, wrote the Justices from the perspective of a cleric ministering to the needs of men dying of AIDS. He reported an upsurge of anti-gay violence following the Court's opinion. Everywhere he went, "I find appalling and irrational hatred and bigotry toward homosexual people as if it were they who created this deadly virus."[44]

Larry Tribe warned: "Despite the majority's disclaimers, [this decision] clearly extends to heterosexuals. Nothing in the approach of the majority opinion should make married people safe." In George Orwell's *1984*, Big Brother prohibited sexual pleasure and deployed cameras in everyone's home to enforce this rule. Sexuality was a life force, a

---

[43] Letter from Arthur G. Wirth to Justice Byron White, July 25, 1986, Blackmun Papers, Box 452, Folder 6; Letter from Steven Cantor to Justice Lewis Powell, August 11, 1986, Blackmun Papers, Box 452, Folder 1; Letter from Barbara Shor to Justice Byron White, July 2, 1986, Blackmun Papers, Box 452, Folder 5.

[44] Letter from Reverend Robert Nugent, S.D.S., to Justice Harry Blackmun, July 1, 1986, Blackmun Papers, Box 452, Folder 4; Letter from Reverend Kenneth A. Bastin to Justice Harry Blackmun, June 15, 1987, Blackmun Papers, Box 452, Folder 1.

fundamental liberty pervasively threatening to despotic totalitarian governments, Orwell was saying. Thus, reactionary governments suppress sexuality as an exercise in despotic self-preservation. In Hardwick's case, Georgia looked like a bizarre amalgam of Big Brother and the Keystone Kops. If the police could barge into Hardwick's bedroom on trumped up charges and cart him and his sexual partners off to jail, who is safe in America? Within days of the opinion, cartoons appeared in hundreds of newspapers, depicting five Justices (with varying resemblances to those

Los Angeles Times

The knock on the bedroom door.

in the *Bowers* majority) knocking at the doors of married couples, luridly peering through the windows of their bedrooms, and even making themselves at home in marital beds. Editorial writers feasted on *Bowers* like famished dieters.[45]

The Georgia authorities reassured Atlanta residents that Big Brother had no interest in exposing *anyone*'s sex lives. "What we said to the Supreme Court," Attorney General Bowers announced, "was that if this law would have applied to a married couple, there would be significant constitutional difficulties." This was particularly reassuring to Keith Torick, who apparently engaged in sodomy with his wife.[46] Bowers did not say whether heterosexual cohabiting or dating couples had anything to worry about. But the Georgia Department of Corrections reported that only four of 16,900 prison inmates in 1985 were in jail for sodomy, including two men for sodomy with a child and two women for sodomy for compensation. District Attorney Slaton reiterated that he would *not* prosecute Hardwick. Major J.E. Oliver, head of the Atlanta police's vice division, said: "If I walk into somebody's home with a warrant, say for narcotics, and [sodomy] is there, sure we'll charge them. But otherwise I don't see any reason to go into a house looking for sodomy."[47]

Bowers and Hobbs were certain that Big Brother did not lurk in the Supreme Court's decision and that Hardwick was wrong to be angered by it. From their point of view, the Court was merely reaffirming state authority to create a regulatory regime supporting marriage. The state supports marriage by celebrating it and by showering married couples with many legal advantages and subsidies—but also by criminalizing non-marital sexual expression. They also agreed with the American Enterprise Institute's Bruce Fein, that the real punch line lay in civil exclusions. Under *Bowers*, "the government can say, 'We don't want to hire you because being a government employee sends a message to the public as to what kinds of people we approve of.'" Several years after

---

[45] Jim Galloway, *High Court Upholds State Sodomy Law*, ATLANTA J. CONST., July 1, 1986, at A1 (quotation in text).

[46] Tracy Thompson, *Homosexuals Fear Sodomy Ruling Will Have Far–Reaching Effect*, ATLANTA J. CONST., July 6, 1986 (Bowers quotation). Keith Torick had left the Atlanta police force in 1983. Soon thereafter, he interviewed for a job with the police department in Roswell, a gay-free, racially segregated zone twenty miles from the heart of Atlanta. Roswell required a polygraph test, which included the question: "Have you ever broken the law?" Torick allegedly "flashed on the sodomy statute, which [he assumed] includes married couples, and asked that the question be rephrased as 'a serious undetected felony,' like robbing a bank. He passed." Harris, supra note 7, at C4 (account of Torick's lie detector test).

[47] Thompson, supra note 46 (prison statistics); Galloway, supra note 45 (Oliver statement).

the decision, Attorney General Bowers withdrew a job offer to Robin Shahar, a brilliant young lawyer, because she was planning to marry another woman. Although Shahar should not be subject to criminal sanctions, Bowers feared that her lesbian self-identification, which she flaunted through her wedding, made her a presumptive law-breaker unsuited for service in a law enforcement office.[48]

Unlike the Georgia authorities, many fundamentalist Christians viewed *Bowers* as a great reaffirmation of moral values in American law. The night *Bowers* was handed down, Reverend Jerry Falwell appeared on *Larry King Live* to announce a moral renaissance in this country, where church and state would be partners in an enterprise to wean Americans from the soulless hedonism represented by homosexuality and other sins. Falwell's sentiments were expressed more brutally in church meetings and even letters to the Court. Matt Millen of Crown Point, Indiana wrote Justice Blackmun: "You voted recently for queers having the freedom to practice their 'lifestyle' even privately. I think it is a shame and disgrace that such people would have a right to destroy the basic principles on which our republic rests. No country has ever survived as a free country when sodomites were welcomed as normal." Carl Laurent wrote: "Does this mean you are homosexual? If so, this explains why you are also for murdering babies." Most blunt of all was Mrs. H.F. Mitchell of Homestead, Florida: "You are an old man and may die soon. If you don't repent, you will wake up in Hell." None of the anguished letters from homosexuals to Justices White, Burger, and Powell was as hateful as the many letters Justice Blackmun received from these Christians.[49]

Academic Critiques of Bowers v. Hardwick

As a decision by the Supreme Court denying a fundamental constitutional right to gay people, *Bowers* was a landmark decision. But it was also important as a statement by the Court's conservative majority that the privacy right should not be further expanded; this invited new efforts to narrow or even overrule *Roe*. Any decision of such importance would inevitably bring the closest scrutiny from law professors and commentators.

---

[48] Interview with Michael Bowers, in Atlanta, Georgia (Buckhead) (Jan. 4, 2004); Telephone Interview with Michael E. Hobbs (Jan. 5, 2004); Letter from Michael E. Hobbs, Deputy Attorney General, Georgia, to William N. Eskridge, Jr., March 7, 2005; Thompson, supra note 46 (Fein quotation); Shahar v. Bowers, 114 F.3d 1097 (11th Cir. 1997) (en banc).

[49] Letter from Matt Miller to Mr. Harry A. Blackmun, July 5, 1986; Letter from Carl Laurent to Justice Blackmun, July 5, 1986; Letter from Mrs. H.F. Mitchell to Justice Harry Blackmun, August 23, 1986. All of these letters, and others like them, are in Blackmun Papers, Box 452, Folders 8–9.

Progressive constitutional scholars, many of whom had been involved in the civil rights and women's rights movements, were predictably critical of the Supreme Court's decision—but so were some of the
nation's most eminent conservatives, including Judge Richard Posner, a
Chicago School law and economics scholar, and George H.W. Bush
Administration Solicitor General Charles Fried. Posner and Fried believed that if you take the Court's privacy precedents seriously, there has
to be some protection for gays as well as straights, at least within their
own homes. As Blackmun had argued, it was a retreat from privacy's
libertarian bearings for the Court to have cabined the privacy right to
decisions relating only to family, procreation, and child-rearing. As
Stevens had argued, it was a violation of equal protection for the Court
to allow Georgia to focus only on homosexual sodomy, while assuring all
its other citizens that the law did not apply to their conduct. Almost all
law professors who wrote on the topic agreed with this criticism, and
most went considerably further.[50]

Moreover, the history upon which the *Bowers* Court relied was
substantially wrong. White and Burger treated the criminalization of
"homosexual sodomy" as a phenomenon reaching back to Roman times.
As Stevens had said in *Bowers*, however, the crime against nature in
both England and America always had applied to different-sex as well as
same-sex couples, and even to married couples. If history were the guide,
Georgia and the Court were wrong to assume that married couples could
not be prosecuted. Professor Anne Goldstein demonstrated, further, that
there was not even a concept of "homosexuality" or "homosexual
sodomy" until the late nineteenth century and that the conduct Hardwick was arrested for—oral sex—was *not* a crime against nature in
England or the United States until the same period, decades after the
Fourteenth Amendment was ratified.[51]

---

[50] Academic criticisms of Bowers include WILLIAM N. ESKRIDGE, JR., GAYLAW: CHALLENGING
THE APARTHEID OF THE CLOSET (1998); CHARLES FRIED, ORDER AND LAW: ARGUING THE REAGAN
REVOLUTION 81–84 (1991); KENNETH L. KARST, BELONGING TO AMERICA: EQUAL CITIZENSHIP AND THE
CONSTITUTION 201–06, 226–27 (1989); RICHARD A. POSNER, SEX AND REASON 341–50 (1992);
DAVID A.J. RICHARDS, THE CASE FOR GAY RIGHTS 73–87 (2005); EVE KOSOFSKY SEDGWICK, THE
EPISTEMOLOGY OF THE CLOSET 6–7 (1990); LAURENCE TRIBE, AMERICAN CONSTITUTIONAL LAW (2d ed.
1988); Sylvia Law, *Homosexuality and the Social Meaning of Gender*, 1988 WIS. L. REV. 187;
Frank Michelman, *Law's Republic*, 97 YALE L.J. 1493 (1988); Rhonda R. Rivera, *Our
Straight–Laced Judges Twenty Years Later*, 50 HASTINGS L.J. 1179 (1999); Jed Rubenfeld,
The Right of Privacy, 102 HARV. L. REV. 737 (1989); Kendall Thomas, *Beyond the Privacy
Principle*, 92 COLUM. L. REV. 1431 (1992); see also Earl Maltz, *The Prospects for a Revival of
Conservative Activism in Constitutional Jurisprudence*, 24 GA. L. REV. (1990) 629, 645 n.95
(citing thirty-three law review articles critical of Bowers).

[51] Bowers, 478 U.S. at 214–16 (Stevens, J., dissenting); Anne Goldstein, *History,
Homosexuality, and Political Values: Searching for the Hidden Determinants of Bowers v.
Hardwick*, 97 YALE L.J. 1073 (1988).

So not only was White's opinion a slanted understanding of precedent, but it was also sloppy history. As I demonstrated in a follow-up to Goldstein's article, no English-speaking jurisdiction considered oral sex to be sodomy until Pennsylvania did so by statute in 1879, more than a decade after the Fourteenth Amendment was ratified. Most states have never clearly regulated sex between two women. Moreover, the original purposes legitimately served by nineteenth century sodomy laws—protection against public indecency and sexual assaults—did not suggest application against private activities between consenting adults. (Other plausible nineteenth century purposes are no longer legitimate ones, as explained below.)[52]

Thus, the Court's originalist approach to the Fourteenth Amendment (apply it *only* to strike down innovative statutes the Framers in 1868 would probably have disapproved) stood in stark contrast not only to the Court's failure to follow an originalist approach in the contraception and abortion cases, but also to Justice White's wildly non-originalist (not only dynamic, but ungrounded in any serious research) approach to the sodomy laws he charged the Framers with knowing and approving. It would not have occurred to any Framer that the crime against nature involved oral sex or sex between women or could be prosecuted against consenting adults without third-party witnesses.

Ultimately, White's opinion re-justified the application of sodomy laws to consensual private conduct on the basis of an anti-homosexual sentiment that was not only unknown to the 1868 Framers, but also a questionable modern justification for criminal sanctions.[53] Were there respectable moral arguments condemning homosexual but not heterosexual sodomy? In *The Laws*, Plato condemned same-sex sodomy because it was nonprocreative and degraded the passive male partner to the status of a woman. But *Griswold* and *Eisenstadt* are probably obstacles to the state's outlawing consensual activities in order to require procreation. And preservation of rigid gender roles (man-inserter, woman-insertee) as a state goal is inconsistent with the Court's sex discrimination jurisprudence. Perhaps the best argument for criminalizing only homosexual sodomy is that its necessary separation from procreative marital intercourse renders it a naked embrace of a philosophy of sex for pleasure alone, and therefore obliterates all moral distinctions in matters of sex between consenting adults. But even under that philosophy, of course, the question remains: Should *the line* be drawn at homosexual sodomy?

---

[52] William N. Eskridge, Jr., *Hardwick and Historiography*, 1999 U. ILL. L. REV. 631; see Ronald Hamowy, *Preventive Medicine and the Criminalization of Sexual Immorality in Nineteenth Century America*, in ASSESSING THE CRIMINAL, 39–41 (Randy Barnett & John Hagell, III eds., 1977).

[53] Bowers, 478 U.S. at 200–05 (Blackmun, J., dissenting); RICHARDS, supra note 50, at 81–83.

Natural law philosophy, the primary basis for anti-sodomy discourse, condemns all sodomy and also condemns anti-homosexual discrimination. Criminalizing homosexual sodomy while leaving heterosexual sodomy unregulated may be an expression of anti-homosexual anxiety and prejudice, rather than a serious statement of moral philosophy. This deep normative problem rendered *Bowers v. Hardwick* vulnerable from the very beginning.[54]

The Rule of Law as a Basis for Deregulating Consensual Sodomy

That the *Bowers* majority misunderstood almost everything—moral philosophy as well as the legal history of the crime against nature—does not mean that the Georgia sodomy law was unconstitutional as applied to consenting activities within the home. But Lewis Powell and his clerk Bill Stuntz thought there was a case to be made. I do, too. The core purpose of the Fourteenth Amendment is to preserve the rule of law in a democracy. Section 1 of the Amendment advanced three principles essential to such a rule of law: legality, liberty, and equality. The Georgia sodomy law, as enforced by Keith Torick and defended by Michael Bowers, was inconsistent with these principles and therefore with the Fourteenth Amendment's core purpose.

1. The Legality Principle.

The notion that the state should exercise power predictably and neutrally, and only when authorized by law, applies with special force in criminal cases. Specifically enforceable under the Due Process Clause, the legality principle requires that criminal statutes give clear notice so that citizens know what conduct is illegal and police understand that they cannot apply the law selectively, to terrorize citizens they do not like. In a society where three-quarters of the citizens engage in oral sex, a law imposing a mandatory one-year prison sentence could not be enforced against everyone—and this fact required the police to exercise discretion, which they inevitably but unpredictably used to harass and persecute despised minorities.[55]

---

[54] For moral condemnation of the passive role for men, see PLATO, LAWS, BOOK VIII, 835d–842a; PETER BROWN, THE BODY AND SOCIETY: MEN, WOMEN, AND SEXUAL RENUNCIATION IN EARLY CHRISTIANITY 382–83 (1988). For current natural law theory's condemnation of both sodomy and anti-homosexual prejudice, see, e.g., Cardinal Josef Ratzinger, Congregation for the Doctrine of the Faith, Letter on the pastoral care of homosexual persons (Oct. 1, 1986).

[55] McBoyle v. United States, 283 U.S. 25 (1931) (due process requires notice to the citizenry as to what conduct is criminal); Cox v. Louisiana, 379 U.S. 559, 579 (1965) (due process regulates selective enforcement of vague statutes).

In *Papachristou v. City of Jacksonville* (1972), the Supreme Court invalidated an ordinance making it a crime to be "vagabonds," "habitual loafers," and so forth. The police arrested two interracial couples for driving around town, "loafing" under this ordinance. A unanimous Court ruled that the "archaic" law violated the Due Process Clause, because it "makes criminal actions which by modern standards are normally innocent," and was therefore enforced mainly against "noncon-formists." This was exactly the problem with the Georgia sodomy law, whose mandatory minimum penalty was greater than the maximum allowed under the *Papachristou* ordinance. Consensual activities within the home have, since colonial times, been legally "innocent," and the state's focus on "homosexual sodomy" alone was evidence that the brunt of its bar to consensual sex was borne by "nonconformists." A *Papachristou*-based theory would have been a better legal basis for Powell's intuitions, for it would have allowed the Court to dispose of *Bowers* on narrow grounds.[56]

2. The Liberty Principle.

As historically understood, the liberty principle provides a plausible foundation for Hardwick's privacy argument. Nineteenth-century America vigorously regulated sexual assaults and public conduct (including cross-dressing), but there is no evidence that the state officially enforced the crime against nature between consenting adults in the home.

Hardwick's problem arose from the fact that the state today is pervasive, a phenomenon completely unanticipated by the Framers. Given current circumstances, the purpose of constitutional "liberty" is to mark off arenas of potential regulation that are least likely to serve public purposes and most likely to harm its targets' ability to flourish as individuals. The state can regulate these marked spaces only when it can demonstrate a tangible public need, such as protection of public health. Within this understanding, *Griswold* remains a paradigm case, because its complete ban of contraceptives was poorly linked to public purposes, such as preventing disease or premarital sex, while its potential effect was to undermine women's ability to control their own lives and plan their own families. Although *Griswold* suggested the privacy line could be drawn around marriage, *Eisenstadt* backed away from such a line. Another precedent provides surprising illumination.

Although no one paid it much attention, *Skinner v. Oklahoma* (1942) offers striking parallels to *Bowers v. Hardwick*. In 1934, Oklahoma provided for sterilization of men convicted of two or more crimes (including sodomy) involving "moral turpitude." As Victoria Nourse

---

[56] Papachristou v. City of Jacksonville, 405 U.S. 156, 161–62, 163–64, 170 (1972) (quotations in text); see Smith v. Goguen, 415 U.S. 566, 575–76 (1974).

shows, this sterilization law was the apotheosis of that era's body politics—yet the Supreme Court struck it down. "The power to sterilize, if exercised, may have subtle, far-reaching and devastating effects. In evil or reckless hands it can cause races or types which are inimical to the dominant group to wither and disappear. There is no redemption for the individual whom the law touches. Any experiment which the State conducts is to his irreparable injury. He is forever deprived of a basic liberty." The ability of the modern state to control an individual's sexuality, against his will and his best interests, is the deepest assault on liberty and can extend beyond sterilization. For sexually active women, state bars to birth control impeded their ability to plan their lives as well as their families. For homosexuals, the crime against nature as presented by the *Bowers* Court was a state effort to commandeer their sexual lives, either forcing them into celibacy or the closet, to achieve highly symbolic or speculative state goals.[57]

Admittedly, Powell and White could not have seen this parallel, because they understood homosexual sodomy to have no connection with family or other productive human relationships; it was, at best, an "addiction." Yet it was clear, by 1986, that theirs was a mistaken attitude. Not only was there a medical consensus that human flourishing required sexual expression, including homosexual expression for many persons, but there was a growing literature demonstrating that lesbians and gay men formed committed relationships whose intimacy involved the crime against nature. Powell and White were unaware of this literature, not because it went unmentioned in the case (it was prominently featured in amicus briefs), but because they were emotionally unable to process it. Such an impulse is understandable for men of their generation, but it is an unacceptable basis for interpreting the liberty protections of the Constitution.

3.   The Anti–Class Legislation Principle.

Skinner was an equal protection, and not just a liberty, case. Similar to *Papachristou*, the Court's decision in *Skinner* emphasized that the statute was aimed at the dispossessed and, as a matter of drafting, exempted white-collar criminals from its extreme sanction. Accordingly, *Skinner* illustrates how the legality, liberty, and equality principles of the Fourteenth Amendment overlap, and how they can work together to yield a verdict against particular state laws. *Bowers'* focus on homosexu-

---

[57] Skinner v. Oklahoma, 316 U.S. 535 (1942); Victoria Nourse, In Evil or Reckless Hands: Science, Crime, and Constitution in New Deal and War—The History of Skinner v. Oklahoma (unpublished manuscript, 2006). For arguments that the privacy cases should protect gay people against the state commandeering their lives, see KARST, supra note 50, 201–06, 226–27; Rubenfeld, supra note 50, at 737–807.

al sodomy reflected a more profound intrusion into equality than the Oklahoma sterilization law had been.

In 1868, there was no social group of "homosexuals" (the term did not even exist). By 1986, homosexuals were a coherent social group in large part because governments had declared their characteristic conduct to be the crime against nature and, based upon that conduct, imposed an array of civil penalties. In Georgia and other states of the South, the open homosexual as a presumptive felon could be excluded from participation in an array of social, economic, and political rights, including: voting and jury service (if convicted of sodomy or even solicitation); military service; opportunities to be municipal police officers, firefighters, or other civil servants; professional licenses; housing (under leases stipulating termination for felonious behavior); public accommodations; civil marriage to one's true love; judicial enforcement of contractual promises or testamentary bequests to a committed lesbian or gay partner; adoption; and raising one's own biological children, where a straight co-parent sought full custody.

The openly lesbian or gay person was an *outlaw*, living outside most of the protections of the rule of law. This regime was not nearly as oppressive as race-based apartheid had been in Georgia, because most homosexuals could avoid these exclusions by remaining in the closet or being discreet in their interactions with state officials. But this *apartheid of the closet* did create a subordinate class potentially excluded from ordinary civic life, based on a stigmatizing trait (homosexuality) that was no more malignant than race or color had been. As Abby Rubenfeld argued in *Bowers*, this regime was a violation of the Fourteenth Amendment's anti-class legislation purpose. This was a conclusion Powell would not have been comfortable announcing in 1986, but it is the strongest *originalist* indictment against consensual sodomy laws. Indeed, the Court reasoned along these lines when it overruled *Bowers* seventeen years later in *Lawrence v. Texas*.[58]

* * *

Sodomy laws are best understood as rejecting the moral acceptability of sexual activities (like drug use) for pleasure alone. Ironically, few of the participants took pleasure from their involvement in *Bowers v. Hardwick*. Retiring from the Court weeks after the decision, Chief Justice Warren Burger felt it was a fitting legacy for his leadership—but

---

[58] Lawrence v. Texas, 539 U.S. 558 (2003) (ruling that the Texas Homosexual Conduct Law violated the right to privacy, and overruling Bowers v. Hardwick, but recognizing the equal protection features of the law's operation). On the civil discriminations against admitted homosexuals or convicted sodomites, see Nan D. Hunter et al., The Rights of Lesbians and Gay Men: The Basic ACLU Guide to a Gay Person's Rights (3d ed. 1992); Rhonda R. Rivera, supra note 50. On the eerie parallel structure of America's anti-homosexual legal regime and that of Nazi Germany, see ESKRIDGE, supra note 50, at 80–83.

in retrospect it epitomized much of what was wrong about Burger's leadership. Along with *Plessy v. Ferguson* (which upheld apartheid), *Bowers* is the most criticized Supreme Court decision of all time that *upheld* a law against constitutional attack. Most of the decisions that have gotten the Court into hot water are those striking down laws, such as *Roe*, which Burger also joined. As *Plessy* had been, the Court's decision in *Bowers* was not just overruled but was repudiated by the *Lawrence* Court.

Poor Byron White did not derive even temporary joy from denying Hardwick's constitutional claim. He took no particular delight in disparaging homosexuals. Yet White's brusque and thoughtless opinion raised the stakes of the culture wars: some traditionalists felt authorized by the Constitution to treat homosexuals like *outlaws*, a proposition that many progressives denounced as lawless as well as ignorant and disrespectful. It is unfair that the only majority opinion history will remember from White will be the sloppy one he dashed off in less than a week to decide *Bowers v. Hardwick*.[59]

William Brennan and Thurgood Marshall were appalled that their votes had enabled the case to get to the Court. Harry Blackmun and John Paul Stevens were disappointed that their arguments had not persuaded more colleagues. Lewis Powell publicly regretted his vote. In a question-and-answer session after delivering the annual James Madison Lecture at NYU's Law School in October 1990, a student asked if there were votes Powell would like to take back. Yes, the vote in *Bowers*. Powell confirmed the answer with a reporter, "When I had the opportunity to reread the opinions a few months later, I thought the dissent had the better of the arguments."[60]

The winning counsel in one of the biggest constitutional cases of the century, Mike Hobbs was happy with his work. He was the slow but sure tortoise who beat the speedy hare, Larry Tribe. (Powell's notes taken during oral argument list Hobbs, "*good lawyer*," a high compliment from the former President of the American Bar Association. After Tribe, Powell wrote: "Torrent of words!") Tribe considers *Bowers* the most disappointing loss of his career, and Bill Stuntz, now Tribe's colleague at the Harvard Law School, unfairly blames himself for not coming up with a better theory to support Powell's intuition. Like Tribe and Stuntz,

---

[59] For varying assessments, compare DENNIS J. HUTCHINSON, THE MAN WHO ONCE WAS WHIZZER WHITE (1998) (White was willing to protect the rights of unmarried fathers but not homosexuals); Meyer, supra note 31 (although poorly informed, White was applying a consistent jurisprudence of restraint in Bowers and other cases); Kate Stith, *Byron R. White, Last of the New Deal Liberals*, 103 YALE L.J. 19, 21–22 (1993) (similar).

[60] Anand Agneshwar, *Ex-Justice Says He May Have Been Wrong*, NAT'L L.J., Nov. 5, 1990, at 3; JEFFRIES, supra note 25, 530.

Kathy Wilde did a brilliant job seeking justice in Hardwick's case and
laments the loss. That her side came so close to winning makes the
disappointment keener.

What of the parties? Prosecutor Lewis Slaton and Police Commissioner George Napper, both of whom dropped out of the case, lamented
the Court's opinion in *Bowers*, because they thought the law was a relic
of a past best forgotten. Hardwick and Bowers regretted the glare of
publicity, as both were rather private men. For the openly straight
Attorney General, it is ironic that "gay rights" and "sodomy" will
always be associated with his name, as generations of law students will
still read the case the Supreme Court has short-handed as *Bowers*. His
political career ended in 1998 when he lost a race for governor, shortly
after his confession to *The New York Times* that he had been engaged in
a long-term adulterous affair while the state's chief legal officer. After a
decade of distinguished work in private practice, including representation of people of color who had been victims of race discrimination,
Bowers was in 2006 voted a Leadership Award by the Atlanta Bar
Association. Even this honor was soured, in small part, by objections
from the Stonewall Bar Association that the award should not be
granted because of Bowers's "discriminatory and hypocritical legacy."[61]

Michael Hardwick found his life's calling after the Supreme Court
decision: he became a successful scene designer for events held in
southern Florida, to which he returned soon after his arrest. He believed
that his constitutional experience, and the astounding Supreme Court
defeat, liberated his artistic imagination; his new-found visibility enabled
him to succeed as an "optical alchemist," the occupation listed on his
black-trimmed business card. Working mostly with chicken wire and
paper mache, Hardwick designed fabulous party spaces in bars and
discotheques all over southern Florida. The Fort Lauderdale bar Squeeze
hired him as its permanent set designer, and he created an "atomic
garden" for the club. "In this place illuminated by black light, Hardwick's glowing green vines, with leaves as large as elephant ears, curl
through purple-blue rafters. Sensuous flowers dot the vine. Giant red
heliconias stand in a vase by the door. A phorphorescent green pterodac-
tyl hovers overhead."[62]

As his artistic work flourished, however, Hardwick became more
personally reclusive. His experiences in Atlanta "had a chilling effect on
me. I have not had a steady relationship since then," he recalled in 1990.
Hanging out with just family members (such as his nephew Robert) and

---

[61] Kevin Sack, *Georgia Candidate for Governor [Bowers] Admits Adultery and Resigns
Commission in Guard*, N.Y. TIMES, June 6, 1997, at A1.

[62] Jill Young Miller, *The Metamorphosis of Michael*, MIAMI SUN-SENTINEL, Sept. 10, 1989,
at E1, E4 (quotation in text).

his white shepherd dog Jumbo, Hardwick spent long hours creating art, often with the music of celloist YoYoMa in the background. At the same time Hardwick was finding peace in his soul, he was losing his body. Within a year of the Court's decision, he had thrush around his neck. His immune system was severely compromised by 1989, and Michael became frail. In 1990, his mother and his sisters Alice and Susan moved him to live with them in Archer, Florida. His once-athletic body wasted away, shriveling to sixty-five pounds. On June 13, 1991, Michael Hardwick died of complications associated with AIDS. His mother Kitty and brother Patrick sprinkled his ashes in the Gulf of Mexico near Naples, Florida.[63]

---

[63] Tracie Cone, *Landmark by Design*, MIAMI HERALD, Dec. 17, 1990, at 1C–2C (quotation in text); Interview with Robert Hardwick Weston (Michael Hardwick's nephew), in New York City (West Village) (Jan. 22, 2004); Telephone Interview with Susan Browning Chriss (Michael's sister) (Oct. 6, 2006).

"Michael Hardwick, 1954–1991"

9

Lynda G. Dodd*

DeShaney v. Winnebago County: Governmental Neglect and "The Blessings of Liberty"

I. Joshua DeShaney and the "Blessings of Liberty"

On March 8, 1984, almost two weeks before his fifth birthday, Joshua DeShaney fell into a coma after suffering a brutal beating at the hands of his father.[1] When brain surgery was performed to save Joshua's life, doctors discovered evidence of repeated head trauma and bruises all over his body. In the constitutional litigation that followed, the courts concluded that the state authorities should not be held liable for failing to protect Joshua from the abuse that ultimately left him partially paralyzed and profoundly brain damaged.[2]

---

* Thanks to Jessica Davidson for her research assistance, and to the editors of this volume for their helpful comments.

[1] Paul Reidinger, *Why Did No One Protect This Child?* A.B.A. JOURNAL 48 (Dec. 1, 1988).

[2] *DeShaney v. Winnebago County Dep't of Soc. Servs.*, 489 U.S. 189 (1989). The facts presented here and in the following paragraphs are derived from Chief Justice Rehnquist's opinion, Judge Posner's opinion for the Seventh Circuit, *DeShaney v. Winnebago County Dep't of Social Servs.*, 812 F.2d 298 (7th Cir. 1987); the unpublished opinion of the district court below, *DeShaney v. DeShaney*, No. 85–C–310, slip op. at 3–14 (E.D. Wis. June 20, 1986), reprinted in the Appendix to the Petition for Certiorari at 35–53, *DeShaney*, 489 U.S. 189 (No. 87–154); the Brief for Petitioner, *DeShaney*, 489 U.S. 189 (No. 87–154); the Brief for Respondent, *DeShaney*, 489 U.S. 189 (No. 87–154); and the Joint Appendix to the merits briefs, *DeShaney*, 489 U.S. 189 (No. 87–154). The lengthy Joint Appendix is a particularly important resource for background information on the *DeShaney* case. The Joint Appendix compiles a number of sources of factual details not mentioned in the legal briefs and court opinions, such as notes from DSS caseworker Ann Kemmeter's case files

The courts absolved the state authorities of all responsibility despite the fact that, for the fourteen-month period before that final beating, Joshua had been under the care and supervision of the Winnebago County Department of Social Services (DSS).[3] In fact, DSS received its first notification of suspected abuse more than two years before Joshua's final beating. This initial report came in January 1982, when the lawyer handling divorce proceedings for Joshua's stepmother, Christine DeShaney, called the Neenah, Wisconsin Police Department to inform them that Joshua's father, Randy DeShaney, was abusing his son. After a brief investigation, DSS decided against taking any action.[4]

One year later, in January 1983, Joshua had suffered such serious injuries that Randy DeShaney's new girlfriend—his former sister-in-law, Marie DeShaney—took Joshua to the local hospital, the Theda Clark Regional Medical Center, for treatment of multiple bruises and abrasions. Marie explained to the doctors that the bruises might have been caused by another toddler hitting Joshua in the forehead with a metal toy truck. His medical report, however, indicated there were bruises and abrasions on Joshua's forehead, cheek, scalp, spine, arms, buttocks, penis, upper thighs, ankles and heel.[5]

When the emergency room physician and hospital social worker notified DSS of suspected child abuse, the agency finally took action and obtained an order from a Wisconsin juvenile court placing Joshua in the temporary custody of the hospital.[6] The county assigned a Child Protection Team—which included a pediatrician, psychologist, police officer, a Winnebago County assistant corporation counsel, and DSS caseworkers—to review Joshua's case.[7] After a three-day investigation, including interviews with Randy, Marie, and Christine DeShaney, the Child Protection Team concluded that the child abuse allegations were "unfounded."[8] However, before officially relinquishing custody of Joshua, they negotiated a voluntary contract with Randy, asking him to seek counseling, to move Marie out of his house (there was some suspicion that she had caused the injuries),[9] and to ensure that Joshua would be placed in a

and excerpts from over 3700 pages of depositions taken during the course of the *DeShaney* litigation.

[3] *DeShaney,* 489 U.S. at 192.

[4] Brief for Petitioner, *supra* note 2, at 8; Joint Appendix, *supra* note 2, at 159–60, 163–64.

[5] Joint Appendix, *supra* note 2, at 107–8, 111.

[6] *Id.* at 107–8.

[7] *Id.* at 45–46.

[8] *Id.* at 107–14.

[9] *Id.* at 59, 63.

Head Start preschool program, where presumably his well-being would be more closely monitored.[10] Randy DeShaney agreed to those requests and Joshua was returned to his custody.

In the internal report filed by DSS, Joshua's new caseworker, Ann Kemmeter, indicated in a notation that, while the allegations against the DeShaneys were dismissed, she would "refer it back into Court should there be any further injuries to this child of an unexplained origin."[11] Just a few weeks later, on March 15, 1983, Joshua was again sent to the emergency room for treatment. Although the hospital social worker filed another report to notify DSS that Joshua had suffered another blow to his head, Kemmeter concluded there was no basis for action.[12]

For the next year, Kemmeter conducted home visits to monitor Joshua's care. She kept detailed notes regarding suspicious injuries—including bruises and bumps on Joshua's forehead, a scratched cornea, and cigarette burns—but she did not attempt to investigate their cause.[13] When she learned that Marie had joined Randy and Joshua in a move to a new home in Oshkosh, Wisconsin, Kemmeter still did nothing to intervene, accepting without question their claims that their relationship had improved following the move.[14]

On November 30, 1983, Joshua was once again taken to the emergency room. Hospital officials at Mercy Medical Center in Oshkosh notified DSS of a head injury, a bloody nose, a swollen ear, and bruised shoulders.[15] After Randy DeShaney offered the explanation that Joshua had injured himself in the bathroom, Kemmeter again decided not to intervene.[16]

During this same period, a Head Start social worker, Ruth Davis, visited the DeShaney home and found that Joshua had been left alone and unsupervised. Davis tried repeatedly to contact DSS to inform Joshua's caseworkers of this incident, but received no immediate response from the agency.[17]

---

[10] *Id.* at 112–14, 170–71.

[11] *Id.* at 170.

[12] *Id.* at 115, 120–21.

[13] *Id.* at 114–21; see also the lengthy summary of incidents and injuries at *id.* at 132–37.

[14] *Id.* at 114–15. From the time the DeShaneys moved to Oshkosh in June 1983 to January 1984, the police responded to at least five complaint calls reporting domestic disputes in the DeShaney household. *See id.* at 6–7, 151.

[15] *Id.* at 119–120.

[16] *Id.* at 121.

[17] Petition for Certiorari at 8, *DeShaney*, 489 U.S. 189 (No. 87–154); Joint Appendix, *supra* note 2, at 186–87. Kemmeter later asserted that she scolded the Head Start social

On each of her next two monthly visits to the DeShaney home, Kemmeter was told that Joshua was either sleeping or too ill to see her. She made no further inquiries, although her social services review report in January 1984 offers for the first time some evidence of her growing suspicions about Joshua's "accident-prone" behavior. She attached to her case notes the domestic violence reports from the Oshkosh Police Department, and she described her suspicion that Marie may be retaliating against Joshua out of frustration resulting from Randy's abusive behavior towards her.[18] Yet Kemmeter made no further attempts to investigate, even when she was told that Joshua was unable to see her during her visits to the DeShaney home in February and March.[19] Indeed, she had not seen Joshua in person since the previous November. The next time she would see Joshua, on March 8, 1984, his bruised body would be lying unconscious in a hospital bed.

When the Mercy Medical Center phoned Kemmeter to notify her of Joshua's catastrophic head injury, she drove to the hospital and met first with Marie DeShaney, who told her that Joshua had fallen down four basement stairs and hit his head. Kemmeter later asserted that she then expressed concern about Joshua's numerous accidental injuries, but Marie insisted that was the true explanation.[20] In Kemmeter's case notes, she reports that she then encountered Randy DeShaney, who approached her crying, shaking violently, clearly upset, stating that if anything happened to Joshua he would have no reason to live. Kemmeter attempted to help calm Randy, and she arranged for him to receive a sedative from the hospital staff.[21]

Kemmeter then called the Oshkosh police department to report the incident. While waiting for the officers to arrive, she visited Joshua's room, and she reports in her notes that she observed that Joshua had bruises on his cheeks, as well as a "line type bruise" across his neck.[22] When the two Oshkosh police officers, Detective Novotny and Officer Kronenwetter, arrived, both Marie and Randy were sitting by Joshua's side. Still crying but sedated, Randy was stroking Joshua's hair when the

---

worker for not calling the police if she truly believed that Joshua was in any danger that afternoon. When following up on the report, Kemmeter apparently accepted the explanations of Randy and Marie DeShaney, who claimed that they had just left Joshua alone for fifteen minutes while they went to the corner to use a pay phone. Brief for Respondent, *supra* note 2, at 11, n. 7; Joint Appendix, *supra* note 2, at 188–90.

[18] Joint Appendix, *supra* note 2; *Id.* at 120–21.

[19] *Id.* at 133–35.

[20] *Id.* at 122.

[21] *Id.* at 122–23.

[22] *Id.* at 124.

officers entered the room.[23] Randy repeatedly asked Kemmeter why it
was necessary to speak to the police, and though he eventually cooperated with the request, Randy reminded her, "Ann, you know Joshua
bruises easily."[24]

Kemmeter and the detectives then met with Joshua's surgeon, who
told them that Joshua had a 25 percent chance of surviving the surgery
that evening. Detective Novotny phoned the district attorney's office to
inform them there was a likely homicide case.[25]

It was at this point that Kemmeter spoke with Joshua's mother,
Melody DeShaney, for the first time. During all the months that Kemmeter had been monitoring the situation with Joshua, she knew that his
mother still resided in Cheyenne, Wyoming, where Joshua was born and
where his parents divorced.[26] Although she had never notified Melody
about the abuse allegations, Kemmeter finally decided to notify Melody
to tell her that her son would likely die.[27] Melody and her mother, Myrna
Bridgewater, later claimed that Kemmeter had confided to them, soon
after their arrival at Mercy Medical Center, "I just knew one day I would
pick up the phone and learn that Joshua was dead."[28]

After the surgery, Kemmeter and the DeShaneys were told that a
large portion of Joshua's skull had been removed in order to relieve
pressure on his brain, and that he would remain in the intensive care
unit indefinitely. His surgeon, Dr. Marc Letellier, predicted that it could
be weeks before Joshua could wake up, if he ever did regain consciousness. The surgeon then met with the Oshkosh police detectives, Kemmeter, DSS supervisor Cheryl Stelse, and other Mercy staff members. He
told the group that there was no indication of any stress fracture on
Joshua's skull, which indicated to him that the explanation that Joshua
fell down the stairs was false. Instead, there appeared to be several areas
of older bruising, which were evident only after Joshua's head was
shaved in preparation for surgery. During the surgery, Dr. Letellier
discovered that a group of blood vessels had been detached from Joshua's

---

[23] *Id.* at 124.

[24] *Id.* at 124.

[25] *Id.* at 125.

[26] When Joshua was fourteen months old, Melody DeShaney agreed to surrender
custody to his father, but she continued to send monthly child support payments and
apparently made numerous attempts to contact Randy to check on Joshua's care. *See id.* at
73–82.

[27] Petition for Certiorari, *supra* note 17, at 10–11. In her case notes, Kemmeter states
that she first received Melody's phone number from Randy DeShaney after Joshua suffered
his final beating. Joint Appendix, *supra* note 2, at 136.

[28] Petition for Certiorari, *supra* note 17, at 11; Joint Appendix, *supra* note 2, at 104–05.

skull, resulting in severe internal bleeding. According to the surgeon, this type of injury is consistent with injuries produced by severe, violent shaking.[29] Because these injuries required a physically strong perpetrator, the Oshkosh detectives began to focus their investigation on Randy DeShaney.[30]

Following this meeting, Joshua was again placed in the temporary custody of the hospital. The assistant corporation counsel for Winnebago County, John Bodnar, was notified of the new abuse allegations, and the Oshkosh Police Department began its own investigation. Detective Novotny first conducted a series of interviews with the staff of Mercy Medical Center. The treating pediatrician, Dr. B.F. Kayali, who initially examined Joshua after his arrival at Mercy on March 8, told Novotny that, in addition to older bruises covering most of Joshua's body, there were also fresh deep purple bruises, on his face, buttocks and upper thighs. Dr. Kayali estimated that the new bruises covered 50 to 75 percent of Joshua's lower body, and he would later testify during Randy DeShaney's criminal trial that he had never observed physical injuries as alarming as those suffered by Joshua DeShaney.[31]

The Oshkosh police detectives also interviewed associates and neighbors of the DeShaneys, and they were able to gather corroborating testimony describing the abuse of Joshua by both Randy and Marie DeShaney that had occurred over the past several months.[32] On May 30, Randy DeShaney was arrested and charged with two counts of child abuse, one count of conduct regardless of life, and five counts of misdemeanor battery against Marie (these last charges were later dropped after Marie refused to cooperate with the prosecutors).[33] In December of 1984, Randy entered an "Alford" plea, which allowed him to accept a plea bargain without admitting to being guilty of the two felony charges against him. At the February, 1985 sentencing hearing,

---

[29] *Id.* at 127.

[30] LYNNE CURRY, THE DESHANEY CASE: CHILD ABUSE, FAMILY RIGHTS, AND THE DILEMMA OF STATE INTERVENTION 65 (2007) (discussing the criminal case against Randy DeShaney).

[31] CURRY, *supra* note 30, at 63.

[32] Joint Appendix, *supra* note 2, at 151–54.

[33] CURRY, *supra* note 30, at 66, 76. Wisconsin's criminal provision 940.201, " 'Abuse of Children,' defined 'child' as a person under sixteen years of age and defined the crime of abuse as a Class E felony, applicable to 'whoever tortures a child or subjects a child to cruel maltreatment, including, but not limited to, severe bruising, lacerations, fractured bones, burns, internal injuries or any injury constituting great bodily harm....' " Those found guilty could be punished with a fine of $10,000 or a prison sentence of not more than two years, or both. *Id.* at 66. Detective Novotny later recalled recommending that his investigation had uncovered enough evidence to charge Randy DeShaney with attempted manslaughter, but the district attorney declined to pursue the charge. *Id.* at 76.

the judge sentenced him to the maximum penalty of two years for each count—four years in total. Randy entered the Dodge Correctional Institution in Waupun, Wisconsin the following week. He was paroled after two years and seven months, and served the remainder of his sentence in a local drug treatment facility.[34]

Joshua's condition improved slightly in the weeks following the final incident, but he remained in the Pediatric Unit from late March until June 5, 1984. One of the brain scans performed during his stay at the Mercy Medical Center showed that he was brain dead on the right side of his brain, but after a second surgery to insert a metal plate in his head where a large portion of his skull had been removed in the first surgery, there was an immediate improvement in Joshua's condition. This second surgery produced some hope that, with extensive physical therapy, his cognitive and physical skills might improve significantly.[35] Upon his release from the hospital, Joshua was sent to the Central Wisconsin Center for the Developmentally Disabled, a state-supported institution in Madison, Wisconsin.[36] As his condition improved, the staff at Central Center recommended that he be transferred to the Gillette Rehabilitation Center in St. Paul, Minnesota, where his recovery proved to be slower than expected. In September of 1984, Joshua remained partially paralyzed and unable to speak or respond to verbal commands, but after months of physical therapy he was able to regain some use of his limbs on the right side of his body.[37] Joshua later left the Gillette Center, and had spent a number of years living in a series of foster homes when the Supreme Court heard his case in 1988.[38] Today, Joshua lives in a Wisconsin group home for severely disabled adults.[39]

Years later, looking back on these events, Ann Kemmeter told a reporter, "I am very sorry for Joshua, but the bottom line is, I'm not the one who abused him ... given the information we had at the time as it was given to us, I don't think there was anything we could have done differently."[40]

II. Civil Rights Litigation and "Constitutional Torts"

In her recent book on the *DeShaney* case, historian Lynne Curry traces the development of child protective services bureaucracies, focus-

[34] *Id.* at 79–81.

[35] Joint Appendix, *supra* note 2, at 139–40.

[36] *Id.* at 139.

[37] *Id.* at 140–41; CURRY, *supra* note 30, at 78.

[38] CURRY, *supra* note 30, at 82.

[39] Joint Appendix, *supra* note 2, at 144.

[40] Nat Hentoff, *No Comment from Joshua*, WASH. POST, Mar. 18, 1989, at A27.

ing especially on their assignment of dual roles to caseworkers, like Ann Kemmeter, who must simultaneously offer therapeutic services to families while also serving as the government's chief investigator.[41] It is certainly true that a careful review of Kemmeter's case files suggests that she had considerable difficulty shifting from the role of family advocate to skeptical investigator. Explaining why such failures to intervene remain so common today, however, requires more attention to the *legal* dimensions of these cases, especially the role of civil rights litigation in efforts to hold the government accountable for the injuries inflicted on children like Joshua.

When Joshua's mother, Melody DeShaney, sued the Winnebago County DSS in order to seek compensatory damages on behalf of her son, she, like thousands of other plaintiffs do every year, relied on 42 U.S.C. § 1983—the primary statutory vehicle individuals use to vindicate their constitutional rights against state and local government officials and municipalities. For civil rights advocates, constitutional tort litigation is an indispensable tool of civil rights enforcement in the modern administrative, welfare state.[42] Because the development of government programs designed to protect children from abuse[43] coincided with the growth of civil rights litigation, it is not surprising that, throughout the 1980s, an increasingly large category of § 1983 cases targeted governmental efforts to protect abused and neglected children.

In these lawsuits, plaintiffs sued child welfare and other governmental agencies for their "failure to protect" them from harm. For a number of doctrinal reasons,[44] these "failure to protect" claims were rarely successful. Under the existing two-step framework for § 1983 litigation, the first hurdle plaintiffs must pass over requires establishing the existence of a constitutional violation. The next step is showing the government entity or official defendant is liable for the injury. The problem with failure to protect cases is that the first hurdle is deemed insurmountable, because in most of these cases, the direct source of the injury or harm is typically a *private* actor, like Joshua DeShaney's

---

[41] Curry, *supra* note 30, at 8.

[42] For an overview of the law of § 1983, see Sheldon H. Nahmod, Civil Rights and Civil Liberties Litigation: The Law of Section 1983 (2006 ed.).

[43] *See* Lela B. Costin et al., The Politics of Child Abuse in America Ch. 4 (1996) (providing an overview of federal child abuse and neglect legislation).

[44] Whether due to concerns about docket pressures resulting from the dramatic growth of cases brought under § 1983 or fears about the consequences of expanding governmental liability, the law of § 1983 has been interpreted in a pervasively anti-plaintiff manner in recent years. For more on these developments, see Lynda Dodd, Securing the Blessings of Liberty: The History and Politics of Constitutional Torts Litigation Ch. 4 (2004) (unpublished Ph.D. dissertation, Princeton Univ.) (on file with author).

father. When there is no state actor serving as the direct cause of the harm, courts have concluded that the "state action requirement" for a Fourteenth Amendment violation cannot be satisfied. The inquiry generally ends at this point, and so all of the remaining questions related to the second step—the liability inquiry addressing such issues as individual officer immunity defenses or the municipal policy or custom requirement—are never even reached.[45]

This focus on the state action requirement is understandable. The protections of the Constitution have traditionally been understood to provide *constraints* on government—not affirmative duties with which the government must comply. Because the principal aim of liberal constitutionalism is to protect citizens from arbitrary abuses of government power, the conventional wisdom has long held that constitutional rights are meant to limit state action, and that the Constitution is thus properly deemed a "charter of negative liberties."[46] Constitutional rights discourse has largely consisted of charging the government with negative duties of non-interference, rather than positive, affirmative duties or guarantees, in order to establish a protected "realm" of private authority.

However, in a series of cases during the 1970s and 1980s, lower federal courts recognized exceptions to this general approach. This is a crucial issue because, if the government has an affirmative duty to protect, then *the failure to act* could satisfy the state action requirement under the Fourteenth Amendment. The key issue in these cases concerns what circumstances would trigger a governmental affirmative duty to protect individuals like Joshua DeShaney from private violence. In these affirmative duties cases, federal judges introduced two major doctrinal theories holding the government responsible for failures to act: (1) the custody limitation and (2) the state-created danger requirement.

A. "Special Relationships" and the Custody Limitation

The "custody doctrine" is based on the acknowledgment that the state's physical custody of individuals gives rise to governmental affirmative duties to protect individuals from harm. The rationale for this exception to the general rule against affirmative duties focuses on the

[45] In *DeShaney*, as with other failure to protect cases, even if the first hurdle had been overcome, the individual defendants likely still would have won because Kemmeter and Stelse could claim a qualified immunity defense, on the grounds that the due process doctrine for failures to protect was not clearly established. It also would have been difficult to satisfy the post-*Monell* doctrinal tests for determining whether a "policy or custom" of the government agency caused the injury. *See* Brief for Respondent, *supra* note 2, at 57–64 (applying the qualifying immunity and "policy or custom" doctrines to the *DeShaney* case).

[46] Bowers v. De Vito, 686 F.2d 616, 618 (7th Cir. 1982).

state's assumption of complete control over the individual.[47] In such circumstances, the state enters into a "special relationship" with the individual in custody, which in turn triggers the assignment of an affirmative duty upon the state to make certain that basic needs are met. The Supreme Court first acknowledged this special relationship in *Estelle v. Gamble*, a case involving the affirmative duty of prison officials to provide medical care to prisoners.[48] In *Youngberg v. Romeo*, the Court extended this custody-based affirmative duty doctrine to apply to patients committed to state mental health institutions.[49]

When applying this doctrine to cases involving abused children, the lower federal courts divided on the issue of the custody limitation's scope.[50] A few circuits—including the Fourth Circuit in *Jensen v. Conrad*[51] and the Third Circuit in *Estate of Bailey by Oare v. County of York*,[52]—held that child welfare agencies could be held responsible for failing to protect children under their supervision, even if they remained in the physical custody of their parents.

In *Jensen v. Conrad*, the Fourth Circuit asserted in dicta that "a right to affirmative protection need not be limited to a determination that there was a 'custodial relationship.' "[53] Because the court disposed of the case on qualified immunity grounds, it did not take the opportunity to offer a full assessment of the circumstances that might trigger an affirmative duty to protect, but the opinion did offer a list of additional factors it considered relevant to the inquiry, including whether the state had expressly stated its desire to provide affirmative protection to a particular class or specific individuals, and whether the state knew of a victim's plight.[54]

---

[47] Youngberg v. Romeo, 457 U.S. 307, 317 (1982) (holding that a duty is triggered when the person is "wholly dependent on the State").

[48] 429 U.S. 97, 106 (1976) (limiting liability under the Eighth Amendment to cases involving "deliberate indifference to serious medical needs").

[49] 457 U.S. 307 (1982). *Youngberg* is also significant because the Court acknowledged that the affirmative duty to protect doctrine encompassed not only Eighth Amendment violations but also claims relying on the substantive due process clause.

[50] The Second and Eleventh Circuits extended the custody analogy to the foster care system, holding that the government has an affirmative duty to protect children placed in the care of foster parents. *See* Doe v. N.Y. City Dep't of Soc. Servs., 649 F.2d 134, 141 (2d Cir. 1981) ("Doe I"); Doe v. N.Y. City Dep't of Soc. Servs., 709 F. 2d 782 (2d Cir. 1983) ("Doe II"); Taylor v. Ledbetter, 818 F.2d 791 (11th Cir. 1987).

[51] 747 F. 2d 185 (4th Cir. 1984).

[52] 768 F.2d 503 (3d Cir. 1985).

[53] 747 F. 2d at 194 (citing Fox v. Custis, 712 F. 2d 84 (4th Cir. 1983)).

[54] *Id.* at 195, n.11.

LYNDA G. DODD   195

In the *Estate of Bailey* case, child protection workers were accused of
failing to protect a five-year-old girl, Aleta Bailey, from abuse by her
mother and her mother's boyfriend. Despite receiving reports from
relatives and physicians about the abuse, the child's social workers
released her to the custody of her mother and then failed to ensure that
the mother's boyfriend moved out of the residence. According to the
complaint, the agency never followed up with an additional investigation
of Aleta's welfare, and just one month later she died from injuries caused
by her mother and the boyfriend.[55] The Third Circuit applied the *Jensen*
factors to Aleta's case—focusing in particular on the agency's awareness
of a special danger to Aleta—and vacated the district court's dismissal of
the complaint.[56]

B.   State–Created Danger Theory

As developed in a series of Seventh Circuit opinions, the "state-
created danger" doctrine focuses on the state's involvement in placing
the individual in a position of danger.[57] No analogies to custodial relationships are required and the state-created danger need not involve any
formal relationship between the government and the victim. Under this
approach, even if it is a private actor that later causes an injury, so long
as the state *created* the danger, it can be held liable for failing to protect
the individual. In Judge Richard Posner's view, "[i]f the state puts a
man in a position of danger from private persons and then fails to
protect him, it will not be heard to say that its role was merely passive;
it is as much an active tortfeasor as if it had thrown him in a snake
pit."[58]

The doctrine was significantly limited in subsequent Seventh Circuit
opinions to emphasize that the danger must be *imposed* by the state and
that if individuals encouraged the creation of the danger, they voluntarily assumed the risk of any ensuing injuries. As Judge Frank Easterbrook
pithily concluded in *Walker v. Rowe*, "[t]he state must protect those it
throws into snake pits, but the state need not guarantee that volunteer
snake charmers will not be bitten."[59]

---

[55] 768 F.2d at 505.

[56] *Id.* at 510–11.

[57] An early example of this approach can be found in *White v. Rochford*, where the
Seventh Circuit applied a state-created danger theory to a case involving police officers who
arrested the driver of a car containing three child passengers. When the police took the
driver into custody and abandoned the children, they became liable for subjecting the
children to a "health-endangering situation." White v. Rochford, 592 F. 2d 381, 382 (7th
Cir. 1979).

[58] Bowers v. Devito, 686 F.2d 616, 618 (7th Cir. 1982).

[59] Walker v. Rowe, 791 F.2d 507, 511 (7th Cir. 1986).

The state-created danger theory is vague enough that it remains susceptible to varying applications. Consider the facts at issue in *Jackson v. City of Joliet*,[60] a case involving a car accident that resulted in the car bursting into flames. A Joliet police officer came upon the scene, where, after calling the fire department, he began directing traffic away from the area. He never attempted to check the status of the car's passengers, nor did he call an ambulance. It is possible to describe the police officer's actions in directing possible sources of help away from the scene as a state-created danger, but Judge Posner offered a different analysis. He conceded that botched rescue efforts may make victims worse off, but he distinguished *White v. Rochford* and other state-created danger cases on the grounds that here, in the *Joliet* case, the victims were already in grave danger before the police officer arrived on the scene. Because the state played no role in the initial car crash, it should not be held liable for the events that followed.[61] From these initial cases, it appeared that the Seventh Circuit was eager to prevent the state-created danger doctrine from becoming a fruitful legal theory for plaintiffs seeking to hold the government accountable for its failures to protect.

III. Lower Court Proceedings

Given these Seventh Circuit opinions, the prospects for DeShaney's lawsuit appeared dim. But Melody DeShaney was determined to find a way to provide for Joshua's care and to ensure that nothing similar ever happened to another child in Winnebago County.[62] After she returned from her visit to Oshkosh, she contacted a local personal injury lawyer, Donald J. Sullivan, and met with him to discuss Joshua's situation. He told her that, compared to a tort claim in state court, her prospects for winning a federal civil rights lawsuit were much lower, but the ability to sue for full compensatory as well as punitive damages could make a federal lawsuit worth attempting.[63] Because the case was filed in the Federal District Court for the Eastern District of Wisconsin, Sullivan

---

[60] Jackson v. City of Joliet, 715 F.2d 1200 (7th Cir. 1983).

[61] 715 F.2d at 1204; *see also* Archie v. City of Racine, 847 F.2d 1211, 1215 (7th Cir. 1988).

[62] William Glaberson, *Determined to Be Heard: Four Americans and Their Journey to the Supreme Court*, N.Y. TIMES MAG., Oct. 2, 1988, at 34. A state law tort claim was thought to be a much less attractive option, because, at the time when Joshua DeShaney was injured, the damages cap for claims against the state of Wisconsin was set at $50,000. The *annual* costs of Joshua's medical care would far exceed the cap on total damages imposed by the state.

[63] CURRY, *supra* note 30, at 84. *See also* Joint Appendix, *supra* note 2, at 17–18 (reproducing the *DeShaney* complaint, which requests $50 million in compensatory damages and $50 million in punitive damages).

arranged for local co-counsel, Curry First, the litigation director for the Legal Aid Society of Milwaukee, Wisconsin, to join the case.[64]

Their legal strategy centered on the recent opinions in *Jensen*[65] and *Estate of Bailey*,[66] both of which had endorsed an expansion of the custody limitation by assigning to the government an affirmative duty to protect children under the care of their child protective services agencies. These opinions had emphasized that sufficient awareness by the government of the dangers faced by the child could trigger an affirmative duty to protect. So, in order to show that the Winnebago County DSS had sufficient knowledge of the serious dangers Joshua faced, Sullivan and First early on realized the importance of discovery: they decided to conduct extensive depositions, and to gather extensive exhibits, including photographs and videotapes of Joshua, medical evidence such as x-rays and CAT scans, and other illustrations and diagrams to explain the extent of Joshua's injuries.[67] Their greatest hope was for a favorable ruling in the district court that would pave the way for serious settlement negotiations.[68]

These hopes were soon defeated. Judge John W. Reynolds (former governor of Wisconsin and now chief judge of the United States District Court for the Eastern District of Wisconsin) was assigned to the *DeShaney* case. In January of 1986, Mark Mingo and Wayne Yankala, the lawyers representing the Winnebago County DSS, Kemmeter, and her supervisor, Cheryl Stelse, filed a motion to dismiss.[69] In their motion, they argued that no special relationship existed between Joshua and the Winnebago County DSS. They emphasized that the social services agreement between DSS and Randy DeShaney was a purely voluntary one, and that neither DSS nor Kemmeter had retained any control or responsibility for the events that occurred during the period they offered services to the DeShaney family. They also argued that Kemmeter and Stelse enjoyed a qualified immunity defense from the lawsuit, because the law regarding the duty to protect was not clearly established at the time the injuries occurred.[70]

[64] CURRY, *supra* note 30, at 89–90.

[65] 747 F.2d 185 (4th Cir. 1984).

[66] 768 F.2d 503 (3d Cir. 1985).

[67] CURRY, *supra* note 30, at 94.

[68] *Id.* at 101. Both lawyers realized they had little chance of winning on appeal, because the Seventh Circuit was filled with appellate judges known to be hostile to their arguments.

[69] The Wisconsin Attorney General represented the other public defendants—the State of Wisconsin, the Wisconsin Department of Health and Social Services, and its Secretary, Linda Rivetz. The claims against these defendants were soon dismissed on Eleventh Amendment state sovereign immunity grounds.

[70] CURRY, *supra* note 30, at 96.

After receiving the motion to dismiss, Judge Reynolds informed the parties that he intended to convert the filing into a motion for summary judgment. This procedural step allowed Reynolds to consider additional materials, and he gave the parties thirty days to submit any other briefs, affidavits, and depositions they had prepared. The DeShaneys' lawyers were dismayed by these developments. They believed that the legal questions in the case—centering on whether a special relationship existed—depended on the full development of a factual record.[71]

On June 20, 1986, Judge Reynolds granted the defendants' motion for summary judgment, finding that there was no special relationship established between the Winnebago County DSS and Joshua Deshaney.[72] He agreed that an affirmative duty to protect may be triggered by a custodial relationship or a state-created danger, but he concluded that neither existed in this case.[73] Reynolds also specifically declined to accept the plaintiffs' proposal to expand the definition of a special relationship in the manner of the Third Circuit's *Estate of Bailey* opinion, which had focused in particular on the state's knowledge of the danger Aleta Bailey faced.[74] Describing the *Bailey* approach as "unsound," Reynolds emphasized the slippery slope problem he considered to be inherent in the *Bailey* expansion of the special relationship doctrine—the result that every social welfare program would become "a charter of constitutionally sanctioned social and economic 'rights' . . . ."[75]

First and Sullivan filed their appellate briefs in the Court of Appeals for the Seventh Circuit in September, 1986, and the *DeShaney* oral argument was scheduled for January 13, 1987. The three-judge panel assigned to the case included Judges Richard Posner, John Coffey, and Robert Grant, sitting by designation from the Northern District of Indiana.

The Seventh Circuit panel issued its opinion on February 12, 1987. Judge Posner wrote the opinion rejecting Joshua DeShaney's claims, citing the "well established" case law in the Seventh Circuit holding that the state's failure to protect individuals from private violence is not a

---

[71] *Id.* at 98.

[72] *DeShaney v. DeShaney*, No. 85–C–310, slip op. at 3–14 (E.D. Wis. June 20, 1986), reprinted in the Appendix to the Petition for Certiorari, *supra* note 2, at 35–53.

[73] Appendix to the Petition for Certiorari, *supra* note 2, at 46.

[74] *Id.* at 46–47.

[75] *Id.* at 48.

deprivation of a constitutional right.[76] According to Posner, in order to establish a due process violation, the plaintiff needed to show a state actor "deprived" him of his liberty. The social workers employed by the Winnebago DSS certainly did not *directly* cause Joshua's injuries. Nor, according to Posner, were they indirectly responsible. Because "deprivation implies causation," the plaintiffs needed to establish that DSS in some way "increased the probability of Joshua's injuries."[77] In assessing such an argument, Posner posed a hypothetical, asking whether Joshua would still have sustained his injuries if DSS had never existed. Posner surmised that he would have: "It is unlikely that Ann Kemmeter's well intentioned but ineffectual intervention did Joshua any good at all, but it is most unlikely that it did him any harm. She merely failed to protect him from his bestial father."[78]

Posner acknowledged that Kemmeter acted recklessly when she failed to act on the growing evidence of abuse, but he also stressed that, by that point, Joshua was in the lawful custody of his father.[79] At this later stage, when the abuse recommenced, the state itself did not *create* the danger. It "merely" failed to protect him from an abusive family environment the state had no responsibility for creating.[80] Thus, in Posner's view, what occurred to Joshua was "botched rescue," not a deprivation by the state.

In his discussion of the "botched rescue" argument, Posner emphasized that the traditional common law tort theory of detrimental reliance—focusing on the idea that the rescuer's botched or negligent attempt made it less likely other potential rescuers would make an attempt—should not be applied in a *constitutional* tort claim:

> "Constitutional tort law, ... which ties a defendant's liability to *depriving* the plaintiff of some right, cannot follow this path of expansion.... [A] constitutional tort requires deprivation by the defendant, and not merely a failure to protect the plaintiff from a danger created by others."[81]

Just as he had done previously in his *Jackson v. City of Joliet* opinion,[82] Posner distinguished situations involving a "botched rescue" from those resulting from a state-created danger, cases where "the state

---

[76] DeShaney v. Winnebago County, 812 F.2d 298, 301 (7th Cir. 1987).

[77] *Id.* at 302.

[78] *Id.*

[79] *Id.* at 303.

[80] *Id.*

[81] *Id.* at 302.

[82] Jackson v. City of Joliet, 715 F.2d 1200 (7th Cir. 1983).

places the victim in a situation of high risk, thus markedly increasing the probability of harm and by doing so becomes the cause of the harm."[83] Posner rejected the argument that, by returning Joshua to his father's custody in January 1983, DSS had recklessly placed him in a position of great danger. At that point, Posner emphasized, the state was weighing the evidence available to it, as it was required to do under Wisconsin law, and taking into account as well that Randy DeShaney might well have sued DSS for violating his parental rights.[84]

Finally, Posner offered an assessment of the arguments in the Third Circuit's *Bailey* opinion,[85] which held that a special relationship and an affirmative duty to protect arose whenever a state becomes aware of the danger that a particular child may be abused and took steps to intervene. Rejecting the *Bailey* expansion of the special relationship category, Posner distinguished physical custody cases like *Estelle*[86] and *Youngberg*[87] on the grounds that, in those cases, the state had deprived individuals of their liberty and prevented them from exercising self-help, and so once having done so "cannot shrug off all responsibility when the danger materializes and injury results."[88] The key difference between the custody situation and a case like DeShaney's was that, according to Posner, the state had not entirely removed Joshua's ability to protect himself.

IV. The Supreme Court

On July 17, 1987, Sullivan and First filed a petition for a writ of certiorari, which the Supreme Court granted on March 21, 1988. Throughout the spring and summer, there was much speculation about the impact of Justice Anthony Kennedy's arrival on the Court. The press coverage of the Court focused in particular on the fact that the 1988–1989 Supreme Court Term would be the first in over forty years in which conservative justices held a majority on the Court.[89] The Court's

---

[83] 812 F.2d at 303 (citing White v. Rochford, 592 F.2d 381 (7th Cir. 1979)).

[84] 812 F.2d at 303; *see also id.* ("To place every state welfare department on the razor's edge, where if it terminates parental rights it is exposed to a section 1983 suit (as well as a state-law suit) by the parent and if it fails to terminate those rights it is exposed to a section 1983 suit by the child, is unlikely to improve the welfare of American families, and is not grounded in constitutional text or principle.").

[85] *Id.*

[86] 429 U.S. 97 (1976).

[87] 457 U.S. 307 (1982).

[88] 812 F.2d at 303.

[89] On the significance of the 1988 Term, see Erwin Chemerinsky, *The Supreme Court, 1988 Term: Foreward: The Vanishing Constitution*, 103 HARV. L. REV. 43 (1989); DAVID G.

docket soon filled with an unusually large number of potentially land-mark constitutional and other civil rights cases.[90] In the midst of all this media attention, the *DeShaney* case received extensive coverage from both television and print journalists.

In their brief, the DeShaneys' lawyers appeared mindful of concerns that their argument would lead to a slippery slope of unmanageable liability for public agencies. Even so, the brief argued once again in favor of returning to the broader definition of "special relationship" endorsed in the Third Circuit's *Bailey* opinion[91] and rejected by Judge Posner in the Seventh Circuit *DeShaney* opinion.[92] They argued that a special relationship could arise in contexts other than involuntary custody in state institutions, but at the same time they attempted to avoid implying that state agencies would enter a "special relationship" every time they undertook to help vulnerable citizens. DSS "knew of" his peril *and* initiated a relationship, and that is enough to establish a special relation-ship.[93]

Because the Supreme Court had recently introduced a heightened state-of-mind requirement for due process claims,[94] Sullivan and First focused on the argument that "more than mere negligence" was in-volved in the government's failure to protect Joshua from the abuse.[95] In order to satisfy a "deliberate indifference" standard, for example, plain-tiffs typically must show there was knowledge or notice of the danger, and a deliberate failure to respond to protect the plaintiff. The DeSha-neys' lawyers argued that the deliberate indifference standard was easily met. Indeed, they argued that Kemmeter's failure to act was such a reckless failure of care that it approached an "intentional deprivation of liberty."[96]

SAVAGE, TURNING RIGHT: THE MAKING OF THE REHNQUIST SUPREME COURT Ch. 8 (1993); EDWARD P. LAZARUS, CLOSED CHAMBERS: THE FIRST EYEWITNESS ACCOUNT OF THE EPIC STRUGGLES INSIDE THE SUPREME COURT (1998).

[90] *See, e.g.,* Webster v. Reproductive Health Servs., 492 U.S. 490 (1989); Michael H. v. Gerald D., 491 U.S. 110 (1989); Texas v. Johnson, 491 U.S. 397 (1989); Penry v. Lynaugh, 492 U.S. 302 (1989); Stanford v. Kentucky, 492 U.S. 361 (1989); City of Richmond v. J. A. Croson Co., 488 U.S. 469 (1989); Patterson v. McLean Credit Union, 491 U.S. 164 (1989); Wards Cove Packing Co. v. Antonio, 490 U.S. 642 (1989).

[91] 768 F.2d 503 (3d Cir. 1985).

[92] 812 F.2d 298 (7th Cir. 1987).

[93] Brief for Petitioner, *supra* note 2.

[94] *See* Davidson v. Cannon, 474 U.S. 344 (1986); Daniels v. Williams, 474 U.S. 327 (1986).

[95] Brief for Petitioner, *supra* note 2.

[96] Brief for Petitioner, *supra* note 2.

The lawyers for the defendants, Mark Mingo and Wayne Yankala, sought the assistance of a well-regarded Washington, D.C. appellate firm, Onek, Klein, and Farr, to assist with their brief and to help prepare for the oral argument. Their brief underscored the voluntary nature of the services provided by DSS to the DeShaney family and claimed that the record of Kemmeter's voluntary assistance could not be characterized as deliberate indifference or recklessness. Emphasizing that Kemmeter and her employers were in no way responsible for Joshua's plight, the brief concluded that the petitioners' argument "stretches the Due Process Clause well beyond the breaking point."[97]

If one measure of the importance of a Supreme Court case is the willingness of interest groups to spend the time and resources preparing amicus briefs, *DeShaney* was an important case, drawing a number of amicus briefs filed by prestigious legal groups.[98] Many of these amicus briefs presented legal arguments that largely tracked the positions of the parties in their merits briefs. Others, such as the amicus brief filed by a coalition of state and local government organizations, addressed the potential impact of liability for failures to protect, relying on policy arguments that were not emphasized in the merits briefs.[99]

The American Civil Liberties Union's Children's Rights Project, which focused its work on class actions to protect children in foster care systems, had followed the *DeShaney* litigation through the federal courts, and was preparing an amicus brief in support of the petitioners.[100]

---

[97] Brief for Respondent, *supra* note 2.

[98] *See, e.g.,* Gregory A. Caldeira & John R. Wright, *Amicus Curiae Before the Supreme Court: Who Participates, When, and How Much?* 52 J. OF POL. 782 (1990); Paul M. Collins, Jr., *Friends of the Court: Examining the Influence of Amicus Curiae Participation in U.S. Supreme Court Litigation*, 38 LAW & SOC'Y REV. 897 (2004). For the *DeShaney* case, six amicus briefs were filed by various coalitions of organizations. The overall number of briefs filed in *DeShaney* was not extraordinary, especially when compared with other cases during the Supreme Court's 1988 Term. In *Webster v. Reproductive Health Servs.*, 492 U.S. 490 (1989), for example, a record seventy-eight briefs, sponsored by over 400 organizations, were filed. *See* Susan Behuniak–Long, *Friendly-Fire: Amici Curiae and* Webster v. Reproductive Health Services, 74 JUDICATURE 261 (1991).

[99] Brief of Amici Curiae The National Association of Counties, Council of State Governments, U.S. Conference of Mayors, National Conference of State Legislatures, National League of Cities, and International City Management Association at 21–29, *DeShaney*, 489 U.S. 189 (1989) (No. 87–154). The other amicus briefs on behalf of the respondents were filed by the solicitor general, a coalition of state attorneys general, and the National School Boards Association.

[100] Eventually, a coalition of advocacy groups signed on to the ACLU brief. *See* Brief of Amici Curiae The American Civil Liberties Union Children's Rights Project, The ACLU of Wisconsin, Legal Services for Children, The Juvenile Law Center, Bay Area Coalition Against Child Abuse, and The National Woman Abuse Prevention Project, *DeShaney*, 489

Impressed by their work on the amicus brief, Curry First proposed to Donald Sullivan that the ACLU, with their more experienced appellate litigators, should take over as the DeShaneys' counsel and argue the case before the Supreme Court.[101] Sullivan, however, insisted on remaining lead counsel and arguing before the Supreme Court.[102]

Sullivan's insistence on this matter resulted in considerable dissension within the *DeShaney* team. In June of 1988, after the Supreme Court had already granted certiorari in *DeShaney*, Sullivan announced his candidacy for a seat in the Wyoming state legislature. After succeeding in the August primary, he began campaigning for the general election, which was to take place on November 8, just six days after the oral arguments in the *DeShaney* case. Melody DeShaney, who was then living in Phoenix, Arizona, became concerned about the amount of time Sullivan was spending campaigning, and she was frustrated that he was not returning her calls seeking assistance for travel to Washington, D.C. for the Supreme Court oral arguments. She even mailed a handwritten letter to Chief Justice Rehnquist to express her dissatisfaction with her attorneys, and to inform the Court that she wanted to have them replaced. Although they were able to resolve their issues through a conference call just four days before the oral arguments, First later described this period as "the lowest point in my life as a lawyer."[103]

First also recalled the concerns he felt on November 1, the day before the oral arguments, when he met with Sullivan to practice and became alarmed when Sullivan appeared unprepared and nervous.[104] And he was right to worry: the following afternoon, at the oral argument in the *DeShaney* case, Sullivan's presentation to the Court was not impressive, and some of his statements during oral argument appear nowhere in the petitioners' merits briefs.[105] He apparently wanted to emphasize that the proposed affirmative duty to protect could be limited to the child welfare context: the petitioners, he asserted, were not arguing for affirmative duties to protect the public, nor were they assigning to the state the duty to protect all children, only those under the care and supervision of child welfare agencies. He repeatedly referred to the

---

U.S. 189 (1989) (No. 87–154). The Massachusetts Committee for Children and Youth filed a separate amicus brief on behalf of the petitioners.

[101] CURRY, *supra* note 30, at 110.

[102] *Id.* at 111.

[103] *Id.* at 112–13.

[104] *Id.* at 117.

[105] The audio recording of the *DeShaney* oral argument is available at the Oyez website, http://www.oyez.org/media/item?type=audio & id=argument & parent=cases/19801989/1988/1988_87_154.

"enmeshment" of DSS and the DeShaney household, a choice of terminology that appeared to both confuse and annoy Chief Justice Rehnquist. Justice O'Connor attempted to draw his attention to the question of the special relationship doctrine and the arguments in favor of expanding it beyond the custody context. But Sullivan was unfocused. In his oral argument notes, under the section for Donald Sullivan, Justice Blackmun wrote, simply, "hostile questions."[106]

Mark Mingo then presented the arguments for the respondents, focusing in particular on (1) the need to uphold the custody limitation on affirmative duties to protect and, (2) the lack of evidence in the record to support finding that Kemmeter acted recklessly or with deliberate indifference. Justice O'Connor asked whether his position would be different if Joshua had been placed in foster care, and suffered abuse at the hands of his foster family. Mingo conceded that the foster care context presents a much closer question, and could fall within either the custody limitation or the state-created danger doctrine. But he also sought to highlight the differences between Joshua and other children placed in foster homes. Mingo suggested that Kemmeter and DSS had done nothing to increase the danger Joshua faced from Randy DeShaney, because the state had merely returned Joshua to his original status when it transferred him back to the custody of his father. He also emphasized that parental custody is itself protected by the Constitution. At this point, Justice Blackmun interjected: "Which is more important than the abuse to poor Joshua?" "Poor Joshua!"[107]

In December, the justices began exchanging opinion drafts and memos for the *DeShaney* case. Chief Justice Rehnquist's initial draft of the majority opinion was circulated, and he incorporated minor suggestions for revisions in subsequent drafts until Justices Stevens, O'Connor,

---

[106] Oral Argument Notes, *DeShaney v. Winnebago County* (No. 87–154), November 2, 1988 (Library of Congress, Harry Blackmun Papers, Supreme Court File, Box 514, Folder 3: *DeShaney v. Winnebago County*, 1989). Neither side earned high marks on Blackmun's eight-point grading scale for oral arguments: Donald Sullivan and Mark Mingo were each assigned a four out of eight (only thirty-eight percent of the lawyers appearing before the Court earned scores of four or lower from Justice Blackmun). *See* Timothy R. Johnson, et al., *The Influence of Oral Arguments on the U.S. Supreme Court*, 100 Am. Pol. Sci. Rev. 99, 105, tbl.7 (2006).

[107] This dramatic interruption in the presentation was incorporated in Justice Blackmun's dissenting opinion, and his evident concern for Joshua's plight would become, by the time of his retirement in 1994, a much remarked upon episode in Blackmun's long tenure on the Court. In a post-retirement interview with Dean Harold Koh, Justice Blackmun explained that he had become frustrated listening to the *DeShaney* oral argument: "Sometimes we overlook the individual's concern, the fact that these are live human beings that are so deeply and terribly affected by our decision." Transcript, The Justice Harry A. Blackmun Oral History Project, Library of Congress, at 397, http://lcweb2.loc.gov/cocoon/ blackmun-public/page.html?FOLDERID=D0901 & SERIESID=D09.

White, Kennedy, and Scalia joined the final version.[108] The constitutional claims made on Joshua DeShaney's behalf were apparently so weak, it took Rehnquist a mere nine pages to dismiss them entirely.[109]

In the first part of his opinion, Rehnquist focused on the state action requirement.[110] Rehnquist asserted that this causal prerequisite was not satisfied in Joshua's case because Randy DeShaney, not the state, inflicted the injuries. According to Rehnquist, "nothing in the language of the Due Process Clause itself requires the State to protect the life, liberty, and property of its citizens against invasions by private actors."[111] Using an analysis nearly identical to that developed by Judge Posner, Rehnquist focused particular attention on the due process clause's reliance on the word "deprive" and emphasized that this choice of words requires that *action by the state* cause the injury in order to claim a constitutional violation.[112]

In the second part of his opinion, Rehnquist examined the leading theories of affirmative duties to protect—the custody requirement and the state-created danger doctrine—and he concluded that neither theory applied to the facts of this case.[113] The state would have been obligated to ensure that Joshua's basic needs were met only after he had been placed in the physical custody of DSS, but Joshua never had been permanently removed from his home.[114] Rehnquist emphasized that the state's role in returning Joshua to his father's custody was not enough to establish a special relationship: "[T]he State does not become the permanent guarantor of an individual's safety by having once offered him shelter."[115]

With respect to the state-created danger theory, Rehnquist concluded that, because the state did not itself *create* the abusive environment nor did it make Joshua's situation worse, it could not be liable for failing to protect him from the abuse.[116] According to Rehnquist, "[w]hile the State may have been aware of the dangers that Joshua faced in the free

---

[108] See Library of Congress, Harry Blackmun Papers, Supreme Court File, Box 514, Folder 2: Draft Opinions, *DeShaney v. Winnebago County*, 1989.

[109] 489 U.S. at 194–203.

[110] *Id.* at 194–95.

[111] *Id.* at 195.

[112] *Id.*

[113] *Id.* at 197–202.

[114] *Id.* at 199–201.

[115] *Id.* at 201.

[116] *Id.*

world, it played no part in their creation, nor did it do anything to render him more vulnerable to them."[117]

Rehnquist's majority opinion centered on his characterization of the government's behavior as state inaction rather than action.[118] This assessment of the facts was subjected to much criticism.[119] Justice Brennan, for example, argued in his dissenting opinion that any choice to characterize the facts as involving state action or inaction is subject to manipulation, depending upon how far back in the chain of events one chooses to go.[120] It is just as easy, and just as valid, Brennan argued, to portray the *DeShaney* case as one involving governmental action. By instituting a set of child protective services, Winnebago County displaced alternative sources of private assistance. The resulting monopoly on the provision of sources was an "act" which could render Joshua more vulnerable if the county subsequently "failed to act" or acted incompetently.[121]

In Brennan's view, Kemmeter interacted often enough with the DeShaneys that it was fair to characterize her behavior as recklessly disregarding apparent dangers to Joshua's safety. By the time Joshua suffered his final beating at the hands of Randy DeShaney, DSS had been monitoring his case for well over a year. After Joshua had been taken into temporary custody at the Theda Clark Medical Center in January 1983, DSS decided to return Joshua to his father's custody, but only after negotiating a set of conditions with Randy DeShaney. Despite learning that none of these conditions had been met—after hearing numerous far-fetched explanations for Joshua's injuries and "accidents," receiving reports from hospital social workers, and obtaining notice of a series of domestic violence reports—Kemmeter did little more than include this information in her case files.[122]

---

[117] *Id.*

[118] *Id.* at 203 ("The most that can be said of the state functionaries in this case is that they stood by and did nothing when suspicious circumstances dictated a more active role for them.").

[119] *See, e.g.,* David A. Strauss, *Due Process, Government Inaction, and Private Wrongs,* 1989 SUP. CT. REV. 53, 61–63; Aviam Soifer, *Moral Ambition, Formalism, and the 'Free World' of* DeShaney, 57 GEO. WASH. LAW. REV. 1513, 1518–19 (1989).

[120] 489 U.S. at 205–06 (Brennan, J., dissenting).

[121] 489 U.S. at 207–08 ("Wisconsin law invites—indeed, directs—citizens and other governmental entities to depend on local departments of social services such as respondent to protect children from abuse."); *see also* Soifer, *supra* note 120, at 1518 ("[Rehnquist] ignores the powerful preemptive quality of the state's initial protective decision, thereby ousting other institutions that might provide such services.").

[122] 489 U.S. at 208–09.

Brennan forcefully argued that it was state action that made Kemmeter's inaction so consequential. Once the state "acted" by establishing a child protective services system that left Kemmeter with the sole authority to initiate investigations and refer cases to the juvenile court, the result was that all of her subsequent "failures to act" had far more pernicious consequences than they might otherwise have had, if other observers—the nurses, doctors, neighbors, and police officers—who were concerned for Joshua's safety had the authority to intervene. The failures of DSS in all likelihood left Joshua more vulnerable to his father's violence than if the agency had never existed. Brennan ended by chiding the majority for failing to see that government "oppression can result when a State undertakes a vital duty and then ignores it."[123]

Justice Blackmun wrote a brief but passionate separate dissenting opinion, criticizing the Court's "sterile" formalistic approach and arguing in favor of a "compassionate" jurisprudence that does not shy away from the moral ambition that the pursuit of justice requires. He lamented the result of this case, concluding that it was "a sad commentary upon American life, and constitutional principles—so full of late of patriotic fervor and proud proclamations about 'liberty and justice for all'—that this child, Joshua DeShaney, now is assigned to live out the remainder of his life profoundly retarded."[124]

Neither of these dissenting opinions endorsed the Third Circuit's approach to expanding the duty to protect in the *Estate of Bailey* case. Instead, Brennan's analysis can be likened to a more generous version of the state-created danger theory.[125] In contrast to Rehnquist's majority opinion,[126] the dissenters' approach would accept that botched rescues can sometimes constitute state-created dangers. Whenever the state establishes a monopoly of some type of protective service—by intervening to help and excluding or discouraging others from assisting—it creates a "danger" of sorts by inducing reliance on the government. In such situations, if the state botches a rescue, then there may be a deprivation of due process.[127] For example, battered women seeking

---

[123] 489 U.S. at 212.

[124] *Id.* at 213.

[125] Brennan suggested that his analysis relied on the framework of *Estelle* and *Youngberg*, but his argument clearly sweeps far beyond the custody context. *See id.* at 207 (suggesting that these cases "stand for the much more generous proposition that, if a State cuts off private sources of aid and then refuses to aid, it cannot wash its hands of the harm that results from its inaction").

[126] Rehnquist's analysis followed Judge Posner's distinction between botched rescues and state-created dangers.

[127] Even if the dissenters' constitutional analyses were accepted, both the qualified immunity and the "policy or custom" doctrines would remain powerful obstacles for § 1983 plaintiffs.

orders of protection from the state would likely have a claim if the police failed to enforce their protection order. Likewise, public school students would be able to sue school officials who failed to protect them from bullying or harassment by their fellow students.

V. *DeShaney*'s Legacy

The Court's ruling in *DeShaney* prevented such claims from going forward. Cases involving failures to enforce protection orders for battered women have been dismissed on the grounds that *DeShaney* limited the establishment of special relationships to the custody context.[128] In the public school cases, federal appellate judges have generally rejected the use of a custody analogy to support claims that schools have an affirmative duty to protect students from harm inflicted by one another.[129] Although courts have extended the custody analogy to cases involving governmental failures to protect children placed in the foster system,[130] they have continued to apply *DeShaney* to reject claims involving the failure to protect children who have been injured or killed while in their parents' custody.[131]

DeShaney has imposed enormous burdens on civil rights plaintiffs attempting to hold the government liable for its failures to protect. Given these broad-ranging effects, no analysis of *DeShaney* should ignore the real-world consequences of the Court's ruling. The paradoxical result of Rehnquist's *DeShaney* reasoning deserves special emphasis: his enthusiastic endorsement of the "charter of negative liberties" view of the Constitution ultimately serves to advance the interests of the state,[132] by eliminating its exposure to liability in almost all cases involving failures to protect. Civil rights plaintiffs like Joshua, meanwhile, are left without any means of obtaining full compensation for their injuries.

---

[128] *See* Balistreri v. Pacifica Police Dept., 855 F.2d 1421 (9th Cir. 1988), *rev'd in light of DeShaney*, 901 F.2d 696 (9th Cir. 1988); *see also* Pinder v. Johnson, 54 F. 3d 1169 (4th Cir. 1995) (rejecting special relationship analysis in case involving a verbal promise by police rather than court-issued order of protection).

[129] *See, e.g.*, Leffall v. Dallas Indep. Sch. Dist., 28 F.3d 521, 529 (5th Cir. 1994); Graham v. Independent Sch. Dist. No. I–89, 22 F.3d 991 (10th Cir. 1994); D.R. ex rel. L.R. v. Middle Bucks Area Vocational Technical Sch., 972 F.2d 1364 (3d Cir. 1992); J.O. v. Alton Cmty. Unit Sch. Dist. 11, 909 F.2d 267, 272 (7th Cir. 1990).

[130] *See, e.g.*, Norfleet v. Arkansas Dep't of Soc. Servs., 989 F.2d 289 (8th Cir. 1993); K.H. through Murphy v. Morgan, 914 F.2d 846 (7th Cir. 1990); Taylor v. Ledbetter, 818 F.2d 791 (11th Cir. 1987).

[131] *See, e.g.*, S.S. v. McMullen, 225 F.3d 960 (8th Cir. 2000).

[132] *See* Chemerinsky, *supra* note 90, at 58 (observing that "in forty-seven non-unanimous decisions in constitutional cases during the 1988–1989 Term, Chief Justice Rehnquist voted against the government only twice").

In the years following *DeShaney*, social services agencies continued to face criticism for their failures to protect vulnerable children. Some of these children's names are well known, due to widespread media coverage following their deaths: six-year-old Elisa Izquierdo of New York City, abused and beaten to death by her mother in 1995;[133] twenty-three-month-old toddler Brianna Blackmond of Washington D.C., killed by her mother's roommate in 2000;[134] and seven-year-old Nixzmary Brown of Brooklyn, abused by her mother and murdered by her stepfather in 2006.[135]

When such horrific cases of abuse become front-page news stories, the resulting public outrage typically produces a flurry of reform proposals to improve the child welfare system. These efforts have produced mixed results. Both the causes of these agencies' failures and the reforms required to improve the child welfare system are extraordinarily complex subjects, and they remain today the focus of intense debates among children's rights advocates and public policy experts.

For these reasons, one must be careful not to overstate the impact of *DeShaney*. The ability to bring failure to protect claims under § 1983 would not generate perfect outcomes in every child abuse case. At the same time, the additional deterrent effect produced by claims for damages under § 1983 should not be underestimated.[136] These private lawsuits could have provided a unique type of check on the performance of social services agencies.

---

[133] Lizette Alvarez, *A Mother's Tale: Drugs Despair and Violence*, N.Y. TIMES, Nov. 27, 1995, at B1; Nina Bernstein and Frank Bruni, *Seven Warnings: She Suffered in Plain Sight But Alarms Were Ignored*, N.Y. TIMES, Dec. 24, 1995, at A1.

[134] Sari Horwitz, *'Failure After Failure'; Foster System Betrayed Brianna*, WASH. POST, FEB. 21, 2000, at A1; Scott Higham and Sari Horwitz, *Brianna, Buried in System's Mistakes*, WASH. POST, Dec. 16, 2000, at A1.

[135] Leslie Kauffman, *Signs of Trouble at Agency Assigned to Protect Children*, N.Y. TIMES, Jan. 13, 2006, at B5; Leslie Kauffman and Jim Rutenberg, *Agency Suspends Supervisors After Girl's Death*, N.Y. TIMES, Jan. 19, 2006, at A1.

Only a few of these children receive such extensive media attention. The National Child Abuse and Neglect Data System ("NCANDS") reported an estimated 1490 child fatalities in 2004 alone, although it is important to note that only 12.4% of these cases involved children had been placed under the supervision of a child protective services agency at some point during the five years prior to their deaths. *Of these fatalities, 78.9% were the product of parental abuse or neglect. Maltreatment 2004* (U.S. Dep't of Health and Human Servs., 2006), http://www.acf.hhs.gov/programs/cb/pubs/cm04/index.htm.

[136] For examples of empirical work examining the deterrent effect of civil rights litigation under § 1983, *see* Charles Epp, Do Rights Matter? Exploring The Impact of Legal Liability on Administrative Policies, Presented at the Annual Meeting of the American Political Science Association (2001); Margo Schlanger, *Inmate Litigation*, 116 HARV. L. REV. 1555 (2003).

The Court's refusal in *DeShaney* to assign any constitutional duties to child welfare agencies instead closed the federal courthouse doors to all plaintiffs seeking to use § 1983 litigation to hold these agencies accountable for their failures to protect them from abuse by their parents. Joshua, and all other children abused by their parents and let down by the government, are left without any constitutional rights to enforce. For these children, the notion that *DeShaney*'s vision of the Constitution helps promote "the blessings of liberty" surely offers little solace.

10

Caroline Bettinger–López and Susan Sturm*

International Union, U.A.W. v. Johnson Controls: The History of Litigation Alliances and Mobilization to Challenge Fetal Protection Policies

I. Introduction

On August 9, 1982, Johnson Controls, the nation's largest manufacturer of car batteries, instituted a new "Fetal Protection Policy." This policy banned all fertile women working in the company's United States Globe Battery Division, regardless of age or personal circumstances, from working in jobs that involved exposure to lead. Lead, an integral component of batteries, was abundant in battery manufacturing facilities. Johnson Controls explained its policy shift as a response to scientific evidence linking lead exposure before and during pregnancy with birth defects in children, and noted that several workers had recently shown lead levels that exceeded the OSHA standard for pregnant women. Johnson Controls' policy followed the practice of other companies in the chemical and heavy metal industry which, fearing mounting tort liability for employees' children born with lead-associated birth defects, had adopted similar policies in the preceding decade.

Almost overnight, life changed dramatically for most of the Globe Battery Division's 275 female employees in 14 plants across the country.

---

* The events recounted in this chapter were drawn from the extensive secondary literature on *Johnson Controls* and from conversations with key participants in the litigation and advocacy efforts. We particularly relied upon the comprehensive study of *Johnson Controls* in JULIANA S. GONEN, LITIGATION AS LOBBYING: REPRODUCTIVE HAZARDS AND INTEREST AGGREGATION (2003).

Johnson Controls' Fetal Protection Policy left most female production and maintenance employees with an agonizing choice: either get surgically sterilized and continue working in a production/maintenance job that in the blue collar world paid top dollar and came with excellent benefits, or accept a transfer to a lower-paying, lower-prestige job that had reduced benefits and opportunities for promotion and overtime but lower lead exposure levels. The new policy also meant that a female employee's very presence on the shop floor exposed an intimate detail about her life—her infertility—to her male co-workers.

Some women, such as 34–year–old Gloyce Qualls, opted for sterilization. Qualls was making $450 a week burning lead posts into large industrial batteries at Johnson Controls' Milwaukee, Wisconsin plant. In August 1982, when the company enacted its fetal protection policy, she had just bought a new car, moved into a new apartment, and was planning to marry a man with four children. Two weeks after company officials told her that they would transfer her to a new $200–a–week position, pursuant to the new fetal protection policy, she underwent tubal ligation.[1] Many women workers like Qualls were juggling tangible hazards in their lives—domestic violence, health problems, and poverty—and needed the financial and professional cushion their factory jobs provided. They had tried to reduce their exposure to lead by wearing protective gear, maintaining good hygiene, and requesting temporary transfers to reduce body lead levels. Such measures, however, were no longer an option under the new fetal protection policy.

Others decided against sterilization. This was the case for Virginia Green and other older female employees, many of whose doctors warned of serious risks associated with such surgery for women over age 50. Although Green was aware of the dangers lead posed to fetuses, she was not particularly concerned about this risk affecting her, as she was 50 years old, divorced, and not planning on having any more children. After eleven years on the shop floor, Green was transferred from the battery assembly line, where she was making nine dollars an hour plus time and a half overtime, to a job as a respirator sanitizer, "a glorified laundress," where she made far less money and became the butt of male co-workers' fertility jokes.[2]

Across the country, Johnson Controls employees, mostly female, trickled into the local bargaining units of their union, the United Auto Workers (UAW), to file grievances. The grievances culminated in a class

---

[1] Estes, Florence, *Supreme friends: Battery workers pulled together to pursue the right to their jobs*, CHI. TRIB., Apr. 28, 1991; *Supreme Court: Health Fears No Excuse For Bias; Fertility issue could affect 20 million*, USA TODAY, Mar. 21, 1991.

[2] David L. Kirp, *Fetal Hazards, Gender Justice, and the Justices: The Limits of Equality*, 34 WM. & MARY L. REV. 101, 104 (1992).

action lawsuit against Johnson Controls. The individual complainants represented a cross-section of employees: Elsie Nason, a fifty year old divorcee; Mary Craig, who elected to be sterilized in order to ensure her job; and Donald Penney, who requested but was denied a three-month leave of absence in order to lower his blood lead levels to enable him to safely father a child, and who was subsequently "harassed and intimidated" by the plant's personnel manager. Both the District Court and the Court of Appeals dismissed the case on summary judgment, and the Supreme Court granted certiorari. On March 21, 1991, the Supreme Court held that sex-specific fetal protection policies violate the prohibition on sex discrimination in employment contained in Title VII of the 1964 Civil Rights Act. The Court found Johnson Controls' policy, which explicitly categorized employees on the basis of their potential for pregnancy, constituted impermissible facial discrimination that could not be defended as a bona fide occupational qualification (BFOQ).[3]

Johnson Controls is best known as a great victory for women's rights and reproductive freedom. It is the culmination of a long legal campaign to invalidate restrictions on women's employment based on pregnancy. It decisively narrows the use of Title VII's BFOQ exception to situations where "sex or pregnancy actually interferes with the employee's ability to perform the job."[4] The case shows the potency of litigation to mobilize alliances aimed at achieving legal change. *Johnson Controls* brought together a remarkable coalition of labor, women's rights, and workplace safety activists. The case also illustrates the impact of relationships among repeat players in the legal advocacy community, particularly the strong relationships between labor attorneys in the UAW and feminist attorneys in national women's rights organizations. The history of this litigation alliance can be tracked through organizations' participation as amici in appellate and Supreme Court cases involving women's rights. These cases powerfully demonstrate the use of amicus briefs as opportunities to link the efforts of groups with overlapping agendas and to shape the Supreme Court's understanding of the surrounding empirical, social and political context.

But *Johnson Controls* also provides important lessons about the narrowing effects and fragility of litigation-centered mobilization. The issue framed in the courts necessarily zeroed in on the unfairness of excluding only women from dangerous jobs based on the potential impact on fetuses. But the problem, as it was experienced by women (and men)

---

[3] *Int'l Union, UAW, et al. v. Johnson Controls, Inc.*, 499 U.S. 187 (1991). The BFOQ provision set forth in Title VII allows employers to discriminate on the basis of sex "in those certain instances where ... sex ... is a [BFOQ] reasonably necessary to the normal operation of the particular business." 42 U.S.C. § 703(e)(1).

[4] 499 U.S. at 204.

was far broader and more complex. As the stories of the *Johnson Control* plaintiffs illustrate, gender bias permeated the way many industries and unions responded to hazardous workplace conditions. It also shaped scientific research on reproductive hazards. Moreover, removing fetal protection policies did not address the underlying health and safety issues threatening the reproductive health of both men and women. But like much test-case litigation, the *Johnson Controls* coalition was organized to win the case at hand. Once the legal victory at the national level was achieved in the courts, the national labor-women's rights coalition assembled to achieve that goal proved difficult to sustain, particularly in light of the increasingly conservative political and regulatory environment. The anti-discrimination goals of the national advocacy groups organized around test-case litigation had been met. The workplace health issues that remained could not easily be addressed as discrimination issues in court. Administrative agency support for addressing those issues did not exist at the national level. At this point, the national groups disbanded and moved on to a new set of issues.

The *Johnson Controls* story poses questions that have taken on much greater urgency in the current legal and political environment. What does this litigation-centered orientation mean for how problems are defined and addressed? How does it determine who participates in and influences the course of the advocacy and change process? Does a national law reform campaign have the capacity to sustain public attention to problems not addressed by the legal claim? Are there ways to connect litigation to a broader mobilization strategy that keeps problems' multiple dimensions in view and sustains crucial alliances when litigation ends?

Interestingly, the federal mobilization story has a state-level analogue, which adopts a different strategy for connecting litigation to mobilization. In the 1980s, California employment, women's rights, labor and public health advocates mobilized at the state level to address the threat posed by workplace reproductive hazards and industry's response to them. Like their federal counterparts, this coalition used litigation as a tool, successfully challenging Johnson Controls' fetal protection policy in California state court. But the California initiative defined its agenda as developing long-term solutions to the complex problems these hazards posed. They found venues beyond the courts to come together and advocate for changes in employer practices affecting workers, including educational arenas and media. They cultivated working relationships with non-lawyer partners to keep the focus on issues broader than those defined by the legal standard. For California advocates, the court victory did not fully solve the problem, and thus was only a step toward the larger goal. Taking advantage of the more hospitable political and regulatory environment and the diverse stakeholders at the table, the

California coalition undertook to mobilize in a way that would enable repeat players with long-term interests to sustain their participation so that the problem, as experienced by workers, would be addressed.

II. Historical, Regulatory and Judicial Backdrop
A. The Origins of a Labor and Women's Rights Alliance

Workplace fetal protection policies that emerged in the 1970s were one chapter in a long history of women's exclusion from hazardous but higher paying jobs. They were rooted in the stated goal of protecting the health and safety of women and their offspring. A century of this state protectionist legislation and a longstanding tradition of male-dominated unions had effectively precluded women in the past from accessing physically demanding and high-paying factory jobs.[5] Indeed, before the 1960s, women's absence from these jobs had become largely normalized in the national psyche.[6] Many unions had opposed women's entry into traditionally male positions and supported protectionist legislation and policies.

With the passage of new civil rights laws in the 1960s, however, industries and unions faced legal challenges to the exclusion of women from these jobs. The civil rights and women's rights movements gave rise to landmark civil rights legislation, including the Equal Pay Act of 1963 and the Civil Rights Act of 1964, and the creation of administrative agencies, such as the Equal Employment Opportunity Commission (EEOC) and the Office of Federal Contract Compliance Programs (OFCCP). The law now required employers and unions to admit women to employment unless their exclusion could be justified.

Many groups formed in the wake of this legislation, which had opened up new avenues for mobilization, activism, and litigation. After the passage of Title VII, employers and unions seeking to preserve the status quo focused on pregnancy and argued for a broad BFOQ exception that would exclude women from jobs perceived as posing risks to them or their unborn children. When major unions like the AFL–CIO and the International Union of Electrical, Radio, and Machine Workers (IUE)[7] hesitated to advocate on behalf of labor women in the 1960s, women formed their own groups to challenge employers' restrictive practices. Some unions, responding to the demands of a growing female member-

---

[5] See Mary E. Becker, *From* Muller v. Oregon *to Fetal Vulnerability Policies*, 53 U. CHI. L. REV. 1219, 1221–22 (1986); *see also* GONEN, *supra* note 1, at 24 (citing JUDITH BAER, THE CHAINS OF PROTECTION: THE JUDICIAL RESPONSE TO WOMEN'S LABOR LEGISLATION (1978)); J. RALPH LINDGREN & NADINE TAUB, THE LAW OF SEX DISCRIMINATION (1988).

[6] ALICE KESSLER-HARRIS, IN PURSUIT OF EQUITY: WOMEN, MEN AND THE QUEST FOR ECONOMIC CITIZENSHIP IN 20TH CENTURY AMERICA (2001).

[7] GONEN, *supra* note 1, at 22, 46.

ship, changed their position and challenged policies discriminating based on pregnancy. This mobilization included a developing alliance between segments of the labor movement and women's rights advocates.

In contrast to other unions, the UAW had historically been active in the women's and civil rights movements. In 1944, the UAW became the first union to establish a Women's Department, and as early as the 1960s it was lobbying the EEOC to oppose protectionist legislation.[8] In 1966, Betty Friedan, former EEOC commissioners, a UAW Women's Committee representative, and members of state women's status commissions formed the National Organization for Women (NOW) in reaction to a lax EEOC response to sex discrimination.[9] In 1974, a UAW leader became the first president of the Coalition of Labor Union Women (CLUW), a group of women who felt powerless within their unions and sought to develop a women's agenda within the established labor movement.[10] Many UAW lawyers had a background in and commitment to women's rights and connections with women's rights organizations across the country.

Women's groups celebrated several judicial, legislative, and administrative agency victories in the Title VII arena in the early 1970s. A new crop of women's rights groups soon emerged, looking to make these victories the beginning of something larger.[11] All of these groups came to play an important role in developing litigation, legislative, regulatory, and other advocacy strategies to promote women's rights, and they became important players in the events producing the Supreme Court's decision in *Johnson Controls*.

B. Mobilization Around Supreme Court Losses

Several Supreme Court decisions in the 1970's threatened women's progress toward workplace equality, and defined the mobilization agenda for women's groups and their sympathetic labor partners. These cases became the focus of a sustained law reform campaign. Pregnancy discrimination—reflected in a constellation of employers' policies including forced leave, loss of seniority, lack of medical coverage, and outright dismissal for pregnant workers—was one of the first issues that this new

---

[8] *Id.* at 45.

[9] *Id.* at 21–22.

[10] *Id.* at 47–48.

[11] These groups included: the NOW Legal Defense and Education Fund (NOWLDEF); the ACLU Women's Rights Project (WRP); the Women's Legal Defense Fund (WLDF); the National Women's Law Center (NWLC); the Women's Law Fund; the Women's Equity Action League (WEAL) litigation fund; the Women's Rights Litigation Clinic at Rutgers Law School; the Women's Law Project; and Equal Rights Advocates (ERA).

coalition of women's groups tackled.[12] The first major case in this area was *Geduldig v. Aiello*,[13] an unsuccessful 1974 equal protection challenge to California's refusal to grant disability benefits to pregnant women. Foreshadowing what would soon become a familiar amicus lineup, the ACLU, AFL–CIO, EEOC, IUE, Physician's Forum, and WEAL filed an amicus brief arguing that the policy was unconstitutional.

In the years following *Geduldig*, women's groups looked to Title VII, rather than the Constitution, as a means to combat pregnancy discrimination. In *General Electric v. Gilbert*,[14] the Supreme Court rejected IUE's Title VII challenge to General Electric's disability plan which, like California's, did not grant disability benefits to pregnant women. The Court held that, under Title VII as well as the equal protection clause, pregnancy discrimination was not sex discrimination.

Women's groups immediately mobilized in response to *Gilbert* and, alongside labor and civil rights groups and churches, soon formed the 300–plus member Campaign to End Discrimination against Pregnant Workers (CEDAPW) with the express goal of legislatively overruling *Gilbert*. In 1978, Congress passed the Pregnancy Discrimination Act (PDA), which amended Title VII to include discrimination based on pregnancy, childbirth, or related medical conditions.

In 1983, the Supreme Court again saw the familiar lineup of amici from *Geduldig* and *Gilbert* in *Newport News v. EEOC*, where the Court found that a corporate policy granting better pregnancy benefits to female employees than to the wives of male employees violated Title VII.[15] Four years later, in *California Federal Savings & Loan v. Guerra*, the Court ruled that policies that treated pregnancy more favorably than other disabilities were lawful under the PDA, since Congress intended the PDA to promote equal employment opportunities for women and to be a floor, not a ceiling.[16] Significantly, *Guerra* produced a rift amongst the nation's women's rights groups. East Coast organizations, including the ACLU WRP, NOW LDEF, the Women's Law Project, NWLC, and WLDF, feared the implications of promoting measures that could be viewed as "special protections" for women and thus submitted "equal treatment" amicus briefs in support of neither party and that advocated treating pregnant women the same as other disabled individuals. West

---

[12] GONEN, *supra* note 1, at 26.

[13] 417 U.S. 484 (1974).

[14] 429 U.S. 125, 136 (1976).

[15] 462 U.S. 669 (1983).

[16] 479 U.S. 272, 285 (1987).

Coast organizations, including the Legal Aid Society–Employment Law Center (LAS–ELC), ERA, the California Teachers' Association, the Mexican–American Legal Defense and Education Fund (MALDEF), the Northwest Women's Law Center, and the San Francisco Women Lawyers Alliance, as well as Betty Friedan and CLUW, submitted "special treatment" amicus briefs in support of the respondent emphasizing the importance of recognizing the real differences between men and women and the harms suffered by women whose employers ignored their pregnancy-related needs. Several years later, as the *Johnson Controls* case worked its way up to the Supreme Court, these groups united in a common effort to eradicate fetal protection policies.

At the same time that PDA-related litigation was winding through the courts, litigants were struggling to define the scope of Title VII's BFOQ exception. In 1977, the Supreme Court found in *Dothard v. Rawlinson* that a prison could properly assert a BFOQ defense to justify the prison's decision to hire only male guards in contact areas of maximum security male penitentiaries.[17] The Court found that "[t]he likelihood that inmates would assault a woman because she was a woman would pose a real threat not only to the victim of the assault but also to the basic control of the penitentiary and protection of its inmates and the other security personnel."[18] Because maintaining safety and order were related to the "essence" of the employer's business, the Court found that it could categorically exclude women from certain jobs.[19] Several federal courts, relying on *Dothard*, subsequently permitted airlines to use the BFOQ defense to justify layoffs of pregnant flight attendants, on the ground that the airlines' policies were necessary to ensure the safety of passengers.[20]

Dothard had opened the door to widening the BFOQ standard by permitting sex stereotypes to be a legitimate basis for excluding women from jobs. Advocates wondered whether *Dothard* could jeopardize their momentous gains on the pregnancy discrimination front. In particular, they worried that the case could lead to legal recognition of the fetus as a "third party" whose safety was placed at risk by its mother's employment. The concern was that courts would permit employers to exclude women based upon concerns for fetal safety.

---

[17] Dothard v. Rawlinson, 433 U.S. 321 (1977).

[18] *Id.* at 335 n.21.

[19] *Id.* at 333.

[20] Harriss v. Pan American World Airways, Inc., 649 F. 2d 670 (9th Cir. 1980); Condit v. United Air Lines, Inc., 558 F. 2d 1176 (4th Cir. 1977), *cert. denied*, 435 U.S. 934 (1978); In re National Airlines, Inc., 434 F. Supp. 249 (S.D. Fla. 1977).

C. The Failure of Regulatory and Litigation Efforts Proceeding Under Workplace Health and Safety Requirements

Statutes and regulations governing health and safety offered another avenue for tackling the reproductive hazards facing women and men in the workplace. These efforts, however, were thwarted by agency paralysis and litigation failures.

On December 29, 1970, after much political wrangling, President Nixon signed the Occupational Safety and Health Act (OSH Act),[21] creating an Occupational Safety and Health Administration (OSHA) that was charged with promulgating workplace health and safety standards and conducting inspections to monitor compliance with these standards.[22] Between 1971 and 1984, OSHA implemented fifteen standards regulating toxic substances, including lead.[23] Chronic overexposure to lead through inhalation or ingestion, the agency found, could cause severe damage to the blood-forming, nervous, urinary, and reproductive systems of men and women.[24] In order to avoid the risks posed to workers by exposure to lead throughout a working lifetime, the agency stated, worker blood lead levels should be maintained at or below 40 [mu]g/100g, and the blood lead levels of all workers who intend to have children should be maintained below 30 [mu]g/100g "to minimize adverse reproductive health effects to the parents and to the developing fetus."[25]

In November 1978, OSHA passed a controversial new lead standard that required employers to remove from the workplace any employees—female and male—with abnormally high blood lead levels or actual physical impairment from lead exposure, to place these employees in

---

[21] P.L. 91–596.

[22] *Id.* at § 6(b)(5).

[23] GONEN, *supra* note 1, at 33 (citing CHARLES NOBLE, LIBERALISM AT WORK: THE RISE AND FALL OF OSHA (1986)).

[24] With respect to the reproductive system, OSHA found:

Overexposure to lead may result in decreased sex drive, impotence and sterility in men. Lead can alter the structure of sperm cells raising the risk of birth defects. There is evidence of miscarriage and stillbirth in women whose husbands were exposed to lead or who were exposed to lead themselves. Lead exposure also may result in decreased fertility, and abnormal menstrual cycles in women. The course of pregnancy may be adversely affected by exposure to lead since lead crosses the placental barrier and poses risks to developing fetuses. Children born of parents either one of whom were exposed to excess lead levels are more likely to have birth defects, mental retardation, behavioral disorders or die during the first year of childhood.

29 C.F.R. § 1910.1025, App. A, § (II)(B)(2).

[25] *Id.* at § (II)(B)(3).

low-exposure workplaces or on leave, and to continue to grant them the earnings, benefits, and seniority rights of their original jobs for at least 18 months.[26] The impact of the new lead standard reverberated throughout the United States, where industry consumed annually over one million tons of lead and at least 800,000 workers, representing 120 occupations in over 40 industries, were exposed to airborne lead on the job.[27]

Although OSHA's lead standard addressed both male and female-mediated harm resulting from workers' exposure to airborne lead, the majority of the studies upon which it relied focused on female-mediated risk. Importantly, the biological mechanism by which paternal transmission of a toxin to a fetus occurs is scientifically difficult to identify. Scientists in the 1970s and 80s studying the effects of exposure to toxic substances in the reproductive context had focused almost exclusively on teratogenic effects—the effects of maternal transmission to a developing fetus—and had largely overlooked the effects of paternal environmental exposure on offspring.[28] Moreover, science is not immune to the gender stereotypes and biases that pervade other fields and industries. Many scientists researching reproductive hazards have mistakenly assumed that only the fittest sperm can and will fertilize an egg, or that there is an exclusive link between birth defects and maternal transmission of toxins.[29] Recent data indicate these assumptions are incorrect, and that both paternal and maternal exposure to numerous chemical, physical, and biological agents can cause spontaneous abortions or birth defects.[30]

OSHA's increased attention to the health hazards associated with lead and the growing scientific research linking maternal lead exposure with birth defects in children alarmed many corporations in the chemical and heavy metal industries. Corporate lawyers feared that the growing focus on lead would result in the filing of multi-million dollar lawsuits on behalf of children with lead-related birth defects, since the workers' compensation system, which bars employees from suing employers on their own behalf for health problems associated with workplace hazards, does not foreclose litigation on behalf of a fetus. Doctors employed by industry advocated protecting women from potential toxic exposure as a

---

[26] 29 C.F.R. § 1910.1025(k)(1)(iii)-(v), (k)(2) (1979).

[27] United Steelworkers v. Marshall, 647 F.2d 1189, 1204 (D.C. Cir. 1980).

[28] SUZANNE UTTARO SAMUELS, FETAL RIGHTS, WOMEN'S RIGHTS 59 (1995). Wendy W. Williams, *Firing the Women to Protect the Fetus: The Reconciliation of Fetal Protection with Employment Opportunity Goals under Title VII,* 69 GEO. L.J. 641, 661 (1980–81).

[29] SAMUELS, *supra* note 29, at 59.

[30] *Id.* at 59; Williams, *supra* note 29, at 661.

matter of public health and to avoid medical malpractice lawsuits.[31] Corporate executives were concerned about the ethical dilemmas posed by risking harm to a fetus by exposing pregnant (or "potentially" pregnant) workers to lead. Managers and industry scientists were convinced that it was not technologically or economically feasible to clean up workplaces enough so that all workers would have blood lead levels below OSHA's standard.[32] Male factory workers and supervisors continued to resist women's entry into traditionally male jobs. In response to these considerations, many major automobile, chemical, tire, and photographic manufacturing companies adopted fetal protection policies throughout the 1970s that, despite the dictates of the new OSHA lead standard, transferred or banned women (without compensation) from jobs in which they were exposed to airborne lead and other toxic substances.[33]

Fetal protection policies, initiated around the same time that protectionist legislation was being dismantled nationwide, effectively re-segregated (by gender) many of the forty-plus industrial workplaces nationwide in which employees were exposed to lead. By the time the PDA was enacted in 1978, fetal protection policies marked a growing trend amongst industry leaders, one that commentators thought signaled "the emergence of a major new civil rights and civil liberties issue that poses medical, legal, economic, and moral dilemmas."[34] The issue involved not only women's rights in the workplace, but also "the more portentous question" of the reproductive harms caused to both men and women by exposure to toxic substances at work.[35]

Women's rights and labor advocates initially enlisted OSHA's support in both invalidating fetal protection policies and reducing health risks to women and men. This mobilization began with a challenge to American Cyanamid Company's fetal protection policy. In January 1978, just four years after women were first hired on the production floor of the company's lead pigment plant in Willow Island, West Virginia, American Cyanamid instituted a policy barring women from all jobs on the factory floor except those who underwent surgical sterilization.[36] Five

[31] Kirp, *supra* note 3, at 114 (citing interview with Dr. Benjamin Culver, medical consultant to the Johnson Controls Fullerton, California plant).

[32] *See, e.g.*, Philip Shabecoff, *Job Threats to Workers' Fertility Emerging as a Civil Liberties Issue*, N.Y. TIMES, Jan. 15, 1979, at A1.

[33] *See* Laura Oren, *Symposium: Institutional Barriers to Women in the Workplace: Protection, Patriarchy, and Capitalism: The Politics and Theory of Gender–Specific Regulation in The Workplace*, 6 UCLA WOMEN'S L.J. 321, 340 (1996).

[34] Shabecoff, *supra* note 33, at A1.

[35] *Id.*

[36] Bill Richards, *Women Say They Had to Be Sterilized to Hold Jobs*, WASH. POST, Jan. 1, 1979, at A1; Oren, *supra* note 34 at 349.

female employees, aged 26 to 43, chose sterilization over job loss. When they returned to work, male co-workers taunted them for having been "spayed" by the veterinarian.[37]

Workers filed complaints with their union, the Oil, Chemical and Atomic Workers Union (OCAW), and the union went public with the story of the sterilization in late 1978. "No More Willow Islands" became a "rallying cry" of unions and interest groups.[38] Soon, more than 44 feminist, labor, civil rights, and civil liberties organizations[39] joined together to form The Coalition for Reproductive Rights of Workers (CRROW), whose statement of purpose read:

> To resist sex-biased sex-specific policies from the outset; to push corporations to eliminate hazards affecting all workers, regardless of sex or occupation; and to devise compensatory strategies, such as voluntary "reproductive leave" or transfers, with full pay and benefits for both female and male workers in jobs where hazards still exist.[40]

CRROW initially framed the problem broadly. Reflecting the breadth of its membership's interests, the coalition sought to link the pursuit of substantive workplace safety precautions with eliminating sex discrimination.

OCAW and CRROW teamed up to respond to American Cyanamid, and the first step in their advocacy strategy was to lobby OSHA—at the time a friendly ally, having recently lowered its blood lead level standards and denounced fetal protection policies as an unacceptable response to concerns about workplace health—for action.[41] In May 1979, OSHA levied fines against Cyanamid for overexposing workers to lead and cancer-causing chromates,[42] and in October 1979, the agency charged

---

[37] Rachel Roth, Making Women Pay: The Hidden Costs of Fetal Rights 37 (2000).

[38] Oren, *supra* note 34, at 351.

[39] These groups included the Amalgamated Clothing and Textile Workers Union, International Brotherhood of Painters and Allied Trades, International Chemical Workers Union, UAW, United Rubber Workers, United Steelworkers, Coalition of Black Trade Unionists, CLUW, ACLU WRP, ERA, Center for Constitutional Rights, Center for Law and Social Policy, National Lawyers Guild, Committee for Abortion Rights and Against Sterilization Abuse, League of Women Voters, NOW, WLDF, Alan Guttmacher Institute, the Reproductive Rights National Network, and Planned Parenthood Federation of America. Oren, *supra* note 34, at 351; Gonen, *supra* note 1, at 36.

[40] Oren, *supra* note 34, at 351.

[41] Oren, *supra* note 34, at 343, 352.

[42] Bill Richards, *Lead Level at Pigment Plant Too High, Inspectors Charge*, Wash. Post, May 6, 1979, at A17.

Cyanamid with violating the "general duty clause"[43] of the OSH Act, which obligates employers to provide safe workplaces to employees, by subjecting female employees to the "hazards" of sterilization as a condition of employment.[44] After extensive administrative litigation, in which OCAW and CRROW were intimately involved, the independent Occupational Safety and Health Review Commission (OSHRC) vacated the citation on April 29, 1981,[45] finding that that the decision to be sterilized was due to external economic factors for which the company was not responsible and concluding that "the [fetal protection] policy is not a hazard within the meaning of the general duty clause."[46] OCAW appealed to the D.C. Circuit.

Before the case was heard on appeal, Joan Bertin from the ACLU Women's Rights Project filed and settled a companion case that challenged American Cyanamid's fetal protection policy under Title VII. Bertin had also assisted OCAW in developing the factual record and expert testimony in the OSHA case. On appeal, the three-judge panel, which included then-Judges Bork and Scalia, unanimously affirmed the OSHRC's decision.[47] Judge Bork wrote for the majority, finding that American Cyanamid's women workers had no remedy under the Occupational Safety and Health Act for being "put to the most unhappy choice" between sterilization and discharge in a case such as this, where the employer complied with OSHA's lead-level standard and still did not eliminate the risk of serious harm to fetuses carried by women employees.[48]

In the wake of *American Cyanamid*, CRROW and its members pressured the EEOC and other executive agencies to propose guidelines

---

[43] 29 U.S.C. § 654.

[44] The text of the citation read:

The employer did not furnish *employment and a place of employment which were free from recognized hazards that were causing or were likely to cause death or serious physical harm to employees*, in that: The employer adopted and implemented a policy which required women employees to be sterilized in order to be eligible to work in the areas of the plant where they would be exposed to certain toxic substances.

OCAW Int'l Union v. American Cyanamid Co., 741 F.2d 444, 447 (D.C. Cir. 1984) (quoting 29 U.S.C. § 654 (a)(1) (1982)) (emphasis added); *OSHA Puts Its Power to a Test*, Bus. Wk., Oct. 29, 1979, at 162T.

[45] American Cyanamid Co., 9 OSHC (BNA) 1596, at *16 (1981); *see also American Cyanamid*, 741 F.2d at 447–48.

[46] *American Cyanamid Co.*, 9 OSHC (BNA) 1596, at *14. *See also OSHA Puts Its Power to a Test, supra* note 45, at 162T.

[47] *American Cyanamid*, 741 F.2d at 449.

[48] *American Cyanamid*, 741 F.2d at 450.

on workplace reproductive hazards and fetal protection policies.[49] In 1980, the EEOC proposed guidelines that permitted single-sex exclusionary policies temporarily and as a last resort, and forbade use of the BFOQ defense in the context of fetal protection policies. OSHA assisted with the development of the guidelines and initially agreed to provide technical assistance with enforcement.[50] These guidelines prompted grievances from groups on both sides of the aisle, and the Carter-appointed EEOC, fearing that the incoming Reagan administration would significantly alter the guidelines, withdrew them and instead issued a simple statement that discrimination claims related to fetal protection policies should be resolved on a case-by-case basis.[51] The EEOC subsequently drafted a supplement to its 1981 Compliance Manual directing field offices to coordinate with OSHA and other agencies to evaluate scientific data relevant to a claim. However, this section was also withdrawn after budget cuts at OSHA precluded it from participating in this collaboration.[52]

From 1981 to 1988, the EEOC had no guidelines for evaluating claims related to fetal protection policies, and claims that were filed during this period were often left unresolved.[53] In 1988, the EEOC issued a Policy Statement which provided that the business necessity test, rather than the more rigorous BFOQ test, should be the appropriate measure of the legality of a fetal protection policy under Title VII. Contemplating a far less prominent role for OSHA, the 1988 Guidelines directed the EEOC to OSHA's expertise "whenever possible," but declined to characterize OSHA's determinations about workplace hazards as binding on the EEOC.[54]

The 1988 guidelines also declared that, in cases where there was inconclusive evidence about the effects of workplace hazards on male workers—even if this paucity was due to the fact that this evidence did not exist (rather than some inconsistency in existing evidence)—the EEOC could consider the claim as if the hazard was "substantially confined to female employees."[55] Because the limited scientific data that existed focused far more on the effects of maternal transmission of toxins to a fetus than on the effects on a fetus of paternal exposure to

---

[49] GONEN , *supra* note 1, at 37.

[50] SAMUELS, *supra* note 29, at 85–86; GONEN, *supra* note 1, at 37.

[51] SAMUELS, *supra* note 29, at 87.

[52] *Id.*

[53] *Id.* at 87, 93.

[54] *Id.* at 89.

[55] EEOC Policy Guidance 1988, 9 *in* SAMUELS, *supra* note 29, at 88–89.

such toxins, these guidelines operated as a disincentive to employer-sponsored research on paternally-transmitted risks and ultimately encouraged employers to exclude women from the workplace.[56]

The EEOC was not alone in responding passively in the 1980s to the growing corporate fetal protection policy trend. The Office of Federal Contract Compliance Programs (OFCCP), which is specifically authorized under Executive Order 11246 to require non-discrimination for private employers who contract with the federal government, did little in the 1980s and instead deferred to the EEOC as the appropriate agency to take action in the area.[57] Similarly, the Environmental Protection Agency repeatedly delegated responsibility for investigating chemicals used in the workplace to OSHA.[58] The EEOC's unwillingness to incorporate health and safety concerns into its anti-discrimination approach seemed to deflate the robust coalition of these interests. Subsequently, CRROW does not appear much in the Johnson Controls story. Advocates increasingly focus their challenges to fetal protection policies on anti-discrimination arguments.

Throughout the 1980s, OSHA, the EEOC, EPA, and OFCCP "engaged in a balancing approach forced by political exigency,"[59] industry pressure, inadequate funding, and the looming abortion issue. The Reagan administration cut agencies' budgets and operating staffs and their ability to formulate policy and enforce existing regulations, and Congress was not interested in taking on the fight against this deregulation. The retreat of both Congress and executive regulatory agencies from the fetal protection debate created a policy vacuum in which agencies maintained out of date standards and only minimally enforced their own regulations, and in which employers knew they could get away with using toxic chemicals and adopting fetal protection policies, even if doing so might technically violate agency guidelines.

In this context, advocates turned once again to the courts as a potential avenue for dismantling fetal protection policies. This time, however, they avoided litigating under OSHA and turned instead to the Title VII sex discrimination framework. This move began the process of narrowing from a multi-prong, problem-oriented coalition to an alliance focused on winning a test case.

D. The Development of a Litigation Strategy Under Title VII

Between 1982 and 1990, five federal appeals courts heard Title VII challenges to sex-specific fetal protection policies.[60] Ordinarily, a policy

---

[56] SAMUELS, *supra* note 29, at 58–59; Williams, *supra* note 29, at 661.

[57] SAMUELS, *supra* note 29, at 99–100.

[58] *Id.* at 130–31.

[59] *Id.* at 135.

[60] *See* Wright v. Olin Corp., 697 F.2d 1172 (4th Cir. 1982); Zuniga v. Kleberg County Hosp., 692 F.2d 986, 991, 994 (5th Cir. 1982); Hayes v. Shelby Memorial Hosp., 726 F.2d

that specifically excludes women from the workforce will be considered intentional discrimination under the Title VII "disparate treatment" framework. An employer can justify such an employment practice only in "those certain instances where [sex] is a bona fide occupational qualification [BFOQ] reasonably necessary to the normal operation of that particular business or enterprise."[61] Courts considering fetal protection policies, however, repeatedly reasoned that these cases presented new and unique issues that justified straying from traditional proof rules. Instead, most courts applied a "disparate impact" analysis, under which neutral policies or practices that have a disproportionate and adverse impact on any protected class constitute discrimination. An employer can justify an employment practice that has a disparate impact with a lesser showing that it is "job related for the position in question and consistent with business necessity."[62]

Some courts indicated that the "valid business necessity" defense could cover employers' legitimate business interests in avoiding tort lawsuits filed by the children of lead-exposed mothers.[63] Others emphasized that fetal protection policies were most justifiable if intended to protect the safety of third parties—in this case, the "unborn children" of female employees.[64] Over time, corporate defendants increasingly focused on this moral/public policy justification for adopting fetal protection policies and deemphasized the financial considerations related to tort liability. These decisions energized the women's rights and labor advocates that had already been working together on fetal protection issues and marked a new phase in the movement.

Various members of the now-familiar cast of characters—labor, civil, and women's rights groups on one side, and corporations, pro-business groups, and anti-abortion advocates on the other—participated in PDA-related advocacy in the 1970s and fetal protection-related litigation in the 1980s as attorneys for the parties and as amici.[65] Marsha Berzon, the Associate General Counsel of the AFL–CIO, who argued the *Johnson*

1543 (11th Cir. 1984); Int'l Union, U.A.W. v. Johnson Controls, 886 F.2d 871 (7th Cir. 1989); *but see* Grant v. General Motors Corp., 908 F.2d 1303 (6th Cir. 1990).

[61] 42 U.S.C. § 703(e)(1).

[62] 42 U.S.C.S. § 2000e–2(k)(1)(A)(i).

[63] *See, e.g., Zuniga*, 692 F.2d 986, at 992 n.10; *Wright*, 697 F.2d 1172, at 1190 n.26; *Johnson Controls*, 886 F.2d 871, at 884.

[64] *Hayes*, 726 F.2d 1543; *Wright*, 697 F.2d 1172, at 1189–90.

[65] GONEN, *supra* note 1, at 53.

Controls case before the Supreme Court, was a principal drafter of the PDA, which, she said, had been deliberately drafted with sex-specific fetal protection policies in mind.[66] Another major figure representing the anti-fetal protection policy position was Joan Bertin of the ACLU Women's Rights Project, who had spent much of the decade working on *American Cyanamid* and other projects to lay the groundwork for a Supreme Court case challenging fetal protection policies. Bertin has been described as the "mastermind" behind the campaign against fetal protection policies[67] The alliances she created with other advocates set the wheels in motion for a challenge to Johnson Controls' company policy, and the UAW was positioned to take a leading role in representing employees across the country who sought to challenge a policy they viewed as discriminatory, unfair, and arcane. This law reform campaign was characterized by participants as the equivalent of the NAACP strategy in *Brown v. Board of Education.* The long range strategic plan was to have this issue determined favorably in the Supreme Court.[68]

III. Johnson Controls: The National Story

Johnson Controls initially adopted a policy in 1977 that warned fertile women of the potentially harmful effects of lead on a fetus but stopped short of excluding them from the workplace.[69] Five years later, in 1982, the company decided to rethink its approach. Corporate executives at Johnson Controls publicly explained that the policy shift was implemented in response to increasing scientific research pointing to risks of fetal harm associated with lead and upon realizing that its current program was not effectively protecting workers' fetuses. However, rumors were circulating that the company, like others in the industry, initiated the new policy in response to rising fears of tort liability. Lead was an essential component of batteries, so the company could not simply stop using lead in battery production. Johnson Controls had spent $15 million since 1978 on new equipment to remove lead from factory air, but the company believed that reducing airborne lead to a safe level for fetuses would be extremely costly, if not technologically impossible.[70]

As a result, Johnson Controls implemented its exclusionary fetal protection policy relatively late in the game in comparison to other giants in the chemical and heavy metal industries. This triggered the

---

[66] *Id.* at 60.

[67] *Id.* at 53.

[68] *Id.* at 56.

[69] *Johnson Controls,* 886 F.2d 871, at 876 (quoting policy).

[70] *See Risk to Fetus Ruled as Barring Women From Jobs,* N.Y. TIMES, Oct. 3, 1989.

litigation that became the capstone of the effort to overturn fetal protection policies and narrow the scope of the BFOQ.

A. *Johnson Controls* litigation in the lower courts

The UAW's assistant general counsel filed EEOC charges on behalf of 8 individual plaintiffs under Title VII, and the agency issued right-to-sue letters in early 1984. The plaintiffs then filed suit in federal court in the Eastern District of Wisconsin. In early 1985, the district court granted class certification to the UAW and its 2,109 production and maintenance employees (of whom only 275 were female).[71] From the beginning, the case was worker-driven. Beverly Tucker, a UAW attorney, described the workers as "adamant" about pursuing the case even when the attorneys who represented them expressed initial reservations after learning of new research that showed harmful effects of even lower lead exposure levels than previously thought.[72] The UAW filed the complaint in *Johnson Controls* with the plan that it would be a "test case, a policy case" that could eventually get to the Supreme Court.[73] In January 1988, the Eastern District of Wisconsin, relying on a disparate impact framework, granted summary judgment for Johnson Controls.[74] Later that year, the EEOC published its first "Policy Guidance on Reproductive and Fetal Hazards," which pronounced that an exclusionary fetal protection policy could constitute a business necessity if an employer could prove that a workplace toxin posed a "substantial risk of harm" to the fetus, that this risk only occurred through maternal exposure, that the policy effectively eliminated the risk of harm, and that no less restrictive alternatives existed.[75]

By the time the case was appealed in February 1988, it had attracted considerable outside attention. The LAS–ELC, the ACLU, and the American Public Health Association (APHA) each filed separate amicus briefs in support of the UAW, and Joan Bertin from the ACLU began assembling amici for a potential appeal to the Supreme Court.

In September 1989, the Seventh Circuit Court of Appeals affirmed the lower court's decision in *Johnson Controls* in a sharply divided 7–4

---

[71] *See* Int'l Union, United Auto., etc. v. Johnson Controls, 680 F. Supp. 309, 310 (E. D. Wis. 1988), *rev'd and remanded*, Int'l Union, United Auto., etc. v. Johnson Controls, Inc., 499 U.S. 187 (1991).

[72] GONEN, *supra* note 1, at 57, 65.

[73] GONEN, *supra* note 1, at 58.

[74] JOHNSON CONTROLS, 680 F. Supp. 309.

[75] "EEOC's Policy Guidance on Reproductive and Fetal Hazards," Daily Lab. Report (BNA), No. 193 at D–1 (Oct. 5, 1988).

en banc decision.[76] The Seventh Circuit found that the company's fetal protection policy was valid under disparate impact and disparate treatment frameworks, becoming the first court of appeals in the country to hold that women's infertility could be a BFOQ for certain jobs.[77] The court found that Johnson Controls had demonstrated a valid business necessity—"the industrial safety-based concern of protecting the unborn child from lead exposure"—for its fetal protection policy.[78] Moreover, the court disregarded the OSHA lead standard and discounted animal studies on the effects of paternal exposure to lead as inconclusive.[79] Employing the reasoning of the recent Supreme Court case *Wards Cove Packing Co. v. Antonio*,[80] the Seventh Circuit placed the burden of proving discrimination, and disproving the company's claimed business necessity, on the plaintiffs.

Judges Richard Posner and Frank Easterbrook dissented. Judge Posner took an intermediate approach to the case, noting that the "the most sensible way to approach it at this early stage is on a case-by-case basis," and upon a full examination of the facts at trial.[81] Judge Posner left room for the possibility that under certain circumstances, fetal protection policies could be "reasonably necessary to the normal (civilized, humane, prudent, ethical) operation of [a] particular business" and could constitute grounds for a BFOQ of infertility.[82]

Judge Easterbrook went several steps further, concluding that the fetal protection policies at issue were facially discriminatory and that, under the PDA, Johnson Controls only had available to it a narrow BFOQ defense—not the business necessity defense that previous appellate courts had applied in similar cases. He concluded that the company's stated objectives—concern for the welfare of the next generation—did not meet that test because they were not related to its ability to make batteries or to any woman's "ability or inability to work."[83] Picking up on a creative argument advanced by the plaintiffs, he noted that "[r]e-

---

[76] Johnson Controls, 886 F.2d 871 (7th Cir. 1989) *rev'd and remanded*, Int'l Union, United Auto., etc. v. Johnson Controls, Inc., 499 U.S. 187 (1991).

[77] Johnson Controls, 886 F.2d 871. *See also* Johnson Controls, Inc., *499 U.S. at 196* (1991).

[78] *Johnson Controls*, 886 F.2d 871, at 899.

[79] *Id.* at 876 n.10, 880, 889, 899.

[80] 490 U.S. 642 (1989) (placing greater burden on plaintiffs to disprove business necessity defense).

[81] 886 F.2d 871, at 908 (Posner, J., dissenting).

[82] *Id.* at 905–06.

[83] *Id.* at 912 (Easterbrook, J., dissenting).

moving women from well-paying jobs (and the attendant health insurance), or denying women access to these jobs, may reduce the risk from lead while also reducing levels of medical care and the quality of nutrition."[84] Judge Easterbrook, perhaps sending a signal to the Supreme Court, noted that *Johnson Controls* was "likely the most important sex-discrimination case in any court since 1964, when Congress enacted Title VII. If the majority is right, then by one estimate 20 million industrial jobs could be closed to women, for many substances in addition to lead pose fetal risks."[85]

The sharply divided Seventh Circuit decision in *Johnson Controls* caught the attention of the EEOC, which, in January 1990, issued revised policy guidance on workplace reproductive hazards that criticized the Seventh Circuit's reasoning and asserted that (1) fetal protection policies were facially discriminatory; (2) that the employer should be held to a narrow BFOQ defense, rather than that of business necessity; and (3) that the burden of proof should be on the employer, not the employee.[86] The guidance indicated that, outside the Seventh Circuit, the EEOC would require employers to show that such policies were reasonably necessary to the normal operation of the business, based on objective evidence, and that a good-faith intention or effort to avoid liability would be an insufficient defense. The new EEOC guidelines were issued just two days before the UAW's deadline for filing its certiorari petition to the Supreme Court. These guidelines served as a *de facto* substitute for an amicus brief (since governmental agencies generally do not submit amicus briefs on certiorari petitions).[87]

B. Litigation before the Supreme Court

The UAW filed a petition for certiorari. The ACLU, APHA, and 54 other groups and individuals filed an amicus brief supporting that petition, arguing that the case presented issues of great public importance in the equal opportunity and public health arenas, particularly to working women and their families, and that a Supreme Court decision resolving the conflicting circuit opinions was needed. In March 1990, the Supreme Court agreed to hear the case.[88] In the months before oral argument, the California Court of Appeal and the Sixth Circuit came down with the first two rulings rejecting a BFOQ defense and finding

---

[84] *Id.* at 918.

[85] *Id.* at 920.

[86] "EEOC Policy Guidance on Seventh Circuit Decision in United Auto Workers v. Johnson Controls, Inc.," Daily Lab. Report (BNA), No. 18 at D–2 to D–3 (Jan. 26, 1990).

[87] *See, e.g.,* GONEN, *supra* note 1, at 104.

[88] *Id.* at 61.

that fetal protection policies that excluded lead-exposed female employees constituted unlawful sex discrimination under a disparate treatment theory.[89]

The plaintiffs reassembled their legal team to handle the Supreme Court briefing and argument, bringing on two experienced Supreme Court litigators from the AFL–CIO, including Associate General Counsel Marsha Berzon. The UAW followed a fairly traditional approach in its briefing on the merits, focusing on questions concerning the interpretation of Title VII, the PDA, and the BFOQ exception, and leaving its amici to highlight the economic and social impact of exclusionary sex-specific fetal protection policies on working women. The union pointed to the PDA and OSHA standards and the California *Johnson Controls* case in support of its argument, emphasizing that under Title VII, the Court must look only to whether or not women could perform the job—not at Johnson Controls' purpose, however benign, in adopting an exclusionary policy.

Johnson Controls responded by arguing that a company's interest in avoiding harm to third parties, including fetuses, was reasonably necessary to the company's normal business operations under Title VII and thus justified its implementation of an exclusionary fetal protection policy. The BFOQ analysis, Johnson Controls argued, was not only limited to a worker's ability to perform the job; a valid BFOQ defense could also include potential tort liability against the company for a fetal injuries.

The UAW responded by noting, as it had in earlier disputes, that Johnson Controls had not presented any evidence that men were *not* at risk for contributing to fetal injuries; that the company could not, under the BFOQ defense, institute a policy of zero risk for fetuses and not for adult workers; that female workers must make their own personal risk assessments; and that responsible employers would not be liable in tort for prenatal harm.

C. Amicus mobilization

After the Supreme Court granted certiorari, Bertin, who had consulted with the UAW in the early stages of the case, assumed the pivotal role of amicus brief coordinator.[90] Working closely with Berzon and others, she spearheaded a comprehensive amicus strategy that mobilized a broad-based coalition of influential amici to rally behind the sex

---

[89] Johnson Controls v. California Fair Employment and Housing Comm'n, 267 Cal. Rptr. 158 (1990); Grant v. General Motors, 908 F.2d 1303 (6th Cir. 1990).

[90] GONEN, *supra* note 1, at 66; Email from Joan Bertin, Executive Director, National Coalition Against Censorship, to Caroline Bettinger–López, Post–Doctoral Research Scholar, Columbia Law School (Feb. 11, 2007, 4:55 p.m.).

discrimination principles at stake in the case and to frame those principles in the context of their broader institutional agendas. This amicus mobilization had several functions. First, securing such diverse and overwhelming opposition to fetal protection policies from experts and other credible sources, Bertin and Berzon felt, would convey a powerful message to the Supreme Court about the importance of the issue and the strength of the empirical and normative consensus behind the union's position. The amicus briefs also provided a comprehensive picture of the harmful effects of fetal protection policies on women and offered arguments to the Court that were more far-reaching and nuanced than those presented by the UAW. Furthermore, the very process of developing a group of amici could reaffirm existing ties between organizations that had previously participated in CRROW, CEDAPW, and other related initiatives, and could spur and sustain, during and after the Supreme Court litigation, new relationships between advocates interested in reproductive and workplace hazards and sex equality. Ultimately, over 110 organizations and individuals signed onto ten amicus briefs in support of the plaintiffs.

1. Communicating Credibility and Consensus

One goal of the amicus mobilization was to show the Court that a broad array of prominent interest groups and experts viewed exclusionary fetal protection policies as unlawful sex discrimination and embraced the narrow BFOQ standard articulated by the UAW plaintiffs. With this goal in mind, Bertin and Berzon successfully courted many groups with longstanding experience litigating before the Supreme Court and a background in women's and/or workers' rights advocacy.

The ACLU, the most active amicus party in the case, had actively participated in Supreme Court challenges to sex discrimination, pregnancy discrimination, and reproductive hazards since the early 1970s, when Ruth Bader Ginsburg founded the Women's Rights Project. Its *Johnson Controls* amicus brief argued that Title VII, as amended by the PDA, represents a comprehensive legislative attempt to eradicate gender discrimination and recognize the serious socio-economic and health consequences of unemployment and occupational segregation on women and families, and that fetal protection policies, offering "neither workplace safety for men nor equity for women," violate these clear objectives. Thirteen scientists and experts, and forty-one organizations (including unions, labor organizations, and civil, women's, and workplace rights advocates, some of whom—such as LAS—ELC, the National Women's Law Center, and NOW LDEF—were repeat players in the pregnancy discrimination arena) signed onto the brief, which Bertin authored.[91]

---

[91] GONEN, *supra* note 1, at 67.

Well-known women's rights organizations also signed onto another amicus brief authored by Equal Rights Advocates (ERA), which argued that the PDA intended to classify pregnancy-based exclusions as facial discrimination, that only an employee's ability to perform the job—and not fetal health—was relevant in considering the BFOQ exception, and that fetal protection policies could only be legally adopted if they were sex neutral. With such strong legislative history, Berzon thought this brief would be "our real ace in the deck."[92]

Another notable set of amici was comprised of state governments. The State of California submitted an amicus brief urging the Supreme Court to model its decision on the California *Johnson Controls* case, which California's Fair Employment and Housing Commission had recently litigated with LAS–ELC. The Massachusetts Attorney General, joined by several other states, filed an amicus brief addressing the public health, gender, and socio-economic dimensions of the case and underscoring the dangers posed to male reproductive systems by airborne lead. The United States and the EEOC jointly filed an amicus brief focusing on the Title VII framework of the case. Interestingly, the U.S./EEOC's amicus brief argued that under certain circumstances—including when the health or safety of a fetus is at risk—an employer could justify its sex-based fetal protection policies under the BFOQ test. This was a much more cautious approach than the policy guidance on the fetal protection issue that the EEOC had issued just two days before the UAW filed its certiorari petition, and was likely due to the Solicitor General's involvement in the litigation.

A final set of amici were public health and environmental groups such as the APHA and the Natural Resources Defense Council (NRDC). These groups' briefs emphasized the validity and importance of animal studies, a topic the Court had only previously considered in passing.

The prominence of many amici and their nuanced understandings of the vast implications of the *Johnson Controls* case lent a sense of legitimacy to the amicus mobilization. Although the Court never specifically acknowledged any particular amicus brief, it is worth noting that the opinion emphasized the legislative history of the PDA, the topic of the ERA's amicus brief.

2. Providing a Context for Understanding Fetal Protection Policies' Harmful Effects on Women

In *Johnson Controls*, the UAW could not, for the most part, draw the Court's attention to the important health and safety issues underlying the case because these issues were tangential to the sex discrimination questions before the Supreme Court. Bertin, understanding and

---

[92] GONEN, *supra* note 1, at 87.

appreciating the seriousness of these issues, capitalized upon the recognized expertise and legitimacy of well-known public interest organizations to address the intersections between gender, economic and social power, and workplace health and safety via amicus briefs. She realized, for instance, that scientific evidence or public health data would be presented more effectively by groups such as the NRDC and the APHA than by the ACLU and women's rights organizations. The amicus briefs in support of the plaintiffs fell into roughly two different (though sometimes overlapping) categories: women's rights/anti-discrimination and public health.

Some of the more far-reaching arguments set forth in the amicus briefs addressed the socio-economic and public health implications of fetal protection policies. The ACLU, ERA, and Attorneys' General briefs noted that fetal protection policies would cause women's unemployment or employment in lower-strata, non-unionized jobs that do not offer medical insurance and other important benefits. The NAACP LDF brief observed that this result "may be more harmful than the potential hazard to uncontemplated future offspring posed by working in a job which may involve exposure to hazardous substances." Notably, the NAACP LDF, known for its legal challenges to racially discriminatory policies, entered the reproductive health arena for the first time with *Johnson Controls*. Marianne Lado, the LDF attorney who authored its amicus brief in *Johnson Controls*, described the case as a "bridge case into the reproductive rights area," which ultimately resulted in LDF coming to see reproductive health issues as "squarely within its area of expertise."[93]

3. Building Organizational Alliances

Through the amicus briefs, Bertin, Berzon, and their colleagues reinvigorated and gave voice to the alliance that had formed between labor, workplace health and safety groups, and women's and civil rights organizations over the past two decades through the formation of groups such as CRROW and CEDAPW, via concerted advocacy efforts surrounding the passage of the PDA and related policies before OSHA and the EEOC, and by way of amicus briefs in fetal protection and pregnancy discrimination cases. These groups collectively produced a broad policy statement through their amicus briefs and advocacy in *Johnson Controls* that addressed health and safety, sex discrimination, job and benefits retention, socio-economic mobility, and other complex dimensions of the problems posed by fetal protection policies and workplace toxins.

The question remained, though, whether their involvement as amici would make a difference to any mobilization or advocacy that occurred

---

[93] GONEN, *supra* note 1, at 101.

afterwards. The ACLU WRP had been preparing for a fetal protection/sex discrimination test case for a decade, and if the plaintiffs' challenge in *Johnson Controls* succeeded, it was unclear who, if anyone, would push ahead on the remaining health and safety issues after the litigation was over.

IV. The Supreme Court Decision & Its Aftermath

On March 20, 1991, the Supreme Court issued a 9–0 decision overruling the Seventh Circuit's decision and finding that Johnson Control's fetal protection policy was facially discriminatory because it categorized employees on the basis of their potential for pregnancy, which was prohibited by Title VII, as amended by the PDA. The BFOQ defense was not available to Johnson Controls, Justice Harry F. Blackmun wrote for the majority, because fetuses were neither customers nor third parties (following *Dothard* and *Harriss*) whose safety was essential to the normal operation of the business.[94] Furthermore, the Court found, a benevolent motive, such as concern for fetal harm, could not justify female sterility as a BFOQ. Justice Blackmun opined that employer liability "seem[ed] remote at best" if the employer adequately warns the employee about the risk and has not acted negligently.[95] In any event, the Court thought, tort liability could not justify a discriminatory policy under Title VII.

In concurrence, Justice White, Kennedy, and Rehnquist asserted that Justice Blackmun's "speculation" about tort liability would be "small comfort to employers," and that an employer who was able to set forth evidence that fertile women's presence in a workplace made the company susceptible to serious tort liability could have a valid BFOQ defense if it chose to exclude fertile women from its workforce.[96] Justice Scalia concurred separately, asserting that a court may take costs to a company into account when ruling on a BFOQ defense.

The Supreme Court's decision made nationwide headlines. Women's rights groups and organized labor celebrated the decision as a victory for millions of working class women. The business community decried the decision as creating a "catch–22" situation for industry, and expressed grave concerns about future corporate tort liability.

The EEOC, following its pattern of issuing guidelines in response to judicial decisions, issued new policy guidance in June 1991 that replaced its old policy guidance and adopted the Supreme Court's ruling in *Johnson Controls*. The new policy stated that employer policies excluding

---

[94] Int'l Union, U.A.W. v. Johnson Controls, Inc., 499 U.S. 187, 202–06 (1991).

[95] *Id*. at 208.

[96] *Id*. at 213 (White, J., concurring).

only members of one sex from the workplace for the purpose of fetal protection "cannot be justified under Title VII," regardless of whether toxic substances in the marketplace posed a health danger to the fetus or whether the employer would incur higher costs as a result of hiring women.[97]

Congress, too, was supportive of the Court's decision. A 1990 Congressional study issued a "scathing indictment" of the EEOC's response to fetal protection policies in the preceding decade.[98] One year later, Congress passed the 1991 Civil Rights Act[99] to, among other things, mitigate the chilling effects of repeated federal court decisions (especially *Wards Cove*) that restricted plaintiffs' ability to bring Title VII disparate impact suits.

* * *

Judges, scholars, and journalists alike have ranked *Johnson Controls* among the most significant Title VII and PDA cases. The Court's decision reaffirmed the broad scope of the PDA and the narrow scope of the BFOQ defense under Title VII. Employers quickly complied, at least *de jure*, with the Court's decision, and advocates witnessed a relatively smooth and speedy end to the sex-specific, exclusionary corporate fetal protection policies that they had vigorously opposed for over a decade.[100]

Johnson Controls' concrete holding and immediate impact have, in fact, made it more a darling of law review articles than the courts. A Westlaw search reveals that only 207 courts, compared with 900 law review articles, have cited to *Johnson Controls*. Despite this outpouring of scholarship, the academic literature has paid little attention to the unique nationwide coalition of labor, workplace health and safety advocates, and women's rights lawyers that formed in the late 1970s and early 1980s to collectively oppose fetal protection policies. How this group came together, and ultimately dissolved, is its own significant story that speaks volumes about legal mobilization and the sustainability of reform efforts.

---

[97] "Guidance on the Supreme Court Decision in International Union, United Automobile, Aerospace 7 Agricultural Implement Workers of America, UAW v. Johnson Controls, Inc.," EEOC Notice No. N–915.064, Sec. 625 at 3971–3973, EEOC Compliance Manual (June 28, 1991).

[98] *See* SAMUELS, *supra* note 29, at 78 (citing interview with Greg Watchman, General Counsel for Majority Staff, U.S. House of Representatives, Committee on Education and Labor, Washington, D.C., Dec. 3, 1990).

[99] 42 U.S.C. § 2000e–2 (2004).

[100] Telephone Interview with Pat Shiu, Vice President for Programs, Legal Aid Society of San Francisco–Employment Law Center, in San Francisco, CA (Dec. 21, 2006).

Mobilizing these diverse interest groups to attack fetal protection policies—a relatively narrow problem that affected a relatively small number of people—took a tremendous amount of energy. Joan Bertin from the ACLU had been largely responsible for this nationwide mobilization. Once the Supreme Court decision came down in *Johnson Controls*, however, these groups "declared victory and retreated to their traditional issue areas."[101] Bertin, exhausted from nearly a decade-long battle, left the ACLU and entered academia. Women's rights organizations and advocates turned to focus on the developing cause of action for sexual harassment, which would enter into Supreme Court litigation in the 1990s.[102] Unions and health and safety groups were left to advocate for the workplace rights of the blue-collar work force, even though the past decade had, in a sense, shown them that no branch of government was willing to tackle workplace health and safety issues in a holistic way. Moreover, *Johnson Controls* illustrated that improving the terms and conditions of work for the labor force required presenting the public and the courts with a problem that had shock value—like an exclusionary fetal protection policy that resulted in sterilization—and that was couched within a viable doctrinal framework—like sex discrimination.[103] General concern over unsafe working conditions, particularly when couched within an OSHA framework, would just not cut it.

Unions had limited success in winning legislative, judicial, and regulatory protections for workers in the 1990s. The ultimate survival of the OSHA lead standard against court challenges provided economic protection and independent medical review for male and female workers involuntarily removed from or hoping to be removed from lead exposure and lead hazards were much abated by other provisions of this standard.[104] While advocates were ultimately successful in convincing OSHA to promulgate rules on bloodborne pathogens, cadmium, lead and asbestos in construction and confined spaces, a host of other regulatory proposals continually languished before the agency.[105]

---

[101] Interview with Joan Bertin, Executive Director, National Coalition Against Censorship, in New York City (Nov. 13, 2006).

[102] *See* Harris v. Forklift Systems, 510 U.S. 17 (1993); Oncale v. Sundowner Offshore Services, 523 U.S. 75 (1998); Faragher v. City of Boca Raton, 524 U.S. 775 (1998); Burlington Industries v. Ellerth, 524 U.S. 742 (1998).

[103] Interview with Joan Bertin, Executive Director, National Coalition Against Censorship, in New York City (Nov. 13, 2006).

[104] Email from Frank Mirer, Professor, Environmental and Occupational Health Sciences, Hunter School of Health Sciences, to Caroline Bettinger–López, Post–Doctoral Research Scholar, Columbia Law School (Feb. 12, 2007, 11:16 a.m.).

[105] *See The Labor Movement's Role in Gaining Federal Safety and Health Standards to Protect America's Workers,* prepared by the AFL–CIO Safety and Health Department, April

Unique coalitions that formed during and after the *Johnson Controls* era faced repeated setbacks, especially after the second Bush administration took office in 2001. The problem of protecting reproductive health for women (and men) who might have sought relief from known reproductive health hazards—such as infectious disease in childcare and healthcare settings, anaesthetic gases and radiation in healthcare settings, and solvent exposure in dry cleaning—was never addressed.[106] After the Bush administration overturned a proposed ergonomics standard, more than 50 labor, occupational safety and health, public health, civil rights, religious, women's, and other organizations collectively petitioned the Secretary of Labor in April 2001 to issue an alternative standard, but the Labor Department never responded.[107] Similarly, after a 15–year dialogue between industry groups, unions, and state and federal agencies on improving injury and illness recordkeeping and data, a revised regulation was issued in January 2001. In June 2003, the Bush administration deleted key elements of the regulation, despite opposition from the unions.

V. A Contrasting Model: The California Example

While the specific goal of advocates at the national level was to establish, through litigation, the illegality of exclusionary fetal protection policies under Title VII and to affirm the narrowness of the BFOQ defense, a coalition of California advocates emerged in the 1980s with a problem-centered orientation and a broader set of goals to develop a long term strategy for addressing the reproductive health risks and needs of women and men working in hazardous industries. They adopted a holistic approach that included but also extended beyond the discrimination framework.

Even before the *Johnson Controls* decisions (the California Court of Appeals' and the Supreme Court's), Patricia Shiu from the LAS–ELC convened an ad hoc committee, designated The Workplace Reproductive Hazards Policy Group, to develop a strategy for tackling the intersecting issues of economic and social power, gender, and workplace health and safety that had clearly emerged in the fetal protection debate. At the table were diverse stakeholders—including experts in reproductive technology, occupational medicine and health, employment discrimination

---

2003 (provided to authors by Frank Mirer, Professor, Environmental and Occupational Health Sciences, Hunter School of Health Sciences).

[106] Email from Frank Mirer, Professor, Environmental and Occupational Health Sciences, Hunter School of Health Sciences, to Caroline Bettinger–López, Post–Doctoral Research Scholar, Columbia Law School (Feb. 12, 2007, 11:16 a.m.).

[107] Letter from AFL–CIO and others to Elaine Chao, Secretary of Labor, Request for a Standard in Ergonomic Hazards to Protect Workers from Work–Related Musculoskeletal Disorders (Apr. 25, 2001) (on file with authors).

law, and workers' compensation and tort liability law—representing the LAS–ELC, the Santa Clara Center for Occupational Safety and Health (SCOSH), the California Department of Health Services' Occupational Health Program, the School of Public Health at the University of California, Berkeley, and the California Fair Employment and Housing Commission (which, along with Shiu, brought the California state court lawsuit against Johnson Controls).

The California committee members shared the sentiments of national advocates who had litigated the Supreme Court *Johnson Controls* case that exclusionary fetal protection policies constituted unlawful sex discrimination, and they celebrated the *Johnson Controls* decisions as an "important first step towards eradicating occupational reproductive hazards."[108] Like their national counterparts, they also realized that "[e]xisting federal and state antidiscrimination law provides a very incomplete set of protections for workers exposed to reproductive hazards,"[109] and that as a result, the national mobilization over sex-specific fetal protection policies, and the *Johnson Controls* decisions themselves, did not (and probably could not) address the larger challenges faced by many low-income, non-unionized women and men of childbearing age who worked in contaminated workplaces.

The California initiative had several distinct advantages that allowed it to address intersectional issues of health and safety and women's rights. First, California offered a political climate that provided some, albeit limited, possibilities for regulatory and legislative reform in the workplace health and safety arena. Also, the California committee members were affiliated with organizations whose wide-ranging, intersectional mandates embraced broad long-term goals and advocacy strategies that ultimately allowed for organizational cross-pollination that was sustainable beyond a particular issue or campaign. Finally, the California group was guided by Shiu, who was well-connected with diverse stakeholders and was deeply committed to a strategy that took account of the mutual and sometimes divergent interests at the table. For Shiu, it was essential that advocates embracing a sex discrimination analysis also be "sensitive to the economic differences between poor and working class women and women [who] might have a greater ability to resist and challenge fetal protection policies because of their wage-earning capacity."[110] Shiu also saw the connection between health and safety issues and

---

[108] The Workplace Reproductive Hazards Policy Group, *Reproductive Health Hazards in the Workplace: Policy Options for California*, in California Policy Seminar brief, Vol. 4, No. 1 (Feb. 1992), at 4, http://www.ucop.edu/cprc/rephlthhzd.pdf.

[109] *Id.* at 5.

[110] Email from Pat Shiu, Vice President for Programs, Legal Aid Society of San Francisco–Employment Law Center, to Caroline Bettinger–López, Post–Doctoral Research Scholar, Columbia Law School (Feb. 11, 2007, 8:51 a.m.).

women's rights as "primarily one of economic justice and education,"[111] since many working poor women, a large proportion of whom were racial and language minorities, "were ill-informed about the effect of the toxins with which they worked, the legal implications for agreeing to work with those toxins, and the potential, probable and likely health outcomes for themselves and their families."[112]

After both *Johnson Controls* decisions, and at the request of California Assemblymember Jackie Speier, the California group analyzed federal and California law and policy in the reproductive health arena from several perspectives: occupational health regulation, equal opportunity and sex discrimination, disability law and the principle of "reasonable accommodation," and tort liability and workers' compensation.[113] After a "series of lively discussions,"[114] the group published a white paper in early 1992 recommending legislative and political responses to the continuing challenges faced by Californians who are exposed to reproductive hazards at work. The white paper focused on key questions concerning these challenges: What reproductive health issues do women working in contaminated worksites continue to confront? What types of scientific data are necessary to fill in research gaps concerning reproductive technology? What are potential remedies (e.g., statutory, tort, workers compensation) for workers exposed to reproductive hazards on the job?[115] After *Johnson Controls*, would employers feel entitled to invoke the Supreme Court decision as their rationale for exposing pregnant women to workplace contaminants as a condition of employment?

The California coalition proposed a set of policy recommendations to address the issues raised in its white paper.[116] Around the same time, the group also drafted and successfully advocated for the passage of an amendment to California's Fair Employment and Housing Act that required employers to provide reasonable accommodations to pregnant women who work in hazardous workplaces. Such accommodations would, for example, permit pregnant employees to take temporary paid leaves of absence from toxic workplaces or temporarily transfer to less

---

[111] *Id.*

[112] *Id.*

[113] *Reproductive Health Hazards in the Workplace: Policy Options for California*, supra note 108, at 3.

[114] Telephone Interview with Pat Shiu, Vice President for Programs, Legal Aid Society of San Francisco–Employment Law Center, in San Francisco, CA (Nov. 14, 2006).

[115] Email from Pat Shiu, Vice President for Programs, Legal Aid Society of San Francisco–Employment Law Center, to Caroline Bettinger–López, Post–Doctoral Research Scholar, Columbia Law School (Feb. 11, 2007, 8:51 a.m.).

[116] *Id.*

toxic worksites while maintaining their economic benefits, seniority status, and advancement opportunities.

The California experience is instructive as an alternative to the model of mobilization and advocacy embraced by the national coalition in the lead-up to the Supreme Court's decision in *Johnson Controls*. The California group embraced a problem-oriented approach to address reproductive hazards in the workplace, using litigation and the sex discrimination framework as only one component of a long-term strategy that involved public education and outreach, legislative advocacy, and regulatory reform. With this structure and vision, the California coalition was able to link the *Johnson Controls* litigation to the health and safety issues that national advocates had also identified. In contrast to the national mobilization, which centered around litigation and largely disbanded after the Supreme Court victory, the California advocates hit the ground running after the *Johnson Controls* decisions, prepared to tackle, through a multifaceted advocacy strategy, the next piece of the reproductive hazards puzzle.

VI. Conclusion: Significance and Legacy of *Johnson Controls*

Johnson Controls is a story of the strengths and limitations of mobilizing a broad set of interest groups and institutional agendas in the context of impact litigation, and the possibilities for reform that emerge from such mobilizations. On the one hand, the mobilization of diverse groups around a narrow issue can have a powerful impact, as evidenced in *Johnson Controls*. Several groups representing a wide range of interests supported a common position in the case. The diversity of these groups' interests, coupled with the uniformity of their message, effectively demonstrated a widespread problem to the Supreme Court and undoubtedly had some impact on the Court's ruling reaffirming key anti-discrimination principles.

On the other hand, narrowly-focused impact litigation often produces limited results that do not address a problem holistically. As some commentators have suggested, *Johnson Controls* affirmed an important anti-discrimination principle but ironically left women with the right to work in unsafe workplaces. It did not, for example, address the flip side of the fetal protection question: what protections did the law offer women factory workers who *wanted* to take time off or be transferred in order to protect fetal health? The national groups that mobilized to support the UAW were neither equipped nor (in some cases) interested in addressing this and other questions that naturally followed from the *Johnson Controls* decision. The example of California, discussed above, contrasts with the federal picture, and is instructive for thinking through these limitations and about potential solutions.

Johnson Controls is also a story about how political realities shape advocacy efforts. Many members of the group that represented plaintiffs and amici before the Supreme Court had experienced firsthand the ineffectiveness of OSHA and the EEOC in addressing workplace lead exposure and reproductive hazards issues, and remembered clearly when the D.C. Court of Appeals issued a crushing blow to the plaintiffs in *American Cyanamid*. These unsuccessful efforts left advocates with few options to address their concerns about fetal protection policies. In the political climate of the 1980s, the sex discrimination framework appeared much more viable than did agency lobbying or an OSHA cause of action.

In the context of repeated political and litigation setbacks, a diverse set of stakeholders, each with different institutional priorities, came together to communicate a unified message: exclusionary fetal protection policies violated Title VII and the PDA, and could never fall within the BFOQ exception. After their victory before the Supreme Court, these stakeholders understood that a larger battle lay ahead to compel employers to clean up unsafe workplaces and grant the requests of fertile employees who sought leave from these unsafe workplaces in order to reduce the risk of reproductive harm caused by workplace toxins. Yet although these groups understood this larger battle, most of them did not participate in it—at least not as a member of this same coalition. Rather, for the most part, groups retreated to their traditional issue areas, recognizing that political realities precluded another large-scale mobilization to address these larger issues.

Broadly-defined mobilizations focused on the narrow goal of winning a case in court may be successful in the short term and may establish important legal principles, but may not be sustainable as a way to address long-term and complex realities, particularly in the lives of marginalized and disempowered populations. The upshot of such narrowly focused mobilizations may be that, as in *Johnson Controls*, concerted mobilization wins an important battle for a client or institution or both, but is not sustainable beyond a specific moment in time.

As federal courts become less available as a site for affirmative progress, social justice advocates must address problems involving race and gender in the context of broader structural dynamics in order to make a difference on the ground. Public interest organizations must rethink their litigation-centered strategies to find new sites of mobilization and ways of sustaining coalitions that cut across different interests and locations. The *Johnson Controls* story provides some insight into the challenges and opportunities for making this transition.

11

Tomiko Brown–Nagin[*]

Missouri v. Jenkins: Why District Courts and Local Politics Matter

To many civil rights advocates, *Missouri v. Jenkins* (1995) (*Jenkins III*) stands as one of three cases from the 1990s in which the Supreme Court struck final blows against *Brown v. Board of Education*.[1] The case involved Kansas City, Missouri's "showcase" school desegregation plan, commonly described as the most comprehensive and expensive in the history of school desegregation litigation. The twin objectives of the remedy were to raise the academic performance of Kansas City Missouri School District's (KCMSD) overwhelmingly black student population and attract white student matriculates from private and suburban schools. In its 1995 decision, a slim majority of the Supreme Court rejected the plan and dashed Kansas City's hopes of creating that rare phenomenon in this country—a world-class school system that also is racially diverse.

Jenkins III was decided at a pivotal moment in the Court's history. By the mid–1990s, the Court's guard had changed. Gone were liberal icons William Brennan and Thurgood Marshall. Their retirements heralded a shift in the Court's ideological alignment. Clarence Thomas's appointment as successor to Thurgood Marshall, the Court's first Afri-

[*] The author extends thanks to Daniel Nagin, Michael Klarman, and Jim Ryan for reading and commenting on prior drafts of this chapter.

[1] In addition to *Jenkins III*, 515 U.S. 70 (1995), the trilogy included *Board of Oklahoma School District v. Dowell*, 498 U.S. 237 (1991) (return to local control is proper goal of school desegregation litigation and desegregation decrees may be dissolved after school district eliminates racial disparities to the extent practicable) and *Freeman v. Pitts*, 503 U.S. 467 (1992) (federal court may relinquish supervision of school district in incremental stages before full compliance has been achieved in every area of school operations). *Jenkins I*, 491 U.S. 274 (1988), concerned attorneys' fees. *Jenkins II*, 495 U.S. 33 (1990), concerned the court's authority to order tax increases to fund the school desegregation remedy.

can American justice and the NAACP's chief litigator during the *Brown* years, was the single most important personnel change during this period. Marshall's retirement, and Thomas's elevation to the Court, marked the end of an era of liberal domination of the national conversation about race. Thomas, a vocal critic of traditional civil rights remedies, was appointed over the objection of the NAACP. His ascension to the Court gave national prominence to black conservative thought for the first time since the turn of the twentieth century, when Tuskegee University President Booker T. Washington had President Theodore Roosevelt's ear. Thomas provided the fifth vote against the KCMSD desegregation plan in *Jenkins III*.[2]

Racial liberals reacted with outrage to the Court's decision and Thomas's role in it. Editorials with titles such as "On Race–Rehnquist's Been Waiting 40 Years," "On Race, It's Thomas v. An Old Ideal," and "The Supreme Court Lurches Backwards" appeared in leading newspapers. Commentators saw the decision as illustrative of the Rehnquist Court's hostility to civil rights, and as proof that Thomas would provide the crucial vote to undo the constitutional revolution that Thurgood Marshall had made. Other cases from the October 1994 term framed liberal reaction to *Jenkins III*. The case was decided in the same term as *Adarand v. Pena*, in which the Court struck down an affirmative action program, and *Miller v. Johnson*, in which the Court struck down a majority black congressional district. To many, *Jenkins III* heralded a general retreat by the Supreme Court from its presumed role as guardian of racial justice.

Yet *Jenkins III* did not constitute a deviant strain in the Court's school desegregation jurisprudence. From *Brown* forward, few, if any, of the Court's school precedents have been entirely pro-plaintiff. It was only because observers had long overestimated the Supreme Court's role as a protector of minority rights that *Jenkins III* struck them as extraordinary. *Brown*—the very case that spawned the cult of high expectations surrounding the Court's race jurisprudence—had itself been flawed. *Brown* lacked a clear and robust conception of equality.

Though pilloried by civil rights activists, Justice Thomas's concurring opinion in *Jenkins III* laid bare some of *Brown*'s weaknesses. School desegregation left blacks in the role of supplicants to whites. Desegregation, a narrow conception of equality, proved short-sighted when whites avoided racially mixed schools in ways deemed beyond judicial reach. *Brown* also fomented resentment among some African Americans, who

---

[2] Both Brennan and Marshall had sided with the school district in *Jenkins II*, a split decision from 1990 in which the majority held that federal courts could require school districts to levy tax increases in excess of state-imposed limits to adequately finance school desegregation remedy. *See* Missouri v. Jenkins, 495 U.S. 33, 48–52 (1990).

sought better schools, if nothing else from *Brown*—only to find that the landmark case apparently had not guaranteed even this basic form of relief. Just as Thomas suggested, *Brown*'s conceptual weaknesses haunted all the school desegregation litigation that followed it.

The outcome in *Jenkins III* was rooted in features of the Warren and Burger Court's anti-discrimination jurisprudence. Sensitivity to local political dynamics, including white resistance to racial mixing in schools, loomed large in the Burger Court's jurisprudence. The same had been true of the Warren Court's desegregation cases. Hence, when observers reacted as if the pro-defendant standards in *Jenkins III* issued peculiarly from the minds of the Rehnquist majority, they were wrong.

Jenkins III also reveals the agency that individual actors—from a lowly housekeeper to governors of Missouri—exercised in the life of the case. We learn of a trial judge whose hostility inspired profound fear in plaintiffs' counsel, but who also was visibly moved by African Americans' testimony about the educational deprivation they experienced under Jim Crow. But we also see that same judge reject many of the plaintiffs' claims and craft a remedy vulnerable to reversal. We learn, too, that despite the powerful evidence that plaintiffs adduced to demonstrate Jim Crow's hold on Kansas City's school system, the outcome of the case ultimately turned on questions of resources and time. Whites asked whether the expenditure of public monies in an attempt to remedy black educational disadvantage was a good investment. Others expressed impatience with the amount of time that it would take to remedy inequality, or implied that past wrongs simply could not be undone. Fighting tirelessly for Kansas City's black students, civil rights lawyers insisted that the plaintiffs deserved the money and time that it would take to redress years of racial discrimination against them. But in the end, the plaintiffs' hope for meaningful and long-lasting relief were dashed.

I. *Jenkins* in Local Context

The *Jenkins* litigation began in 1977. In that year, long after *Brown* had become the law of the land, several African American families joined in an unusual alliance with the Kansas City school board. The parties filed a lawsuit against the state of Missouri and a range of federal, state, and local housing, transportation, and finance agencies. The plaintiffs claimed that these defendants had spun a web of school and residential discrimination that denied black students their right to equal educational opportunity. Missouri's wrongdoing extended back to the antebellum era. The state had decreed schooling slaves a crime. It had mandated separate schools beginning in 1865, just as the slaves gained the right to live freely among whites. The provision of Missouri's constitution mandating Jim Crow schools was not repealed until 1976. The plaintiffs alleged that the state and school district had done little to implement

Brown at any time prior to their suit. African American students were limited to inferior, racially homogenous schools. Given the tremendous duration and scope of discrimination and segregation in the Kansas City schools, the plaintiffs requested comprehensive relief. They asked for the merger of the metropolitan area's city and suburban school districts so that black students could receive an education comparable to that available in majority white schools.[3]

The trial spanned a remarkable seven months. United States District Judge Russell Clark presided. Judge Clark's presence loomed large over the proceedings. His skepticism of the plaintiffs' claims showed from the outset of the trial. Arthur Benson II, the lead attorney for the plaintiffs, described the worry that set in among the plaintiffs' lawyers as the trial proceeded:

> During the first three months of the trial [Judge Clark] was overtly antagonistic to plaintiffs and repeatedly threatened to hold us, the lawyers, in contempt if we kept calling witnesses to describe their interdistrict experiences with segregation from the 1930s to the then-present. We said we'd stop when the State stipulated that the number of students affected was not *de minimis*. The State would not agree, so we kept calling witnesses.

Worry morphed into dread with each new threat by Judge Clark to find the lawyers in contempt of court for merely trying their case. Eventually, terror set in at the counsel's table. Benson recalled: "Some of the young lawyers from the NAACP LDF were so nervous and afraid of Judge Clark that before they called a witness, they would go into the bathroom and vomit." But the lawyers' persistence in attempting to show the depth of Jim Crow's impact on Kansas City blacks, despite Judge Clark's open hostility, paid off. Over the course of the trial, the judge's attitude changed. Benson explained the metamorphosis:

> Over time, the emotional impact of these witnesses grew on Judge Clark and he came to realize how devastating segregation had been to blacks, leaving life-time effects. I recall he was particularly moved by the testimony of an older black woman who testified that as a young girl she wanted to grow up to be a doctor. She went to a rural one-room, all-black elementary school with a "professor" as her teacher and learned Latin, biology, and much more. At the end of 8th grade, there was no school for blacks so her family sent her 50 miles to Kansas City to live with a distant relative she had never

---

[3] *See* Jenkins v. Missouri, 593 F. Supp. 1485, 1488–90 (W.D. Mo. 1984) (citing stipulation and witness testimony); *see also* Adams v. United States, 620 F.2d 1277, 1280 (8th Cir.) (en banc), *cert. denied*, 449 U.S. 826 (1980) (finding that St. Louis schools remained segregated in the late 1970s); Brief of Respondents Jenkins et al. in Opposition to Certiorari at 4–5, Missouri v. Jenkins, 515 U.S. 70 (1995) (No. 93–1823). In 1978, KCMSD was realigned as a defendant, making the school district a "friendly adversary" of the plaintiffs.

met. She graduated from high school with high honors. Did you realize your dream to become a doctor? No. What do you do for a living? I clean houses. By the end of the 92–day trial, Judge Clark had changed sides!

"Linwood School for Whites, Kansas City, Mo., circa 1930–50" and
"Dunbar School for Blacks, Kansas City, Mo., circa 1930–50"

In September, 1984, Judge Clark issued an order finding that Jim Crow's reach in the KCMSD had been wide and deep, with profound consequences. The school system was physically and pedagogically decimated. Facilities had "literally rotted," with safety and health hazards widespread. The curriculum was poor, and the district's teachers were the least experienced and credentialed in the area. These conditions existed within a rigidly segregated community. Before and after *Brown*, the state and KCMSD had gerrymandered school attendance zones and manipulated school site selection decisions to perpetuate racial isolation. In addition, Missouri had encouraged real estate, banking, and insurance practices that reinforced residential segregation. Consequently, "A large percentage of whites do not want blacks to reside in their neighborhood and a large percentage of blacks do not want to reside within a neighborhood in which they are not wanted." The segregated residential patterns reinforced the state's and school district's discriminatory school assignment policies.

The overall educational impact of these unlawful acts was devastating. Unconstitutional conduct had produced a "system-wide reduction" in black students' achievement. The low achievement levels, in turn, had far reaching life consequences, limiting students' employment opportunities and causing poverty. The court found both the state and KCMSD liable for the condition of Kansas City's schools, but of the two parties, it heaped most blame on the state. The school district had not mandated separate schools for blacks and whites itself, but merely enforced a policy handed down from above by state officials and willed from below by the white citizens of Missouri. "The people of the state of Missouri through constitutional provisions and the General Assembly through legislative enactment mandated that all schools for blacks and whites in the state were to be separate," he wrote.[4]

Judge Clark's opinion offered sweeping rhetoric about the state's complicity in KCMSD's failures, but his holdings regarding liability were, by comparison, timid. His conversion to the plaintiffs' cause had been incomplete. Despite the culpability that he laid at the feet of the state of Missouri for KSMSD's discrimination, and the breadth of the violations that he found in the metropolitan area's school system, Judge Clark ruled that the plaintiffs' evidence had fallen short of establishing defendants' liability for an *inter-district* (metropolitan-wide) constitutional violation. He was unconvinced that a finding of inter-district liability against the range of federal, state, and local school, housing, transportation, and financial entities that the plaintiffs had sued (and the merger of the city and suburban school systems) was justified. Consequently, he dismissed the federal agencies and outlying, suburban school districts from the case; he found the state and KCMSD liable for an *intra-district* violation, or for causing segregation within KCMSD, only. Judge Clark's findings rested on 1974's *Milliken v. Bradley (Milliken I)*. In *Milliken I*, the Court held that suburban districts could not be required to help remedy inner city school segregation, absent a finding of state or suburban culpability for racial isolation in the city schools. As the majority and concurring opinions in *Jenkins III* would show, the district court's limitation of its finding to intra-district, rather than inter-district liability, was the single most critical development in the litigation.[5]

Judge Clark's expansive rhetoric returned in remedial orders issued in 1985 to "eliminate the vestiges of segregation" from KCMSD. The court's purpose, he wrote, was to "make the constitutional ideal of equal justice under the law a living truth." He quoted *A Nation at Risk*, the National Commission on Excellence in Education's alarming 1983 report calling on the nation to recommit itself to educational achievement or risk losing preeminence to world competitors. "All, regardless of race or class or economic status, are entitled to a fair chance and to the tools for developing their individual powers of mind and spirit to the utmost.... Segregation in KCMSD has resulted in this promise going unkept."[6]

Judge Clark set about giving KCMSD students the opportunity for success through remedial initiatives designed to improve the physical plant of schools in the KCMSD, raise the achievement levels of black

---

[4] *Jenkins v. Missouri*, 593 F. Supp. at 1504–06; *see also* Email Interview with Arthur Benson II, Partner, Benson & Associates (Oct. 7, 2006).

[5] *Milliken v. Bradley*, 418 U.S. 717 (1974).

[6] *Jenkins v. Missouri*, 639 F. Supp. 19, 24 (W.D. Mo. 1985).

students closer to national norms, and attract white students into the district. To achieve these ends, the court ordered a multi-faceted remedy including: an array of capital improvements, a comprehensive, state-of-the-art magnet school program, new curricula, faculty and staff salary increases, a reduction in class sizes, full-day kindergarten, summer school for elementary students, before and after school programs, and voluntary intra- and inter-district transfer policies. The transfer polices allowed black students to attend predominantly white schools, and white students to attend predominantly black schools. The curricula improvement feature of the remedy, or quality education programs, was an outgrowth of *Milliken II*, the Court's 1977 decision upholding remedial educational programs for students victimized by school segregation. The pupil reassignment and transfer policies were inspired by the District Court's conclusion that racial isolation was deleterious to African American students. At the same time, the court recognized that achieving even a small degree of racial diversity would be a precarious endeavor. Few white students attended KCMSD, consistent with data showing that whites generally are unwilling to attend schools with large concentrations of African American students. Hence, the court approved programs designed to attract voluntary white student enrollees from schools within and outside of KCMSD to the district's majority black schools. The comprehensive remedy was costly, with the capital improvements alone projected to cost between fifty and seventy million dollars. Judge Clark ordered the state and school district to finance all aspects of the remedy, with the state—the primary wrongdoer—bearing the largest share of the costs. The court enjoined the operation of a state tax levy rollback so that KCMSD could fund its initial share of the remedial expenses.[7]

As Missouri's Republican attorney general from 1976 to 1985 and governor from 1985 to 1993, John Ashcroft, who would go on to serve as a United States senator and United States attorney general under George W. Bush, led a fierce campaign against Judge Clark's order.[8] While Missouri's attorney general, Ashcroft opposed state spending on the *Jenkins* remedy, arguing that KCMSD's admittedly dilapidated physical plant was not linked in any way to segregation. As a gubernatorial candidate, Ashcroft campaigned on an anti-busing platform: at every turn, Ashcroft trumpeted his opinion that suburban Kansas City students should not be torn away from their neighborhood schools for the sake of integration. Soon after Judge Clark issued remedial orders in the case, Governor Ashcroft's attorney general's office filed the first of several appeals attacking the state's financial obligations for the *Jenkins*

---

[7] *Id.* at 24–45. *Milliken v. Bradley II* is found at 433 U.S. 267 (1977).

[8] John Ashcroft's role in opposing the KCMSD desegregation plan imperiled his nomination to be United States attorney general. Protestors rallied in opposition to his confirmation, but he ultimately prevailed.

remedy as an abuse of judicial discretion, grossly excessive, and a threat
to Missouri's financial health. Yet, in 1988, while the initial appeal was
pending, the *St. Louis Post–Dispatch* reported that the state was flush
with cash. Due to federal tax revisions, Missouri had experienced a
budget "windfall" totaling $178 million, leaving state legislators to
wonder what to do with the excess funds. Eventually, some of the money
was used to finance the Kansas City (and St. Louis) school desegregation
plans. Ashcroft publicly lamented the expenditure. Many Democratic
legislators joined Ashcroft and his fellow Republicans in opposing the
remedial expenditures ordered by the district court. As funds were
disbursed for the remedy, officials repeatedly questioned whether the
state ought to comply with the court's orders. The director of social
services wondered whether building schools in Kansas City was "worth
it" given how much doing so "sure is hurting the rest of the people in
this state."

The politicians' fiscal position was popular with constituents, many
of whom paid tax levies earmarked for the school desegregation plan
"under protest." When the Supreme Court, in *Jenkins I*, upheld the
district court's authority to order local authorities to increase taxes to
support the school desegregation remedy, Mel Hancock, a Missouri
congressman, proposed that Congress strip the federal courts of the
power to order tax increases. Hancock claimed that such judicial orders
constituted "taxation without representation," and thus, "tyranny." He
was joined by a bipartisan coalition of Missouri congressmen and garnered more than one hundred other congressional sponsors. Ultimately,
Hancock's jurisdiction-stripping proposal failed. Nevertheless, the proposal's popularity demonstrated the local and national influence of
Ashcroft's narrative that the *Jenkins* remedy was an overpriced and
unwarranted intrusion upon suburban families.

Save the occasional newspaper editorial and aside from a few local
activists, few Missourians spoke out about the historic and contemporary
racial discrimination at issue in the case or championed the remedial
costs as a necessary step in making the plaintiffs whole. The one voice
consistently addressing these issues in public was Arthur Benson II, the
plaintiffs' attorney. Benson dismissed as dishonest and hypocritical the
persistent complaints about the costs of the *Jenkins* remedy. Judge
Clark had only overhauled KCMSD with expensive educational program-
ming and capital improvements because of white resistance to increased
educational opportunities for blacks, Benson argued. And this resistance
persisted even in the face of Judge Clark's orders. Moreover, he noted,
some of the most expensive remedial measures were adopted because
they appealed to and benefitted white suburban students.

The essential truth of Benson's claims were indisputable. In 1986,
Judge Clark had learned that all twelve majority white suburban dis-

tricts surrounding KCMSD had refused to accept any of the hundreds of black students who had expressed interest in a voluntary city-suburban pupil transfer program. The court admonished the state for its part in the failure. Missouri had offered little support for the program—an unsurprising fact, given that Governor Ashcroft, an avowed opponent of such plans, remained in office. Despite the district court's warnings, the state's obstruction of the school desegregation effort persisted. In 1990, the Eight Circuit found that "not a single suburban school district has admitted a single black student from the KCMSD," in large part because the state refused to pay for the program's costs. The state's open defiance of Judge Clark's order led the appeals court to question whether racial animus was the root cause of the foot-dragging. Further delay "cannot be countenanced," the Eighth Circuit ruled. Even after this warning and the state's eventual assurance that it would cover the costs of the transfer program, suburban districts were slow to accept black applicants. By 1992, only 10 city students attended suburban Kansas City schools under the voluntary desegregation program; by comparison, in St. Louis, which had reached a judicially-coerced settlement of its school desegregation litigation in 1983, suburban districts accepted 14,-000 black students in the voluntary majority-to-minority transfer program. On the eve of the *Jenkins III* decision, little had changed. By 1995, suburban Kansas City had accepted just 20 black students under the transfer program (compared to 14,700 in St. Louis). The magnet school program, aimed at attracting whites into KCMSD from outlying areas, had netted only 2,000 students. Observing these figures, Benson charged that the state had wasted millions of dollars fighting school desegregation to appease white constituents—a claim that officials heatedly rejected.[9]

II. *Jenkins* at the Supreme Court

When *Missouri v. Jenkins* reached the Supreme Court for the third time, Benson saw first hand how the justices would resolve the conflicting claims about wasted money, white resistance, and discrimination against black students. The Court's grant of certiorari grew out of Missouri's failed bid to have KCMSD declared unitary rather than segregated, a finding that would relieve the defendants from the Court's ongoing jurisdiction and remedial powers. Under the standard enunciated by the Court in 1991's *Oklahoma City v. Dowell* and 1992's *Freeman v. Pitts*, a district can be declared unitary if it has complied in "good faith" with an outstanding remedial decree and eliminated the vestiges of segregation "to the extent practicable." In its petition for certiorari and subsequent legal briefs, the state framed the question presented as

---

[9] *See* Jenkins v. Missouri, 639 F. Supp. 19, 51 (W.D. Mo. 1985); Jenkins v. Missouri, 904 F.2d 415, 419 (8th Cir. 1990).

whether KCMSD should be declared unitary, given the "unprecedented" expenditures provided to KCMSD over the course of the *Jenkins* litigation. In the state's view, the comprehensive *Jenkins* remedy was proof positive that it had fulfilled its remedial obligations under *Freeman*, notwithstanding continuing black academic underachievement and racial isolation in KCMSD. Missouri claimed that the district court had wrongly pegged KCMSD's success in eliminating the vestiges of segregation to African American students' performance on national achievement tests—a benchmark that far exceeded what was required under *Dowell* and *Freeman*. All it had to do to make up for past segregation was provide educational opportunities, the state argued, not guarantee particular educational outcomes on standardized tests. The state also asked the Court to review Judge Clark's order requiring salary increases for KCMSD faculty and staff, including non-instructional employees. This, too, went beyond what *Dowell* and *Freeman* required, the state argued.[10]

KCMSD claimed that the state's framing of the issues constituted an attempt to bamboozle the Court. The state was trying to re-litigate the long-settled issue of liability and the overall scope of the district court's initial remedial orders. The state had seized on *Dowell* and *Freeman* as "the latest weapon in its public crusade against" the KCMSD remedy, based on its perception that the political environment was now favorable to such an assault. The state's claim that the courts below had made particular scores on standardized tests a benchmark for unitary status also was a ruse, KCMSD argued. The opinion in which the state claimed the national test score benchmark had been established nowhere mentions the words "standardized test scores," "national averages," or anything of the kind. KCMSD charged that the entire test score line of argument was designed to convince the public and the Court that proponents of the KCMSD desegregation plan were wholly unreasonable. The one facet of the remedy that was legitimately before the Court—whether raises for non-instructional employees were justified—should be decided in its favor, KCMSD argued. These salary increases ensured the success of the desegregation plan; the increases were predicated on the district court's finding that near-market salary levels were necessary to ensure the district's "desegregative attractiveness," or its appeal to white families.[11]

Signaling how momentous the Supreme Court's decision would be, numerous organizations submitted amicus curiae briefs supporting

---

[10] *See* Petition for Certiorari at 12–26, *Jenkins*, 515 U.S. 70 (No. 93–1823); Brief for Petitioners at 23–32, *Jenkins*, 515 U.S. 70 (No. 93–1823).

[11] Brief for Respondents Kansas City, Missouri School District at 2, 31, 40–49, *Jenkins*, 515 U.S. 70 (No. 93–1823); *see also* Brief for Respondents Jenkins et al. at 20–22, *Jenkins*, 515 U.S. 70 (No. 93–1823).

KCMSD's bid for continuing state support for the school desegregation remedy. The Clinton administration's solicitor general, Drew S. Days, the American Civil Liberties Union, the National Jewish Congress, the National Urban League, and the Children's Defense Fund, among others, sided with the school district. Their briefs predicted dire consequences if the Court struck down the *Jenkins* remedy. The justices' decision in *Jenkins III* would determine nothing less than whether *Brown* remained a precedent with enduring relevance.

The Majority Opinion

It was clear from the first few pages of the majority opinion that KCMSD and the collection of amicus filers had lost their case, for Chief Justice Rehnquist accepted the state's framing of the issues. The majority opinion held that the district court's orders went far beyond the scope of the plaintiffs' rights under *Brown* and related precedents. The lower court could not require Missouri to finance the challenged elements of remedial order, Chief Justice Rehnquist held, because the nexus between the order and the state's and city's prior history of *de jure* segregation was too tenuous.

The Court's holding was based on several deficiencies in the district court's findings of fact. Judge Clark had held both Kansas City and the state of Missouri liable for the school system's prior *de jure* segregation, but he had issued no finding that the surrounding school districts had ever perpetuated school segregation. To the contrary, Judge Clark had dismissed the suburban districts from the case. Aspects of the district court's order that nevertheless aspired to suburban participation in the remedy, even on a voluntary basis, were an impermissible end run around *Milliken I*, Rehnquist wrote. In light of *Milliken I*'s high evidentiary bar for requiring suburbs to help remedy inner city segregation, the district court's goal of desegregative attractiveness, in as much as it aspired to lure students from suburban districts into KCMSD, was improper. It followed that any element of the judge's orders justified on this basis was improper, as well. Justice Rehnquist placed broad swaths of the *Jenkins III* remedy in this category, including state financing of the voluntary inter-district pupil desegregation program, the magnet school system that was the lure for these students, and across-the-board salary increases.

The quality education programs aimed at raising black students' achievement levels fell due to insufficient factual findings of a different sort. Here the problem was that the district court had not identified the exact extent to which achievement had been adversely affected by segregation. Without a "precise statement" regarding how much underachievement could be attributed to segregation, Justice Rehnquist held, it was impossible to identify any particular benchmark that would satisfy the state's duty to ameliorate achievement deficits caused by segregation. Thus, Missouri could not be required to fund special programs for black students even if their scores consistently fell below national norms. (After all, as Justice Scalia had scoffed during the oral argument in the case, "Half the country is below national norms!")[12]

The opinion's rhetoric suggested that the expense of the remedy and the amount of time (seven years) that it had been in place were critical factors in the majority's conclusion that Judge Clark had strayed from the proper remedial course. The Court called the KCMSD remedy the most expensive in history and noted that it had resulted in the district having "facilities and opportunities" purportedly "unavailable elsewhere in the country." In striking this note, the majority opinion tracked the complaint that John Ashcroft and other state officials had lodged against Judge Clark's remedial orders since 1985—they were overkill. The price of the remedy for Missouri's racial past literally was too high; thus, it was time to lay the past to rest. Justice Rehnquist remanded the case to the district court with instructions that all but required it to declare KCMSD unitary. Judge Clark's duty was not only to remedy the vestiges of discrimination, the majority wrote, but also to "restore state and local authorities" to control of the school system.[13]

Observers inside and outside of the Court attacked the majority opinion's scope and substance. Critics charged that Chief Justice Rehnquist had gutted aspects of the *Jenkins* remedy that the state had not contested previously and the Court had not reviewed in two prior iterations of the case. The dissents were particularly pointed.

For Justice Souter, the majority's sweeping review constituted a breakdown of "orderly adjudication" and ruled out "any confidence" that the results were sound "in fact or in law." Most significantly, the outcome repudiated *Hills v. Gautreaux*, a landmark housing discrimination precedent from the Burger Court that both the majority and Judge Clark had dismissed. *Gautreaux*, a unanimous decision, established the permissibility of inter-district relief for an intra-district violation in the housing context. The *Gautreaux* Court upheld an order requiring the U.S. Department of Housing and Urban Development, which had been found guilty of discrimination against African Americans in the city of Chicago, to create housing opportunities for blacks in Chicago's suburbs. The suburbs had not been found guilty of discrimination. The *Gautreaux* Court distinguished *Milliken I* by holding that interdistrict relief was permissible for the intradistrict violation because it did not infringe on the powers of suburban authorities not guilty of unlawful conduct. *Gautreaux* supported the interdistrict school desegregation order in

---

[12] *See Jenkins*, 515 U.S. at 86–102.

[13] *Jenkins*, 515 U.S. at 102.

Jenkins III, Souter argued, because it was *voluntary*. Consistent with *Gautreaux*, the *Jenkins III* remedy did not impinge on suburban Kansas City districts' authority in any way.

The majority took issue with Justice Souter's interpretation of *Gautreaux*. The remedy in *Gautreaux* did not "go[] beyond the geographical or political boundaries of its violation," Chief Justice Rehnquist wrote. Likewise, he concluded, the *Jenkins III* remedy must be limited to the scope of the violation. Had Judge Clark found an inter-district school violation, *Gautreaux* might have supported *Jenkins III*'s inter-district school remedy. But Judge Clark had found neither an inter-district school violation nor an inter-district housing violation; the Court had determined that the plaintiffs' evidence was inadequate to support the kind of inter-district remedy imposed in *Gautreaux*.

Justice Souter also pointed out that the majority had ignored a crucial part of *Milliken I*. The *Milliken I* Court had left open the possibility of interdistrict relief even in instances where a court only found an intradistrict violation. Intra-district segregation could produce effects beyond its own boundaries of such significance that they could support the imposition of an inter-district remedy. *Gautreaux*, when read with the part of *Milliken I* that discussed the spillover effects of intradistrict violations, supported the inter-district transfer program in *Jenkins III*, Justice Souter insisted. The majority did not even engage this aspect of Souter's dissent.

Justice Ginsburg's dissent also focused on the relatively low costs imposed on surburbia by remedies for urban school segregation, versus the high costs that the plaintiffs had paid historically on account of their race. Justice Ginsburg's dissent chastised the majority for suggesting that seven years of remedial intervention were sufficient to cure the constitutional violation that KCMSD students had suffered. Compared with "more than two centuries of firmly entrenched official discrimination," Ginsburg wrote, the remedial experience had been "evanescent."

The ruling in *Jenkins III* "devastated" Arthur Benson and many other members of the civil rights bar. William Taylor, an expert school desegregation litigator, referred to the Court's decision to strike down the quality education programs as relying on the "It's a Wonderful Life test." "You'd need a guardian angel to come down to tell what the world would have looked like were it not for segregation," he complained. Many news and law review commentators counted *Jenkins* a grave setback for civil rights. One asked whether the decision constituted the second "Missouri Compromise," referring to the deal that allowed Missouri to enter the Union as a slave state. By contrast, conservatives cheered the decision. Joan Biskupic, writing for the *Washington Post*, summed up the reason for conservative glee. "This is the Supreme Court that Ronald Reagan wanted but didn't get."[14]

In reality, though, the story of *Jenkins III* was more complex. True, the decision underscored the increasing power of the conservative wing of the Court in race cases. But to conflate the decision's political and legal meanings is to understate the continuity in the Court's school desegregation precedents over time, well before conservatives were so dominant. *Jenkins III* did not move the law far from where it had been before. It is difficult, for example, to fault the Rehnquist majority, more than the district court or the Burger Court, for the collapse of the inter-district transfer program. Granted, *Milliken I* did not specifically address voluntary, as opposed to mandatory, pupil reassignment policies. And true enough, *Gautreaux* approved an inter-district remedy. But the *Gautreaux* housing remedy rested on a district court finding of liability against a federal agency—a finding of the sort that Judge Clark rejected. "Here, unlike the desegregation remedy found erroneous in *Milliken,* a judicial order directing relief beyond the boundary lines of Chicago will not necessarily entail coercion of uninvolved governmental units, because ... HUD ha[s] the authority to operate outside the Chicago city limits," the *Gautreaux* Court had stated. Given the crucial relevance of the federal agency's culpability to the *Gautreaux* Court's endorsement of an interdistrict remedy, and *Milliken I*'s generally dim view of suburban participation in remedies for inner city school desegregation, Judge Clark's remedial orders stood on infirm ground. Inter-district relief could be ordered, but both *Gautreaux* or *Milliken I* indicated that broad findings of liability would be the safest anchor for any kind of inter-district remedy in the *Jenkins* litigation, whether voluntary or mandatory. Yet, Judge Clark had pointedly rejected the considerable amount of evidence plaintiffs proffered to support a finding of inter-district school segregation, or a finding of interconnected housing and school segregation.

Thus, to criticize *Jenkins III* for rejecting Judge Clark's inter-district remedies is mainly to lament Judge Clark's own constrained view of the evidence and long-standing precedent. The main culprit is *Milliken,* decided by the Burger Court more than twenty years before *Jenkins III* (with Rehnquist, a recent addition to the court, in the majority). But even *Swann v. Charlotte–Mecklenburg Board of Education,* the Burger Court's most expansive statement about the district courts' power to remedy school segregation, acknowledged constraints on courts' authority. Though *Swann* counseled that district courts should strive to desegregate the schools, it never mandated that judges disre-

---

[14] *See* 515 U.S. at 138 (Souter, J., dissenting); 515 U.S. at 175 (Ginsburg, J., dissenting); *see also* Floyd G. Delon et al., *The Implementation of* Missouri v. Jenkins III; *The New Missouri Compromise?*, 125 ED. LAW REP. 263 (1998); Joan Biskupic, *Court's Conservatives Make Presence Felt,* WASH. POST, July 2, 1995 at A1.

gard local context. All of the justices, including liberal holdovers from the Warren Court, signed on to *Swann*.

Indeed, the most famous example of the Court's deference to local prerogatives was issued by the liberal-dominated Warren Court. In 1955's *Brown II*, the Warren Court took up the question of when and how must segregation cease. *Brown II* answered that desegregation should occur "with all deliberate speed," that famously ambiguous phrase. It concluded that district courts should take into account the logistical difficulties that school boards would face in the transition to desegregated schools. From *Brown II* forward, the Court, regardless of ideological tilt, has balanced the equities in school desegregation cases in ways that ensure defendants play a large role in deciding whether and how victims receive recompense for infractions against their rights. Thus, Justice Rehnquist's decision in *Jenkins III* was not invented out of whole cloth, but constituted an extension of the Court's always circumspect approach to implementing *Brown*.[15]

Yet, *Jenkins III* did not forbid inter-district desegregation remedies. As in *Milliken I*, the rules reiterated in *Jenkins III* left intact precedents equating educational equality with pupil desegregation and permitting curricular improvement as a remedy for discrimination. But district courts generally have been reluctant to mandate broad relief for school segregation. Most of these judges, like Judge Clark, have treated *Milliken I* as an iron-clad bar to school desegregation remedies encompassing city and suburban school systems. As we have seen, however, *Milliken I* did not entirely foreclose interdistrict remedies; on the few occasions when district courts have ordered inter-district relief, the orders typically have withstood appellate scrutiny, despite *Milliken I*. Similarly, after *Jenkins III*, district court judges still have discretion in crafting remedial decrees. But judges have been jettisoning school desegregation cases at a remarkable clip. After *Jenkins III* and its sister cases, federal courts received and granted dozens of "unitary status" requests from school districts across the nation. The districts asked courts to limit the scope of remedies earlier imposed for *de jure* segregation or to remove themselves altogether from the business of monitoring their compliance with *Brown*. The courts granted all but one of these requests during the period 1992 to 2002, according to one analysis. The study concluded that "the award of unitary status seems almost guaranteed" if school districts seek it, even if racial disparities remain in the schools. Rather than testing the boundaries of *Jenkins III* (and *Milliken I*), district courts all but gave up on school desegregation.[16]

---

[15] *See* Brown v. Bd. of Educ. II, 349 U.S. 294 (1955); Swann v. Charlotte–Mecklenburg Bd. of Educ., 402 U.S. 1 (1971).

[16] The study of post-*Jenkins* cases is Wendy Parker, *The Decline of Judicial Decision Making; School Desegregation and District Court Judges*, 81 N.C. L. Rev. 1623, 1633, 1645

Thomas's Concurring Opinion

Jenkins III's fame turns as much on Justice Thomas's role in its outcome as anything else. His concurrence marked Justice Thomas's emergence as a jurist with a distinctive and impassioned voice on the Court. Justice Thomas's opinion introduced a remarkable new perspective to the Court's race jurisprudence. Thomas openly challenged the core remedial principle of *Brown*—that the cure for *de jure* school segregation is desegregated education. His critique was powerfully rendered. Thomas began, "It never ceases to amaze me that the courts are so willing to assume that anything that is predominantly black must be inferior." With this opening salvo, he proceeded to reject the stigma theory of educational inequality undergirding *Brown*. That rationale was captured in the well-known phrasing from *Brown* that separate schools, even if equal in terms of facilities and other indicia of quality, could never be equal under law. The fact of separation itself was the constitutional problem, Chief Justice Earl Warren had written in *Brown*, because it "usually [is] interpreted as denoting the inferiority of the negro group" and this "sense of inferiority ... has a tendency to [retard] the educational and mental development of Negro children." *Brown* cited sociological literature, including the Kenneth and Mamie Clark doll study, to support this premise. The Clark study showed that black children in segregated schools strongly preferred white over black dolls; the youngsters' embrace of the white figures demonstrated self-hatred and the harms of racially segregated schools, the Clarks concluded.

Thomas dismissed this data as "questionable" and lamented its socio-legal consequences. *Brown*'s scientifically shaky stigma concept had inspired federal judges to attempt to desegregate schools that had not been officially racially segregated for years. But as Thomas saw it, *de jure* segregation was remedied once a state ceased classifying schools by race; after that, the racial make-up of a school's student body was constitutionally inconsequential. For Thomas, the disastrous school desegregation experiment that had followed *Brown* had been to the detriment of black students.

The *Jenkins* litigation, in Thomas's view, painfully illustrated the point. Costly attempts to achieve racial balance such as the elaborate magnet school system and the voluntary inter-district transfer policies that Judge Clark imposed on Missouri demonstrated how far federal courts could stray on the faulty belief that "[b]lacks cannot succeed without the benefit of the company of whites." Thomas insisted that these efforts all had been futile (despite evidence to the contrary).

(2003) (ten-year study showing that of the dozens of requests for unitary status made by school districts all but one were granted by federal courts during the period from June 1, 1992 through June 1, 2002).

Desegregation had failed to produce "predicted leaps forward in black educational achievement," had deflected African Americans' attention from achieving by their own devices, and worst of all, had kept blacks in the role of supplicants, begging white students to learn with them. This madness was unquestionably an abuse of judicial discretion, according to Thomas, and contrary to the intentions of the Constitution's framers.[17]

Justice Thomas's concurrence substantiated the perception among some that he was an unrelenting ideological foe of civil rights claims, but his opinion served a useful purpose in at least one respect. The justice's strongly-worded opinion reminded us that African Americans had rarely spoken in one voice on the issue of school desegregation. Thomas eloquently brought to light the diversity of views about school desegregation that had emerged over time. To be sure, skepticism about policies that compel students to attend racially diverse schools typically is voiced by conservative whites. But many whites and some blacks *across the political spectrum* make choices that indicate skepticism about the utility of school integration. In 1985, when the district court initially entered its remedial decrees in *Jenkins*, KCMSD was 68.3 percent African American. Yet the school-aged population was 60 percent white, and whites lived in census tracts that were 99 percent white. As is true across America, most people in Kansas City clustered in racially homogenous enclaves and, in urban areas especially, attended schools lacking in racial diversity. This is so despite polls indicating that more than 90 percent of Americans support integrated education *in principle*. But both demographic and poll data show that far fewer Americans support school integration *in practice*. In 1994, only 25 percent of whites, compared with 57 percent of blacks, expressed support for federally mandated school integration. Moreover, although a majority of African Americans surveyed still backed federal intervention to achieve integrated schools, the percentage of blacks expressing this view has declined markedly over time; in 1964, 82 percent of black supported such policies.

Leading black intellectuals, in particular, have frequently aired skepticism about school desegregation over the years. One contemporary legal scholar, Derrick Bell, has gone so far as to argue that rather than declaring segregation inherently unconstitutional in *Brown*, the Supreme Court should have reaffirmed *Plessy v. Ferguson* and required separate-but-equal schools in fact. W.E.B. Du Bois, the eminent sociologist, had cautioned African Americans against viewing integrated schools as a panacea as early as 1934.

---

[17] *See* Brown v. Board of Educ., 347 U.S. 483, 494 & n.11 (1954). Justice Thomas's first articulated some of the ideas expressed in his *Jenkins III* concurrence in *United States v. Fordice*, 505 U.S. 717, 745 (1992) (Thomas, J., concurring).

Whatever one thinks of Thomas's conclusion that the *Jenkins* remedy was unconstitutional, his concurrence tracks a large store of public doubt about school desegregation. His opinion poses a pressing question—whether the decades-long debate over court-ordered pupil desegregation impoverishes the judicial and political conversations about what equality in education might look like, beyond the goal of racial balance.[18]

Thomas undermined the overall force of his opinion, however, with his sweeping conclusion that African American students in Kansas City and elsewhere would be better off without desegregation decrees. Reciting the truism that the existence of *de jure* segregation in 1954 does not necessarily establish that *de facto* segregation existing years later is unlawful, Thomas wrote that the factual record in *Jenkins III* "could not have supported a finding of liability against the State." Thomas could only have reached that conclusion by ignoring much of the record in the case. As Justice Ginsburg stated in her dissent noting the "deep, inglorious history of segregation in Missouri," Judge Clark had found that Missouri and KCMSD intentionally segregated black students into substandard schools well after 1954. Justice Thomas left this part of the record out of his analysis, substituting his judgment for that of the legitimate fact finder in the litigation.

Thomas also ignored data that calls into question his dim view of the educational benefits of school desegregation. Many scholars now question the Kenneth and Mamie Clark doll study, as Justice Thomas pointed out. But numerous, more recent studies that Thomas failed to cite show that attending a school with an economically and racially diverse student body can enhance the life prospects of some minority students.

By emphasizing only those facts that supported his view of school desegregation, Justice Thomas substantiated an old saw: many criticisms of structural remedies in institutional reform cases derive from objections to the underlying right, above all else.[19]

Conclusion

Soon after the Supreme Court's decision in *Jenkins III* was announced in 1995, Ashcroft's Democratic successor as governor, Mel Carnahan, initiated settlement talks. In attempting to bring an end to the case, Carnahan said, "It's time for the court phase of the desegregation fight to end. [P]arents and educators—not the courts and lawyers—[should] be running the Kansas City Schools." Arthur Benson expressed interest in settling the case, as well. In 1996, the parties reached an

[18] On demographics in Kansas City, see *Jenkins v. Missouri*, 855 F.2d 1295, 1302, n.5 (8th Cir. 1988); *Jenkins v. Missouri*, 593 F. Supp. 1485, 1491 (W.D. Mo. 1984).

[19] See 515 U.S. 114, 116 (1995); *see also id.* at 176 (Ginsburg, J., dissenting).

agreement that released the state from further liability in exchange for a multi-million dollar lump sum payment to the district.[20]

But the saga of *Jenkins v. Missouri* continues. Even after the settlement and a finding by the district court that KCMSD was unitary—intended to end the case once and for all—the Eighth Circuit rejected the finding and reversed. As a result, the district court embarked on renewed efforts to close the black/white "achievement gap" in KCMSD and ameliorate the ongoing racial isolation in its schools. New initiatives included redesigned leadership, assessment, curriculum, recruitment and instructional policies. In 2003, some eight years after *Jenkins III*, KCMSD finally achieved unitary status. Even so, the federal courts still monitor the erstwhile defendants' treatment of KCMSD and its students. In June 2006, the district court entered an order, now on appeal to the Eighth Circuit, enjoining the state from diverting money from the property tax levy to charter schools until 2014 or such time as the desegregation bonds have been repaid. The final chapter of *Jenkins v. Missouri* has not yet been written.[21]

Even as *Jenkins* goes on, it reminds us that as important as Supreme Court decisions are to the enforcement of constitutional rights, majoritarian politics, occurring in local contexts, play an enormous role in civil rights litigation. Surely the Court's opinion in *Jenkins III*, together with *Dowell* and *Freeman*, reinforced barriers to the implementation of *Brown*. But the standards articulated in *Jenkins III* only tell part of the story. The steadfast opposition of John Ashcroft and Missouri officials of both political parties to the *Jenkins* remedial decrees frustrated the plaintiffs' efforts to obtain meaningful relief. The federal district court was a part of the local political environment. More than any other fact, Judge Clark's decisions regarding liability—made at the very outset of the case—proved fatal to the plaintiffs' remedial ambitions. The district court's findings made Chief Justice Rehnquist's decision in *Jenkins III* possible and probable.

Judge Clark's timidity comes into even sharper focus by comparing his actions to those of the trial judge in the St. Louis school desegregation case. The two cases involved much of the same evidence, with the state of Missouri bearing much of the blame for the school segregation existing in both cities. But recall that in St. Louis, thousands of black

---

[20] *See* Lynn Horsley & Mark Morris, *Settlement Unlikely on School Case*, KANSAS CITY STAR, Oct. 22, 1995 at B5; Patricia Corrigan & William H. Freivogel, *Judge Signs KC Accord On Desegregation Plan*, ST. LOUIS POST-DISPATCH, Feb. 22, 1995, at 1A; Kim Bell & William H. Freivogel, *State, KC Schools Make Deal*, ST. LOUIS POST-DISPATCH, July 6, 1995, at 1A.

[21] *See* Jenkins v. Missouri, 73 F. Supp. 2d 1058 (W.D. Mo. 1999), *rev'd* 205 F.3d 361 (8th Cir. 2000); *see also* Joe Robertson, *Ruling Upsets Legal Battles*, KANSAS CITY STAR, June 16, 2006, at B5.

students attended suburban schools under a majority-to-minority transfer programs, whereas few did in Kansas City. The radically different
educational options available to black students in these sister cities
resulted from the different perspectives that the presiding judges
brought to similar evidence. In St. Louis, on the eve of trial, Judge
William Hungate gave suburban districts that were skeptical of voluntary transfer programs a tremendous incentive to settle. He explained
that he would consolidate the St. Louis city and suburban districts and
order a mandatory inter-district remedy if he found an inter-district
constitutional violation. Judge Hungate's warning made the outlying St.
Louis districts amenable to a settlement featuring a voluntary inter-
district school desegregation remedy. Under the guidance of a court-
appointed special master, the St. Louis city and suburban districts went
on to develop the largest school choice program in the country.[22]

By contrast, in Kansas City, Judge Clark gave the suburban school
districts no such incentives. He had started off hostile to the plaintiffs'
claims and ended up imposing a remedy that did not fully address the
breadth of the wrongs committed against them.

Ultimately, *Jenkins III* is most remarkable in the way it reminds us
of two related truths: the basic consistency over time in the Supreme
Court's school desegregation cases, and the tremendous extent to which
majoritarian politics, showcased in various local contexts, have mediated
that doctrine. William Rehnquist, writing as a law clerk to Justice
Robert Jackson, captured this reality in a 1952 bench memorandum on
the constitutionality of the segregation cases. *Plessy v. Ferguson* "was
right and should be reaffirmed" despite the NAACP's arguments, Rehnquist wrote, explaining:

> To the argument made by Thurgood not John Marshall that a
> majority may not deprive a minority of its constitutional right,
> the answer must be made that while this is sound in theory, in
> the long run it is the majority who will determine what the
> constitutional rights of the minority are.

During his confirmation hearings to become Associate and Chief Justice
of the Supreme Court, Rehnquist claimed that the then-impolitic state-

---

[22] Judge Hungate's announcement regarding his intentions followed on the heels of the
Eighth Circuit's stinging reversal of an earlier decision, issued by a different district judge,
for the St. Louis school board; the Eighth Circuit's decision critically influenced the
outcome of the St. Louis litigation, as well. *See* Adams v. United States, 620 F.2d 1277 (8th
Cir. 1980); Liddell v. Board of Educ., 546 F.2d 768 (8th Cir. 1976); Liddell v. Board of
Educ., 491 F. Supp. 351 (E.D. Mo. 1980).

ment did not represent his personal views. But *Jenkins III* reveals the essential truth of the statement: minority rights *often are* subject to a majority veto.[23]

---

[23] The Rehnquist quote is cited in MARK V. TUSHNET, MAKING CIVIL RIGHTS LAW: THURGOOD MARSHALL AND THE SUPREME COURT, 1936–1961 189–190 (1994).

*

12

Cornelia T.L. Pillard*

United States v. Virginia: The Virginia Military Institute, Where the Men are Men and So are the Women

. . .

The curious thing about the constitutional challenge to the exclusion of women from the Virginia Military Institute is that it ever became a major civil rights case in the first place. VMI is, after all, a tiny, rather eccentric and anachronistic military college in Virginia. Most Americans who were even aware of the Institute's existence before the litigation responded, at least in part, with a kind of shoulder-shrugging puzzlement about why anyone—male or female—would ever want to go to a college like VMI. The chance to become one of approximately 1300 cadets, marching around a toy-castle campus in uniforms, crew cuts, and silly hats, living in Spartan, grey barracks devoid of privacy, spending most of freshman year as a "rat" (the "lowest form of life") at upper-classmen's beck and call, being shouted at, insulted, ordered to drop for push ups at the slightest infraction, and subjected to frat-boy-style antics at all hours hardly seems like the kind of opportunity from which anyone should worry much about being excluded. Given the other problems facing American women, like entrenched economic inequality and rampant sexual exploitation and violence, admission to VMI might seem low on the list of priorities for the United States government's civil rights enforcers and the big guns of the women's rights bar.

---

* The title of this article is based on a quip made by one of the first female students to attend VMI, as reported in LAURA FAIRCHILD BRODIE, BREAKING OUT: VMI AND THE COMING OF WOMEN 202 (2000).

Male cadets in dress uniform near VMI barracks.

Although VMI's admissions policy might have seemed like a small fish, at least it looked like one that could be shot in a barrel. So it is also surprising that the challenge to VMI's exclusion of women became a major, drawn-out litigation that went all the way to the United States Supreme Court. VMI was exclusively male when it was founded in 1839. At that time, colleges trained men alone for the male dominated public sphere. Women would lack even the vote for another 80 years. Academic study was believed superfluous to woman's distinct social role and even risky to her health.[1] VMI was established specifically to serve militiamen at a time when it was unthinkable to include women in military education. The constitutional doctrine against sex discrimination that developed in the 1970s and '80s targeted just the kinds of overbroad, stereotyped notions about men's and women's different roles and abilities that VMI's male-only policy reflected. Virginia, meanwhile, never really came up with a better reason why VMI should remain all-male. By the mid–1980s, the case against VMI seemed to be the missing twin to the successful 1981 Supreme Court challenge to exclusion of men from the nursing school at the Mississippi University for Women.[2]

---

[1] United States v. Virginia, 518 U.S. 515, 536–37 & n.9 (1996).

[2] Mississippi Univ. for Women v. Hogan, 458 U.S. 718 (1982).

The fact that this dispute over a tiny college became a big deal shows the importance of symbolism and stigma to the law of sex equality, and more generally to the social construction of gender. Small and eccentric as it may be, VMI takes itself very seriously and is taken seriously by many people, especially in Virginia, as a last bastion of true masculinity and a rigorous proving ground for powerful leadership positions in the public and private sector. How, in this day and age, could the tough and influential VMI shut its gates to women and keep them from showing that they can hack it alongside the men, and thereby join the exclusive VMI alumni circle? After all, it is not as if men have a monopoly on the qualities VMI requires and celebrates. Many women are emotionally and physically stronger than many men, are more drawn to a culture of physical stress, discipline, and loyalty, and would be better suited to a military-style education than many men. After a generation of women had already graduated from West Point and from the Naval, Air Force, and Coast Guard Academies, and served with distinction in active military duty, VMI's exclusion of women became insufferable. One mother of a female army reserve medic who was shipped to Saudi Arabia for Operation Desert Storm decried "the indignity which we suffer from the statement of women's inequality which VMI makes to the world."[3] Even women (and men) who would never have applied to VMI in any event felt personally insulted by VMI's exclusion of women.

Doctrinally, the length and magnitude of the *VMI* litigation attests to the inadequacies of the "intermediate scrutiny" standard of constitutional review of sex-based policies and laws, such as VMI's male-only admissions policy. As the divergent analyses of the parties and the judges in the *VMI* litigation show, there was startlingly little agreement on how to apply intermediate scrutiny. A key requirement of that standard is that stereotypes about the distinct characteristics of the sexes cannot justify sex-based different treatment, but "real" differences between the sexes may. The lower courts in *VMI* repeatedly misapplied intermediate scrutiny, first in upholding VMI's male-only policy, and then in sustaining a constitutionally offensive remedy for women's exclusion. What struck one person as a sex-role stereotype often seemed like a real sex difference to another.

Finally, the story of the *VMI* case is bound up with that of Justice Ruth Bader Ginsburg, and not only because it was she who was to write the Supreme Court opinion that opened VMI to women. For many years before Ginsburg was appointed to the bench she had been the nation's leading sex discrimination lawyer; when President Clinton nominated Ginsburg to the Supreme Court, he aptly compared her contributions to the women's movement to former Supreme Court Justice Thurgood

---

[3] PHILIPPA STRUM, WOMEN IN THE BARRACKS: THE VMI CASE AND EQUAL RIGHTS 96 (2002).

Marshall's efforts on behalf of the rights of African Americans. If there was one issue that shaped Ginsburg's career as a lawyer, it was her drive to establish that sex is a suspect classification entitled to strict constitutional scrutiny. Many view her opinion in *VMI* as having accomplished just that.

Where Soldiers Were Men and Women Were Ladies

The Virginia Military Institute, a small, public, military college in Virginia, devoted itself for over a century and a half to "drawing out the man" in an often rambunctious and underperforming set of boys.[4] VMI championed masculinity, with a stress on southern values of chivalry and militarism. The Institute prided itself on being unique among colleges. By 1990, virtually every other college in the country—military or civilian, public or private, the military service academies included— had moderated highly gendered traditions, modernized behavioral assumptions, and embraced coeducation.[5] With a Rebel's dedication to lost causes, VMI clung to what it saw as an increasingly threatened set of masculine values, and it had, not coincidentally, the strongest determination to exclude women.

VMI's strident militarism dates to its establishment in 1839 as a means to discipline and keep busy the rowdy group of young militiamen assigned to guard weaponry stored at the Lexington Arsenal following the War of 1812. VMI became the nation's first state-sponsored military school. Dubbed "the West Point of the South" even before it opened, 94 percent of VMI's then-alumni fought for the Confederacy during the Civil War. The enrolled cadets fought, too, suffering ten deaths and many serious injuries at the Battle of New Market, Virginia. The VMI campus is rife with statues, paintings, buildings and other memorials to its Civil War heroes, and an annual VMI ceremony commemorates New Market to this day. VMI's early science faculty boasted Professor Thomas Jonathan Jackson—later known as Confederate war hero "Stonewall" Jackson. VMI's most renowned graduate was the World War II five-star General George C. Marshall, who remained an active alumnus. VMI's more recent graduates are disproportionately influential and well-to-do, but none rivals the stature of Generals Jackson or Marshall. Part of VMI's devotion to tradition no doubt reflects its striving to maintain a connection to the giants of its past.[6]

---

[4] *See* HENRY A. WISE, DRAWING OUT THE MAN: THE VMI STORY (1978).

[5] The Citadel and VMI, the last single-sex public colleges, are now coeducational, and only a handful of private colleges remain single sex. *See generally* Rosalind Rosenberg, *The Limits of Access: The History of Coeducation in America*, *in* WOMEN AND HIGHER EDUCATION IN AMERICAN HISTORY 107, 107–29 (Faragher and Howe eds. 1986).

[6] Dianne Avery, *Institutional Myths, Historical Narratives and Social Science Evidence: Reading the "Record" in the Virginia Military Institute Case*, 5 S. CAL. REV. L. & WOMEN'S

Despite its military history and ethos, VMI is not, strictly speaking, a military school; only about 15 percent of its graduates enter the military.[7] VMI instead uses its militaristic regimen, dubbed the "adversative method," to graduate "citizen-soldiers, educated and honourable men who are suited for leadership in civilian life and can provide military leadership when necessary."[8] Through "physical rigor, mental stress, absolute equality of treatment, absence of privacy, minute regulation of behaviour, and indoctrination of desirable values,"[9] VMI aims to break down the incoming students, shear away their false confidence, and build them up again on a firmer foundation. It seeks to show cadets that they are capable of surpassing their previously self-imposed limits and thereby creating a new "sense of self-efficacy through meeting challenges, developing self discipline, meeting rigor and dealing with it, and having successes."[10] Militarism pervades the school's culture, discipline, and "co-curricular" life. Students live four-to-a-room in Spartan, panopticon-style "barracks" with no shades and windowed doors that minimize privacy, they wear uniforms at all times, and they participate in military drills and obligatory ROTC. VMI's faculty are all officers in the Virginia Militia or the United States Military.[11]

The most distinctive and controversial aspects of VMI—and the aspects that VMI asserts are the most important—are administered not by the faculty and staff, but by the students themselves, and are centered not in the classroom, but in the barracks. The highly ritualized, student-run activities and institutions include the freshman "rat line" or "rat training," a "tough physical training program" that is "comparable to Marine Corps boot camp in terms of both the physical rigor and mental stress of the program" and is "designed to foster self confidence and physical conditioning"; the "class system," which assigns hierarchical roles to each year of cadets and uses peer pressure to inculcate "desired values and behaviors"; an associated "dyke system," in which seniors mentor freshman while treating them as peons; and an honor code, providing that a cadet "does not lie, cheat, steal nor tolerate those

STUD. 189, 249 (1990); STRUM, *supra* note 3, at 18–20. The fifteen VMI alumni who fought for the Union left no such mark on VMI's identity.

[7] United States v. Virginia, 518 U.S. at 522.

[8] United States v. Virginia, 976 F.2d 890 (4th Cir. 1992), *rehearing denied*, 976 F.2d 900 (4th Cir.), *cert. denied*, 508 U.S. 946 (1993).

[9] United States v. Commonwealth of Virginia, 766 F. Supp. 1407, 1421 (W.D. Va. 1991).

[10] United States v. Commonwealth of Virginia, 44 F.3d 1229, 1234 (4th Cir. 1995); *see generally* United States v. Commonwealth of Virginia, 766 F. Supp. at 1421–22.

[11] *See* VIRGINIA MILITARY INSTITUTE, 2006–2007 CATALOGUE (2006).

who do," enforced by the sole sanction of expulsion for its violation, and administered by a student Honor Court.[12]

With a student body self selected for macho, militaristic zeal, the student-run activities can take on a kind of Lord of the Flies aspect. As former VMI faculty wife Laura Fairchild Brodie describes it, upperclassmen sometimes subject their juniors to demeaning, humiliating, and even sadistic treatment. Hazing is forbidden at VMI and is against the law in Virginia (largely in response to excesses at VMI), but students traditionally conduct much of what they refer to as the "co-curricular" program without close supervision. VMI is not only distinctively Southern, militaristic, and masculine, but often also notably adolescent.[13]

At VMI, masculinity was often defined in terms of male superiority and female inferiority, and sometimes in crudely gendered ways that reasonable women would find denigrating. Sexist jokes and gendered profanity were common. Desks in VMI's classrooms were covered with obscene graffiti. Cadets routinely used harshly gendered epithets, like bitch, whore, cunt, pussy, or even simply "woman," as a way to break one another down.[14] Peeling apart the stiffly starched legs of a new pair of trousers was, to VMI cadets, "raping your virgin ducks."[15] When, preparing for coeducation, VMI hired a female U.S. Army Major as Assistant Commandant, hundreds of male VMI cadets responded by drumming her out of the barracks with cries of "bitch" and "whore."[16] According to one history professor, the classroom atmosphere at the all-male VMI included "a lot of hooting and macho stuff going on that had nothing to do with being in a classroom."[17] Some of the professors themselves contributed to the sexist atmosphere, with one explaining that, in a lesson on parts of speech, "I would say 'Look folks, the participle is a virgin. You don't change her. You don't trifle with her. You do all your playing around, all your trifling, all your manipulation with the helping verb. She's the whore.' "[18] The courts were to hear plenty about VMI's history of military and civilian prestige, but the most extreme sexist and misogynistic aspects of VMI's vaunted adversative

---

[12] United States v. Commonwealth of Virginia, 766 F. Supp. at 1422–23; Avery, *supra* note 6.

[13] Avery, *supra* note 6, at 247–48; LAURA FAIRCHILD BRODIE, BREAKING OUT: VMI AND THE COMING OF WOMEN 41, 168–69,182–83 (2000).

[14] *Id.* at 73, 82–83, 175, 252.

[15] *Id.* at 80.

[16] *Id.* at 175.

[17] *Id.* at 326.

[18] *Id.* at 327.

culture were kept under wraps and never made it into the litigation record.

Origins of a Lawsuit

Even without its seamy underside exposed, the brazenly male-only VMI smacked of an equal protection violation when the United States Justice Department took up the matter in 1989. Virginia had no public, single-sex college for women. A constant theme of VMI's defense was that the school's time-tested "uniqueness" would be destroyed by coeducation, but the emphasis on uniqueness underscored that VMI's benefits were unavailable anywhere else to the excluded women. Part of VMI's value was that it was an "elite" institution for distinctly non-elite males. Academic stars and top athletes had other choices. VMI, meanwhile, took a swath of the mediocre middle among male high-school graduates and fashioned them into leaders, especially in the male-dominated fields of business, engineering, politics and the military. VMI's longstanding trial-by-fire ethos bred extraordinary alumni success and loyalty, leading to the highest per capita college endowment in the nation and an active network of connections that buoyed the careers of VMI's graduates. A VMI education was a valuable opportunity indeed for the few who got it, and women, too, thought they could benefit.

VMI had no analogue to Shannon Richey Faulkner, the female student who captured the public imagination after she was mistakenly admitted to The Citadel (where they thought "Shannon," on paper, was a boy), and sued for the right to attend. VMI instead was sued by the federal government under a statute that authorized the Department of Justice to litigate based on an anonymous complaint from an excluded young woman.[19] That statutory authority helpfully shielded the complainant from the wrath of VMI's defenders, but not without costs. The litigation might have had more appeal from the start had the case had the public face of competent and appealing women like the intrepid band who eventually commenced coeducation at VMI. Nor was there the added legal firepower of any nongovernmental legal team like the ACLU, which represented Faulkner in tandem with the Justice Department in the Citadel case. (There was also less embarrassment in the *VMI* case; Faulkner forced open the Citadel's doors only to exit in emotional and physical exhaustion a week into her first semester.) The lack of an individual plaintiff probably also made it easier for VMI to cast itself as the beleaguered victim of over-zealous federal civil rights enforcement. The male cadets were captured in the media, ringing old states-rights themes still so resonant in the South; no female plaintiff shouted back.

---

[19] 42 U.S.C. § 2000c–6 (1972).

For all its outrage at the legal challenge, VMI saw it coming. The faculty, administration, and Board of Visitors had long known that the Institute was vulnerable. Simmering doubts at VMI reached a high point following the Supreme Court's 1982 decision forcing the women-only nursing school of the Mississippi University for Women (MUW) to admit men. Justice Sandra Day O'Connor, the first woman to sit on that Court, wrote the majority opinion in *Mississippi University for Women v. Hogan*[20] less than six months after her confirmation. The five-member majority rejected Mississippi's asserted compensatory rationale and concluded that MUW's single-sex policy instead unconstitutionally reflected the "stereotyped view of nursing as an exclusively woman's job" and, by excluding men, made "the assumption that nursing is a field for women a self-fulfilling prophesy."[21] *Hogan* reached that conclusion under the "intermediate scrutiny" standard that VMI would, at a minimum, have to meet in order to remain all male. Virginia would have to show "an exceedingly persuasive justification" for VMI's male-only policy, a burden met only if excluding women "serves important governmental objectives" and if the exclusion is "substantially related to the achievement of those objectives."[22] *Hogan* emphasized that the governmental interest must not itself reflect "archaic and stereotypic notions" such as a desire to "exclude or 'protect' members of one gender."[23]

After *Hogan,* it was obvious that VMI needed a powerful argument if it were to continue to exclude women. The VMI Board of Visitors appointed an *ad hoc* committee to evaluate VMI's male-only admissions policy. During 1984–1986, the committee visited West Point and the U.S. Naval Academy at Annapolis, VMI's near neighbour, the College of Washington and Lee, and the all-male Citadel in South Carolina. Back in Lexington, the Mission Study Committee reported that, if women were admitted, there would have to be "some adjustments" made to military and physical demands, and that "[b]ecause many of these demands contribute to the ethos of which the Virginia Military Institute is proud and which, it is firmly believed, contributes to the unity of the corps, there is doubt that the same spirit could be maintained at the same level in the same way if women were introduced into the Corps."[24] In other words, pride, male bonding, and a spirited disinclination to change seemed to be the principal reasons for continuing to exclude women.

---

[20] *Hogan*, 458 U.S. 718.

[21] *Id.* at 729–30.

[22] *Id.* at 724.

[23] *Id.* at 725.

[24] United States v. Virginia, 776 F. Supp. at 1429.

When the press reported in 1986 that, notwithstanding *Hogan*, VMI would not budge, Judith Keith, a career trial lawyer in the Education Section of the Civil Rights Division of the United States Department of Justice (DOJ), read about it in the *Washington Post*. She responded with a fighting spirit that, eventually, got the better of VMI. Keith kept her eye out for three years until a complaint arrived at DOJ in 1989 from a Northern Virginia high school student rejected from VMI because of her sex. Even political appointees in the DOJ of George H.W. Bush approved of the lawsuit: If the conservative creed maintains that women, like minorities, are not supposed to get "special treatment," women should have the chance to prove their mettle on the same terms as men. [25]

Upon learning that DOJ was planning to sue, VMI performed a preemptive strike to assure an advantageous judicial venue. Plaintiffs typically have some leeway in choosing where to sue, so VMI raced to the courthouse for a declaratory judgment that VMI's admissions policy did *not* violate equal protection. Seizing the plaintiff role, VMI sidestepped the northern Virginia courts it feared DOJ might select, in favor of Roanoke, near VMI's Lexington home. Only one federal judge sat in Roanoke: Judge Jackson L. Kiser, a reliable skeptic of sex discrimination claims.

Leading the litigation team for the VMI Alumni Association and its Board of Visitors (both private entities) was Robert H. Patterson, Jr., a senior partner at an establishment Richmond law firm and a devoted VMI alumnus. He was fortunate to have as a law partner another true believer and able lawyer—this one female. Anne Marie Whittemore, a 1970 graduate of Yale Law School and a *summa cum laude* Vassar College graduate, had been dismayed by Vassar's decision to admit men. Whittemore believed that women and men learn differently and benefit from different kinds of single-sex education, and she saw her own views as consistent with "the cutting edge of feminist theory."[26]

A public entity like VMI itself is ordinarily represented, not by private counsel, but by the state's attorney general, and the governor and legislature, not college officials, have the last word on state educational policy. Virginia Attorney General Mary Sue Terry was the first woman elected to Virginia state-wide office, one of only two women state attorneys general nationwide, and a path breaker at the University of Virginia (which resisted admitting women and lost an equal protection lawsuit in 1970). Terry probably held her nose as she took on the representation of VMI.[27] Soon, however, L. Douglas Wilder was elected in

[25] *VMI Runs Rear–Guard Action Against Admitting Women*, WASH. POST, June 1, 1986, at A22; STRUM, *supra* note 3, at 35, 84–87.

[26] STRUM, *supra* note 3, at 97–98.

[27] *Id.* at 91; Kirstein v. Rector and Visitors of Univ. of Virginia, 309 F. Supp. 184 (E.D. Va. 1970).

Virginia as the nation's first African American Governor, and his public declaration that "no person should be denied admittance to a State supported school because of his or her gender" became the official state position on VMI.[28] With no public policy to stand on in defending VMI, Terry moved to withdraw from the case—a motion that Judge Kiser allowed only on the condition that VMI not be left without counsel. Patterson's team gladly stepped in. When the dust settled, the DOJ suit was consolidated with VMI's declaratory judgment action into a single case in front of the alumni and board's chosen judge, Jackson Kiser. The private legal team, rather than any publicly accountable government attorney, controlled the litigation.

The Lower Courts Bungle Intermediate Scrutiny

Judge Kiser held a six-day trial in the spring of 1991, and two months later he issued a lengthy opinion ruling in VMI's favor in every respect. He began with reference to the Civil War conflict at New Market, remarking that "The combatants have again confronted each other, but this time the venue is in this court."[29] Judge Kiser knew which side he was on.[30] It was Kiser's 26 pages of factual findings that were most significant because, although the United States could argue the legal points on a clean slate on appeal, the trial judge's findings of fact would bind the appellate courts unless shown to be "clearly erroneous," i.e. wrong in some obvious way.

Several of Judge Kiser's findings would bedevil the United States all the way to the Supreme Court. The lack of evidence of any preexisting, non-discriminatory state interest in VMI's exclusion of women was glaring, yet Kiser managed to cobble together a finding that "system-wide diversity" in higher educational options is a legitimate state objective.[31] He determined that some students, both male and female, can benefit from single-sex colleges, and that offering single-sex education for males at VMI thus served the system-diversity objective. Judge Kiser further found that VMI's distinctive, "adversative" method added to system-wide diversity, but that the adversative method would not work for women. Plunging into the quagmire of sex stereotyping, he explained

[28] Brief for the Cross–Respondent, Virginia v. United States, 518 U.S. 515 (1996) (U.S. No. 94–2107).

[29] United States v. Virginia, 766 F. Supp. at 1408.

[30] STRUM, *supra* note 3, at 173.

[31] Perversely, Kiser relied on affirmative-action and academic-freedom cases, including *Regents v. Bakke*, 438 U.S. 265 (1978), and *Sweezy v. New Hampshire*, 354 U.S. 234 (1957) cited in United States v. Commonwealth of Virginia, 766 F. Supp. at 1409, which stand, not for the benefits of diversity among types of schools, but diversity within student bodies, which VMI most decidedly lacked.

that women and men are physiologically different in as much as most men have less body fat, and greater explosive power, lifting capacity, and running speed than most women. Relying heavily on the videotaped testimony of Harvard University sociology professor emeritus David Riesman, the judge found that typical women and men also are developmentally different and, consequently, that they "learn differently." "Males tend to need an atmosphere of adversativeness or ritual combat in which the teacher is a disciplinarian and a worthy competitor. Females tend to thrive in a cooperative atmosphere in which the teacher is emotionally connected with the students." Kiser concluded that admission of women would require some changes, but that change to any aspect of VMI's eccentric method would "affect the educational experience as a whole." Given those facts, he effectively held single-sex education categorically self-justifying, and especially so at VMI: VMI presumably benefited its students; its single-sex status and method differentiated it from other colleges; system diversity is good; and VMI's distinctiveness would be lost if it admitted women. In Judge Kiser's words, "VMI truly marches to the beat of a different drummer, and I will permit it to continue to do so."[32]

The factual findings did, however, contain a few morsels favorable to the United States. Stepping into a hole that VMI's own lawyers had dug, Judge Kiser found that VMI is "unique." "The system of education at VMI is not offered elsewhere in the United States. Therefore women have no opportunity anywhere to gain the benefits of this education." Moreover, Judge Kiser's findings about physical and developmental differences between the sexes were, importantly, only findings of *average* differences. He found that some women would be "capable of all the individual activities required of VMI cadets," and that some women "would want to attend [VMI] if they had the opportunity." A "critical mass" of 10–40 percent female enrolment would be needed to provide a good educational environment for women at a formerly all-male school, and Judge Kiser found that VMI could reasonably expect at least 10 percent female enrolment. Those findings would eventually provide critical footing for the federal government.[33]

President Bush's Solicitor General, Kenneth W. Starr, provided the requisite go-ahead for the appeal.[34] The United States Court of Appeals

---

[32] United States v. Virginia, 766 F. Supp. at 1434, 1422, 1415, 1421.

[33] *Id.* at 1412, 1414, 1431, 1422.

[34] *See* Cornelia T.L. Pillard, *The Unfulfilled Promise of the Constitution in Executive Hands*, 103 MICH. L. REV. 676, 705 (2005) (explaining the responsibilities and duties of the solicitor general).

**In pre-enrollment summer session, incoming VMI students (including
Kimberly Haft, left) prepare for the first year of coeducation
under the famed Rat system. Photo by Nancy Andrews**

for the Fourth Circuit, which hears all appeals from federal courts in
Virginia, had a reputation as the most ideologically conservative Circuit
in the nation, and the court proved true to form. At oral argument, one
judge ignored the finding that some women could hack VMI and insisted
"we know that women can't endure the type of first-year or maybe even
second-year training the VMI offers."[35] Another comment from the
bench suggested that "[i]t all traces back to maleness, physical vigor,
that ability to withstand adversity, the ability to withstand invasions of
privacy. Everything that is said about the mission, it seems to me, comes
back to the absolute necessity that it be male, and all male, and
untraveled by anything not male."[36]

The Fourth Circuit's opinion showed that it understood *Mississippi
University for Women v. Hogan* to be a more significant obstacle for VMI
than had Judge Kiser, but the court pointed a different way around it.
For all the potential benefits of single-sex education, Virginia lacked a
convincing reason for providing "this unique educational opportunity to
men only," so the court found an equal protection violation and vacated
and remanded for remedial proceedings.[37] The twist was that, in the
court of appeals' view, VMI need not admit women "if adequate alternatives are available."[38] Virginia "might properly decide to admit women to
VMI and adjust the program to implement that choice"—clearly not a
route the court was inclined to push—or, alternatively, "it might estab-

---

[35] STRUM, *supra* note 3, at 192.

[36] *Id.* at 193.

[37] United States v. Virginia, 976 F.2d 890 (4th Cir. 1992), *rehearing denied*, 976 F.2d
900 (4th Cir.), *cert. denied*, 508 U.S. 946 (1993).

[38] *Id.* at 892, 900.

lish parallel programs, or it might abandon state support of VMI, leaving VMI the option to pursue its own policies as a private institution," or, indeed, VMI might come up with "other more creative options or combinations."[39] VMI had not asked to go private or set up a sister school, but once the court of appeals signalled its receptiveness, VMI's remedial preference was clear.

In a Different Place: The Virginia Women's Institute for Leadership

VMI quickly turned to Mary Baldwin College, a small, private, liberal arts college for women thirty-five miles down the road from the Institute, and invited it to consider establishing a female-only counterpart to VMI. MBC, facing its own financial challenges, welcomed the invitation, sweetened as it was by VMI's initial promise of $6.5 million to help with building renovation, scholarships, and endowment.[40] A task force of MBC senior administrators, faculty, and one student set to work on plans for a Virginia Women's Institute for Leadership (VWIL) at MBC.

The Task Force never sought to produce a female mirror image of VMI, nor did it consult anyone at VMI in planning VWIL's curriculum. It aimed instead to develop "the optimum environment for the education and training of women leaders"[41]—albeit with strategically inspired VMI-style overtones. According to the Task Force, "a military model and, especially VMI's adversative method, would be wholly inappropriate for educating and training most women for leadership roles."[42] (Whether VMI was appropriate for training most men for leadership was a question never pursued.) The Task Force found that "young women will be for the foreseeable future products of a culture which encourages them to find their sense of self in relationships," so that they would benefit from "a cooperative method which reinforces self-esteem rather than the leveling process used by VMI."[43]

The VWIL program would not be a holistic, barracks-oriented military college but would instead be equivalent to a curricular minor designed to explore various aspects of women's leadership for a select few MBC women. VWIL's only military aspects would be 2–4 hours per week of ROTC training and participation in a new, largely ceremonial Virginia Corps of Cadets. VWIL's mission statement parroted the core

---

[39] *Id.* at 900.

[40] STRUM, *supra* note 3, at 201–02.

[41] *Id.* at 207–08.

[42] United States v. Virginia, 852 F. Supp. 471, 476 (W.D. Va. 1994).

[43] *Id.*

VMI objective of producing "citizen-soldiers," but the Task Force reject-ed every one of the components of the VMI system that the courts had found to be so integral to VMI's "unique" educational method, eschew-ing the class and dyke systems, strict honor code, and barracks life that had been hailed as so instrumental to the leveling and bonding of cadets at VMI. Instead of the rat line, VWIL women would receive "training in self-defense and self-assertiveness through a Cooperative Confidence Building program."[44] VWIL would not have VMI's math or science focus, it would not offer engineering, nor would it offer a Bachelor of Science degree. VWIL's faculty and facilities would be far less extensive and of lower caliber than those at VMI.[45]

The United States promptly challenged the adequacy of the VWIL plan as a remedy for VMI's unconstitutional exclusion of women. Follow-ing an evidentiary hearing, Judge Kiser approved the VWIL remedial plan.[46] Judge Kiser acknowledged that the proposed VWIL "differs substantially from the VMI program," but he found the differences to be "justified pedagogically" based on "developmental and emotional differ-ences between the sexes."[47] Judge Kiser expanded his Civil War meta-phor in a way that would become his opinion's tag line in the press, concluding that "[i]f VMI marches to the beat of a drum, then Mary Baldwin marches to the melody of a fife and when the march is over, both will have arrived at the same destination."[48]

The United States again appealed and again lost before the same Fourth Circuit panel, this time garnering a dissenting opinion. VMI also cross-appealed its liability, insisting that the excluded women were not entitled to anything beyond the status quo, but that if they were, VWIL sufficed. The panel majority, by Judge Paul V. Niemeyer, a Reagan district court appointee elevated to the court of appeals by George H.W. Bush, concluded that *Hogan*'s two requirements were readily met by the VWIL remedy. VMI had established that "providing the option of a single-gender college education" was an important governmental inter-est, and excluding women from VMI was "by definition necessary for accomplishing the objective."[49] That approach had the troubling effect of seeming to require "little or no scrutiny" of single-sex education, so the court created a "special intermediate scrutiny" test with a third analytic

---

[44] Brief for Petitioner at 8–9, United States v. Virginia, 518 U.S. 515 (1996) (No. 94–1941).

[45] *Id.* at 8–11.

[46] United States v. Virginia, 852 F. Supp. at 471.

[47] *Id.* at 473, 480.

[48] *Id.* at 484.

[49] United States v. Virginia, 44 F.3d 1229 at 1237–38 (4th Cir. 1995).

step, requiring that the benefits separately provided to each sex be, not equal, but "substantively comparable."[50] Acknowledging that VWIL "differs substantially" from VMI, and that a VWIL degree would lack VMI's history and prestige, the court was nonetheless satisfied because VWIL's "goals are the same" and it "aimed at achieving similar results" as VMI; prestige would inevitably take time.[51] The court thus allowed defendants, in the context of fending off admission of women, to insist that every detail of VMI's unique program was essential, but when it came to what Virginia owed the excluded women, the court settled for general claims about VWIL's likely overall outcomes at some undefined future time. Judge James Dickson Phillips, Jr., a decorated WWII combat veteran, dissented. It was clear to him that the real reason for the separate and different programs was simply to keep VMI all-male. VWIL was, moreover, patently unequal, and its "catch-up game [was] an impossible one" given VMI's enormous head start.[52] Judge Diana Gribbon Motz, one of only two women on the 13–member Fourth Circuit and the first female judge to opine on the case, wrote a powerful dissent from denial of rehearing en banc explaining why the panel's application of *Hogan* was "confused and contrary to both law and logic."[53]

In the Supreme Court: Authenticating Objectives and Smoking Out Stereotypes

Not satisfied with the dual-school solution, VMI pursued its challenge to liability all the way to the Supreme Court while awkwardly professing a genuine interest in women's education at VWIL. The United States, meanwhile, assailed the VWIL remedy as a new equal protection violation in itself. With a new administration in office, President's Clinton's Supreme Court litigator, Solicitor General Drew S. Days, III, took over from the Civil Rights Division's appellate staff. VMI hired as Supreme Court counsel conservative heavy-hitter Theodore B. Olson, who would later successfully argue for George W. Bush in *Bush v. Gore*, and become the second President Bush's solicitor general.

Solicitor General Days, a Yale Law School Professor who once headed up the Civil Rights Division, made a major strategic decision at this point to argue for strict constitutional scrutiny for sex-based classifications. During the six years of the *VMI* litigation, the lower federal courts applying intermediate scrutiny had upheld an exclusionary policy that was, in the Justice Department's view, obviously unconstitutional.

---

[50] *Id.* at 1237.

[51] *Id.* at 1240–41.

[52] *Id.* at 1250.

[53] United States v. Virginia, 52 F.3d 90, 92 (1995) (Motz, J., dissenting from denial of rehearing en banc, joined by Hall, Murnaghan, and Michael, JJ.).

The solicitor general proposed strict scrutiny as the analytically correct standard, needed to avoid the kind of "ambiguity about the general illegitimacy of sex-based classifications" that had stymied the lower courts.[54] To minimize the implication that the plaintiff could not win without the more searching standard, Days briefed it as an alternative ground and kept that point short.[55]

Elevated constitutional scrutiny applies to governmental decisions based on characteristics, like race or sex, that have historically triggered pervasive discrimination. Such scrutiny, whether strict or intermediate, is designed to "smoke out" discrimination by examining the sincerity and importance of the governmental objective and the "fit," or degree of relevance, of the characteristic to meeting the objective. Relying on race as a way to find the most reliable managers, or sex to find the best day care workers, for example, would fail the requirement of close "fit" by unnecessarily invoking overbroad generalizations or stereotypes instead of individualized consideration of relevant qualifications.

The bar against stereotyping is a key aspect of elevated constitutional scrutiny, and it accounts for much of the difference between intermediate scrutiny of sex-based decisions and the stronger, strict scrutiny of race. Whereas the Court deems race virtually irrelevant, it has in a few cases viewed sex characteristics as non-stereotypical, "real" differences that are relevant to and constitutionally permissible in governmental decision making. The lower courts in *VMI*, drawing on expert witness testimony that women were unsuited to VMI's adversarial method and were better served by VWIL's cooperative confidence building, characterized those average tendencies as real sex differences, not stereotypes. The record showed, however, that some women wanted to and could succeed at VMI. If excluding them cleared the intermediate-scrutiny stereotyping bar, the Justice Department wanted a higher bar.

As an advocate decades earlier, Ruth Bader Ginsburg had made it her mission to rid the state and federal statute books of laws that treated women differently, and to persuade the Court to recognize sex as a suspect ground of classification that, like race, warranted strict constitutional scrutiny.[56] She aimed high, and initial progress was quick and dramatic. Ginsburg co-authored the brief in the 1971 case, *Reed v. Reed*,[57] in which the Supreme Court for the first time, and by a

---

[54] Brief for Petitioner at 36, United States v. Virginia, 518 U.S. 515 (1996) (No. 94–1941).

[55] *Id.* at 33–36; Brief for Cross-Respondent at 9, 16–17, United States v. Virginia, 518 U.S. 515 (1996) (No. 94–2107).

[56] STRUM, *supra* note 3, at 63.

[57] 404 U.S. 71 (1971).

unanimous vote, invalidated an overtly sex-based law under equal protection. That same year, the ACLU established a Women's Rights Project (WRP) and persuaded Ginsburg, then a new professor at Columbia Law School, to lead the WRP on a part-time basis. On behalf of the ACLU, Ginsburg shared oral argument time in *Frontiero v. Richardson*,[58] a case challenging a statutory presumption that spouses of male but not female service members are dependents eligible for benefits. Ginsburg devoted her entire argument to the reasons supporting strict scrutiny. A four-member plurality was persuaded. Justice Brennan's lead opinion in *Frontiero* adopted strict scrutiny and paid Ginsburg the signal compliment of relying explicitly on her brief.[59]

Four justices do not a majority make, however, and the level of constitutional scrutiny applicable to sex-based classifications soon fell into a holding pattern. Over the persistent objections of Justice Rehnquist, who insisted that the very lowest standard—rationality review—sufficed, a majority of the Court found intermediate scrutiny adequate to invalidate the sex-based laws challenged in a series of cases, including *Craig v. Boren*,[60] *Stanton v. Stanton*,[61] and *Orr v. Orr*.[62] In 1981 in *Hogan*, and in a 1994 jury discrimination case, *J.E.B v. Alabama*, the Court ruled for the sex discrimination plaintiffs and explicitly sidestepped strict scrutiny as unnecessary to resolve those cases.[63] The question whether the Court would ratchet up the standard to "strict" in an appropriate case thus appeared to be an open one when it heard *United States v. Virginia*.

Women's rights groups strongly favored advocating strict scrutiny in *VMI*. One potential downside was that strict scrutiny would pose a higher barrier to sex-based affirmative action, but the advocates noted that courts already effectively imposed the same, strict standard on affirmative action plans based on sex as they used for race.[64] Meanwhile, intermediate scrutiny had proved full of holes, allowing sex discrimina-

[58] 411 U.S. 677 (1973).

[59] *Id.* at 686 & n.17.

[60] 429 U.S. 190 (1976).

[61] 429 U.S. 501 (1977).

[62] 440 U.S. 268 (1979).

[63] Hogan, 458 U.S. at 724 n.9; J.E.B. v. Alabama ex rel T.B, 511 U.S. 127, 136–37 and n.6 (1994).

[64] *See* Adarand Constructors Inc. v. Peña, 515 U.S. 200 (1995) (symmetrically imposing strict scrutiny against benign as well as malign racial distinctions); *see, e.g.,* Brunet v. City of Columbus, 1 F.3d 390, 403–04 (6th Cir. 1993), *cert. denied* 510 U.S. 1164 (1994); Lamprecht v. FCC, 958 F.2d 382 (D.C. Cir. 1992); *id.* at 405–06 (Mikva, J., dissenting).

tion in cases involving pregnancy,[65] statutory rape,[66] and in the military[67] —and in the bungled lower court opinions in *Virginia*. The women's groups also were under the impression that Justice Ginsburg was eager for a chance to apply strict scrutiny to a sex-based classification and would be annoyed if the opportunity were wasted by the parties' failure to ask for it. Several *amici* joined the United States in urging strict scrutiny.[68]

At oral argument, it quickly became apparent, however, that the justices were not interested in strict scrutiny. Justice O'Connor peppered Principal Deputy Solicitor General Paul Bender with questions that were openly hostile to the government's plea for strict scrutiny. Why had the solicitor general even asked for strict scrutiny, when the level of scrutiny was "not exactly an open question"?[69] Bender noted that the Court had repeatedly said that the question *was* open (including in O'Connor's *Hogan* opinion). Justice O'Connor brushed that assertion aside, asking why the intermediate standard did not suffice to decide this case, too. When another justice interrupted with a new line of questioning, Justice O'Connor sat back with knitted brow, evidently unpersuaded.

Theodore Olson framed the case as about "the inescapable central question of whether the States can support single sex education."[70] The justices, and especially Justice O'Connor, bore down on Olson about how he could defend "provid[ing] single sex education to just one sex, to just men," and asked, with some incredulity, "you want to defend that? . . . You want to say it is not a violation of the Constitution to provide a single sex education just for men?"[71] Olson pointed to the finding, which the federal government had not contested, that single-sex education could be beneficial for some members of both sexes and to the work of "education experts" in devising the right program at VWIL (though they had done no such thing at VMI).

The most dramatic moment in the argument came when Justice Scalia pressed Paul Bender about why the United States thought VWIL

---

[65] Geduldig v. Aiello, 417 U.S. 484 (1974).

[66] Michael M. v. Superior Court of Sonoma County, 450 U.S. 464 (1981).

[67] Rostker v. Goldberg, 453 U.S. 57 (1981).

[68] *See, e.g.*, Brief for National Women's Law Center et al. as Amici Curiae Supporting Petitioner, United States v. Virginia, 518 U.S. 515 (No. 94–1941); Brief for Employment Law Center et al. as Amici Curiae Supporting Petitioner, United States v. Virginia, 518 U.S. 515 (No. 94–1941).

[69] Transcript of Oral Argument at 11–13, United States v. Virginia, 518 U.S. 515 (1996) (No. 94–1941).

[70] *Id.* at 28.

[71] *Id.* at 31.

was an inadequate remedy. As Bender responded, the courtroom fell silent. Bender hypothesized:

> [W]hat if a State set up a State law school in 1839, all for men, because at that time only men could be lawyers, and over 150 years it developed an extremely adversarial method of legal education, the toughest kind of Socratic teaching, tremendous time pressures, tremendous pressures in exams, tremendous combativeness by the faculty, tremendous competitiveness among the students, and developed a reputation for that.

> And ... it was a place that was known as hard to succeed at, and a third or so of the people flunked out in the first year, and the graduates of that school who survived that process became known as expert leading lawyers and judges in that State and Nationwide.

> And then as women came into the legal profession and started to apply to the school, to ask it to change its admission policy, the school made a judgment that most women really wouldn't be comfortable in this environment, and the faculty would have trouble cross-examining them in the same way they cross-examine men, and other students would have difficulty relating to them in the same competitive way, and so it's better not to let women into the school.

> What we'll do is, we'll set up a new women's law school, and it won't have the tough Socratic method, it will have a much warmer, a much more embracing environment, and it won't have large classes with a lot of pressure, it will have seminars, and it won't have tough exams, it will have papers, and things like that—

> (Laughter.)

> .... I think we all understand that that is not by any means equal treatment of women with regard to their access to the legal profession.[72]

None of the justices interrupted. They had studied law when the law schools were just beginning to accept women. They were well familiar with stereotypes about women and lawyering. Perhaps they were sobered by awareness of the bias that Justices Ginsburg and O'Connor had surmounted in their own legal careers. Bender's analogy to early exclusion of women from the bar would surface in the opinion ruling in the United States' favor.[73]

---

[72] *Id.* at 22–24.

[73] United States v. Virginia, 518 U.S. at 532 n.5, 556.

The Court decided *United States v. Virginia* by a 7–1 majority, over the lone dissent of Justice Scalia, with Justice Thomas (whose son attended VMI) recusing himself. The standard the Court announced was a demanding one. Justice Ginsburg saw it as the practical equivalent to what women would have obtained had the Equal Rights Amendment succeeded.[74] Even Chief Justice Rehnquist's separate concurrence providing the seventh vote underscored the strength of the majority, both because the majority had brought the reluctant Chief Justice around, and because no other justice signed on to his less skeptical approach.[75]

The Chief Justice would ordinarily decide which justice would write the opinion, and could have assigned it to himself. Because Chief Justice Rehnquist had voted with VMI in the Court's post-argument conference, however, Justice Stevens, the most senior member of the initial majority, had authority to assign, and gave the opinion to Justice Ginsburg. Fearing a strict scrutiny opinion would not garner maximal consensus among the justices, she did not even mention the United States' bid for strict scrutiny. Ginsburg instead declared "skeptical scrutiny" to be the appropriate standard for sex-based classifications, attaching that new moniker to the "exceedingly persuasive justification" requirement of Justice O'Connor's opinion in *Hogan* and Justice Kennedy's in *J.E.B.*[76]

The opinion's analysis, however, effectively blurs the line between intermediate and strict scrutiny, narrowing the gap between the standards applicable to sex- and race-based classifications. It strengthens anti-stereotyping doctrine, jettisoning the term "stereotype," with its narrowing connotations of the archaic or denigrating, to instead bar sex-based "over-generalization." Under *Virginia*, even a sex-based generalization that is statistically accurate, and thus "real" as to "most women" or "women as a group," cannot "justify denying opportunity to women whose talent and capacity place them outside the average description."[77] Under that approach, the presumption of irrelevance of sex is almost as strong as that applied to race under strict scrutiny.

---

[74] STRUM, *supra* note 3 at 287 n.27 (quoting Jeffrey Rosen, *The New Look of Liberalism on the Court*, N.Y. TIMES, Oct. 5, 1997 (Magazine)).

[75] Chief Justice Rehnquist started out on the other side both in the initial voting on the *VMI* case itself, Strum, *supra* note 3, at 282, and on the general question whether sex based classifications deserve any heightened scrutiny whatsoever. *See, e.g.*, Hogan, 458 U.S. at 735–45 (Powell and Rehnquist, JJ., dissenting); Craig v. Boren, 429 U.S. at 217-228 (Rehnquist, J., dissenting); Frontiero, 411 U.S. at 691 (Rehnquist, J., dissenting); *see generally* Reva B. Siegel, *"You've Come a Long Way Baby": Rehnquist's New Approach to Pregnancy Discrimination in* Hibbs, 58 STAN. L. REV. 1871 (2006).

[76] United States v. Virginia, 518 U.S. at 530.

[77] *Id.* at 550.

The *Virginia* opinion also verges toward strict scrutiny by using the analysis of *Sweatt v. Painter*[78] to compare VWIL and VMI. *Sweat,* decided before *Brown* categorically established that racially segregated schools can never be equal, strictly scrutinized the tangible and intangible qualities of Texas's segregated white and black law schools, and found them unequal. *Virginia* applied *Sweatt* and similarly found VWIL to be plainly unequal to VMI. VWIL had lower aggregate student and professor qualifications, fewer curricular options, lesser facilities, endowment, prestige, and alumni power and resources. Justice Ginsburg also reemphasized that intermediate, or "skeptical," scrutiny, like strict scrutiny, requires that courts assess "actual state purposes," not *post hoc* rationales behind challenged classifications.[79] The actual purpose of VWIL was to preserve VMI for men. Despite the majority's silence on the strict scrutiny claim, Justice Scalia in his dissent was not the only observer to read the opinion as having "effectively accept[ed] it."[80]

The first remarkable thing about Chief Justice Rehnquist's solo concurrence was that it was not a dissent. His opinion echoed the "comparability" analysis of the Fourth Circuit, except that, in the Chief Justice's view, VWIL did not provide constitutionally equivalent opportunity because it was "distinctly inferior to the existing men's institution and will continue to be for the foreseeable future." He thought separate schools for each sex could be quite different in character and still be constitutional: "one could be strong in computer science and the other in liberal arts." They need only "offer ... the same quality of education and [be] of the same overall caliber." A state could "consider the public's demand" in setting different curricula, so long as it avoided "assuming demand based on stereotypes." For all its apparent lenience, the Chief Justice's opinion demanded more for women than VWIL offered. In hinting that women might be better served by something other than admission to VMI as it then stood, Rehnquist was also the only justice

---

[78] 339 U.S. 629 (1950).

[79] United States v. Virginia, 518 U.S. at 516.

[80] *Id.* at 569–70, 571, 574; *see, e.g.,* Cass R. Sunstein, *The Supreme Court, 1995 Term— Foreword: Leaving Things Undecided,* 110 Harv. L. Rev. 4, 75 (1996) (contending that "[t]he Court [in *VMI*] did not merely restate the intermediate scrutiny test but pressed it closer to strict scrutiny"); Michael Dorf, *Equal Protection Incorporation,* 88 Va. L. Rev. 951, 963 n.36 (2002) (noting that, in *VMI,* "the Court appeared to apply something like strict scrutiny to a gender classification"); Deborah L. Brake, *Reflections on the* VMI *Decision,* 6 Am. U. J. Gender & L. 35 (1997) (characterizing *VMI* as "crafting a standard with the teeth, if not the name, of strict scrutiny"). *But see* Tuan Anh Nguyen v. INS, 533 U.S. 53 (2001) (nominally applying *VMI* to sustain a sex distinction in the Immigration and Nationality Act that, as Justice O'Connor argued in dissent, should not survive any level of scrutiny higher than rational basis review).

who arguably expressed a glimmer of recognition of how formal equality alone can give short shrift to women.[81]

Alone in dissent, Justice Scalia saw the Court's decision as having adopted strict scrutiny *sub silentio*, sounding the death knell of public funding for single-sex education, public or private. He noted that the majority "creates the illusion that government officials in some future case will have a clear shot at justifying some sort of single-sex public education." In his view, the Court's own analysis foreclosed that chance because "the single-sex program that will not be capable of being characterized as 'unique' is not only unique but nonexistent," and, under the majority's reasoning, "if any program restricted to one sex is 'uniqu[e],' it must be opened to members of the opposite sex 'who have the will and capacity' to participate in it."[82]

"Assimilation" of Women, the VMI Way

Even after the Supreme Court's decisive ruling, VMI remained loath to admit women. In a depressing echo of the emergence of segregated private schools for whites seeking to evade the impact of *Brown*, some VMI alumni mounted a quixotic campaign to raise funds to privatize VMI to keep it exclusively male. The truth was that the Institute was already suffering declining enrolment and could not stay afloat without the one-third of its budget the state provided; the Board of Visitors rejected privatization by a close 9–8 vote.

Members of the last all male VMI class showed their opposition to women's admission by referring to themselves as LCWB, or "last class with balls." They had an arrow added to the "2000" on their class rings to "symbolize the class's manhood." A male cadet, telling a female "you are the reason my school sucks," gave voice to tensions that all the new women undoubtedly felt. Some professors openly resented coeducation, insisting that male students weren't getting the same quality of education at VMI now that coeducation had "ruined" it, or overtly pointing out that they couldn't teach in the way they used to "now that there's a *lady* in the room."[83]

Instead of considering how best to re-create the rigors of VMI for a newly coeducational student body, VMI approached women's arrival with a determination to change as little possible. In some ways, that decision made sense. The litigation and the Court's opinion had focused on the group of women that wanted, not VWIL or something else, but the VMI

---

[81] United States v. Virginia, 518 U.S. at 565–66.

[82] *Id.* at 596; *see also id.* at 569–70.

[83] *Id.* at 253, 327, 343–44.

experience—the experience that had been previously reserved for men.[84] They wanted, as Paul Bender had put it at oral argument, "to demonstrate that they have the same qualities" of toughness as the male VMI graduates, and they wanted the VMI degree "as a mark of [their] ability to survive that program as a member of the, up until now, brotherhood of VMI graduates."[85] The symbolic point that men have no monopoly on toughness and self discipline might not have been won if women's arrival at VMI promptly "feminized" the place, as some VMI men and their boosters like right-wing agitator Phyllis Schlafley had portended.

Newly shorn female "rat" Yulia Beltikova salutes on the parade field during drill practice. Photo by Nancy Andrews.

Changing as little as possible proved tricky, however, for a school that thought women and men were significantly different and that defined itself in such stereotypically masculine terms. VMI administrators obsessed over the cut of the women's hair, uniforms, swimsuits— and even whether it would show impermissible favoritism to dispense tampons free of charge to prevent inconvenience to busy cadets lacking a quarter. Would the incoming women be subjected to the same crew cuts as the men, or would they wear a different short haircut that allowed them to be more readily distinguished and thus "retain their feminini-

---

[84] United States v. Virginia, 518 U.S. at 555.

[85] Transcript of Oral Argument at 9, 17, United States v. Virginia, 518 U.S. 515 (No. 94–1941); *see* United States v. Virginia, 518 U.S. at 550–51 (focusing the remedial inquiry, not on the typical women, but on the women eager and qualified for VMI).

ty"? Unisex gym shorts and T-shirts were no problem, but the men's everyday uniforms included neckties, stout oxfords, and other traditionally masculine accoutrements, and the men's dress uniforms harkened to pre-Civil War days, with a broad chest full of braid and brass buttons, long tails on the jackets, and tall, bucket hats with braid and feathers. Would all cadets wear those same dress uniforms, even to dances, producing an illusion of men dancing with men?[86]

The Institute chose to hew so closely to its masculine dress and grooming standards for the incoming female rats that VMI women were often mistaken for men. A retired servicewoman at a dedication in Washington D.C. for the new Women in Military Service for America Memorial told the VMI women she was "really glad to see you men here supporting us," and the emcee introduced them as a group of West Point men. Time and again female VMI cadets were angrily shooed out of women's public restrooms.[87] There was delicious irony in the way that VMI's insistence that the women do things in the traditional, masculine VMI way was more gender-bending than the approach followed by other coeducational colleges, including the service academies, where women's different uniforms and longer hair signal gender distinction. At VMI, women and men alike were called "brother" rats.

VMI did not, in the end, quite have the stomach for the sartorial project it set for itself. The administrators didn't want "to develop a group of women who were trying to out-butch the guys," and they worried, with thinly veiled homophobia, about attracting "the wrong kind of women," whom they thought of as "Amazons."[88] VMI men expressed their conflicted expectations for the women in many ways, including when VMI cheerleaders took over from the former Mary Baldwin College imports and appeared on the sidelines in short skirts, bare midriffs and buzz cuts. The male cadets thought they were too sexy for VMI, but also grotesque and unfeminine with their shorn heads. These men would be more comfortable with their female peers after they completed the "rat line," when, the administration decided, they would be permitted (and expected) to grow their hair, wear "conservative cosmetics," and have the option to wear gold-post earrings and skirts.[89]

Dress and grooming codes were not the only standards set by and for men that VMI sought to retain. Existing academic standards posed no particular obstacle for the women, but VMI continued to insist that they be evaluated according to physical fitness standards set for men.

---

[86] BRODIE, *supra* note 13, at 123–24, 133–37.

[87] *Id.* at 279–80.

[88] *Id.* at 286, 281.

[89] *Id.* at 132–34, 281, 345–46.

The requirement of five pull-ups in the physical education course, for example, with no partial credit for any fewer, made it quite a lot more difficult for women than men to get A's in physical education, despite the fact that VMI's first women were disproportionately varsity athletes. To the extent that average physical differences meant that physical standards designed specifically for men had a dramatic adverse impact on women's physical education grades, VMI was effectively setting the bar higher for women as a group than for men.

Interestingly, however, most of the new VMI women—admittedly self-selected to want "the VMI experience"—favored the same physical fitness standard for women and men (although they did question its role in their grades). The decision to maintain the standard was made in large part out of conviction that it "would be best for the women's assimilation."[90] Many VMI men were so hostile to women's arrival that they blamed any change, however trivial or unrelated to coeducation, on women. The men's heckling must have helped to make male-oriented standards seem more appealing to the women than any new standard, such as one that incorporated partial credit for both sexes, or used sex-neutral ability grouping.

VMI's determination to change as little as possible may have had some logic to it, but it was also deeply problematic. The Justice Department's initial litigation decision not to question the pedagogical value of VMI's archaic and hyper-masculine traditions is partly to blame. VMI is not just a symbol but an educational institution. However valued may be its traditions by those who built and succeeded under them, the Institute must educate students for life in contemporary society. VMI now belongs to its women as much as to its men. Any coeducational public college, VMI included, should be designed in a way that maximizes educational benefits while minimizing disproportionate adverse impact on any sub-group—in particular one that has been historically subjected to discrimination. A VMI equally devoted to women and men would develop standards that drew out the best in everyone, rather than defiantly adhering to traditional practices avowedly designed by and for men. If the gratuitous machismo of VMI's culture makes it harder for women than for men to fit in and thrive, it is the culture, not just the women, that should adapt. Eventually, there can be little question that VMI will adapt. Over time, a non-misogynistic toughness will take root and displace the swaggering machismo. But the way that the litigation anointed VMI's "adversative" approach as valuable and special—which even the Justice Department and the Supreme Court echoed rather than challenged—make it that much harder for VMI women to seek appropriate responsiveness from VMI now that it is their school, too.

---

[90] *Id.* at 157.

Conclusion

The signal contributions of *United States v. Virginia* to sex equality law are that it strengthens the doctrine against sex-based generalizations and lays down a demanding standard of equality for public, single-sex educational institutions. By insisting that as long as some women could and wanted to make the grade at VMI they must be given the opportunity to do so, the Court assured that conclusions about the general proclivities of a sex will not serve to foreclose opportunity for any person outside the typical mold of her or his sex. By requiring that any educational institution designed separately for women and men be equal in every material respect, *VMI* also assures that single-sex education will not be used as a ruse for inequality, or as a training ground in separate, different, and unequal gender roles.[91]

The equal protection doctrine that ultimately served as the driving wedge to open VMI to women is avowedly individualistic. It is concerned with a rare opportunity for the a-typical woman (or man), not with what might be best for the ordinary woman, or for women as a group. Schools and classes are institutions designed for groups, however, and sex equality in coeducational institutions is appropriately measured, not just by the absence of formal sex-based barriers, but also in terms of freedom from unwarranted obstacles to the equal success of male and female students generally.[92] The *VMI* case lacked a rigorous test of the extent to which the components of VMI's "success," such as its student-run rat line or particular physical requirements, were pedagogically legitimate, or instead gratuitous or worse. To the extent that VMI is dedicated to the propagation of masculinity for men through a four-year bonding ritual, the essence of which is differentiation from women and perceived femininity, merely opening the doors to women is a smaller step toward sex equality at VMI than it might have seemed.

---

[91] In October, 2006, the Department of Education announced new regulations liberalizing the terms under which districts may establish single-sex schools and classes. *See* 71 Fed. Reg. 62,529 (Oct. 25, 2006). The new rule, codified at 34 CFR Part 106, encourages a trend that was already occurring in the face of significant legal uncertainty: Nationwide, the number of single-sex public schools has risen from 3 in 1995 to 241 in 2006. Diana Jean Schemo, *Change in Federal Rules Backs Single–Sex Public Education*, N.Y. Times, Oct. 24, 2006, at A1. While it lessens regulatory obstacles, the new rule invites serious constitutional problems under *VMI*.

[92] Title IX of the Education Amendments of 1972 and its implementing regulations, to the extent that they prohibit practices with unjustified disparate impact on women, reflect that group-focused norm. The Supreme Court has not determined, however, whether disparate-impact regulatory prohibitions exceed statutory authority, and there is disagreement on the issue in the lower courts. *See* David S. Cohen, *Title IX: Beyond Equal Protection*, 28 Harv. J.L. & Gender 217, 276 (2005).

Megan Smith, in the first class of women admitted to VMI, being subjected to the "rat line." Photo by Nancy Andrews.

An unspoken shame of the *VMI* litigation was the way that it denigrated the Virginia Women's Institute for Leadership established for women at Mary Baldwin College, and in so doing implicitly cast aspersions on woman-conscious educational standards generally. VWIL certainly lacks the resources of VMI and does not provide for women what VMI does. Images of women organizing speaker series, keeping journals, and engaging in confidence building exercises at VWIL, juxtaposed with those of men drilling, commanding, dressing down their "brother rats," and complying with a high-stakes honor code at VMI all made for much eye-rolling over the patent sex-based over-generalizations and inequality. Stereotyping and inequality there was, and the Supreme Court decision rejecting it was entirely correct. The point should not be lost, however, that for all its relative paucity of resources and power, VWIL at least attempted to provide an educational experience designed to make women succeed; VMI did not. One wonders whether a well-endowed coeducational school with a pedagogical approach like VWIL's might be more successful for both sexes than a coeducational VMI. We are unlikely to know the answer to that question any time soon. VWIL continues to operate for a small group of women. The taint of femininity, however, together with the reality that male institutions like VMI wield more social and economic power than female institutions like VWIL, likely will deter a male plaintiff from seeking to integrate VWIL in the near future.

The *VMI* case, properly understood, did not achieve equality for women, either at VMI or in the law more generally. Opening to women male bastions of power like VMI is, undeniably, a critical step. The case also shows how further steps are called for to question and renovate historically and stereotypically male characteristics of existing institutions, standards, and uses of power. Kevin Trujillo, who was the peer-elected president of the graduating class the year women arrived at VMI, gave cause for optimism in explaining that he saw the arrival of women at VMI as "a chance to professionalize" VMI by amending some of the more adolescent and destructive rituals of VMI, and thereby improving it for both sexes.[93] Such change was not required by the lawsuit, but we should hope that it will be the eventual result. Meeting male standards is what got women into VMI, but until those standards, however demanding, are genuinely egalitarian and no longer palpably male, women at VMI will not have truly arrived.

---

[93] BRODIE, *supra* note 13, at 216.

13

By Serena Mayeri*

Civil Rights on Both Sides: Reproductive Rights and Free Speech in *Schenck v. Pro–Choice Network of Western New York*

Introduction

Since the Supreme Court decided *Roe v. Wade* in 1973, abortion has been the subject of passionate debate not only in courtrooms and legislatures, but also on the streets of American cities and towns. Though frequently and sometimes cynically manipulated for political gain, the abortion controversy may be the quintessential example of a dispute in which activists on both sides act out of deep, often immovable moral conviction. To advocates of reproductive choice, the availability of safe, legal abortions is central to women's ability to control their lives and destinies, and to achieve equality and dignity as human beings. To opponents of abortion, the procedure is antithetical to every human value, a desecration of body and soul that is morally equivalent to murder.

Beginning in the mid–1980s, abortion clinics became the site of picketing and protest. Abortion clinic protest tested the limits of the First Amendment in a society torn between its commitment to protect the constitutional rights of women seeking reproductive health services, and its dedication to freedom of speech and assembly. *Schenck v. Pro–*

---

* I am grateful to Laurence Behr, Marilynn Buckham, Rev. Paul Schenck, Yolanda Wu, and especially Lucinda Finley, for graciously sharing their recollections of the events recounted here. Drew Days, Myriam Gilles, and Risa Goluboff provided valuable comments and support for this project. All errors are mine.

Choice Network of Western New York, filed in 1990 and decided by the Court in 1997, was one of many constitutional challenges to injunctions that sought to strike a balance between these competing values. *Schenck* provides a particularly vivid and revealing glimpse into the world of abortion clinic protest and its impact on American communities. *Schenck* also provides a classic example of a case in which both parties saw themselves as defending civil rights against attacks potentially fatal— both literally and figuratively—to their respective causes. Both pro-choice and pro-life advocates proclaim themselves heirs to the legacy of the civil rights movement, with its courageous stance against injustice and for basic human rights amid a climate of violence and fear.

"A Troublemaker and a Crazy"

It was a humid Sunday in the summer of 1987 that transformed twenty-eight-year-old Paul Schenck into an anti-abortion activist. He had just finished delivering his morning sermon at the New Covenant Tabernacle Church in Tonawanda, New York, when two members of his congregation approached him with a look of urgency in their eyes. They needed to speak with him right away, the husband and wife said. The husband held a nondescript bag tightly in his hands.

Inside the bag, Schenck and his parishioners were horrified to find, were what they believed to be the remains of four aborted fetuses, unceremoniously discarded in a dumpster across the street from the couple's home in a Buffalo suburb. When calls to the police and the local health department proved unavailing, Schenck and his parishioners appealed to the public conscience. They obtained burial sites in Mount Olivette Cemetery and held religious services to mourn what they felt were the cruel murder and ignominious disposal of unborn children. "Before that," Schenck recalled, "I called myself pro-life by conviction and pro-choice by default. I had not taken into account the unborn child as a victim until that event."[1]

Shortly after the symbolic burial, a group of Schenck's parishioners informed him that they would be holding a prayer meeting in front of a local reproductive health clinic to voice their opposition to abortion. "I was very, very reluctant," Schenck remembered. "I knew the mayor and local officials by their first names. I had a lot of entrée into local government, and was afraid I would lose some of that access, that I would be considered a troublemaker and a crazy."[2] He agonized over the matter at length with his wife, Rebecca. If you don't join the protest, she said finally, I will.

---

[1] Interview with Paul Schenck, Apr. 19, 2000.

[2] *Id.*

The next day, the Schencks were among one hundred protesters gathered at the front and back entrances of a downtown reproductive health clinic, situated between a hairstyling salon and a pizza joint. When the police arrived and asked the demonstrators to disperse, they refused. The protesters were arrested and transported to a nearby ice skating rink, where they were given their court papers. That evening, Schenck found himself sharing dinner with the world-renowned evangelical preacher Billy Graham. It was a day he would not soon forget.[3]

Paul Chaim Schenck was born in 1959 in Grand Island, New York, to a Reform Jewish family, liberal in their politics and proud of their Jewish identity. He and his twin brother Robert were young teenagers when they became acquainted with members of a local Methodist youth group. "I saw in their lives a very sincere faith," Paul recalls, "and so I began to explore the claims of Christianity. I subsequently became convinced that the claims that Jesus made to fulfill Old Testament prophecies, to be the Jewish Messiah, were truthful." At sixteen, he was baptized, and joined the Methodist Church in Orchard Park. "I did not feel that I was repudiating my Jewish identity.... I saw Christianity as fulfilling the promises of Judaism. And still today I don't feel that I've rejected my Jewish heritage; I have fulfilled it."[4]

A few months after Schenck's first abortion protest, another young evangelical Christian New Yorker founded what would become the most famous—and infamous—anti-abortion group in the nation. Twenty-nine-year-old used car salesman Randall Terry's Operation Rescue, based in Binghamton, wasted no time in bringing the pro-life cause to national attention. Terry attracted hundreds of people to Atlanta, site of the Democratic National Convention, in July, 1988, including Paul Schenck. Schenck promptly founded the Northeastern Clergy Council, a group of clerics "on call" to minister to women considering abortion. Meanwhile, demonstrators numbering in the hundreds refused to identify themselves to police, going to jail in the names of Baby Jane Doe and Baby John Doe, attracting precious media attention and straining city resources.[5] Their success in Atlanta galvanized anti-abortion leaders to launch a nationwide crusade. The cities and towns of upstate New York were among Operation Rescue's first targets.

By 1990, thousands of protestors had been arrested throughout the country, many of them for physically blockading clinics.[6] Seeing their

---

[3] *Id.*

[4] *Id.*

[5] *See* Ronald Smothers, *Atlanta Protests Prove Magnet for Abortion Foes,* N.Y. TIMES, Aug. 13, 1998, at 6.

[6] *See Nearly 400 Abortion Protesters Arrested,* L.A. TIMES, Nov. 20, 1988, at 2.

cause as analogous to the civil rights struggle, they invoked and used tactics of civil disobedience pioneered in the United States by Martin Luther King, Jr., and even sang civil-rights era spirituals retooled with pro-life lyrics.[7] In one typical incident, four protesters chained themselves to a Kenmore, New York clinic; two of them served time in jail when they refused to post bail, and were cheered by five hundred supporters as they spent over a week fasting in their cells.[8] "We felt there was a compelling need to stop abortions for as long as we could," Schenck recalled, "so that women could receive the help they truly needed, the services they truly needed." He describes pro-life "sidewalk counselors"—"mostly women, some of whom were post-abortive"—providing bibles, information, and prayers to women entering the abortion facilities. "They spoke only loving and caring words and offered services and information to the women."[9]

Marilynn Buckham remembered things very differently. By the late 1980s Buckham was a veteran of reproductive health services, having begun as a receptionist at Buffalo's first abortion clinic in 1972, two years after New York legalized the procedure. Before *Roe v. Wade* made abortion more widely available, women flooded into New York from other states, but by 1983, when Buckham founded her own clinic, Buffalo GYN Womenservices, "It was very low-key. The feeling at that time was that it was possible and desirable to do outpatient abortions, outside of hospitals, and do them safely."[10] Buckham, who had grown up in a Catholic family in Buffalo, had made peace with family and friends about her choice of vocation.[11]

"It was around 1985 when the Christian Right first became quite vocal in picketing the clinic," Buckham recalled.[12] Not one to shrink from a challenge, she was shaken to find her name and phone number plastered on a billboard outside the clinic on Elmwood Street, and that was only the beginning.[13] Soon thereafter, protesters held the mock funeral for aborted fetuses outside the office of Buffalo obstetrician and abortion provider Dr. Shalom Press.[14] Then, in 1988, the first Operation Rescue blockades came to Buffalo. "We were all amazed at the amount

---

[7] EYAL PRESS, ABSOLUTE CONVICTIONS 155–56 (2006).

[8] *See The Nation*, L.A. TIMES, Feb. 27, 1989, at 2.

[9] Interview with Schenck, Apr. 19, 2000.

[10] Interview with Marilynn Buckham, May 17, 2000.

[11] PRESS, *supra* note 7, at 124.

[12] Interview with Buckham, May 17, 2000.

[13] PRESS, *supra* note 7, at 125.

[14] *Id.* at 126–27.

of—" Buckham hesitated for a moment—"terrorism that was happening outside the door of a medical facility. It was very scary, we felt very isolated. We had a pro-life mayor and his police commissioner was not very helpful. He pretty much did nothing."[15]

Frustrated by the inaction of local law enforcement, Buckham and her colleagues decided to take matters into their own hands, founding an organization called the Pro–Choice Network of Western New York. The Network, which later boasted a board of directors and a formidable fund-raising apparatus, began as a grassroots effort intended to provide a small army of pro-choice escorts to accompany women attempting to gain access to Womenservices and other area clinics. After two years of sporadic but large-scale protests, in the fall of 1990 pro-choice groups initiated the case that would come to be known as *Schenck v. Pro–Choice Network of Western New York*. It began the day Buckham found a pamphlet announcing Operation Rescue's intention to organize a blockade that would close down abortion providers all over the western part of the state.

Upon finding the pamphlet, Buckham immediately called Lucinda Finley, a law professor at the State University of New York at Buffalo. The daughter of a labor lawyer and a physician, Finley had graduated from Columbia Law School and taught for a time at Yale before relocating to Buffalo in 1989. Finley had been trying for months, without success, to help procure legal representation for Buckham and the Pro–Choice Network, but lawyers in the Buffalo area were reluctant to take the case. Some demanded too much money up front; others told Finley that they would love to help, but could not disregard the wishes of pro-life firm partners.

While Buckham saw the pamphlet as a frightening premonition of more clinic strife, Finley's lawyerly instincts told her that this was the "perfect smoking gun" to take to a federal judge in pursuit of an injunction.[16] One year earlier, the Court of Appeals for the Second Circuit had ruled in *New York State NOW v. Terry* that women seeking abortions constituted a protected class under the civil rights law codified as 42 U.S.C. section 1985(3), and that health care providers had standing to sue on behalf of their patients.[17] The ruling suggested that pro-choice groups were on solid legal footing if they could show that anti-abortion demonstrators' tactics were depriving women of their right to choose to terminate pregnancies. After the *Terry* decision, Finley had attended meetings with lawyers from NOW Legal Defense and Education Fund

---

[15] *Id.*

[16] Interview with Lucinda Finley, Mar. 31, 2000.

[17] *See* New York State NOW v. Terry, 886 F.2d 1339 (2d Cir. 1989).

and the ACLU to discuss strategies for obtaining injunctions against anti-abortion protesters; now, as she drafted a complaint on the clinics' behalf, she relied on NOW LDEF's complaint and injunction papers to avoid "reinventing the wheel."

But Finley and her colleagues sensed that they were working within a somewhat uncharted area of the law. "Where is the line between free speech and harassment?" Finley wondered aloud to fellow attorney and law professor Isabel Marcus as they worked late one night at Finley's house drafting the complaint. Marcus replied that the law in the area was far from clear. "Do you think this will ever get to the Supreme Court?" she asked Finley. Finley scoffed at the idea, vowing, "If this ever gets to the Supreme Court, I'll go over Niagara Falls in a barrel."[18]

The complaint drafted by Finley and Marcus based their request for a temporary restraining order on section 1985(3) and a number of state law claims. They used the pamphlet Buckham had found, among other evidence, to argue that the planned blockade posed an imminent danger of impeding all access to reproductive services at Buffalo-area clinics. After several unsuccessful attempts at obtaining relief in state court, the plaintiffs hoped that they would find in Judge Richard Arcara of the Federal District Court for the Western District of New York a more sympathetic ear. Arcara, a former U.S. Attorney, was a Catholic Republican appointed by Ronald Reagan. But Finley and her colleagues hoped that Arcara's prosecutorial background would kindle his law-and-order instincts in favor of the pro-choice group.

They were not disappointed. On September 27, 1990, the day before the scheduled clinic blockade, Arcara issued a temporary restraining order containing four main provisions. First, the TRO enjoined the defendants from "trespassing on, sitting in, blocking, impeding or obstructing access to, ingress into or egress from any facility at which abortions are performed in the Western District of New York, including demonstrating within 15 feet of any person seeking access to or leaving such facilities."[19] The injunction provided a key exception to these "buffer zones" for "sidewalk counselors," who were permitted to hold "non-threatening" two-on-one conversations with persons coming in and out of the clinics. But Arcara also included a "cease-and-desist" provision:

> Also provided that no one is required to accept or listen to sidewalk counseling and that if anyone ... wants to leave, or

---

[18] Interview with Finley, Mar. 31, 2000.

[19] Temporary Restraining Order, Pro–Choice Network of W. New York v. Project Rescue of W. New York, 90 CIV–1004A (Sept. 27, 1990) [hereinafter TRO], *reprinted in* Joint Appendix, Schenck v. Pro–Choice Network of W. New York, No. 95–1065, at 21, 23 [hereinafter Joint Appendix].

walk away, they shall have the absolute right to do that, and in such event the persons seeking to counsel shall cease and desist from such counseling of that person.[20]

Finley was particularly fond of this provision, though attorneys at NOW LDEF, experienced in abortion clinic injunction cases, had advised her that First Amendment doctrine would not permit it. But Finley believed she could make a credible argument that, freedom of speech notwithstanding, patients and staff entering and exiting health facilities had a "right to be left alone."[21]

Among other provisions, the TRO also enjoined defendants from "attempting, or inducing, encouraging, aiding, or abetting in any manner, others" to take any of the actions prohibited by the first three sections of the TRO.[22] Pro-life ministers in the Western District vocally protested this provision, announcing that they would continue to use their pulpits to further the cause of anti-abortion resistance. Arcara responded by issuing a statement of clarification on October 4, emphasizing that "it never was intended or expressed by this Court that this order prohibited any clergyman or individual from preaching from the pulpit, quoting from the Bible or practicing any rights protected by the first amendment."[23]

The defendants, who had initially proceeded pro se, had begun to realize that they would need legal representation to effectively challenge the TRO and defend against the contempt motions occasioned by their violations. Serendipitously, one afternoon in early October, 1990, they happened upon James Duane, a Harvard graduate and then a thirty-one-year-old lawyer with a prominent Buffalo firm, in the clerk's office of the U.S. District Court. Shortly thereafter, Duane met with the defendants as a group and agreed to take their case.

"Compliance in Action, Defiance in Speech"

Over the next few months, the protesters deliberately tested the injunction. In a late-night meeting around Christmastime, Paul Schenck, his brother, local pro-life leader Karen Swallow Prior, and the Reverend Johnny Hunter decided that they would attempt to expose what they believed to be the unconstitutionally speech-restrictive nature of the TRO by accentuating the free expression element of their activities. "We decided that our motto would be 'compliance in action but defiance in speech,' " Schenck recalled. "My brother and I would go in front of the

---

[20] *Id.*

[21] Interview with Finley, Mar. 31, 2000.

[22] *Id.* at 24.

[23] *Id.*

clinics and do what we had always done, approach people with literature." The brothers wished to emphasize the religious, rather than the
specifically anti-abortion element of their speech, so as to demonstrate
that constitutionally protected prayer and religious exhortation were the
injunction's true victims.[24]

The Schencks' activities are characterized rather differently in the
court proceedings that ensued when, in early 1991, the plaintiffs instituted contempt charges against the Schencks and four other defendants.[25]
According to Judge Arcara's findings of fact, the Schenck brothers
pursued one woman from the parking lot to the alcove in front of the
clinic, "exhort[ing] her not to have an abortion," telling her "with raised
voices" that "she should not enter the clinic, she should not have an
abortion and she should not kill her baby."[26] The two then stood
"shoulder to shoulder" in the alcove, effectively blocking the clinic
entrance.[27] After following another woman to the entrance, Paul Schenck
continued to shout at her through the closed glass door of the clinic.[28] A
short time later, when a car with out-of-state license plates attempted to
enter the clinic driveway, Paul "placed himself directly in front of the
vehicle on the driver's side of the hood in order to block the vehicle from
entering."[29] Other Project Rescue demonstrators crowded around the
driver's door, exhorting her to open the window. The vehicle was forced
to slow down almost to a complete stop so as not to run over Schenck. In
general, requests by patients and their "pro-choice escorts" to cease and
desist apparently fell on deaf ears as the Schencks pursued several more
women to the door of the clinic.[30]

Judge Arcara did not rely solely upon eyewitness testimony for these
findings: the demonstrators themselves had captured them on videotape
as part of their strategic challenge to the injunction and, pro-choice
advocates believed, as part of their campaign of intimidation against
clinic patients and staff. The Schenck brothers did not give an entirely
ingenuous on-camera performance. Exploiting their virtually identical
features, the twins at one point switched eyeglasses and neckties, and

---

[24] Interview with Schenck, Apr. 19, 2000.

[25] Judge Arcara had ordered that the TRO remain in place until he reached a decision
on granting a preliminary injunction.

[26] Decision and Order (relating to contempt proceedings against Robert and Paul
Schenck), Pro–Choice Network of W. New York v. Project Rescue of W. New York, 90 CV–
1004A (Sept. 14, 1992) *reprinted in* Joint Appendix at 121, 129.

[27] *Id.*

[28] *See id.* at 130.

[29] *Id.* at 131.

[30] *See id.* at 132–33.

Paul Schenck held an umbrella between himself and the camera as he impeded the car's ingress to the parking lot.[31] Arguing pro se in the contempt proceedings, the Schencks denied the switch and claimed they could not remember which one of them had obstructed the vehicle.[32] Arcara was having none of this: "[T]he Court finds the Schencks' inability to recollect the incident to be totally incredible,"[33] he wrote in an order finding both Schenck brothers in contempt of court. "In fact, the Court finds that Paul Schenck made false statements under affirmation."[34]

The contempt hearings attracted attention in the Buffalo press and in the legal community. The Schencks' trial was particularly noteworthy for the brothers' pro se argument, which substituted eloquent pronouncements on constitutional principle for legal expertise. "I'm not a lawyer, but I have read the First Amendment," Paul Schenck told the judge. "And this fifteen foot floating zone doesn't sound like the First Amendment to me." Schenck argued that the TRO was analogous to a hypothetical injunction prohibiting atheists from approaching within fifteen feet of his own parishioners. "Arcara didn't buy that argument," Schenck recalls dryly.[35]

But many pro-life observers did. When the contempt proceedings drew public notice, Duane received several phone calls from local lawyers offering their support. One of them was Laurence Behr of the Buffalo firm Barth Sullivan Behr, who had made headlines in Buffalo a few years earlier when he successfully defended the right of local students to hold an after-hours bible study group on public school grounds.[36] Behr had recently founded Western New York Lawyers for Life, and, in 1992, when anti-abortion leaders were gearing up for the "Spring of Life" demonstrations, Behr had already assembled a dedicated cadre of lawyers who stood ready to defend the protesters.[37]

For Behr, representing the pro-life demonstrators was something of a personal mission. A Catholic whose faith had lapsed in his young adult years, Behr remembers vividly his elation when abortion was legalized in New York in the late 1960s. "It was the revolution," he says, a bit ruefully. "We all thought making abortion legal was the best thing that

---

[31] *See id.* at 132–34.

[32] *See id.*

[33] *Id.* at 132.

[34] *Id.* at 133.

[35] Interview with Schenck, Apr. 19, 2000.

[36] That case was brought under the Federal Equal Access Act.

[37] Interview with Laurence Behr, Apr. 20, 2000.

had ever happened." But as Behr witnessed the upheaval of the '60s and '70s—the Vietnam War, the riots, the Attica prison massacre, "one devastation after another"—he became increasingly despondent. "I gradually came to realize that there is no meaning in life without God," he says, "that Jesus is the savior of the world, and that there is no way that He would condone taking life from the womb of a mother. Life is not a choice; no one chooses to be born. Once you have had a close encounter with God, it's impossible to be pro-choice."[38]

"The Need to Protect These Young Vulnerable Women"

In early 1992, anti-abortion groups husbanded their resources in preparation for a renewed campaign to shut down abortion clinics in western New York as they had successfully done in Wichita, Kansas, the preceding summer. The pro-life mayor of Buffalo, Jimmy Griffin, had publicly invited Operation Rescue to his city, energizing anti-abortion activists anew.[39] As plans for the Spring of Life demonstrations began to percolate, Judge Arcara was again contemplating the legal contours of the pro-choice groups' complaints against the pro-life protesters. After hearing twelve additional days of testimony from both sides, the judge issued a preliminary injunction. In addition to the fifteen-foot "floating" buffer zone, the injunction included a new provision added at Finley's behest: a "fixed" buffer zone protecting the clinic entrances themselves.

Arcara's opinion was unambiguous in its condemnation of the protesters' tactics. Findings that the demonstrators had physically obstructed clinic entrances—at times by chaining themselves together—and had "constructively blockaded" health care facilities by behaving in a noisy and disruptive manner were only the beginning.[40] Arcara also found that the practice of "sidewalk counseling," even if initiated peacefully, "often erupts into a charged encounter" in which counselors "turn to harassing, badgering, intimidating and yelling at the patients and patient escorts in order to dissuade them from entering."[41] Arcara chastised the anti-abortion protestors for using video cameras "as offensive weapons to intimidate patients seeking abortions."[42] The judge found that the defendants had "attempted to hinder and interfere with local law enforcement by harassing" police officers, patients, and clinic staff.[43]

---

[38] *Id.*

[39] *See* Andrew Duffy, *Why Abortion Fight Moved to Buffalo*, Toronto Star, Apr. 24, 1992, at A1.

[40] *See* Pro–Choice Network of W. New York v. Project Rescue of W. New York, 799 F. Supp. 1417, 1423–24 (W.D.N.Y. 1992).

[41] *Id.* at 1425.

[42] *Id.*

[43] *Id.*

But the most dire effects of the demonstrations were visited upon patients attempting to enter the health clinics, according to Judge Arcara. Elevated blood pressure, hyperventilation, and agitation were among the symptoms suffered by patients exposed to sidewalk counseling. Women were often too upset to undergo scheduled procedures, and the resulting delays increased the risks associated with abortion. The presence of video cameras aggravated the damage: "Defendants are well aware," Arcara wrote, "that women seeking abortions, especially younger women, are often terrified at the prospect of anyone, especially family members, finding out that they are having an abortion, and that the presence of cameras increases patients' fear that their identities might be revealed."[44] In determining whether the plaintiffs were entitled to a preliminary injunction, the court, Judge Arcara declared, "must balance the need to protect these young vulnerable women from defendants' harassment against defendants' First Amendment rights."[45] By intimidating patients entering the clinics, the defendants had created medical risks for which damage awards could not compensate.

Perhaps most devastatingly, Arcara drew an analogy between the defendants' behavior and the intimidation tactics of southern segregationists in the 1960s:

> During the civil rights movement, segregationists congregated in front of schools and polling places with attack dogs and clubs in order to intimidate blacks into foregoing their constitutional rights to an integrated education and to vote. Here defendants are attempting to prevent women from exercising their constitutional right to choose to have an abortion.... [I]nstead of using dogs and clubs, defendants use cameras and the threat of exposure to scare and intimidate women into foregoing their constitutional rights.[46]

Arcara's rhetoric was a blow to the defendants, who depicted themselves—not the plaintiffs—as the true heirs to the mantle of the civil rights movement.

Indeed, the next issue facing Judge Arcara was the validity of the plaintiffs' section 1985(3) claim, the only federal cause of action in the complaint. The key question—yet to be resolved by the Supreme Court—was whether women seeking an abortion constituted a protected class under the civil rights statute. Drawing an analogy to *Griffin v. Breckinridge*, where the defendants' assault upon black civil rights workers on an interstate highway was ruled a conspiracy to deprive them of their

---

[44] *Id.* at 1426.

[45] *Id.*

[46] *Id.* at 1439.

right to travel, Arcara found that the defendants were indeed engaged in a conspiracy to infringe upon women's right to travel and upon their right to choose abortion. Arcara concluded that the plaintiffs had satisfied the Fourteenth Amendment's state action requirement, finding that "defendants have acted to render local law enforcement officials incapable of keeping the clinics readily accessible to women who choose to have an abortion."[47]

After determining that the plaintiffs were also likely to succeed on the merits of their state law claims, Arcara proceeded to address the defendants' First Amendment challenge to the injunction. The judge ruled that women seeking abortions should be considered a captive audience for the purposes of First Amendment analysis. Though the captive audience doctrine was generally inapplicable to speakers in traditional public fora like a public street or sidewalk, here "[d]efendants' aggressive conduct makes it impossible for women entering the clinics simply to avert their eyes or cover their ears.... The only choice women have if they want to avoid the message is to forego their constitutional right to have an abortion."[48] Finding that the defendants retained "ample alternative channels of communication," Judge Arcara summed up his rejection of every single one of the pro-life side's contentions and issued a preliminary injunction reaffirming the restrictions contained in the TRO.

"You're Not in Kansas Anymore"

This legal setback notwithstanding, Operation Rescue and its local counterparts soldiered on toward the Spring of Life demonstrations, announcing their intention to picket the homes of individual physicians and clinic staff, and to close down abortion facilities in the Greater Buffalo area.[49] The pro-choice forces were determined to prevent another Wichita, where forty-six days of demonstrations in the summer of 1991 had closed down clinics despite the arrest of almost three thousand anti-abortion protesters. They enlisted hundreds of abortion rights activists to form human chains around the clinics to protect access, and consulted with national coordinators at the Feminist Majority Foundation about their experience in defending clinics against blockades.[50] Kit Bonson, a spokeswoman for Buffalo United for Choice, extolled the pro-choice groups' nonviolent clinic defense training, and expressed the hope that

---

[47] *Id.* at 1431.

[48] *Id.* at 1436.

[49] *See* Catherine Manegold, *Protesters Set for Collision on Abortion*, N.Y. TIMES, Apr. 21, 1992, at B1.

[50] *See* Catherine Manegold, *Abortion War, Buffalo Front: Top Guns Use Battle Tactics*, N.Y. TIMES, Apr. 25, 1992, at 1.

SERENA MAYERI   305

damage done by Operation Rescue to clinic access could be minimized.
"If they're not able to succeed here, they're less likely to go to another
city," Bonson predicted.[51] Even before the protests were scheduled to
begin in earnest, pro-choice advocates met before dawn to surround the
Buffalo GYN Womenservices clinic in a protective ring.[52] Events seemed
to prefigure an impending violent confrontation, as Paul Schenck was
shoved and spat upon when he knelt in front of the entrance to the
Womenservices clinic, his Bible knocked from his hands and cigarette
ashes sprinkled on his head.[53] "We'll defend the clinic doors—You're not
in Kansas anymore!" the pro-choice demonstrators chanted.[54]

On April 20, over one thousand anti-abortion advocates gathered for
an opening rally in a local church, where the Reverend Keith Tucci read
the names of local physicians who performed abortions and exhorted his
audience to beg the doctors to stop. Robert Schenck told the *New York
Times* that the pro-life groups had hired private investigators to investigate the "backgrounds, private lives and financial profiles of the doctors" who performed abortions locally.[55] Later that night, Operation
Rescue organizers held a news conference at which they displayed a
twenty-five-week-old fetus they claimed had been aborted. The following
day, Robert Schenck was arrested for brandishing a fetus in the faces of
abortion rights demonstrators, and charged with disorderly conduct.[56]
The police also arrested Paul Schenck when he boarded a police bus
where his brother was being held.[57]

Nevertheless, despite strong turnout by both sides, the demonstrations remained relatively peaceful. The police were out in force, erecting
barriers between abortion rights and anti-abortion protesters. Pro-choice
advocates, armed with radios to monitor the movement of the pro-life
demonstrators, announced in cautious triumph that clinic schedules
remained undisrupted.[58] On the third day of the campaign, two hundred
anti-abortion protesters were arrested when they defied police orders

---

[51] David Treadwell, *Abortion-Issue Activists Clash in Buffalo*, L.A. TIMES, Apr. 22, 1992,
at A1.

[52] *See id.*

[53] *See Abortion Rights Activists Attack Praying Minister*, ATLANTA JOURNAL-CONSTITUTION,
Apr. 19, 1992, at A10.

[54] *See* Manegold, *supra* note 50.

[55] *Id.*

[56] *See Clerics Arrested After Fetus Waved at Buffalo Protest*, ASSOCIATED PRESS, Apr. 22,
1992.

[57] *See id.*

[58] *See* Catherine Manegold, *Rallies Held, Peacefully, Over Abortion*, N.Y. TIMES, Apr.
22, 1992, at B2.

and knelt in the road thirty yards from a clinic entrance, but pro-choice and police barricades kept the clinics open.[59] Both sides compared themselves to civil rights protesters and their opponents to Nazis,[60] but the violent rhetoric rarely spilled into action.

By the third day of protests, pro-life demonstrators seemed increasingly desperate to make headway toward their goal of shutting down clinics. As the Supreme Court was hearing arguments in *Planned Parenthood v. Casey* hundreds of miles away in Washington, in Amherst, New York, protesters attempted to break through a police line outside the Women's Center. Police wrestled them to the ground, using handcuffs to bind the feet of demonstrators like Rev. Johnny Hunter, who had broken through a cluster of abortion rights guards and run toward the clinic door.[61] At the end of the day, Linda Stadler, office manager for Dr. Press, reported that all patients with appointments kept them and were seen by health care providers.[62] After ten days of protests, both sides were declaring victory. "They didn't accomplish a single one of their goals," Marilynn Buckham said, echoing a *Time* magazine story that ridiculed the Spring of Life demonstrations as "Operation Fizzle."[63] Robert Schenck disagreed, delivering a triumphant speech to a standing-room-only crowd at his suburban church.[64] According to Operation Rescue, most of the six thousand demonstrators at Spring of Life were local supporters protesting for the first time. And, they said, at least twenty women changed their minds about terminating their pregnancies. One, sixteen-year-old Stephanie White, the mother of a two-year-old, told whomever would listen that she had decided to "keep her twin babies" after reading a pamphlet distributed by the demonstrators.[65]

For many pro-choice activists, what was at stake in the Buffalo demonstrations was the right of women to control their reproductive destinies. To them, the fiery rhetoric about mangled fetuses and eternal damnation was inextricably intertwined with the "pro-family" ideology promoted by ministers like the Schenck brothers. What was perhaps most alarming to many feminists about anti-abortion rhetoric—besides

---

[59] *See* David von Drehle, *Amid Mass Arrests, Counter–Protests, Buffalo Abortion Clinics Stay Open*, WASH. POST, Apr. 23, 1992, at A14.

[60] *See id.*

[61] *See Nearly 200 Arrested as Buffalo Abortion Showdown Continues*, ATLANTA JOURNAL-CONSTITUTION, Apr. 23, 1992, at A4.

[62] *See* Catherine Manegold, *194 Arrested in Protests at Buffalo Abortion Clinics*, N.Y. TIMES, Apr. 23, 1992, at B9.

[63] *Quoted in All Claim Victory in Abortion Fight*, BALTIMORE SUN, MAY 3, 1992.

[64] *See id.*

[65] *See* Jeannie Ralston & Barbara Maddux, *The Great Divide*, LIFE, July 1992, at 55.

its violent overtones—was its conception of appropriate gender roles. When Paul Schenck extolled a renaissance of pro-family values in America, he called for "overt leadership exercised by the father/husband" and "covert leadership exercised by the mother/wife."[66] At one Operation Rescue rally, when women stood to give testimonials, twenty-one-year-old Toni Denver prayed before a crowd of over one thousand, "Oh please, Lord, break the curse on women's hearts that says we don't need our men. Break that independence. Help men rise up to take positions of leadership and authority that we might submit to them."[67] Katherine Spillar of the Feminist Majority spoke for many women's rights advocates when she called Operation Rescue's ideology a thinly disguised brand of antifeminism. "They want women to put their aprons back on and retreat to the kitchens," she said. "They are very threatened."[68]

Meanwhile, the mostly male abortion providers in the Greater Buffalo area found themselves labeled "baby-murderers" and received constant threats of physical harm and even death. They declared themselves motivated by medical duty and compassion for women who faced difficult and painful choices. Dr. Parviz Taefi had only to remember the horror of OB/GYN practice before legalized abortion to reaffirm his commitment to providing abortion services. "Not a night went by when I didn't see someone in the emergency room dying from a botched abortion," he remembered of the pre-*Roe* era.[69] In 1992, Taefi was performing about twenty abortions per week, a small fraction of his practice. Most of his time was devoted to check-ups, surgeries, and childbirth; among Dr. Taefi's regular patients were the sisters of Robert and Paul Schenck.[70] "The moral question of abortion is a valid one," Taefi acknowledged. "I would always rather deliver a baby. But that's idealistic. Reality is different."[71]

"We Knew What the Truth Was"

Reality in the coming year proved unsettling to both sides in the *Schenck* case. In June, the Supreme Court reaffirmed the central holding of *Roe* in *Planned Parenthood v. Casey*. In November, Paul Schenck

---

[66] Manegold, *supra* note 50.

[67] *Quoted in* Ralston & Maddux, *supra* note 65.

[68] Manegold, *supra* note 50.

[69] *Quoted in* Ralston & Maddux, *supra* note 65.

[70] In fact, when Taefi suffered a heart attack in 1993, Robert Schenck appeared in his hospital room, declaring he would pray for the doctor's recovery out of gratitude for his delivery of his baby niece. *See Off Main Street*, BUFFALO NEWS, Jan. 17, 1993.

[71] *Quoted in id.*

served time in jail for harassing obstetrician and abortion provider Dr. Barnett Slepian the previous year.[72] In January 1993, the pro-choice side suffered its own legal blow when the Supreme Court ruled in *Bray v. Alexandria Women's Health Center* that women seeking abortions did not constitute a protected class under section 1985(3). Over three dissents, Justice Scalia's opinion for the court rejected the pro-choice groups' contention that anti-abortion activities reflected "class-based animus" analogous to the racially motivated hostility targeted by the Ku Klux Klan Act.[73] The decision was a significant defeat, symbolically and strategically, for abortion rights supporters, who could no longer invoke federal civil rights law against groups who attempted to prevent women from seeking abortions.

The Pro–Choice Network had more immediate concerns, however. Following the decision in *Bray*, as pro-life groups announced a new round of protests in western New York, Finley told the U.S. marshal's office that federal assistance might be required to enforce the injunction.[74] In March, to the horror of pro-choice activists and physicians around the nation, abortion provider Dr. David Gunn was shot dead outside a health care facility in Pensacola, Florida. The Schencks and other Buffalo-area pro-life activists immediately issued a joint statement condemning the violence, but clinic staff and physicians admitted they were rattled by the murder. "I've never been this afraid," Marilynn Buckham told a local reporter.[75] Dr. Barnett Slepian spoke with the *Buffalo News* for the first time about the enormous strain associated with performing abortions in a hostile and potentially violent climate. Dr. Gunn's death "hits home," Slepian said, "because it could have been me. For years I've felt, and I still feel, it could happen to me."[76]

Meanwhile, increasingly frustrated with what he perceived as Judge Arcara's personal bias, Behr filed a motion asking the judge to disqualify himself from the *Schenck* case for accepting a Citizen of the Year award from the pro-choice *Buffalo News*. Arcara, in an eight-page decision, rejected the motion, suggesting that the pro-life demonstrators were seeking his recusal "merely to avoid unwelcome rulings."[77] Behr was not

---

[72] *See Rev. Schenck Released from Jail*, BUFFALO NEWS, Nov. 21, 1992.

[73] *See* Bray v. Alexandria Women's Health Ctr., 506 U.S 263, 268–74 (1993).

[74] *See* Jerry Zremski, *Ruling Doesn't Give Abortion Foes Free Rein*, BUFFALO NEWS, Jan. 13, 1993, at 3.

[75] Gene Warner, *Killing of Doctor at Abortion Clinic Spurs Drive for Tougher Laws*, BUFFALO NEWS, Mar. 20, 1993, at 4.

[76] Gene Warner, *Slepian Discusses Pressures Faced in Abortion Work*, BUFFALO NEWS, Apr. 19, 1993.

[77] *Quoted in* Dan Herbeck, *Arcara Rejects Pro–Life Plea, Won't Step Aside in Abortion Case*, BUFFALO NEWS, Mar. 31, 1993.

the only one losing patience; the Schencks' frustration with the on-the-ground anti-abortion struggle was growing by the day. In April, the brothers announced their intention to abandon the Buffalo battle and step onto the national stage—into the mainstream, so to speak. "For the time being," Paul Schenck said, "the effectiveness of blockades is minimal. Therefore, new approaches need to be employed."[78] Those approaches would include addressing public rallies, writing books, and lobbying public officials in the hopes of effecting changes in national policy.

But the Schencks would not be able to escape Buffalo so easily. In April, Amherst Town Justice Sherwood Bestry sentenced Robert Schenck to nine months in jail for disorderly conduct and resisting arrest during the Spring of Life protests.[79] In July, Arcara dismissed the Pro-Choice Network's section 1985(3) claim in light of *Bray*, but to no one's surprise, decided to exercise pendent jurisdiction over their state law claims.[80] That fall, a federal magistrate judge ordered the Buffalo pro-life activists, including the Schencks, to pay over $100,000 in legal fees incurred by physicians and abortion providers as a result of pro-life demonstrations at the Womenservices clinic.[81] Robert Schenck was fined an additional $25,000 for his role in displaying a fetus to then-Governor Bill Clinton during the 1992 Democratic National Convention in violation of a federal court order.[82] Finally, Paul Schenck found himself facing perjury charges for falsely denying under oath the apparel switch with his twin during the videotaped 1990 protests.[83]

For Paul Schenck, the courts' repeated refusals to recognize his heartfelt protests as legitimate, protected expression under the First Amendment was deeply disillusioning. "We were naïve," he says. "We knew what the truth was ... I think we had a very accurate view about what the framers of the constitution had in mind. But we were up against a court that had a view of constitutional rights that included

[78] *Quoted in* Gene Warner, *Schencks Taking Pro-Life Pursuits to National Level*, BUFFALO NEWS, Apr. 2, 1993.

[79] *See* Carl Allen, *Minister Gets Jail in Protest Case*, BUFFALO NEWS, Apr. 20, 1993; *see also* Editorial, *A Just Sentence for Schenck: He'll Pay for What He Did, Not for His Beliefs*, BUFFALO NEWS, Apr. 21, 1993, at 2; Gene Warner, *Pro-Life Minister, On National TV, Targets Amherst Judge, His Family*, BUFFALO NEWS, May 13, 1993.

[80] *See* Pro-Choice Network of W. New York v. Project Rescue of W. New York, 828 F. Supp. 1018 (W.D.N.Y. 1993).

[81] *See* Dan Herbeck, *Pro-Lifers Ordered to Pay Legal Fees*, BUFFALO NEWS, Oct. 2, 1993, at 1.

[82] *See Federal Judge Fines Schenck $25,000 in Fetus-Display Incident*, BUFFALO NEWS, Oct. 14, 1993, at 7.

[83] *See Paul Schenck Charged With Perjury*, BUFFALO NEWS, Nov. 5, 1993, at 1.

abortion trumping the First Amendment.... It was extremely frustrating and discouraging."[84]

The *Schenck* defendants appealed Judge Arcara's injunction to the Second Circuit, where Vincent McCarthy, a long-time First Amendment lawyer with a successful record in other abortion protest cases, took over the case from James Duane, who had accepted a position at the Regent University School of Law in Virginia Beach. McCarthy, as it turned out, would argue the *Schenck* case before an unusually sympathetic panel that included Judges Thomas Meskill and Frank Altimari, as well as Senior Judge James L. Oakes. McCarthy made a straightforward argument to the panel, contending that the sidewalks outside abortion clinics were traditional public fora, requiring a compelling state interest to restrict speech, and that under the established test for content-neutral time, place, and manner restrictions, the injunction's bubble zones and cease-and-desist provisions impermissibly burdened speech.

Three months after the panel heard oral arguments from McCarthy and Finley, the Supreme Court decided *Madsen v. Women's Health Services*, a challenge to an abortion clinic protest injunction in Florida. Chief Justice William Rehnquist's majority opinion for a divided Court established a new test for injunctions: "whether the challenged provisions of the injunction burden no more speech than necessary to serve a significant government interest."[85] It found portions of the Florida injunction, which provided for a thirty-six-foot buffer zone and restricted the extent to which protesters could approach persons coming in and out of the clinic, constitutional, and struck down others as too speech-restrictive. Contrasting the majority's decision with prior rulings in labor picketing and civil rights cases, Justice Antonin Scalia's vitriolic dissent ridiculed the indeterminacy of the *Madsen* test and urged strict scrutiny of injunctions.[86] He decried the "ad hoc nullification machine" he believed to operate in abortion cases and lamented its latest victim, the First Amendment.[87]

Justice Scalia's protestations notwithstanding, it was the *Madsen* test that the appellate panel applied to the *Schenck* injunction, and the very indeterminacy of the new standard worked in favor of the defendants. Judge Meskill, writing for himself and Judge Altimari over Judge Oakes's dissent, struck down both of the buffer zones and invalidated the cease-and-desist provisions. With the panel's decision, Paul Schenck had something to celebrate beyond his recent release from prison. But

---

[84] Interview with Schenck, Apr. 19, 2000.

[85] Madsen v. Women's Health Ctr., 512 U.S. 753, 765 (1994).

[86] *Id.* at 793 (Scalia, J., dissenting).

[87] *Id.* at 785 (Scalia, J., dissenting).

the protesters' victory was short lived. Chief Judge Jon O. Newman stayed the panel's decision pending en banc review. Meanwhile, the willingness of the U.S. Attorney's office to bring criminal charges against some of the demonstrators for their illegal activities "changed our strategy to a large degree," according to Paul Schenck. "Most pro-life people range from poor to middle-income, so an economic penalty had been more symbolic than anything else. But then the question became, should I risk my children losing their father in their most formative years, or take another approach?"[88]

Legally, the *Schenck* case was temporarily stalled as the parties waited seven months for the rehearing, and another five for the en banc court's decision. It was not an uneventful year in the larger abortion debate, however. The Freedom of Access to Clinic Entrances Act (FACE), signed into law by President Clinton the previous May, went into effect, making it a federal crime to physically block access to clinics, damage their property, or injure, interfere with or intimidate patients or clinic staff. On the other hand, after the Republican victory in the 1994 mid-term elections helped elect Dennis Vacco, the pro-life candidate for New York attorney general, the year ended on a terrifying note for those committed to preserving women's reproductive choices. Two days before the New Year, twenty-two-year-old John Salvi, an anti-abortion militant, opened fire at a Boston women's clinic, killing two staff members and wounding seven others. Although advocates on both sides expressed horror at the tragedy, they offered different interpretations of the violence. To pro-choice leaders, the murders were a chilling reminder of their own vulnerability, and an affirmation of the need for more stringent restrictions like FACE. To some anti-abortion sympathizers, the violence was a predictable result of suppressing more peaceful forms of dissent. The Schenck brothers' father, Henry Schenck, had eerily predicted three months before the Boston killings that pro-choice advocates would have "to contend with the more violent residue who, in their frustration, step forward and fill the void left by the nonviolent advocates."[89]

"The Timid Have a Right to Go About Their Business"

The Second Circuit's en banc ruling, authored by Judge Oakes, reversed the panel's decision in an opinion that essentially recapitulated Oakes's earlier dissent.[90] The court upheld both the buffer zones and the

---

[88] Interview with Schenck, Apr. 19, 2000.

[89] *Schenck Brothers' Father Says Sons Following Tradition*, BUFFALO NEWS, Sept. 11, 1994, at 8.

[90] Pro–Choice Network of W. New York v. Schenck, 67 F.2d 377 (2d Cir. 1995) (en banc).

cease-and-desist provision, and in a particularly vehement concurrence, Judge Ralph Winter defended injunctions targeted at "even isolated threats or obstructions," declaring, "The timid have a right to go about their business, and it is no embarrassment for a federal court to say so."[91] Only Judges Meskill and Altimari dissented, with Meskill echoing Scalia's condemnation of the "abortion ad hoc nullification machine,"[92] and Altimari stressing the indeterminacy and overbreadth of the "floating" bubble zone.[93]

McCarthy's petition for certiorari similarly accused the Second Circuit majority of bias against anti-abortion protesters. "[T]he Pro–Choice En Banc Panel flatly and arrogantly in its haste to jump aboard the abortion bandwagon, flouts all constitutional precedent," the protesters' petition charged.[94] In her response, Finley was somewhat constrained by the procedural posture of the *Schenck* case as it reached the Supreme Court. Because the protesters were challenging the preliminary injunction, issued in February of 1992, she was limited to presenting the facts as they stood at that time, even though some of the protesters' most obstructionist activities had occurred later. "It was so frustrating," Finley exclaims. "Because right after the preliminary injunction they went out and blockaded!" Still, Finley continued to emphasize the substantial factual record she did have. The other thorn in Finley's side was the necessity of defending the "floating" bubble zone, a provision that she believed "clutter[ed] up the injunction," and in fact had unsuccessfully petitioned to modify in 1994.[95]

By the time the Supreme Court granted certiorari in *Schenck*, on March 18, 1996, the Schenck brothers themselves had finally managed to leave their Buffalo lives as rabble-rousers behind them and relocate to the nation's capital. As the justices began to examine the injunction that had restrained their protest activities in western New York, Robert Schenck was comfortably installed as the general secretary of the National Clergy Council, and Paul Schenck—despite his status as a convicted felon—had become executive vice president and chief of operations at the American Center for Law and Justice (ACLJ), the Pat Robertson-sponsored public interest law firm helping to represent him before the Court.[96] Having been feted at a national Christian Coalition conference

---

[91] *Id.* at 396 (Winter, J., concurring).

[92] *Id.* at 404 (Meskill, J., dissenting).

[93] *Id.* at 409–11 (Altimari, J., dissenting).

[94] Petition for a Writ of Certiorari, Schenck v. Pro–Choice Network of W. New York, No. 95–1065, at 14 (hereinafter Petition for Cert.).

[95] Interview with Finley, Mar. 31, 2000.

[96] *See* Zremski, *supra* note 74.

only a few months before as "completed Jews,"[97] the Schencks had joined the religious conservative mainstream.

"Peaceful Protesters," "Intimidating Mobs"

Finley was shocked to hear that the Supreme Court had granted "cert." Immediately, her "phone was ringing off the hook with people trying to offer help." Finley accepted NOW LDEF's offer to join her as co-counsel and to coordinate the hordes of amicus curiae interested in filing briefs. Finley and her NOW LDEF colleagues were particularly concerned about attracting the support (or, at least, forestalling the opposition) of two key organizations—the AFL–CIO and the ACLU—whose interests in protecting free speech were at odds with their reliably pro-choice stance on reproductive rights.[98]

The Pro–Choice Network's attorneys knew the AFL–CIO's brief could exert a decisive influence on the outcome of *Schenck*. In *Madsen*, where the group had filed a brief in support of neither party, the Supreme Court had more or less adopted the standard proposed by the labor unions' lawyers.[99] Finley was relieved to discover that Marsha Berzon, then a distinguished San Francisco labor lawyer and longtime women's rights advocate, would author the brief. Finley felt that hours on the phone with Berzon paid off in the end, for while the brief was highly critical of the Second Circuit's reasoning in upholding the injunction, its text and footnotes also acknowledged the strength of the factual record of obstruction compiled by the plaintiffs.[100]

If disaster had been averted on the labor front, the pro-choice side could be even more pleased with the ACLU national office's contribution to the amicus effort. Despite dissent from several state and local ACLU affiliates, the brief submitted by the national ACLU along with other free speech groups and Jewish organizations emphasized both the stringency of the First Amendment standard to which the injunction was subject, and the gravity of the obstruction and harassment that were its target.[101] Amicus support for the Pro–Choice Network more predictably

---

[97] *See* Stephen Henderson, *Family Weekend: Christian Coalition's Faith and Freedom '95 Conference*, 112 CHRISTIAN CENTURY 1102 (1995).

[98] Interview with Finley, Mar. 31, 2000.

[99] *See* Brief of the American Federation of Labor and Congress of Industrial Organizations as Amicus Curiae in Support of Neither Party, Madsen v. Women's Health Ctr., No. 93–880.

[100] Brief of the American Federation of Labor and Congress of Industrial Organizations as Amicus Curiae in Support of Neither Party, Schenck v. Pro–Choice Network of W. New York, No. 95–1065.

[101] *See* Brief of the American Civil Liberties Union, New York Civil Liberties Union, American Jewish Congress, American Jewish Committee, and People for the American Way as Amicus Curiae in Support of Respondents, *Schenck*, No. 95–1065.

included numerous women's rights organizations, a coalition of physicians' groups and reproductive health service providers, and the attorneys general of eighteen states. On the protesters' side were the Rutherford Institute, the Family Research Council, and the Life Legal Defense Foundation.

Putting aside their different doctrinal emphases, the most striking differences between the two sides' positions were their contrasting characterizations of the factual record. The protesters maintained that the fixed and floating buffer zones, which designated areas off limits to protesters, were "factually unjustifiable" and that the "cease-and-desist" provision was indistinguishable from the "no-approach" provision struck down in *Madsen*.[102] In response, the Pro–Choice Network provided a detailed refutation of petitioners' factual discussion, what the brief called a "stark[] dramatiz[ation]" of "the problems posed to law and order when a passionate mob is intent on preventing other people from exercising their constitutional rights, or intimidates and harasses them for doing so."[103] "Part of our strategy," NOW LDEF attorney Yolanda Wu recalled, "was to talk a lot about how non-abortion health services were affected, since several of our clients were facilities that treated patients for all kinds of medical problems, cancer, you name it."[104] The Pro–Choice Network's brief implemented what had been Finley's approach all along—to depict in compelling terms the medical harm suffered by women harassed and threatened by anti-abortion protesters determined to obstruct their access to necessary health services.

Just over six years after Finley filed the original complaint in the *Schenck* case, she was to argue before the Supreme Court, an eventuality she had often quipped would send her over Niagara Falls in a barrel. Her opponent before the Court would be Jay Alan Sekulow, the forty-year-old chief counsel for the ACLJ. Sekulow had risen to prominence in conservative circles after victories in several Supreme Court cases. He was a well-known speaker on the religious right's lecture circuit, making frequent appearances on the Christian Broadcasting Network's "700 Club," and launching his own syndicated radio show, Jay Sekulow Live. In some ways, Sekulow's path to Christian activism was not unlike that of the Schenck brothers. Raised in a Reform Jewish household "very culturally committed" to Judaism, Sekulow converted to Christianity as an undergraduate at Mercer University, a Baptist institution in Atlanta. As he described his religious awakening to the *New York Times* in 1995, "When I really understood [the New Testament] intellectually, and when it translated into my heart—which is the most important part—my

---

[102] Brief for Petitioners at 16, *Schenck*, No. 95–1065.

[103] Brief for Respondents at 20, *Schenck*, No. 95–1065.

[104] Interview with Yolanda Wu, Mar. 15, 2000.

life has never been the same."[105] Now overseeing a staff of almost two dozen lawyers and five hundred attorney-affiliates throughout the country, with an annual budget in the tens of millions and a caseload of almost one thousand cases, Sekulow felt he was beginning to fulfill a moral obligation to restore religious values to American public life. But his goal, ultimately, was "far, far away.... It's a constant struggle. If you let your guard down for a moment, you'll get clobbered."[106]

Sekulow was evidently determined not to let that happen in the *Schenck* oral argument, where he insisted that both the floating and fixed buffer zones squelched protected speech. Despite tough questioning from Justice Ruth Bader Ginsburg about his characterization of the factual record, and an onslaught of queries from the other justices pressing him to explain exactly how the buffer zones limited speech, Sekulow did manage to insert a reference to the petitioners' favorite case, *NAACP v. Claiborne Hardware*, driving home the analogy between anti-abortion protesters and civil rights demonstrators. Finley, too, faced an immediate and unrelenting barrage of questions. Inquiries from Justice Scalia and others about the underlying legal basis for the injunction threatened to devolve into a debate over the proper use of medical evidence as a basis for restricting speech. Justice Anthony Kennedy declared at one point, "I would say that persons who walk through a picket line in order to work despite a strike face extreme stress.... [but labor picketing] cases do not talk about stress to the individual. That's somewhat antithetical to very, very essential First Amendment values." Finley also fielded questions about the implementation of the "floating" bubble zone, the provision she was least enthusiastic about. Finally, Solicitor General Walter Dellinger took the podium to present the Government's case for the injunction's constitutionality. The Court pressed Dellinger to distinguish the *Schenck* case from *Claiborne Hardware*, and to clarify the propriety of using medical evidence as a justification for enjoining protesters.

Overall, the justices seemed skeptical of the floating bubble zone, but the oral argument had barely touched upon the core of the injunction—the fixed buffer zone and the cease-and-desist provision. Finley remained optimistic, believing that a successful challenge to the floating zone might actually work in her clients' favor by justifying a much larger fixed buffer zone. "It may turn out to be a case where the defendants should have been careful what they wished for," Finley told reporters after the argument.[107] The Schenck brothers also emerged from the

---

[105] *Quoted in* Gustav Niebuhr, *Conservatives' New Frontier: Religious Liberty Law Firms*, N.Y. TIMES, July 8, 1995, at 1.

[106] *Quoted in id.*

[107] *Quoted in* Jerry Zremski, *Abortion Protesters May Lose By Winning*, BUFFALO NEWS, Oct. 17, 1996, at 7A.

courtroom confident. Robert Schenck told his brother's former congregation at New Covenant Tabernacle that he felt "the Justices were with us," singling out Justice Scalia for special praise as "our angel on the Court."[108]

The Court's decision, issued on February 19, 1997, earned praise from many commentators for its embrace of the often-elusive middle ground. The ruling upheld the pro-choice groups' precious fixed buffer zone but struck down the provision most offensive to the protesters, the floating bubble zone.[109] On the "cease-and-desist" provision, the Court also found a middle way, upholding the restriction but refusing to endorse the more capacious "right to be left alone" that respondents had urged. Evenhandedness aside, the decision was splintered, with Justices John Paul Stevens, Sandra Day O'Connor, Ginsburg, and David H. Souter in agreement with the Chief Justice on the permissibility of the fixed zone and the unconstitutionality of the floating bubble; Justices Scalia, Kennedy, and Clarence Thomas proclaiming the unconstitutionality of the fixed zone as well as the floating bubble; and Justice Stephen Breyer voting to uphold the entire injunction. Scalia's dissent echoed his screed in *Madsen*, chastising the majority for its "effort to recharacterize th[e] responsibility of special care imposed by the First Amendment as some sort of judicial gratuity."[110]

In the wake of the Supreme Court's decision in *Schenck*, both sides proclaimed victory. Sekulow called the Court's invalidation of the floating bubble a "tremendous victory for free speech,"[111] while Marilynn Buckham declared she was "thrilled about the decision," since the "heart and soul of the injunction remain[ed] in place."[112] Paul Schenck characterized the ruling as "a victory for all people of conscience who object to the wanton killing of innocent human beings."[113] Schenck still maintained three years later that he "felt thoroughly vindicated. Many who support me did not feel that it was a clear win and technically it wasn't. But for what was in my heart it was."[114] Yolanda Wu and Martha

---

[108] *See* Barbara O'Brien, *Schenck Confident of Victory in Abortion Case*, Buffalo News, Oct. 21, 1996, at 1B.

[109] Schenck v. Pro–Choice Network of W. New York, 519 U.S. 357 (1997).

[110] *Schenck*, 519 U.S. at 391 (Scalia, J., dissenting).

[111] *Quoted in* Linda Greenhouse, *High Court Upholds 15–foot Buffer Zone at Abortion Clinics*, N.Y. Times, Feb. 20, 1997, at A1.

[112] *Quoted in* Jerry Zremski, *High Court Voids Part of Order on Buffer Zones*, Buffalo News, Feb. 19, 1997, at 1A.

[113] *Quoted in* David Savage, *Justices Rule Abortion Protest is Free Speech*, L.A. Times, Feb. 20, 1997, at A1.

[114] Interview with Schenck, Apr. 19, 2000.

Davis of NOW LDEF applauded the Court for its balanced ruling, noting that the "proof of victory" would "ultimately rest[] . . . on the impact of the decision on women's access to reproductive choice." They believed pro-choice groups could "take comfort that, in the long term, the decision in *Schenck* will be a win."[115] For her part, Finley saw the decision as "an invitation to ask for a larger fixed buffer zone," since the Court had credited a factual record compiled before many of the largest demonstrations and blockades had occurred. "They were laying the seeds of their own future destruction by acknowledging that evidence of TRO violations would have warranted expanded restrictions," she says. "I thought, that plays right into my hands when we go back to district court."[116] For Finley, the true test of victory would be how expansive an injunction she could win from Judge Arcara. "The Supreme Court was really the tip of the iceberg in all this," she says. "The district court record-building work was 90 percent of it, and the Supreme Court about ten. Well, maybe 80–20."[117]

For the pro-life side, the most cherished triumphs of the *Schenck* case were symbolic. "This decision clearly means that the First Amendment applies to the pro-life message, and there is no longer an exception to the free speech clause when the issue is abortion," Sekulow declared, in tones echoed by other religious conservatives. Pro-choice leaders were not unconcerned about the anti-abortion forces' interpretation of the decision as a moral victory. A California NOW officer expressed a typical worry when she said, "Patients are at risk of being ambushed by zealots."[118] A clinic director in Seattle also had misgivings, saying, "This just gives anti-choice activists more tools to harass women."[119] Davis and Wu noted that the *Schenck* decision left many questions unanswered, including the status of statutes and ordinances creating buffer zones around medical clinics.[120] But those were questions for another day, and another case.

The *Schenck* case, however, was not over. Back in district court, Judge Arcara encouraged the parties to settle their differences. "Although the court fully recognizes that the parties strongly and sincerely believe in the righteousness of their respective causes," Arcara wrote in

---

[115] Martha Davis & Yolanda Wu, *The* Schenck *Decision: A Solomonic Solution*, Nat'l L.J., Mar. 10, 1997, at A18.

[116] Interview with Finley, Mar. 31, 2000.

[117] *Id.*

[118] *Quoted in* Savage, *supra* note 109, at A1.

[119] *Quoted in* Richard Carelli & Ferdinand M. De Leon, *Court Gives Abortion Foes Partial Victory*, Seattle Times, Feb. 19, 1997, at A1.

[120] *See* Davis & Wu, *supra* note 111.

an April 1998 ruling, "it strongly urges them to take a hard, realistic look at their positions and to consider carefully the cost of continuing this litigation."[121] Before any settlement could be reached, however, a tragedy of unprecedented proportions shook the beleaguered and divided Buffalo community.

On Friday, October 23, 1998, Barnett Slepian was standing in the kitchen of his Amherst home with his wife Lynn and two of his four young sons. They had just returned from Sabbath services at a nearby synagogue, where the family had marked the anniversary of Slepian's father's death. Without warning, a bullet shattered the kitchen window, striking the fifty-two-year-old physician in the back. "Did you hear that?" the doctor asked his wife. "Lynn, I think I've been shot." His other two sons rushed into the room as he collapsed to the floor. It was the last time they would see their father; Dr. Slepian died ninety minutes later at a nearby hospital.

"These People Are Ruthless Murderers"

"Please don't feign surprise, dismay, and certainly not innocence," Dr. Slepian had written in an open letter to anti-abortion demonstrators four years before his death, "when a more volatile and less restrained" protester "decides to react to inflammatory rhetoric ... by shooting an abortion provider."[122] After his death, many in the pro-choice community came to agree with him. "This horrendous assassination ... cannot be separated from the virulent and inflammatory language of radical right-wing ideologues who demonize women, abortion and medical providers without regard to the real-life consequences," said Janet Benshoof, president of the Center for Reproductive Law and Policy.[123] "What I feared most had happened," Buffalo clinic director and close Slepian friend Marilynn Buckham said simply. "I can't tell you how deeply sad I am."

Local pro-life leaders were quick to condemn the murder. "For anyone to take it upon himself to be judge, jury, and executioner is nothing but sheer evil," said Karen Swallow Prior, the longtime anti-abortion activist.[124] The Schenck brothers issued a statement "unequivocally condemn[ing] any violence used to end abortion."[125] More radical

---

[121] Quoted in Dan Herbeck, Judge Urges Parties to Settle Abortion–Demonstration Issues, BUFFALO NEWS, Apr. 2, 1998, at 9C.

[122] Quoted in Abortion Doctor Had Warned of Violence, ASSOCIATED PRESS, Oct. 26, 1998.

[123] Quoted in Gene Warner, Activists on Both Sides of Issue Express Horror about Shooting, BUFFALO NEWS, Oct. 25, 1998, at 11A.

[124] Quoted in id.

[125] Quoted in id.

anti-abortion spokesmen expressed no such horror, however. Virginia minister Donald Spitz called the killer "a hero" who ended Slepian's "bloodthirsty" practice. "We as Christians have a responsibility to protect the innocent from being murdered.... Whoever shot the shot protected the children," Spitz declared.[126] Others created resentment when they offered condolences. A bouquet of roses left by Robert Schenck on the steps of the slain doctor's office was returned by Lynne Slepian several days after the murder with an angry note questioning his sincerity and his motives.[127]

In retrospect, Paul Schenck saw Dr. Slepian's death as doubly tragic for the pro-life movement. "First of all, our objective was never to take out an abortionist," he says. "Our objective was to convict him of his sins and bring about his conversion.... As Christians we are committed to peace. The very thought of taking up a firearm even to defend yourself, let alone to bring about vigilante justice was horrific. When you get to know someone, even your opponent, you develop a relationship.... For us it was a profound tragedy." The second element of tragedy for the anti-abortion cause, Schenck said, was that it "gave so much ammunition to the other side. They could say, these people are ruthless murderers—which is what we had been saying about the abortion industry.... I think it scared people away, it made them feel that violence was a potential, that maybe what we were doing was inciting people. I don't think that's true, but some people did."[128]

Marilynn Buckham was one of those who believed that the protesters' speech was an incitement to violence, at least indirectly. "Dr. Slepian's death was not only a dreadful tragedy, I think it made people realize how terrible these people really are ... I think in some ways the protests and the murder are very much connected. If there weren't protests here, no attention would have been brought to this clinic in the first place." If anything positive could be said to come from Dr. Slepian's death, Buckham said, it was to alert federal and local law enforcement to the need for much more vigilant protection of abortion clinics. "The murder of Dr. Slepian was definitely a catalyst," she thought, for more vigorous efforts to control the parameters of anti-abortion protest.[129]

One of these efforts was a new lawsuit, filed by Finley with the help of New York State Attorney General Eliot Spitzer, who had run on a platform promising stricter enforcement of laws against clinic obstruc-

---

[126] *Quoted in* Carolyn Thompson, *Abortion MD Had Deadly Premonition*, Toronto Star, Oct. 26, 1998, at A22.

[127] Press, *supra* note 7, at 209.

[128] Interview with Schenck, Apr. 19, 2000.

[129] Interview with Buckham, May 17, 2000.

tion than that provided by his incumbent opponent, Dennis Vacco. Just one week after Dr. Slepian's death, Operation Rescue leaders Revs. Philip "Flip" Benham and Bob Behn announced that a "Spring of Life Reunion" would take place the following April in Buffalo, bringing anti-abortion demonstrators back to the city where they had convened seven years earlier. A new coterie of pro-life enthusiasts was in charge in Buffalo, smaller but no less determined than their predecessors.

Behr, the *Schenck* attorney representing the new defendants, attempted to settle with Finley and Spitzer, to no avail. A heated meeting in a local church basement with the pro-life protesters exposed the divisions among defendants. "Many of those folks—some of whom were clients in both the *Spitzer* and *Schenck* cases—are just morally opposed to agreeing to anything that would limit their advocacy for the unborn," Behr said. "Even though they might see something as advantageous in a legal sense, they just won't do it. . . . Some of the most dedicated people wanted to settle so they would have greater access, but others, especially several pastors, inveighed against reaching any agreement."[130] Behr and his clients finally decided that those who urged settlement would be let out of the lawsuit, and the rest would continue to oppose any and all injunctions.

In April 1999, after a twenty-three-day trial, Judge Arcara issued a temporary restraining order establishing a sixty-foot buffer zone around western New York abortion clinics. The ruling gave Finley "what was probably my best moment ever as a lawyer." Marilynn Buckham called her the day the TRO took effect, in tears. "She said, I just had my first normal experience going to work in ten years."[131] One year later, Buckham maintained that "the new injunction made all the difference in the world. The patients don't come in crying, they are much less traumatized, the noise problems we had in the operating rooms are greatly diminished, it has made a huge difference for the staff in terms of running a medical facility." But the death of Dr. Slepian and the cumulative horror of years of anti-abortion violence had taken their toll, Buckham said in 2000. "Because of all the protests, the intimidation, the murders, there are many, many fewer doctors who are willing to take the risks involved in providing abortions. You can have all the laws in the world, but without the providers, you cannot get an abortion." On the other hand, Finley said several years later, the murders of physicians and clinic staff seem to have strengthened the resolve of the intrepid few who do brave threats of violence and often travel long distances to ensure the continued availability of abortion.[132]

---

[130] Interview with Behr, Apr. 20, 2000.

[131] Interview with Finley, Mar. 31, 2000.

[132] Interview with Finley, Aug. 24, 2006.

As it turned out, the Spring of Life reunion drew scarcely more than one hundred protesters. Reproductive health clinics also garnered additional protection from FACE. The injunction issued by Judge Arcara in 2000 removed the exception for "sidewalk counseling" after Finley presented extensive evidence that allowing protesters to approach and "counsel" women coming in and out of the clinic had resulted in widespread abuses and obstruction of clinic entrances. A Second Circuit ruling in 2001 scaled back Arcara's new injunction to some degree, and a small but dedicated cadre of picketers still regularly appear at the Buffalo GYN Womenservices clinic, now housed in a new location. Nationally, though, almost a decade after the Supreme Court ruled in *Schenck*, the anti-abortion movement had largely shifted its focus from street-level protest to lobbying, seeking abortion-restrictive legislation at the state and national levels and the appointment of judges who oppose *Roe v. Wade*. Ultimately, the outcome of these legal battles will likely determine the future of on-the-ground abortion protest.

Conclusion

For both sides, the *Schenck* case presented a question of basic civil rights, as advocates for and against reproductive choice struggled to define themselves as the natural heirs to the civil rights movement. For abortion rights proponents, the initial challenge was to frame women seeking reproductive health services as citizens attempting to exercise legitimate constitutional rights in the face of violence, intimidation, and obstruction, and to depict anti-abortion demonstrators as a modern day version of the Ku Klux Klan. Bringing suit under section 1985(3), the civil rights statute aimed at racial violence and intimidation, virtually required the Pro–Choice Network and other reproductive rights organizations to draw this analogy explicitly or implicitly. The rhetorical problem they faced was that while white supremacists acted out of hatred for African Americans and other nonwhites, pro-life demonstrators—many of whom were themselves women—were motivated by what they felt to be love and concern for women and their families. As a legal matter, in *Bray v. Alexandria Women's Health Clinic*, the Supreme Court rejected the notion that anti-abortion demonstrators possessed the kind of "invidious, class-based, discriminatory animus" required under section 1985(3). Justice Scalia wrote, "Whether one agrees or disagrees with the goal of preventing abortion, that goal in itself ... does not remotely qualify for such harsh description, and for such derogatory association with racism."[133]

Anti-abortion demonstrators, meanwhile, sought to portray themselves as heirs to the legacy of Martin Luther King, Jr.'s movement of

---

[133] *Bray*, 506 U.S. at 274.

civil disobedience, which had established many of the free speech precedents that redefined First Amendment law in the postwar period. Schenck, his compatriots, and their attorneys believed that the courts disregarded pro-life protesters' First Amendment prerogatives purely based on the content of their speech, that a pro-choice bias infected judges' assessments of the parameters of free expression. At a more visceral level, many pro-life demonstrators felt themselves to be fighting an injustice every bit as profound and inhumane as racial oppression. Like the abolitionists of the nineteenth century, whose religious conviction led them to place their bodies in harm's way for the sake of ending slavery, pro-life protesters manipulated and even disregarded legal rules and injunctions. If abortion was murder, then the obstruction of reproductive health clinics was a moral imperative, whether or not it was a violation of the law. But the legitimacy of the civil rights movement was grounded in non-violence, and the shootings and bombings at clinics in the 1990s undermined the anti-abortion movement's claim to occupy the moral high ground. In upstate New York, the murder of Dr. Slepian left some dedicated anti-abortion activists shaken and others rhetorically compromised.

In the end, both sides turned to politics. The passage of FACE and the escalation of clinic violence enabled pro-choice advocates to assert the illegality of obstructing clinic access and call upon law enforcement actively to protect women's right to enter health facilities unmolested. The election of George W. Bush and a Congress dominated by conservative Republicans allowed anti-abortion activists to hope that their dream of transforming the courts into allies rather than enemies would be realized, and that legal change would obviate the need for street-level protest and obstruction. Whose vision of civil rights prevails will depend on the outcome of these political battles.

14

By Samuel R. Bagenstos*

US Airways v. Barnett and The Limits of Disability Accommodation

In 1990, Congress adopted the Americans with Disabilities Act by overwhelming margins, and the first President Bush signed it into law.[1] The statute was the result of an extensive and savvy lobbying campaign by a still relatively new social movement—the disability rights movement. Beginning in earnest in the late 1960s and early 1970s, the disability rights movement turned, much more quickly than had the black civil rights movement before it, "from protest to politics."[2]

The ADA, which represented the achievement of the movement's major political goal, appeared to be revolutionary. Not only did it extend antidiscrimination protection to people with disabilities, but it also seemed to expand the notion of discrimination itself.[3] Like earlier civil rights statutes, the ADA prohibits intentional discrimination and the use of facially neutral selection criteria that unjustifiably screen out protected class members as a group.[4] But it goes beyond those statutes. The

---

* Thanks to Michael Romano for helpful research assistance, to Dean Kent Syverud for research support, and, as always, to Margo Schlanger. Some of the discussion of the disability rights movement in this chapter is drawn from Samuel R. Bagenstos, *The Americans with Disabilities Act as Welfare Reform*, 44 WM. & MARY L. REV. 921 (2003); thanks to the William and Mary Law Review for reprint permission.

[1] Americans with Disabilities Act of 1990, Pub. L. No. 101–336, 104 Stat. 328 (1990).

[2] *Cf.* Bayard Rustin, *From Protest to Politics: The Future of the Civil Rights Movement*, COMMENTARY, Feb. 1965, at 25.

[3] *See* Pamela S. Karlan & George Rutherglen, *Disabilities, Discrimination, and Reasonable Accommodation*, 46 DUKE L.J. 1 (1996).

[4] *See* 42 U.S.C. § 12112(b)(1)-(3), (5) (2006). For a summary of the law under earlier civil rights statutes, see Int'l Bd. of Teamsters v. United States, 431 U.S. 324, 335 & n.15 (1977).

ADA treats the failure to "mak[e] reasonable accommodation to the known physical or mental limitations of an otherwise qualified individual with a disability" as prohibited discrimination as well.[5]

Unlike earlier civil rights statutes, which took job duties as they found them, the ADA required employers to consider whether the functions assigned to particular positions were really "essential."[6] That seemed a major intrusion on traditional managerial prerogatives. And the statute gave only certain employees the right to demand changes to non-"essential" job duties or other accommodations—the narrowly defined class of "individual[s] with a disability." The ADA thus seemed to grant one class of employees a right to seek exemption from the general rules their fellow workers must follow. Not surprisingly, the law triggered a backlash.[7]

In *US Airways, Inc. v. Barnett*,[8] the Supreme Court addressed the ADA's requirement of reasonable accommodation in employment for the first time. The Court did so in a fact setting that seemed to pit employees with disabilities against their nondisabled coworkers. *Barnett* ultimately offers a window into three of the most important issues to understand about the ADA's accommodation requirement: the requirement's relationship to more traditional antidiscrimination mandates; its seemingly zero-sum nature; and the limits of its usefulness in a world of reduced job security for everyone.

BACKGROUND

The American Disability Rights Movement

The American disability rights movement had its origins in the depths of the Great Depression, when a group of job-seekers with disabilities in New York City mobilized as the League of the Physically Handicapped to protest discrimination by state and federal relief agencies.[9] New Deal programs—like other programs of poor relief in Anglo–American history[10]—treated disability as a condition that exempts an individual from the ordinary obligation to work.[11] But members of the

---

[5] 42 U.S.C. § 12112(b)(5)(A).

[6] 42 U.S.C. § 12111(8) (2006).

[7] *See* Linda Hamilton Krieger, *Socio–Legal Backlash*, 21 BERKELEY J. EMP. & LAB. L. 476 (2000).

[8] 535 U.S. 391 (2002).

[9] *See* PAUL K. LONGMORE, WHY I BURNED MY BOOK AND OTHER ESSAYS ON DISABILITY 54–101 (2003).

[10] *See generally* DEBORAH A. STONE, THE DISABLED STATE (1984).

[11] I use the male pronoun because women generally were not regarded as authentic workers by poor relief systems at this time. But that's a civil rights story for another day.

League argued that, by labeling people with disabilities as "unemploya-
ble," poor relief programs "simultaneously stigmatized and segregated
them, codifying job market discrimination into law."[12] League members
wanted work opportunities, not charity.

The League of the Physically Handicapped eventually petered out,
but new organizations of people with disabilities arose in its place. The
National Federation of the Blind, founded in 1940, was a notable
example. Federationists favored "independence" for blind people. They
urged states to adopt "white cane laws" (which give blind pedestrians
carrying white canes the right of way when crossing the street) and
"guide dog laws" (which eliminated restrictions on the use of service
animals by blind people). Those laws, and other similar legal developments, were crucial to giving blind people the same freedom of movement as was enjoyed by the nondisabled.[13]

In 1966, the great legal scholar Jacobus tenBroek[14] attempted to
synthesize the legal theory of the emergent disability rights movement.
Professor tenBroek was blind, and he was an important leader of the
National Federation of the Blind.[15] In two articles published in the
California Law Review tenBroek argued that the law should reject a
stance of "custodialism" toward people with disabilities. That stance,
"typically expressed in policies of segregation and shelter, or special
treatment and special institutions," should be supplanted by a policy of
"integrationism."[16] In contrast to custodialism, integrationism "enti-
tl[es] the disabled to full participation in the life of the community and
encourag[es] and enabl[es] them to do so."[17] Custodialism, tenBroek
argued, fostered paternalistic attitudes in nondisabled people, which
imposed a "social handicap" that limited people with disabilities far
more than did their physical impairments.[18]

---

[12] LONGMORE, *supra* note 9, at 79.

[13] *See generally* Jacobus tenBroek, *The Right to Live in the World: The Disabled in the Law of Torts*, 54 CAL. L. REV. 841 (1966).

[14] Professor tenBroek is best known for his contributions to Fourteenth Amendment scholarship. *See* JACOBUS TENBROEK, THE ANTISLAVERY ORIGINS OF THE FOURTEENTH AMENDMENT (1951); Joseph Tussman & Jacobus tenBroek, *The Equal Protection of the Laws*, 37 CAL. L. REV. 341 (1949). Professor tenBroek was also an important poverty law scholar. *See* FAMILY LAW AND THE POOR: ESSAYS BY JACOBUS TENBROEK (Joel F. Handler ed., 1971).

[15] *See* tenBroek, *supra* note 13, at 841 n.*

[16] Jacobus tenBroek & Floyd Matson, *The Disabled and the Law of Welfare*, 54 CAL. L. REV. 809, 816 (1966).

[17] tenBroek, *supra* note 13, at 843.

[18] tenBroek & Matson, *supra* note 16, at 814.

As the 1960s came to a close, Professor tenBroek's "right to live in the world" began to creep into the law. In 1968, a senator with a disabled staffer secured the passage of the Architectural Barriers Act.[19] That law required federal government buildings to become more accessible to people with disabilities. In 1973, a group of Senate staffers working on civil rights issues inserted a provision into the reauthorization of the Rehabilitation Act; the new provision, section 504, prohibited disability-based discrimination by recipients of federal funds.[20] The Architectural Barriers Act was the first rights-oriented federal disability law, and section 504 would become an extremely important vehicle for asserting disability rights.

At roughly the same time, activists in California and New York were coming together in the first significant disability protest groups since the 1930s. In many cases, those modern activists were inspired by the examples of the antiwar and black civil rights movements of the 1960s and the feminist movement of the 1970s. Veterans returning from Vietnam with disabilities added to and further radicalized the movement's ranks. Like the earlier disability activists, participants in the disability rights movement of the late 1960s and early 1970s developed a critique of welfare and charity as paternalistic responses that limited the citizenship of people with disabilities. They argued for civil rights and "independent living," not charity, welfare, and institutionalization.[21]

The rise of the disability rights movement during this period clearly reflected the same broad social forces that led members of Congress and their staffers to push disability rights legislation. But the legislation was not the result of movement pressure. In 1977, however, the two worlds collided. The Ford administration had left the implementing regulations for section 504 of the Rehabilitation Act on the desk of the Carter administration's new secretary of health, education, and welfare (HEW), Joseph Califano. Notoriously headstrong, Califano refused to issue the regulations without extensive further study. Activists were incensed by the refusal, four years after the adoption of section 504, to implement the law. They responded with protests around the country, including a twenty-eight-day sit-in at HEW's San Francisco regional office. Mayor Moscone of San Francisco brought the protesters portable showers, and Representatives Phil Burton and George Miller held a congressional

---

[19] *See* STEPHEN L. PERCY, DISABILITY, CIVIL RIGHTS, AND PUBLIC POLICY 50 (1989).

[20] 29 U.S.C. § 794 (2006). The best history of this provision is RICHARD K. SCOTCH, FROM GOOD WILL TO CIVIL RIGHTS: TRANSFORMING FEDERAL DISABILITY POLICY (2d ed. 2001).

[21] The best sources on the rise of the American disability rights movement in the late 1960s and early 1970s are DORIS ZAMES FLEISCHER & FRIEDA ZAMES, THE DISABILITY RIGHTS MOVEMENT: FROM CHARITY TO CONFRONTATION (2001), and JOSEPH P. SHAPIRO, NO PITY: PEOPLE WITH DISABILITIES FORGING A NEW CIVIL RIGHTS MOVEMENT (1993).

hearing at the scene. The sit-in garnered extensive media attention. Califano relented and issued the regulations.[22]

The disability rights movement had scored its most important political and legal victory to date. For the first time in American law, the HEW regulations recognized that "discrimination" against people with disabilities can take the form of the failure to make accommodations.[23] A building that is constructed without people with disabilities in mind may have its sole entrance placed atop a flight of stairs. That barrier excludes people with disabilities just as surely as the hanging of a "no cripples" sign. The HEW regulations thus acknowledged the point, made by many disability rights activists, that what kept people with disabilities from "living in the world" was often not overt discrimination but instead physical, social, and institutional structures that failed to take account of disability.

But the victory was a limited one: section 504 of the Rehabilitation Act applied only to recipients of federal funding.[24] That was enough to cover universities and most state government entities, but it left people with disabilities without any federal antidiscrimination protection in most of the private economy. Disability rights activists thus turned toward advocacy of a new, comprehensive federal disability discrimination law.

The time was hardly auspicious for a new, broad civil rights measure.[25] As the 1970s came to a close, oil crises and tight budgets led to retrenchment on the domestic policy front. When Ronald Reagan was elected president in 1980, he appointed his vice president, George Herbert Walker Bush, to chair a task force on regulatory reform. One of the task force's first targets? The section 504 regulations.[26]

The still-emergent disability rights community responded fiercely to the threat to what was, at that time, the most important law prohibiting disability-based discrimination. Evan Kemp was a major "point person" for the disability community in its efforts. Kemp, a Republican who was then serving as the director of the Nader-affiliated Disability Rights Center, made a national name for himself in 1981 by attacking Jerry Lewis's Labor Day telethon for its role in propagating patronizing stereotypes of pity and fear of people with disabilities.[27] Making his case

---

[22] See SCOTCH, supra note 20, at 102–16; SHAPIRO, supra note 21, at 64–70.

[23] See SCOTCH, supra note 20, at 68–81.

[24] 29 U.S.C. § 794.

[25] See Samuel R. Bagenstos, "Rational Discrimination," Accommodation, and the Politics of (Disability) Civil Rights, 89 VA. L. REV. 825, 902–08 (2003).

[26] See PERCY, supra note 19, at 88–96.

[27] See Evan J. Kemp, Jr., Aiding the Disabled: No Pity, Please, N.Y. TIMES, Sept. 3, 1981, at A19. For a discussion of the attack on the Jerry Lewis telethon, see SHAPIRO, supra

to Bush and his counsel, C. Boyden Gray, "Kemp used a conservative argument. Disabled people wanted independence, Kemp told Bush. They wanted to get out of the welfare system and into jobs."[28] Bush found this argument (backed by significant political mobilization in the disability community) persuasive, and he decided to leave the section 504 regulations alone.[29]

Bush and Gray ultimately became strong supporters of disability rights (and when Bush became president, he appointed Evan Kemp as chair of the Equal Employment Opportunity Commission). And their successful efforts to win over Bush and Gray gave activists a new strategy that they would put to good use in their efforts to enact comprehensive disability rights legislation: In addition to being the heir to earlier civil rights laws, a disability rights law would serve as a tool of welfare reform. It would get people with disabilities off of the welfare rolls and into the workforce.[30]

In 1983, two leading (Republican) lawyers with disabilities, Christopher Bell and Robert Burgdorf, wrote a report on disability rights for the United States Civil Rights Commission. They argued that antidiscrimination and accommodation rules would more than pay for themselves through "large savings in reduced expenditures of public benefits programs, such as social security disability insurance, supplemental security income (SSI), and State welfare, home relief, and aid to families with dependent children."[31] Burgdorf followed up by drafting a 1986 report for the National Council on the Handicapped (now the National Council

---

note 21, at 20–24. For further discussion, see the three pieces on the telethon issue in the Ragged Edge collection: Anne Finger, . . . *And the Greatest of These is Charity*, in THE RAGGED EDGE: THE DISABILITY EXPERIENCE FROM THE PAGES OF THE FIRST FIFTEEN YEARS OF THE DISABILITY RAG 115 (Barrett Shaw ed., 1994) [hereinafter RAGGED EDGE COLLECTION]; Mary Johnson, *A Test of Wills: Jerry Lewis, Jerry's Orphans, and the Telethon*, in RAGGED EDGE COLLECTION, *supra*, at 120; Julie Shaw Cole & Mary Johnson, *Time to Grow Up*, in RAGGED EDGE COLLECTION, *supra*, at 131.

[28] SHAPIRO, *supra* note 21, at 121. Edward Berkowitz described the events this way:

The handicapped rights movement leader Evan Kemp argued that their goals and those of the Reagan administration were not dissimilar: Both accused big government of stifling initiative; both believed in welfare only for the truly needy; both denounced paternalistic government; and both were "antibureaucratic." In short, both believed in independence.

EDWARD D. BERKOWITZ, DISABLED POLICY: AMERICA'S PROGRAMS FOR THE HANDICAPPED 222 (1987).

[29] *See* BERKOWITZ, *supra* note 28, at 222–23; PERCY, *supra* note 19, at 95–96; SHAPIRO, *supra* note 21, at 120–21.

[30] For an extensive effort to document the deployment of this welfare reform argument in the efforts to obtain passage of the ADA, see Bagenstos, *supra* note *, at 957–75.

[31] U.S. COMM'N ON CIVIL RIGHTS, ACCOMMODATING THE SPECTRUM OF INDIVIDUAL ABILITIES 81 (1983).

on Disability). That report for the first time proposed a comprehensive disability discrimination law, and it again urged that such a law could save billions of dollars in welfare benefits each year.[32] The Commission's chair was Justin Dart, who had had polio and was the son of a prominent Republican contributor. Dart used his own money to cris-scross the country and hold hearings to gather support for the proposed antidiscrimination law. Dart sold the statute as one that would move people with disabilities from being unproductive recipients of public benefits to being taxpaying workers.[33]

Following the National Council's recommendation, Senator Lowell Weicker and Representative Tony Coelho introduced the proposed Americans with Disabilities Act in 1988.[34] Buoyed by the welfare-reform argument, as well as more traditional civil rights support and (ironically) widespread feelings of charity toward people with disabilities, the bill passed 377–28 in the House of Representatives and 91–6 in the Senate. When he signed the bill into law in 1990, President George Herbert Walker Bush—who, along with his attorney general, Dick Thornburgh, had strongly supported its passage—declared: "Let the shameful wall of exclusion finally come tumbling down."[35] The disability rights movement had achieved its most significant policy goal—the adoption of a comprehensive disability discrimination law.

By the time Robert Barnett's case got to the Supreme Court, however, many of the hopes of disability rights activists had been tempered by hard experience. In the employment area specifically, the picture looked particularly bleak: Studies showed that over 90 percent of ADA employment plaintiffs lost their cases—a rate of futility exceeded only by prisoners challenging the conditions of their confinement.[36] And while the Supreme Court had issued some rulings that read the ADA expansively outside of the workplace context,[37] the Court also ruled, in a

---

[32] NAT'L COUNCIL ON THE HANDICAPPED, TOWARD INDEPENDENCE (1986).

[33] See Bagenstos, supra note *, at 965–66.

[34] S. 2345, 100th Cong. (1988); H.R. 4498, 100th Cong. (1988).

[35] Ann Devroy, In Emotion–Filled Ceremony, Bush Signs Rights Law for America's Disabled, WASH. POST, July 27, 1990, at A18.

[36] See Ruth Colker, Winning and Losing Under the Americans with Disabilities Act, 62 OHIO ST. L.J. 239 (2001); Ruth Colker, The Americans with Disabilities Act: A Windfall for Defendants, 34 HARV. C.R.–C.L. L. REV. 99 (1999).

[37] See PGA Tour, Inc. v. Martin, 532 U.S. 661 (2001) (requiring PGA Tour to accommodate its "walking rule" for a golfer with a disability under the ADA's public accommodations title); Olmstead v. L.C. ex rel. Zimring, 527 U.S. 581 (1999) (holding that the public services title of the ADA prohibits unnecessary institutionalization in many circumstances); Bragdon v. Abbott, 524 U.S. 624 (1998) (holding that a dentist might be required to treat a patient with HIV under the ADA's public accommodations title).

trilogy of employment cases in 1999, that the statute reached only a narrow protected class.[38] And the employment rate for people with disabilities had remained stagnant at best.[39]

Robert Barnett's Employment at US Airways

Barnett began working for Pacific Southwest Airlines (PSA) in 1984. PSA got its start in 1949 in California. In 1987, PSA merged with US Air, a carrier formerly known as Allegheny Airlines that had focused its operations on the eastern United States. (At roughly the same time, US Air merged with Piedmont Airlines, a carrier centered in the southeastern United States.)

After the merger, Barnett became a US Air employee. At the San Francisco and Oakland airports, Barnett worked in a variety of different jobs, including "baggage claim, training department, catering, ramp service, ticketing, air cargo, mailroom, ramp supervisor, and acting ramp manager."[40] Like nearly all air carriers at the time, both PSA and US Air assigned workers to jobs according to their seniority with the company; the employee with the longest tenure had the first choice of jobs.[41] Airline employers and workers tended to believe that such systems had advantages for both sides. For the employer, the seniority system encouraged workers to make investments in the company early in their careers and remain loyal once they had acquired experience; for the employee, seniority provided freedom from arbitrary managerial decisions. When Barnett moved from PSA to US Air, his accumulated seniority came over with him.

In January 1990, Barnett was working as a cargo handler in San Francisco's airport. Moving the heavy towbars that are used to push aircraft back from the gate, he felt a twinge in his back and thought he pulled a muscle. But the injury turned out to be much more serious and prevented him from doing any heavy lifting.[42] Because heavy lifting was required of cargo employees, Barnett sought a job in the mailroom, and received his requested transfer due to seniority. Barnett was capable of performing the functions of the mailroom position, and he stayed in it for the next two years.

---

[38] See Albertson's, Inc. v. Kirkingburg, 527 U.S. 555 (1999); Murphy v. United Parcel Service, Inc., 527 U.S. 516 (1999); Sutton v. United Air Lines, Inc., 527 U.S. 471 (1999).

[39] See Samuel R. Bagenstos, Has the ADA Reduced Employment for People with Disabilities?, 25 BERKELEY J. EMP. & LAB. L. 527 (2004).

[40] Petition for Writ of Certiorari at 88a–89a, US Airways, Inc. v. Barnett, 535 U.S. 391 (2002) (No. 00–1250) [hereinafter "Petition for Writ of Certiorari"].

[41] Petition for Writ of Certiorari, supra note 40, at 96a.

[42] Telephone interview with Robert Barnett, August 25, 2006.

The year 1992 saw record losses for the airline industry. As fallout from the first Iraq war and a lingering recession reduced commercial air traffic, United States airlines lost $4.8 billion.[43] US Air alone suffered a net loss of $1.2 billion and laid off 7,000 of its workers.[44] In August of that year, the company put all of its cargo and mailroom positions open for seniority-based bidding.[45] Knowing that he would be "bumped" back to a cargo position if other employees with greater seniority could bid on his mailroom job, Barnett sent a letter to his supervisor asking to remain in his current position. Although the company never responded to his letter, it left Barnett in the mailroom for the next five months.[46]

On January 20, 1993, however, Barnett's manager informed him that he could no longer work in the mailroom. Unbeknownst to Barnett, the company had apparently treated his mailroom position (at least since August 1992) as a limited-duty assignment, and company policy limited such assignments to sixty days. Because Barnett had served in that assignment for five months, the company decided to remove him from the mailroom. The company placed Barnett on "on-the-job injury" leave, effective immediately. US Air continued his salary and benefits for one additional month, but he never returned to duty at the company.[47]

Two days after he was removed from his mailroom position, Barnett suggested two possible accommodations that, he said, would enable him to work in the cargo positions to which his seniority still entitled him. First, he suggested, the company could provide him with what he called "robotics" equipment to assist him in the lifting that cargo work often requires. Second, Barnett suggested, the company could guarantee that he would be assigned to perform only office work in the cargo department, and that he would not have to perform the rotations that required heavy lifting. The company responded, in a letter on March 4, that it had considered but could not accommodate those requests. According to

---

[43] Paul Adams, *Airlines Fear War Would Hit Them Savagely*, BALT. SUN, Sept. 29, 2002.

[44] Joint Appendix at 21a, *Barnett*, 535 U.S. 391 (No. 00–1250).

[45] It remains unclear whether US Air did so as part of a routine practice, as the company said in response to Barnett's EEOC complaint, or US Air instead did so because of the layoffs, as the company said in its Supreme Court briefs. The most likely answer seems to be that the company did have a routine practice of putting all of its positions up for bid, but that the layoffs attached particularly high stakes to the bidding in August 1992. *Compare* Brief for Petitioner at 5, *Barnett*, 535 U.S. 391 (No. 00–1250) (rebidding was "in connection with" layoffs), *with* Brief for Respondent at 2–3, *Barnett*, 535 U.S. 391 (No. 00–1250) (rebidding was normal practice).

[46] *See* Brief for Appellee at 8–9, Barnett v. U.S. Air, Inc., 157 F.3d 744 (9th Cir. 1998) (No. 96–16669).

[47] *See id.* at 9–10; Brief for Appellant at 11–12, Barnett v. U.S. Air, Inc., 157 F.3d 744 (9th Cir. 1998) (No. 96–16669).

Barnett's trial-court counsel, Richard Davis, US Air "wouldn't lift a finger to try to find a way to assist him." Davis said that Barnett was not alone in this regard: "They had other problems in their personnel department with the way they were treating employees with disabilities."[48]

In the meantime, on February 28, 1993, Barnett had filed a discrimination charge with the Equal Employment Opportunity Commission (EEOC). Barnett claimed that his back injury constituted a "disability" under the ADA, and that US Air had failed to provide him the "reasonable accommodation" the statute requires. At the same time, Barnett contacted the Job Accommodation Network (JAN), a federally-funded agency that assists individual employers and employees in developing workplace accommodations. The JAN responded with information about mechanical devices that would help Barnett lift cargo onto and off of pallets and carts. Barnett sent that information to the US Air attorney who was handling his EEOC charge. The company continued to reject the proposed accommodations, however.[49]

LEGAL PROCEEDINGS

District Court

On November 4, 1994, Barnett filed suit in the United States District Court for the Northern District of California. His complaint asserted four causes of action: (1) that US Air violated the ADA by refusing to make an accommodation for his back injury; (2) that US Air violated the ADA by retaliating against him because of his request for an accommodation; (3) that US Air's actions intentionally inflicted emotional distress, in violation of California law; and (4) that US Air's actions *negligently* inflicted emotional distress, in violation of California law.[50]

After just over a year of discovery, US Air filed a motion for summary judgment on January 10, 1996.[51] In two opinions issued over the next six months, District Judge D. Lowell Jensen granted the motion for summary judgment.[52] Judge Jensen ruled that none of the accommodations Barnett requested were "reasonable." To permit Barnett to remain in the mailroom position, when other more senior employees wanted that position, would require overriding the company's seniority system. But Judge Jensen concluded that a modification to US Air's

---

[48] Telephone Interview with Richard Davis, July 31, 2006.

[49] Brief for Appellant, *supra* note 47, at 14.

[50] *See* Petition for Writ of Certiorari, *supra* note 40, at 93a, 104a, 106a.

[51] *See id.*

[52] *See id.* at 79a–109a.

seniority system would not be "reasonable." That system, he noted, "ha[d] been in place for 'decades' and govern[ed] over 14,000 USAir Agents [*sic*].''[53] Such policies were "common to the airline industry.''[54] Altering the seniority system for employees with disabilities, he concluded, would "creat[e] undue burdens on other employees [and] disrupt[] the fundamental structure of the USAir seniority system.''[55]

As to the other accommodations requested by Barnett, Judge Jensen determined that those would not be "reasonable," either. The judge concluded that lifting and moving cargo were "essential" to the cargo position.[56] And he ruled that US Air was not required to grant Barnett's "request for special lifting equipment," because the company already made forklifts "available to cargo department employees to aid in lifting.''[57] Although he held that the ADA required US Air to engage in an "interactive process" to identify accommodations, Judge Jensen ultimately determined that the company had engaged in such a process.[58] The judge also made quick work in dimissing Barnett's ADA retaliation claim and state-law claims.[59]

Court of Appeals

Barnett appealed to the United States Court of Appeals for the Ninth Circuit. The three-judge panel assigned to Barnett's appeal consisted of two conservatives (Judge Pamela Rymer and Judge Charles Wiggins, a former Republican member of Congress from California, best known for his defense of Richard Nixon in the 1974 impeachment proceedings[60]) and one liberal (Judge Betty Fletcher). By a 2–1 vote, the panel affirmed Judge Jensen's decision. Judge Wiggins wrote the majority opinion, joined by Judge Rymer. Allowing Barnett to remain in the mailroom, they held, would grant him a "preference over nondisabled

---

[53] *Id.* at 96a.

[54] *Id.*

[55] *Id.* at 97a.

[56] *Id.* at 97a–98a.

[57] *Id.* at 99a–100a.

[58] *Id.* at 84a.

[59] Judge Jensen found the evidence insufficient to raise a triable issue regarding whether the company retaliated against Barnett, and he concluded that the state's workers' compensation law did in fact preempt the infliction of emotional distress claims. *See id.* at 106a.

[60] *See* Gebe Martinez, *Watergate–Era Members Recall Impeachment Lessons Learned*, WASH. POST., Mar. 24, 1998 (describing Wiggins as "one of the last conservative Republican hold-outs for Nixon on the Watergate panel").

employees" whose seniority entitled them to his position.[61] Because they
read the ADA "as requiring no more than equality among disabled and
nondisabled employees in hiring and reassignment decisions," Judges
Wiggins and Rymer concluded that any request to override a seniority
system was not "reasonable."[62] They also concluded that the "robotics"
equipment Barnett requested would not "provide him with any accommodation of his disability not already provided by the forklifts furnished
in cargo," and that permitting Barnett to perform only desk work in a
cargo position would effectively create a new position, something the
ADA does not require.[63] Unlike Judge Jensen, they held that the ADA
does not impose on employers any independent obligation to engage in
an "interactive process" to determine whether an accommodation is
available.[64] In dissent, Judge Fletcher disagreed with all of these points.

Barnett filed for rehearing en banc, supported by amicus briefs filed
by the EEOC and a collection of disability rights and civil rights
organizations. After hearing oral argument before a packed courtroom
(indeed, an overflow room had to be set up in which spectators watched
the argument on closed-circuit television),[65] the eleven-judge en banc
court issued a ruling on October 4, 2000. This time, Judge Fletcher
wrote the majority opinion, joined by Chief Judge Procter Hug, and
Judges Mary Schroeder, Harry Pregerson, A. Wallace Tashima, Sidney
Thomas, Raymond Fisher, and Ronald Gould (all appointees of Presidents Carter and Clinton). Judges Diarmuid O'Scannlain and Stephen
Trott (appointees of President Reagan), and Judge Andrew Kleinfeld (an
appointee of the first President Bush), dissented.

In her majority opinion, Judge Fletcher ruled that Barnett had
presented sufficient facts to raise a triable issue on each of his ADA
accommodation claims. Her opinion held, first, that the ADA does
impose a mandatory obligation on employers to engage in an "interactive
process" to determine whether accommodations are available, and US
Air had failed to engage in such a process. "Given US Air's failure to
engage in the interactive process," the en banc majority held, "liability
would be appropriate if a reasonable accommodation would otherwise
have been possible."[66] Because there was "conflicting evidence" on
whether the accommodations Barnett requested would have been reason-

[61] Petition for Writ of Certiorari, *supra* note 40, at 59a.

[62] *Id.* at 60a.

[63] *Id.* at 62a–63a.

[64] *Id.* at 66a.

[65] Barnett interview, *supra* note 42.

[66] Petition for Writ of Certiorari, *supra* note 40, at 20a.

able, the majority determined that summary judgment was inappropriate.[67]

Judge Fletcher's majority opinion singled out one possible accommodation for more extensive discussion: Barnett's request that the company permit him to remain in the mailroom. Judge Fletcher noted that the ADA explicitly lists "reassignment to a vacant position" as one possible reasonable accommodation.[68] US Air interpreted that provision as guaranteeing only "the opportunity to apply for and compete for reassignment," but Judge Fletcher adopted the EEOC's position that the provision " 'means that the employee gets the vacant position if s/he is qualified for it. Otherwise, reassignment would be of little value and would not be implemented as Congress intended.' "[69] And she concluded "that a seniority system is not a per se bar to reassignment"; rather a "case-by-case fact intensive analysis is required to determine whether any particular reassignment would constitute an undue hardship to the employer."[70] Because the company had "provide[d] no information concerning the number of ADA claimants at US Air, their seniority, or their need to be accommodated by exceptions to the seniority rules," its claim of undue hardship rested on "[m]ere speculation" insufficient to support summary judgment.[71]

In dissent, Judge Trott, joined by Judges O'Scannlain and Kleinfeld, agreed with the panel opinion written by Judge Wiggins (who died seven months before the en banc court issued its opinion).[72]

On to the Supreme Court

US Air decided to seek review of the Ninth Circuit's en banc decision in the Supreme Court. The company hired a new lawyer, Walter Dellinger, to represent them. Dellinger filed a petition for certiorari, and the Court agreed to decide whether a reassignment that required modification of a seniority position could be a "reasonable accommodation" under the ADA. In his briefing on the merits, Dellinger argued aggressively that a modification to a neutral seniority system would constitute not an "accommodation" but a "preference": Barnett's lack of seniority did not result from his disability, so a modification to the seniority

[67] *Id.* at 21a.

[68] 42 U.S.C. § 12111(9)(B) (2006).

[69] Petition for Writ of Certiorari, *supra* note 40, at 22a (quoting EEOC Enforcement Guidance).

[70] *Id.* at 27a.

[71] *Id.* at 28a.

[72] *Id.* at 36a–40a.

system would not accommodate his disability.[73] Dellinger also contended that a modification of a seniority system could never be a "reasonable" accommodation (and would always cause "undue hardship") in any event.[74]

In the Supreme Court, Barnett was now represented by Claudia Center, an attorney at the Employment Law Center of the Legal Aid Society of San Francisco. Center, whose ten-year legal career had been spent entirely in public interest practice, had filed an amicus brief on Barnett's behalf before the en banc Ninth Circuit, and Barnett brought her on as lead counsel for the Supreme Court proceedings. Her brief disagreed with each of Dellinger's arguments. And Center added an aggressive argument of her own: In determining whether an accommodation is "reasonable," a court should consider only whether that accommodation would enable the employee to perform his or her job duties. Center contended that cost, burden on the employer, and harm to other important interests are not relevant to an accommodation's reasonableness, and that those factors should be considered, if at all, only as part of an employer's "undue hardship" defense.[75]

The Oral Argument in the Supreme Court

The case came up for argument on December 4, 2001. Dellinger went first, and he opened on a conciliatory note. The ADA, he acknowledged, "does more than merely prohibit hostile discrimination against individuals with disabilities." Instead, he continued, "this Act does affirmatively require businesses to lift barriers that might inhibit employment opportunities for those with disabilities."[76] But there was one line he contended that the ADA did not demand that employers cross: "[T]he Act simply does not require an employer to override neutral criteria wholly unrelated to disability in choosing among applicants for a position, and in particular it does not require the employer to set aside the normal operation of a bona fide seniority system."[77]

Justice O'Connor pressed Dellinger on just how settled US Air's seniority system was. She noted the company's own suggestion, in its briefs to the Supreme Court, "that every so often all positions in the category in which this person worked are declared vacant."[78] She also

---

[73] Brief for Petitioner at 10–14, 17–31, *Barnett*, 535 U.S. 391 (No. 00–1250).

[74] *Id.* at 31–44.

[75] Brief for Respondent, *Barnett*, 535 U.S. 391 (No. 00–1250).

[76] Transcript of Oral Argument at 3, *Barnett*, 535 U.S. 391 (No. 00–1250).

[77] *Id.* at 4.

[78] *Id.* at 7.

noted the company's own position "that the seniority policy does not create legally enforceable rights in any employee[.] No employee wanting to come in would be able to sue to get that enforced."[79] Along the same lines, Justice Breyer asked what would happen in "a seniority system that's riddled with exceptions."[80] Justice Ginsburg then pressed Dellinger on the differences between the ADA and earlier civil rights laws like Title VII of the Civil Rights Act of 1964. "Title VII," she noted, "says, thou shalt not discriminate."[81] But "[t]his Disabilities Act gives a starring role to reasonable accommodation, which it truly doesn't have in Title VII."[82] Wasn't it "reasonable," she asked, to leave Barnett in his position? "[C]ouldn't you look at this and say, well, this man was already in the job, and nobody is going to be out of work, so the accommodation is reasonable?"[83] But Dellinger stood his ground.[84]

Now it was Center's turn. She opened with her argument that a "reasonable" accommodation is one that enables the employee to do the job, and that an accommodation's cost, burden, and effect on other employees are not appropriately considered in the reasonableness determination.[85] That position quickly brought her trouble. Justice Scalia noted that Center had conceded that a promotion could never be a "reasonable accommodation" under the Act, and asked how that could be true given Center's reading of the word "reasonable."[86] Center offered a number of possible responses, but none got at that basic tension.[87] It was not until much later in the argument that she stated that, even if the term "reasonable" does account for the interests of other employees, an accommodation to a seniority system would be reasonable; by then, it was too late to discuss the issue at any length.[88]

THE SUPREME COURT OPINIONS

On April 29, 2002, the Supreme Court issued its decision. The *Barnett* case was one of four ADA cases the Court heard that year—a

[79] *Id.* at 8.

[80] *Id.* at 12.

[81] *Id.* at 14.

[82] *Id.* at 15.

[83] *Id.*

[84] *See id.* at 16, 18–19, 22–24.

[85] *Id.* at 24–25.

[86] *Id.* at 25–28.

[87] *Id.*

[88] *See id.* at 43, 48.

fact that led Justice O'Connor to dub the Term the "Disabilities Act Term."[89] In each of the four cases, the Court ruled against the ADA plaintiff.[90] But Barnett was luckier than the others: The Court's ruling was only 7–2 against him (the other cases were decided 9–0), and the justices' various opinions left him an opening to win on remand.

Justice Breyer wrote the opinion of the Court, joined by Chief Justice Rehnquist and Justices Stevens, O'Connor, and Kennedy. Rejecting US Airways' more aggressive argument, Justice Breyer's opinion held "that preferences will sometimes prove necessary to achieve the Act's basic equal opportunity goal."[91] Many neutral rules may limit the opportunities of individual employees with disabilities, and the whole point of the reasonable accommodation requirement is to demand that employers make exceptions to those rules.[92] But Barnett was incorrect, as well, to argue "that the statutory words 'reasonable accommodation' mean only 'effective accommodation.' "[93] As Justice Breyer explained, "[i]t is the word 'accommodation,' not the word 'reasonable,' that conveys the need for effectiveness. An *ineffective* 'modification' or 'adjustment' will not *accommodate* a disabled individual's limitations."[94]

Accordingly, Justice Breyer continued, the question in Barnett's case was whether an accommodation that would violate the rules of a seniority system could be "reasonable." And he concluded that, at least "ordinarily," such an accommodation would not be reasonable.[95] Justice Breyer looked to the important interests a seniority system serves for employers and employees. Any requirement that the employer defend its seniority system against accommodation requests on a case-by-case basis, he said, might itself "undermine the employees' expectations of consistent, uniform treatment."[96] "That," Justice Breyer explained, "is because such a rule would substitute a complex case-specific 'accommodation' decision made by management"—a decision with "inevitable dis-

---

[89] *See* Charles Lane, *O'Connor Criticizes Disabilities Law as Too Vague*, WASH. POST, Mar. 15, 2002, at A2.

[90] *See* Barnes v. Gorman, 536 U.S. 181 (2002) (9–0 decision); Chevron U.S.A., Inc. v. Echazabal, 536 U.S. 73 (2002) (9–0 decision); Toyota Motor Mfg., Ky., Inc. v. Williams, 534 U.S. 184 (2002) (9–0 decision).

[91] *Barnett*, 535 U.S. at 397.

[92] *Id.*

[93] *Id.* at 399.

[94] *Id.* at 400.

[95] *Id.* at 403.

[96] *Id.*

cretionary elements" that "might well take place fairly often"—"for the more uniform, impersonal operation of seniority rules."[97]

But Justice Breyer's majority opinion did leave an opening for accommodations to seniority systems. Employees with disabilities, the Court concluded, may in particular cases "show that special circumstances warrant a finding that, despite the presence of a seniority system (which the ADA may not trump in the run of cases), the requested 'accommodation' is 'reasonable' on the particular facts."[98] For example, the plaintiff could show that the employer changes the seniority system so frequently that employees have reduced "expectations that the system will be followed."[99] Or the plaintiff could "show that the system already contains exceptions such that, in the circumstances, one further exception is unlikely to matter."[100]

The Court vacated the Ninth Circuit's judgment and remanded for application of its legal rulings.[101] In a brief concurrence, Justice Stevens expressed his agreement with the Ninth Circuit's holding "that there was a triable issue of fact precluding summary judgment with respect to whether petitioner violated the statute by failing to engage in an interactive process regarding respondent's three proposed accommodations"—a holding he characterized as "untouched by the Court's opinion today."[102]

Justice O'Connor's concurrence was more interesting. She disagreed with Justice Breyer's reading of the application of the ADA to seniority systems. But she joined it anyway to create five votes for a single interpretation of the statute.[103] In Justice O'Connor's view, the relevant question should be whether the position to which the plaintiff sought assignment was "vacant," because the ADA lists "reassignment to a vacant position" as a possible accommodation.[104] And a position would not be "vacant" if another employee, because of a seniority system, had a legally enforceable claim on it.[105] Accordingly, Justice O'Connor would have held that a seniority system could not be accommodated when, and

---

[97] *Id.* at 404–05.

[98] *Id.* at 405.

[99] *Id.*

[100] *Id.*

[101] *See id.* at 406.

[102] *Id.* at 407 (Stevens, J., concurring).

[103] *See id.* at 408 (O'Connor, J., concurring).

[104] *Id.* at 408–09.

[105] *See id.* at 409–10.

only when, that system was legally enforceable.[106] Although the US Air seniority policy was not legally enforceable,[107] Justice O'Connor nonetheless believed that Justice Breyer's view would "often lead to the same outcome as the test [she] would have adopted."[108]

Four justices dissented, but they did so from two radically different perspectives. Justice Scalia, joined by Justice Thomas, argued that the Court had not gone far enough to reject Barnett's claim. In Justice Scalia's view, *no* accommodation to a seniority system should ever be required by the ADA, because seniority systems "pose no *distinctive* obstacle to the disabled."[109] As Justice Scalia read the statute, it "eliminates workplace barriers only if a disability prevents an employee from overcoming them—those barriers that would not be barriers *but for* the employee's disability."[110] Some people with disabilities might have higher medical expenses than their nondisabled coworkers as well, so paying them the same salary has a "harsher impact upon the more needy disabled employee." But, he noted, that does not mean that the ADA requires that disabled employees receive higher salaries than their nondisabled counterparts.[111] If the ADA were not limited to "disability-related obstacles," Justice Scalia contended, it would become "a standardless grab bag—leaving it to the courts to decide which workplace preferences (higher salary, longer vacations, reassignment to positions to which others are entitled) can be deemed 'reasonable' to 'make up for' the particular employee's disability."[112]

Justice Souter, joined by Justice Ginsburg, dissented from the opposite direction. He argued that the Ninth Circuit's judgment should be affirmed.[113] In his view, the ADA contained no special exemption for seniority systems (at least outside of the context of collective bargaining). While Title VII contained an explicit provision protecting "bona fide" seniority systems, the ADA, to a large extent modeled on Title VII, contained no such provision.[114] And the ADA's legislative history suggested that the difference was intentional.[115]

---

[106] *See id.*

[107] *See id.* at 410.

[108] *Id.* at 411.

[109] *Id.* at 412 (Scalia, J., dissenting).

[110] *Id.* at 413.

[111] *Id.*

[112] *Id.* at 414.

[113] *See id.* at 424 (Souter, J., dissenting).

[114] *See id.* at 421.

[115] *See id.* at 421–22.

THE AFTERMATH

US Airways was pleased with the company's win in the Supreme Court.[116] But Barnett's lawyers also regarded the Supreme Court's decision as a victory on a "very significant issue."[117] The decision left Barnett a clear path to success by showing that the US Airways seniority system did not create settled expectations in its employees. Because the company itself had repeatedly declared that its system was not legally binding, such a showing would be quite plausible. And, as Justice Stevens had emphasized, the Supreme Court's decision did not even call into question the Ninth Circuit's *other* grounds for finding a triable issue of an ADA violation. Barnett later explained that he "was excited" when the Court decided the case, "because of the fact that we were going to trial."[118]

But the feeling of victory did not last. In the aftermath of the terrorist attacks of September 11, 2001, "the U.S. airline industry ... confronted financial losses of unprecedented proportions."[119] On August 11, 2002, four days after the district court spread the Ninth Circuit's mandate on remand from the Supreme Court in Barnett's case, US Airways filed for bankruptcy. With a one billion dollar loan guarantee the next year from the federal Air Transportation Stabilization Board (an agency set up to bail out air carriers after 9/11), the company quickly emerged from bankruptcy.[120] But the company could not achieve financial stability, and it filed for bankruptcy again in September 2004. Because the case could not proceed while US Airways was in bankruptcy, Barnett settled for approximately $3,500.00—what Davis called "cents on the dollar."[121] As of 2004, Barnett was still on on-the-job injury status on US Airways' employee rolls: "They never did fire the gent."[122] But the airline had long since subcontracted its cargo operation at the San Francisco airport, so he could not have returned to his old job in any event.[123]

---

[116] Interview with anonymous US Airways official, August 25, 2006.

[117] Davis interview, *supra* note 48.

[118] Barnett interview, *supra* note 42.

[119] GOV'T ACCOUNTABILITY OFFICE, COMMERCIAL AVIATION: BANKRUPTCY AND PENSION PROBLEMS ARE SYMPTOMS OF UNDERLYING STRUCTURAL ISSUES 1 (2005).

[120] *See* Letter from Daniel G. Montgomery, Executive Director, Air Transportation Stabilization Board, to David N. Siegel, President and Chief Executive Officer, US Airways, Inc., July 10, 2002, *available at* http://www.treas.gov/press/releases/docs/usair.pdf.

[121] Davis interview, *supra* note 48; Email from Claudia Center.

[122] *Id.*

[123] *See* Joint Appendix at 23a, *Barnett*, 535 U.S. 391 (No. 00–1250).

A year or two after the Supreme Court's decision, the company recalled Barnett to work, saying that he now had seniority to bid into an open mail position, but they quickly called back to say they had "made a mistake."[124] During the ten years his case was pending, Barnett estimates that he spent "at least twenty-something hours a week" thinking about, doing research for, and working on his case.[125] He also worked in a number of retail jobs and went back to school and received his bachelor's degree. As of this writing, Barnett is still working in retail, though he is waiting for a job doing background checks of employment candidates.[126]

Since *Barnett*, lower courts have treated accommodations to seniority systems about as one might expect: Where there is no evidence that an employer has ever made an exception to its seniority system, or where a seniority system is the result of collective bargaining, lower courts hold that no accommodation to that system is required.[127] Where an employer has made exceptions to or changed its seniority system, the courts *sometimes* find the kind of "special circumstances" that would make an accommodation to the system reasonable.[128] And although some judges have expressed sympathy with Justice Scalia's dissenting position that "disability-neutral" rules need never be accommodated, they have recognized that Justice Breyer's majority opinion firmly rejected that position.[129]

LESSONS

US Airways v. Barnett was litigated for ten years in the federal courts, but in the end the courts never had a chance to resolve the merits. Davis described it as a case with "a short beginning and a lousy ending."[130] Both the substantive issues addressed by the courts and the ultimate outcome of the litigation raise serious questions about the disability rights project that culminated in the adoption of the Americans with Disabilities Act.

As an examination of the various opinions in the Supreme Court shows, the case certainly raises questions about the purpose and scope of

---

[124] Barnett interview, *supra* note 42.

[125] *Id.*

[126] *Id.*

[127] *See, e.g.,* Medrano v. City of San Antonio, 179 Fed.Appx. 897 (5th Cir.2006); Banks v. Brown–Forman Corp., 84 Fed. Appx. 625 (6th Cir. 2003); Stamos v. Glen Cove Sch. Dist., 78 Fed. Appx. 776 (2d Cir. 2003).

[128] *See, e.g.,* Office of the Architect of the Capitol v. Office of Compliance, 361 F.3d 633 (Fed. Cir. 2004).

[129] *See, e.g.,* Peebles v. Potter, 354 F.3d 761, 768–769 (8th Cir. 2004).

[130] Davis interview, *supra* note 48.

the ADA's reasonable accommodation requirement. For the disability rights movement, as discussed above, the accommodation mandate was emphatically *not* about charity. It was about removing the barriers that keep people with disabilities from working—barriers that exist only because a predominantly nondisabled world does not take people with disabilities into account when designing physical structures, institutions, and work routines. The articulated goal of the ADA's proponents was to *avoid* charity and welfare by giving people with disabilities an opportunity to work and make their own way.

But the facts of *Barnett* put a good deal of pressure on that view of accommodation. Seniority systems do not, in and of themselves, appear to be structures that exclude people with disabilities by failing to take account of them. This seems particularly true for people who acquire disabilities on the job, like Robert Barnett. A flight of stairs disparately excludes people who use wheelchairs; a rule against breaks disparately excludes people with diabetes. But a seniority system would seem to have no particular connection to disability. It excludes anyone who, for whatever reason, has less seniority than the person with whom she is competing. Moreover, unlike the installation of a ramp, an accommodation that overrides a seniority system comes at an obvious cost to the more senior fellow employee who is bumped from or loses an opportunity to move into a desired position. The accommodation Barnett sought, on its face, looks like charity of a particularly troubling kind—charity in the form of a job that one employee is forced to give to another.

Given the facts of *Barnett*, it should not be surprising that Justice Scalia sought to confine the accommodation requirement to cases where individuals seek alteration of "disability-specific obstacles." What might be surprising, though, is that Justice Scalia's restrictive reading carried some interesting disability-rights overtones, particularly in its effort to keep the ADA from serving as a vehicle for judicial decisions of what "preferences . . . can be deemed 'reasonable' to 'make up for' the employee's disability."[131] Although Justice Scalia was taking a position that most disability rights activists opposed, he was speaking their language. His effort, consistent with the goals articulated by disability rights activists themselves, was to ensure that the ADA would remain a civil rights law, rather than a demand for charitable largesse.[132]

Yet the "disability-specific obstacle" principle ultimately cannot do the work Justice Scalia wanted it to. Justice Scalia concluded that the

---

[131] *Barnett*, 535 U.S. at 414 (Scalia, J., dissenting).

[132] For a discussion of how limitations on the accommodation requirement might be seen as serving the disability rights aim to avoid charity, see Samuel R. Bagenstos, *The Future of Disability Law*, 114 YALE L.J. 1, 50–54 (2004). Much of the article offers a critique of that way of thinking.

seniority system was not "disability-specific," because he believed that Barnett's disability had nothing to do with his lack of seniority. But that is not right: Barnett's disability is what made him unable to work in the cargo position and thus put him at the mercy of the seniority system before he had accumulated enough seniority to hold a position that would enable him to keep working. Both Barnett's need for seniority and his lack of seniority at the time he needed it were the product of his disability.

Barnett's case really looks just like a paradigm case for reasonable accommodation. Imagine a nine-person secretarial pool in which all of the secretaries do typing and filing, but one—always the newest hire—is also required to relieve the receptionist at the lunch hour. The pool hires a new secretary, who is deaf. Under Justice Scalia's analysis, the employer would never be required even to consider whether it is reasonable to reallocate the receptionist duties from the new hire to someone else: Sure, her disability is what keeps her from performing the receptionist duties of the secretarial position (just as Barnett's disability kept him from performing the lifting duties of the cargo position), but it's her lack of seniority that forces her to perform the receptionist duties. Many, many accommodations can be described in the same two steps: (1) eliminating job duties that the employee cannot perform; and (2) waiving whatever rules generally prevent the employee from shedding those duties. The fact that the rules in the second step are disability-neutral (like seniority rules) does not change the fact that the job duties are themselves disability-specific obstacles.

To put it another way, even if disability does not limit the amount of seniority a person can accrue, a workplace that took people with disabilities into account as "normal" workers would recognize their more frequent need for flexibility in the application of a seniority system. Lack of flexibility is itself a disability-specific barrier to continued employment. (It certainly was for Barnett.)

Justice Scalia's "disability-specific obstacle" principle was clearly motivated by a desire to avoid giving "preferences" to people with disabilities. But as Justice Breyer emphasized in his majority opinion, the accommodation requirement always demands "preferences" in the sense that it requires employers to make accommodations for people with disabilities that they need not make for other employees. Although inconsistent with Justice Scalia's view that the "Rule of Law" is a "Law of Rules,"[133] the statutory accommodation requirement gives courts little choice but to decide, in a case-by-case common-law fashion, what alterations to workplace rules are "reasonable" to assure that people with disabilities get the same employment opportunities that they would in a

---

[133] Antonin Scalia, *The Rule of Law as a Law of Rules*, 56 U. Chi. L. Rev. 1175 (1989).

world where institutions were designed with them in mind. What made *Barnett* so telling was that it put front and center the burdens the accommodation requirement imposes on other employees. Those burdens are among the most significant causes of the social backlash against the ADA,[134] and Justice Breyer's rule that seniority systems need not ordinarily be modified clearly reflects a fear of exacerbating that backlash.

In the end, though, the most important lesson about the case may highlight the limited power of civil rights laws in a changing economy. Robert Barnett lost his job because US Airways would not modify its seniority system, but it was the company's decision to subcontract its cargo work that left him with no job to which to return. And it was the company's bankruptcy that denied him a full opportunity to seek legal redress. Just as the positive effects of the Civil Rights Act of 1964 were in some ways overtaken by the deindustrialization that took place in the 1960s and 1970s, so too are the positive effects of the ADA likely to be limited by today's trends of reduced job security. And that was a lesson Robert Barnett learned all too well. As he sums it up: "Would I do it again? Yes, I would do it again. But I never expected the company I worked for to go Chapter 11. If it wasn't for that, I think we had enough [to win on] two out of the three [claims of denial of accommodation]."[135]

---

[134] *See generally* Krieger, *supra* note 7.

[135] Barnett interview, *supra* note 42.

15

Thomas B. Metzloff*

The Constitution and the Klan: Understanding the Burning Cross in Virginia v. Barry Black

"I don't want to sound like I'm a bigot. I do want to sound like I'm a racist, because I am a racist. I believe that my pigmentation is my suit of armor. That's my skin. That's my people."

Barry Elton Black

Carroll County, Virginia is nestled in the foothills of the Appalachian Mountains. Located on the border of North Carolina, it is near Mt. Airy, a town made famous as the hometown of the actor Andy Griffith and the inspiration for his television show and its legendary television sheriff Andy Taylor. Hillsville, the county seat, is like Mayberry in many respects—a quiet town where most people know each other. The local sheriff, Warren Manning, even looks and sounds a bit like Andy. It is a very nice place.

But on Saturday, August 22, 1998, a group of people gathered in a field near the town of Cana, in the southern part of the county, to hold a rally to organize a new chapter of the Ku Klux Klan. Carroll County—with a white population of over ninety-five percent and a black population of less than one percent—would be one of the last places where you would expect to see a Ku Klux Klan rally. As is typical at a Klan rally, the forty or fifty people in attendance ended the event by setting fire to kerosene-soaked cloths that had been draped over a metal cross. As the

* All quotes in this chapter are from interviews conducted by the author in Fall 2004 with the principal parties to the case including interviews with Barry Black, Sheriff Warren Manning, Deputy Richard Clark, Dean Rodney Smolla, David Baugh, former State Solicitor General William Hurd, and Commonwealth Attorney Gregory Goad. Those interviews were the source for a documentary about the case that is available in DVD format. For information, see www.voicesofamericanlaw.org.

flames grew higher, they cast a bright glow over the countryside. To those in attendance, it was a traditional ritual; to those seeing it from their homes or hearing about it later, it was a sad reminder of racial hatred and violence.

Field in Cana, Virginia where Klan Rally was held

This Klan rally would end up differently than the scattering of other similar rallies that are held from time to time across the country. Instead of just being the subject of local gossip and concern, Sheriff Manning decided to arrest Barry Black—the leader of the Klan who had come to Virginia from his home in Johnstown, Pennsylvania—for violating a Virginia law that prohibited cross-burning. Black's subsequent conviction eventually made its way all the way to the Supreme Court.

The Rally

The story of *Virginia v. Black* thus begins with interconnected histories of the Ku Klux Klan and Barry Black.

The original Klan emerged in the war-torn South at the end of the Civil War. Many southern whites, upset by occupation by Union troops and the political and economic autonomy given to the freed slaves as part of Reconstruction, formed vigilante groups to attack African–Ameri-

cans and otherwise work to challenge the post-war regime.[1] In many
towns in the South, the Klan succeeded in destabilizing the new government; random acts of violence against blacks became commonplace.
Congress reacted by passing specific laws aimed at eradicating Klan
violence. By 1870, the visible Klan faded, replaced by a new regime of
laws that institutionalized segregation in most of the South.

The "Invisible Empire" re-emerged in the early twentieth century
in part as reaction to the release of the epic movie *The Birth of the
Nation*. That film romanticized the Klan's role in fighting the perceived
oppressions of Reconstruction. Organizers formed Klan chapters in most
states; membership by the early 1920s numbered in the millions.[2] On the
surface, this second coming of the Klan bore the trappings of respectability with community parades, good works, and the like. But some of its
members increasingly turned to violence to further their segregationist
beliefs.

Growing criticism of the Klan's role in supporting violence eventually diminished its public role and it reverted to a more clandestine
organization. Throughout the civil rights era in the United States in the
1950s and 1960s, Klan violence served as a constant threat to those
working towards assuring equal rights to African–Americans. The federal government began to work hard to prosecute Klansmen who committed crimes. As the fabric of segregation unraveled, the Klan's power
waned. But it never completely vanished; individuals and small groups
would emerge that claimed title to the Klan's heritage and traditions.

Barry Black was one of those people. Indeed, he came from a long
line of such people. Black's grandfather had been active in the Klan, and
Black joined the youth corps of the Klan in the early 1960s. He recalls
vividly a trip to Stone Mountain, Georgia for a rally presided over by
James Venable, then the head of the largest Klan organization in the
country. While Venable was talking, Black was whispering with some of
his buddies. Venable stopped his talk, went over to Black, and asked
what he had to say that was so important. Others in the group snickered
at Black's predicament. Venable countered by telling the others to be
quiet, and that while this youngster had a lot to learn, "He will be your
Imperial Wizard someday."

Black took that prediction to heart, and, at the time of the Virginia
rally, he had ascended to the position of "Imperial Wizard" in the
Invisible Knights of the Ku Klux Klan for the "realm" of Pennsylvania.
Black is fairly typical of the modern Klansman, with many issues on his
mind and a willingness to speak openly about them. For example, he is
clearly angry over trade agreements like NAFTA that he believes have
taken jobs away from American citizens; he is also angry about affirma-

---

[1] For a useful history of the Klan, one cited by the Supreme Court in its decision in
Virginia v. Black, see W. WADE, THE KU KLUX KLAN IN AMERICA: THE FIERY CROSS (1987).

[2] *See* NANCY MACLEAN, BEHIND THE MASK OF CHIVALRY: THE MAKING OF THE SECOND KU KLUX
KLAN (1994).

tive action programs that he believes have made it almost impossible for white men to get quality jobs. Black is an ardent supporter of the Second Amendment right to own guns. And he is avowedly a racist in that he believes the races should stay separate. That does not translate in his mind to racial hatred. It is about being with "his people" and his history.

In addition to being Imperial Wizard, Black was also a "kleagle"— an organizer whose job is to evangelize by attending rallies to enlist new members. Accordingly, Black has spent many weekends traveling the country attending Klan rallies to enlist new members. Unlike earlier manifestations of the Klan, the modern-day Klan does not have a clear organizational structure nor a widespread following; there are a number of splinter groups that assert they are the "real" Ku Klux Klan. While sometimes fighting amongst themselves, these groups all claim allegiance to the earlier and more powerful Klan incarnations.

Photo of Barry Black

In the summer of 1998, Black received a call from Joey Sechrist in Cana, Virginia about leading a rally. Joey lived with his mother in a rural area. The mother owned property there and she was willing to let him use it for the rally. There did not seem to be any particular issue that sparked local interest and there had not been any local incidents that were racially charged. Black recalls some discussion about how the "Mexicans" were getting all the jobs down there. (Carroll County has quite a few orchards and many Hispanics are employed as pickers in that industry.) In any event, Black agreed to come. One attraction was that

Carroll County was near Mt. Airy–Andy Griffith's home town. Black had long been a fan and hoped the trip might provide him a chance to visit the town.

The Klan rally in Carroll County that day in August was similar to the many other rallies Black had led over the years. Local organizers had informed possibly interested people in Carroll County and nearby North Carolina about the rally. But it was not publicly advertised; in fact, the organizers had put a piece of plywood near the driveway entrance on which they had written "Private Gathering–Public Not Invited." During the rally, the organizers set up a microphone. Any member of the Klan could get up and say what was on his mind. The remarks covered a number of topics—the number one target of the group's collective wrath was President Clinton and his policies.

At the end of the rally, as is the Klan's tradition, the group participated in the ritual lighting of the cross.[3] Black had the materials to make the cross with him in the back of a small camper. The cross consisted of three six-foot lengths of pipe which could be screwed together with a short cross-piece added and then placed in the ground. It was wrapped in kerosene-soaked cloths and then lit as the culmination of the rally. That is when the trouble began.

The Arrest

On the day of the rally, Sheriff Manning had been out during the day. When he returned home around 6:00 p.m., he had a message telling him that there was a Klan rally going on in Cana and that he had "better get down there." Manning found the news surprising. Carroll County had never had an active Klan that he had known about; he was not aware of any racial issues or problems that would have precipitated local interest in the Klan. He decided he had better drive out to the rally. In a rural area like Carroll County, the Sheriff is expected to be involved personally when something unusual happens.

At about the same time, Deputy Sheriff Rick Clark overheard a police radio report about the gathering. When a follow-up report indicated it was a Klan meeting, he too drove down to Cana. When he arrived, he observed a group of people—mostly men—meeting in an open field along Brushy Fork Road. There were several homes along that stretch of Brushy Fork Road, some of them fairly new. There were also a couple of trailer homes in the area as well as many open fields.

Sheriff Manning arrived around dusk and parked his police cruiser on the side of the road overlooking the field where the rally was being held. He saw several people in white robes. The officers could hear members of the rally speaking through a loudspeaker but could not make out the specifics of what was being said. After talking with Deputy Clark, the Sheriff turned on his blue lights to get the attention of the

---

[3] Members of the Klan do not refer to their ceremony as "burning" the cross; rather for them it is a cross "lighting" or "illuminating."

group and find out what was going on. A few of the men, including Joey Sechrist, who lived on the property, came over. Sechrist told the police that he had invited a Klan leader to come to a rally.

Manning's approach was to keep the situation calm. As far as he could tell, the group was not doing anything illegal. But he wanted to know more about what they were planning to do and he was also concerned about how others might react if they found out about the Klan meeting. "I was going to wait for them and make sure that everything was going to be OK. You don't know what's going to happen when they're having a meeting like that." He could imagine anti-Klan people coming by and shooting out the windows of the Klansmen's cars.

He asked the men how long they were going to be there, and they replied about another hour. Manning said that would be fine. He also decided to stay around.

About forty minutes later, something did happen. Just as Manning and Clark were expecting the rally to end, the "sky just lit up." The cross was near the crest of a hill. The light from the flames was visible for at least a half-mile in each direction. As the cross burned, the crowd joined in singing "Amazing Grace."

What was taking place on the hill in front of them was a carefully coordinated ritual. The leader would have all the torch-carrying Klansmen form a circle around the cross and march clockwise to "take the Klan into the future."[4] The participants would then turn to face the cross, and follow the lead of the head Klansman, who would lower his torch. He would say, "In the name of the Father," and raise his torch; then "in the name of the Son," and raise it again; and then "in the name of the Holy Ghost," and raise it a third time. He would then call out "Klansmen, right face," and they would turn and countermarch back around the cross. This symbolized taking the Klan back into the past in respect for their venerated ancestors. After more marching, the Klansmen would approach the cross. Each would place their torches at the bottom to light it, and then back away.

Once lit, the caller would say "Klansmen, salute." All Klansmen would then open their arms outstretched in the sign of the cross. "Behold the fiery cross, still illuminating the sky brilliantly. We do not light this cross to desecrate this cross, we light this cross to signify that Christ is alive, not only in our hearts but throughout the world. Only fire lights the darkness, only fire purifies the stubble, the wood, the gold

---

[4] It was assumed throughout the proceedings to follow that Barry Black was the leader of the Klan during the cross-lighting ritual. During his interview, however, he stated that in fact he did not preside over the cross-lighting in Carroll County (although he had done so innumerable times in the past at other rallies). On that day, he was suffering from back problems and states that he let someone else preside.

and silver, and purifies it. God give us men! God give us strong, sun-crowned men, God give us men who will not flinch at the call of duty."

Both Manning and Clark were startled when they saw the flames. Manning had never seen a cross-burning other than on television. He was not scared by what he saw, but rather more shocked. It was so unexpected in his community.

Clark's reaction was stronger—he was angry. His father had been a conservative Baptist minister. "When I look at the cross, that represents the saving grace of our Lord and Savior. And they were singing a religious song that I grew up singing and set fire to a cross. It was just an outrage. I didn't want that to happen in my county."

Manning and Clark discussed what to do. Clark had begun his career with the sheriff's office as a dispatcher. When working the midnight shift, he would sometimes read through the Code of Virginia to pass the time. He recalled that there was a prohibition against burning a cross, but he did not recall the specifics of the crime. He called back to the police station to ask the dispatcher to research the issue. After a few minutes, the dispatcher called back—cross-burning was a Class 6 felony in Virginia. While the least serious felony, it still was punishable by a fine and up to five years imprisonment in the state penitentiary.

Manning and Clark then drove onto the property up a dirt road to where the cross was still smoldering. Manning walked over to a group of men that looked like the leaders of the rally and informed them that they were violating the law, and that whoever was responsible would be arrested.

At that point, Barry Black stepped forward. Manning recalls that Black said "I'm the head of the Klan here tonight, so I'll accept responsibility." Black remembers the arrest differently. He recalls Manning flying up the road in his police vehicle and threatening to arrest the elderly woman who owned the land. Black was incensed. He told Manning that he had rented the land for seventy-two hours and that if he was going to arrest anyone, he should arrest Black. In any event, Manning placed Black under arrest.

Deputy Clark drove Black to Hillsville to the courthouse where he was taken before a magistrate judge for booking. The drive took about twenty minutes. According to Clark, Black immediately launched into a "radically racial rhetoric about the blacks and the Mexicans who were taking all the jobs." Clark told him that they could stop at every house between Cana and Hillsville and they would not find a black person.

Clark also recalls a specific reference to black men and white women holding hands walking up and down the sidewalks. Clark replied that there were not any sidewalks in Cana.[5]

The arrest was big news in Carroll County. The local newspaper—the Carroll News—covered the story extensively. Carol Lee Lindsey, the head editor, wrote an editorial expressing outrage at having the Klan meeting in Carroll County. "I had kind of a knee jerk reaction, and my knee jerk reaction was, 'I don't want Carroll County known for something like this. Because I know Carroll County to be a friendly place with caring people." The editorial sounded a theme that would become a common refrain among community members: this was something that was done by outsiders. There was strong sentiment in favor of prosecuting Black for the cross-burning.

The Defense Team

After his arrest, Black contacted a few local attorneys but none of them were interested in representing such an unpopular client. "No one would represent me. They said, 'Well, we know all about the case, but we can't represent you, we'll be ostracized. I won't even be able to be a dogcatcher around here if I represent you.'" Frustrated, Black decided to contact the Virginia chapter of the American Civil Liberties Union ("ACLU").

The ACLU sent out a report of the case to a committee of lawyers who screened potential cases. One of the members was David Baugh, a successful criminal defense lawyer in Richmond. He recalls reading the email about the Klansman arrested for cross-burning. He was interested. "So I read the statute and I went, 'How in the name of all that is good and holy can that pass constitutional muster?' So I called and volunteered to work on the case."

What made Baugh's offer remarkable is that he is African–American. "A lot of people asked, 'How could you defend a Klansman?' It's a no-brainer. I understand that the Constitution is a set of principles and if you're going to protect my right to say what I want to say, I have to defend that guy." As he explained: "Mr. Black had the right to stand up

---

[5] Black also told Clark that he was himself a police officer and that perhaps he could offer some professional courtesy. Clark replied simply that Black had committed a felony and that there were not any courtesies to be offered other than following standard procedures. It turned out that Black had in fact been elected on two occasions as a constable in his home town in Pennsylvania. The position was unpaid; constables were authorized to serve warrants and make arrests if authorized by a judge. Black was first elected in 1991. There were no listed candidates on the ballot, but Black received several write-in votes. He was subsequently stripped of the office when a local district attorney successfully moved to have him removed because of his record of prior convictions. Black filed a legal action asserting that he was being singled out for his membership in the Klan, but the Pennsylvania Supreme Court affirmed his dismissal. He was elected a second time in 1998—this time as the result of a single write-in vote—but he was again ousted from the office.

in the middle of a field and say, 'I hate all African–Americans or I hate all Jews.' He can say that. That should be protected. Well the question is can he *symbolically* make the same statement. And the answer is yes, he can." In fact, Baugh thought he would be the perfect lawyer for Barry Black. A white lawyer ran the risk of others thinking that they might be seen as being supportive of the Klan. No one was going to accuse Baugh of being a "closet Klansman."

Baugh is used to battling for what he believes in: he was attending an historically black school in Virginia when the government made the decision to merge the school with white schools. Baugh was opposed to the decision and, during his senior year, he took part in demonstrations protesting the decision, which led to his expulsion. The local American Civil Liberties Union successfully represented him in challenging the expulsion. Watching his lawyers take on the establishment made an impression, and Baugh decided he would attend law school.

Also volunteering to work on Black's case was Professor Rodney Smolla, a noted constitutional law scholar and Dean of the University of Richmond School of Law. Smolla had authored many articles and a leading treatise on the First Amendment. Like many academics, he was a political liberal and not at all sympathetic to the Klan, but as a constitutional law expert, he thought it important to protect their rights of expression. "I was never defending the content of his message and he knew that from the very beginning. It was the classic, almost cliché, I don't like what you say but I'll defend your right to say it."

An initial issue for the defense team was how to handle the fact that Baugh was African–American. They decided to inform Black about that to make sure it was acceptable to him. Black recalls being surprised that an African–American attorney was willing to work on his case. He asked Baugh one question: "Are you willing to fight for me?" Baugh assured him that he would; Black replied "that's good enough."

As Baugh and Smolla assessed the case, their strategy was simple. They could not argue that Black had not burned the cross; he was at the rally and he had been the head of the Klan that day. Instead, the defense was going to be that the Virginia cross-burning statute was itself unconstitutional. The statute was simple: it made it a crime to burn a cross "for the purpose of intimidating any person." In addition, the law also established a presumption: if you burned a cross, *the jury could assume* that you did so in order to intimidate someone.[6]

---

[6] Such presumptions are fairly common in criminal law; for example, it can be presumed that if you have in your possession more than a certain amount of an illegal drug, then you intended to sell it (making you potentially guilty of not only possession but the separate crime of intending to sell the illegal drug).

Smolla filed a motion to dismiss the case against Black based upon the unconstitutionality of the statute. In his brief, he noted that a prior Supreme Court decision had established a First Amendment right to burn the flag.[7] Thus, the idea that one had constitutional protections even when burning some sacred symbol seemed clearly established. In another recent decision, the Supreme Court had thrown out a conviction of a cross-burner from St. Paul, Minnesota because the local ordinance had singled out certain kinds of conduct for punishment.[8] Smolla was confident of success. "I'm putting together those cases and I'm figuring I can't lose."

The Prosecution

The local prosecutor, Greg Goad, was fully prepared to do what it would take to secure a conviction. Knowing that the ACLU was now involved, he expected the case to go to trial. Moreover, if the prosecution was successful, Baugh and Smolla would certainly file an appeal. As a result, Goad notified the Virginia Attorney General's office about the case. They assigned two lawyers to work with Goad in crafting a reply to Smolla's motion.

One of the attorneys assigned to the case was State Solicitor General William Hurd, one of the top-ranking attorneys in the Attorney General's office. Hurd, like all those associated with the prosecution of the case, was proud of his Southern heritage. But he also understood its destructive history of racism. "I believe the south is a wonderful place. But I know that in the south, like other parts of the country, it's important to preserve harmony between the races. The Ku Klux Klan, for a hundred years has tried to disturb that harmony." Hurd, like Sheriff Manning and the others in Carroll County, very much wanted a conviction. "When this Pennsylvania Klansman came to Virginia, to intimidate citizens in Carroll County, we felt it was important to make sure that the conviction was obtained and that a message was sent that cross burning in Virginia is illegal and will not be tolerated."

In crafting a response to the motion to dismiss the case, Hurd emphasized the historical background of the statute. The cross-burning law dated from 1952, a time when Virginia was still a segregationist

---

[7] *See* Texas v. Johnson, 491 U.S. 397 (1989). In that case, the Court in a 5–4 decision overturned the conviction of protestor who burned a flag outside the Dallas City Hall to protest American policies during the 1984 Republican National Convention. The majority noted: "If there is a bedrock principle underlying the First Amendment, it is that the government may not prohibit the expression of an idea simply because society finds the idea itself offensive or disagreeable."

[8] *See* R.A.V. v. St. Paul, 505 U.S. 377 (1992). For an excellent account of the *R.A.V.* case written by the attorney who represented the cross-burner, see Edward J. Cleary, Beyond the Burning Cross (1994).

state. What prompted the legislative action was a series of cross-burnings throughout Virginia. While it was true that the Virginia legislature at the time supported segregation, it did not support the violence associated with groups like the Ku Klux Klan. This law was justified by the Klan's long history of "vigilante injustice."

The trial judge sided with the prosecution. In the judge's view, the law did not make it a crime simply to burn the cross. Rather, the law was limited to cross burners who had the intent to intimidate others. The judge assumed that the legislature used the term "intimidate" as synonymous with "threaten." There is no constitutional right to threaten someone, in much the same way that there is no constitutional right to yell "fire" in a crowded auditorium. The case would proceed to trial.

The Trial

Black's trial would have received a good deal of publicity simply because it involved the Klan. But with Black being represented by an African–American lawyer, there was even more media interest. Reporters once asked Baugh, "What's it like representing someone who wouldn't invite you to their house for a meal?" Baugh's reply was disarming: "I've *never* been to a client's house for a meal. I've never been to my doctor's house for a meal. It's a professional relationship." Baugh explained that Black had the right to be a bigot. There was no need for an attorney and client to become friends. "We don't have to have a kumbayah moment."

Black's case went to trial in Hillsville on June 23, 1999. The trial itself was short, lasting a single day. Jury selection took longer than in might have in a less controversial case. Baugh asked prospective jurors about their views on the Klan—unsurprisingly, he found a good deal of hostility. The resulting jury was all-white, not because of any choice by Baugh to exclude blacks, but simply because of the demographics of Carroll County.

Goad, the prosecuting attorney, presented a simple case. He began by putting into evidence several pictures showing the field and the approximate location of the cross. He then called Sheriff Manning and Deputy Clark to describe what happened that day. While important testimony, none of it went to the heart of the matter: Did the rally reasonably have the impact of intimidating anyone? Neither Manning nor Clark testified that they were personally frightened by what had happened. Clark testified that he felt "moral outrage." Baugh's follow-up question was, "That's a nice answer, but perhaps you could answer my question. Did you feel threatened?" Clark replied, "For my personal safety, no, sir."

Original Courthouse in Carroll County, Virginia

Clark did testify that while he was observing the rally, a black family drove by on Brushy Fork Road and asked Clark what was happening. When he told them it was a Klan rally, he testified that they seemed upset and sped off. But that was not a personal account. Indeed, Baugh objected when Clark described the family as upset; the judge agreed and that answer was stricken from the record.

The key witness in the case—the only witness who could testify about her own fear caused by the Klan rally—was Rebecca Sechrist. She and her husband had just set up a trailer home on their property which was adjacent to the field where the rally was held. They had been out most of the day, but had returned in the afternoon. She was close enough to the rally to hear what was being said over the speakers. What she heard upset her. Others in the neighborhood had also been upset, but none were willing to testify for fear of possible reprisals by those sympathetic to the Klan. But Mrs. Sechrist, even though she was related to the owner of the property, was willing to testify.

She testified that the rally participants had talked a lot about blacks, and many used the "N" word (she refused to say the word in open court). She also testified that one Klansman stated that "he would love to take a .30/.30 and just randomly shoot blacks." Others criticized President Clinton. Sechrist testified that she was scared.

When the cross was lit, she said it made her feel "awful." She told the jury that "I couldn't begin to put in words how I felt. I cried, I sat there and I cried. I didn't know what was going to happen between everything going on. It was just terrible." She was worried that her new home might be burned or that the group might injure her children.

Baugh's defense was simple. During cross-examination of Sheriff Manning, he got him to admit that there was a sign indicating that it was a private gathering, and that none of the rally participants had disobeyed any orders from the police. He also carefully cross-examined Mrs. Sechrist, getting her to admit that no one made any specific threats to her, that the comments that she objected to were general comments directed at groups like African–Americans and Hispanics. Baugh did not present any witnesses for the defense, and Black did not testify on his own behalf.

After the close of the evidence, the trial judge read a few pages of instructions on the law. Most of the instructions were routine: that the jury's decision must be unanimous; that the defendant is presumed innocent; that he must be proven guilty beyond a reasonable doubt. With respect to the specific crime, the Court instructed the jury that it could only find Black guilty if he burned the cross "with the intent to intimidate" someone. But the subsequent instruction—based upon the statute itself—was potentially critical to the case. The Court read Instruction #9 as follows: "The Court instructs the jury that the burning of a cross by itself is sufficient evidence from which you may infer the required intent." Baugh objected to the reading of that instruction.

During closing arguments, Goad reminded the jury of witness statements that a Klansman at the rally had talked about shooting blacks. Baugh's main argument to the jury was there was no intent to intimidate anyone. The conduct—both the rally itself and the ritual cross-lighting—was not directed against any individual. It was something that they were doing amongst themselves.

The jury, after deliberating for only twenty-five minutes, found Black guilty. In Virginia, unlike most states, the jury also assesses the punishment. The jury could have sent Black to prison for up to five years and assessed a fine up to $2,500. Goad exhorted the jury to punish Black with at least some jail time. He submitted an exhibit that listed seven prior convictions, most of which dated from the early 1970s and included convictions for robbery, as well as escaping from prison. He stressed to the jury the serious threats that had been made during the rally. Black was the one who had taken responsibility for the rally and all that happened there.

Baugh asked the jury to contrast this cross-burning with "the worst case scenario" of a group going to someone's home in the middle of the night, burning the cross, and making explicit threats. This case, he argued, was completely different. There were no threats made against any specific individual. Indeed, the only comment that might constitute even a general "threat" was a statement made by someone other than Black during the rally. They were in the middle of a field in the country having a private gathering. He urged the jury simply to assess a small fine.

The jury deliberated for close to an hour on the penalty. They chose to award the maximum fine possible—$2,500—but not to assess any prison time. Baugh was disappointed with the conviction, but at the same time, "anytime your client walks out of the courtroom that's a victory and Barry Black did walk out of that courtroom." Goad, too, was disappointed; he had hoped that the jury would assess some prison time. Sheriff Manning thought that the jury was inclined to go lightly because no one had been hurt in the incident and Black had cooperated with Manning during the arrest.

The Appeal

Black could have paid the fine and ended the matter. But he wanted to continue the fight. "I couldn't do that, not in my heart and soul, because if I did that, I'm letting my race down. If I would have just said hey, here's $2,500, let's just forget it. I have to make people know that America is still a land of opportunity, that America is still a land of democracy, and that the Constitution of the United States of America still means something." His attorneys filed an appeal to the Virginia Supreme Court. From that point on, Smolla was primarily responsible.

On appeal, Black's case was consolidated with a second cross-burning case from Virginia Beach. In that case, a couple of teenagers had tried to burn a small cross on a neighbor's yard as a result of family dispute.[9] Smolla agreed to handle that case as well. For Hurd, now primarily responsible for representing Virginia, having the second case was useful. It permitted him to argue that Virginia was not targeting one particular group, the Klan, but rather wanted to ban cross-burning by anyone.

---

[9] One of the teenagers had been upset when his neighbors—a racially mixed family— complained to his parents about his shooting a gun near the property. He and some friends were drinking beer at a party and got upset about what had happened. After the party, they lashed two small sticks together and went over to their neighbors' yard. They put this crude cross in the ground and tried to light it. It never caught fire, but it did smolder. They then left. The next morning, the neighbors saw the cross and, understandably upset, called the police. The youths were prosecuted under the same cross-burning law.

Both cases were heard by the Virginia Supreme Court on September 10, 2001. No one in the courtroom knew that the next day would be one of the most infamous days in U.S. history as terrorists attacked the Pentagon and World Trade Center. As Smolla watched the smoldering ruins of the Twin Towers, he knew that the tragedy of September 11 would impact the case: "I was thinking it's going to change the way we think about free speech; it's going to change the way we think about terrorism; it's going to affect the chemistry and the culture surrounding the case." Before September 11, it was easier to dismiss the type of racist diatribe that took place at the Klan rally as unpleasant but basically harmless speech. After the attacks, fewer Americans would accept that view. This was now as much a case about terrorism as it was about the First Amendment.

But Black won his appeal in the Virginia Supreme Court. That Court held that Virginia's statute was unconstitutional because, based upon the U.S. Supreme Court's decision in *R.A.V. v. St. Paul*, Virginia may not regulate expressive conduct based on hostility towards the underlying message. Hurd strongly disagreed with the ruling, and Virginia filed a petition for certiorari to the U.S. Supreme Court.

The Supreme Court granted review. Smolla was not surprised. "We've always struggled and had a real hard time with what you do when the threat's done by abortion protestors, what you do when the threat's done by a civil rights group, what you do when the threat's done by the Ku Klux Klan. Are you really talking about blowing up an abortion clinic, or killing a civil rights activist?" *Virginia v. Black* presented an excellent opportunity for the Court to address those types of questions.

The Supreme Court

In many respects, the case as argued in the Supreme Court transcended its roots. It became much less about what happened on that field in Cana, Virginia, and much more about the significance of the Ku Klux Klan throughout American history.

Hurd's main tact at oral argument was to stress the violent history of the Klan. "The burning cross, based on a hundred years of usage, is a sign of intimidation—a threat of violence soon to come. The Klan has burned crosses because they wanted that message of intimidation." The cross was not just a symbol of hatred, but stood for something far more dangerous: a warning to blacks and other outsiders that "if you don't succumb to what we want you to do, there's going to be violence." To convey to the Justices just how intimidating a burning cross could be, Hurd drew their attention to the grand marble columns before which the Justices sat. As several Justices turned their heads to look, Hurd told them that the flames from the burning cross had risen as high as those majestic columns—some thirty feet into the air—and allowed the that image to slowly sink in. Hurd also argued that the Klan was a terrorist group: "The reason the Klan burned crosses was to intimidate people, to terrorize people, and to give them warning that if they did not capitulate to whatever the demands were, that they would be hurt or would be killed. It was to instill terror."[10]

In response, Smolla emphasized that the Virginia statute singled out one particular act—the burning of the cross—to the exclusion of other acts that could be equally odious, such as burning the Star of David. He used a simple explanation to illustrate what he thought was wrong with the law: "If you imagine someone taking two sticks, dousing them with kerosene, and lighting them and they hold the sticks out apart from one another, they don't commit a crime. But they take the vertical stick and they cross it with the horizontal stick, suddenly they're guilty of a felony." In Smolla's view, this akin was punishing someone just for brandishing a symbol. That would create a dangerous precedent.

Smolla also emphasized that there was no need for a state to punish cross-burning. In those situations where cross-burning was truly part of a directed activity to intimidate someone, the actions could be punished through a law designed to prohibit threats or other laws such as criminal trespass. "If you can prove that somebody burned a cross to threaten somebody, then indict them under a threat law and throw them in jail. No problem."

Many Supreme Court oral arguments are dramatic with the Justices interrupting the usually skilled advocates to ask difficult questions or make key points. But the argument in *Virginia v. Black* is among the most dramatic in recent memory, because just as several of the Justices began to ask the attorneys questions, Justice Clarence Thomas spoke up. This itself would be noteworthy, as Justice Thomas seldom asks questions during oral argument, preferring to reflect on the attorneys' arguments. And, furthermore, Black's lawyers had assumed that Justice Thomas would likely favor their position based upon some of his prior decisions. What followed stunned everyone in the Court that day.

Justice Thomas did not speak against the ban; rather, he spoke powerfully and with great passion in favor of Virginia's law. He noted the hundred years of lynching and violence by the Klan, which he called a "reign of terror." Justice Thomas declared that burning a cross went

---

[10] The United States Government had entered the case in support of Virginia's position, and an attorney from the United States Solicitor General's Office joined Hurd in arguing that a state should be able to single out the burning cross and make it a crime to burn it so long as there was the requisite intent to intimidate—the law was simply punishing threats consistent with the Constitution.

far beyond a mere threat of violence: "My fear is that you are understating the symbolism and effect of the cross; it is unlike any symbol in our society." As Justice Thomas spoke, the tension in the Court was palpable. Smolla recalls that the Justice was "shaking as he's talking, he's eloquent; you could hear a pin drop in the courtroom." Justice Thomas' invective was front-page news the next day.

The Court's Decision

The Supreme Court's decision in *Virginia v. Black* was a compromise. The main opinion, written by Justice O'Connor, decided three key points. First, the Court held that in general, burning a cross *is* protected speech under the First Amendment. Just like burning a flag, the government can not outlaw a symbol just because it is distasteful or even despicable. On this point, Justice Thomas dissented; as signaled by his comments during oral argument, he believed that the burning cross was a unique symbol of hatred that a state could justifiedly ban.

While protected, however, Justice O'Connor went on to hold that the government could prohibit cross burning only if it were done with the intent to threaten or intimidate. The Court in prior cases had noted that "true threats" were not protected by the First Amendment. Accordingly, if cross burning were done in a manner that constituted a real threat, then it could be punished. It was acceptable for the Government to focus on this one particular act and seek to punish it so long as it is only criminalized cross-burnings that directly threatened others.

Finally, the Court said there had to be specific proof of the constitutionally-required intent to threaten or intimidate. The Virginia statute stated that the mere fact that the defendant burned a cross gave rise to a presumption that the defendant intended to intimidate someone. The Court held that the presumption was unconstitutional; there must be proof of the requisite intent to intimidate or threaten. The result was that the Court reversed Black's conviction because the jury had been instructed that it could presume an intent to intimidate from the mere fact of Black having burned the cross.

Both sides felt that they had won. For Black, having his conviction reversed by the Supreme Court was validation of what he had long believed were his rights and the rights of the Klan: "[W]e proved that the law does work yet. That victory went worldwide. I can light a cross anywhere in the United States of America that I want to light it as long as I'm not doing it to intimidate anybody. How they perceive it is how they perceive it." Since the decision, Black has been back to Virginia for another rally that included a cross lighting. He remains defiant and angry at all those involved in the Carroll County incident. He has been talking with lawyers about filing a civil rights case against Sheriff

Manning and Deputy Clark for violating his civil rights. Black is optimistic that the Klan will soon undergo a resurrection and he intends to be an active part of its rebirth.

Smolla was not as jubilant as Black. He recognized that the Supreme Court's decision in *Virginia v. Black* was a difficult one to parse; it clearly was a mixed decision that he finds potentially disturbing. While it has some strong language saying that cross-burning is a protected ritual under the First Amendment, it does not then conclude that states should never be able to have a cross-burning law and should instead just have ordinary threat laws. The decision creates a precedent to allow the Government in the future to pass other laws that penalize other symbols of some religious group, or gang, or even something that we have not yet thought about. "Do you want governments browsing the universe of symbols and starting to pick out those symbols that most scare it? And if you can ban a symbol it is but a short step to banning a word, or a set of words, or a particular message."

Hurd believed that Virginia's position clearly prevailed. The Court expressly said that cross-burning was an especially virulent form of intimidation that could be banned without having to ban other forms of intimidation in the same statute or in the same way. The fact that a part of the statute was struck down was less important. Virginia could obtain convictions in future cases without resort to the presumption. "What is important is that we have set the principle that cross burning with intent to intimidate can be prohibited consistent with the First Amendment and that it may be singled out for the especially harsh treatment that it deserves."

But Hurd and others involved in the prosecution were disappointed that the Supreme Court's opinion precluded a retrial of Black. They remain convinced that Black had intended to intimidate citizens in Carroll County during the rally. Deputy Clark felt that the sole reason Black burned the cross was to intimidate: "It was not a celebration; it's only symbolic of terror. And symbolically, through the ages, if you ask any black person, they'll tell you burning a cross is symbolic of terror. And that was the only reason he burnt that cross was the symbol of terror. He will tell you that it signifies purity, but actually that's just too far-fetched for me to comprehend."

* * *

Barry's Black's case proves the importance of avoiding simple generalizations when thinking about issues of race in contemporary America. The leader of the Klan was not a white racist from the South, but rather a northerner. The citizens of the small, predominately white southern town where the Klan rally was held, far from supportive of the Klan's message, were deeply offended by what had happened. The white police officers and prosecutors were intent on prosecuting the Klansman to the full extent of the law. They were opposed in the courtroom by an African–American lawyer intent on protecting the Klan's freedom of speech. This dispute, rising from its relatively simple origins, provides us with a fundamental challenge as to how to reconcile what we fear and what we value most.

Contributors

Samuel Bagenstos is Professor of Law and Associate Dean for Research and Faculty Development at the Washington University School of Law in Saint Louis, Missouri, where. He teaches constitutional law, civil rights litigation, and labor and employment law courses, and he writes on civil rights, antidiscrimination and social welfare law, with a particular focus on disability law. Among his notable publications on these topics are *The Structural Turn and the Limits of Antidiscrimination Law*, 94 Cal. L. Rev. 1 (2006); *The Future of Disability Law*, 114 Yale L.J. 1 (2004); and *"Rational Discrimination," Accommodation, and the Politics of (Disability) Civil Rights*, 89 Va. L. Rev. 825 (2003). Bagenstos is also a frequent appellate advocate in civil rights cases in the federal courts. He holds a bachelor's degree from the University of North Carolina at Chapel Hill and a law degree from the Harvard Law School. After graduating from law school, he clerked for a year for Judge Stephen Reinhardt on the United States Court of Appeals for the Ninth Circuit, then worked for three years as an attorney in the Appellate Section of the Civil Rights Division of the United States Department of Justice, then clerked for Justice Ruth Bader Ginsburg of the Supreme Court of the United States.

Caroline Bettinger–López is the Human Rights Fellow and Attorney at Columbia Law School's Human Rights Institute and Clinic. Her work focuses on gender and race discrimination, human rights, and violence against women. She engages in litigation and other forms of advocacy before the Inter–American human rights system, United Nations, and state and federal courts. Caroline is lead counsel on the first international domestic violence case against the United States, *Jessica Gonzales v. United States*, and is author of the forthcoming "Jessica Gonzales v. United States: *An Emerging Model for Domestic Violence & Human Rights Advocacy in the United States*," which will be published in the Harvard Human Rights Law Journal in Spring 2008 and featured at the Journal's 2008 symposium, "Human Rights and the United States." She is a member of the International Human Rights Committee of the New York City Bar Association. Prior to joining Columbia, Caroline was a Skadden Fellow at the ACLU Women's Rights Project and a law clerk for the Honorable Sterling Johnson, Jr. in the Eastern District of New York. She is a graduate of Columbia Law School, where she received her J.D., and the University of Michigan, where she received her B.A. in Anthropology. She is author of *Cuban–Jewish Journeys: Searching for Identity, Home, and History in Miami* (Univ. of Tennessee Press, 2000).

Tomiko Brown–Nagin is Professor of Law, Professor of History, and F. Palmer Weber Research Professor in Civil Liberties and Human Rights at the University of Virginia. She holds a Ph.D. in history from Duke University and a law degree from Yale University, where she was a senior editor of the *Yale Law Journal*. She teaches courses on American social and legal history, constitutional law, public interest law, and education law. Brown–Nagin has written widely on civil rights history and law. She has published articles about the NAACP's legal campaign against Jim Crow and contemporary campaigns for racial equality in law and history journals, including the *Columbia Law Review*, the *University of Pennsylvania Law Review*, the *Duke Law Journal*, the *Journal of Law and Education*, and *Women's History Review*. She currently is working on a book that explores African American ambivalence about liberal legalism before and after *Brown v. Board of Education.*

Sheryll Cashin, Professor of Law at Georgetown University, currently teaches Constitutional Law, Local Government Law, and Property. She writes about race relations, government and inequality in America. Her book, *The Failures of Integration: How Race and Class are Undermining the American Dream* (PublicAffairs, 2004) received critical praise in *The New York Times Book Review* and *The Chicago Tribune* among other publications. Her new book, *The Agitator's Daughter: A Memoir of a Family* (forthcoming PublicAffairs, 2008) traces the arc of American race relations through five generations of her family. Cashin has published widely in academic journals and trade publications. She worked in the Clinton White House as an advisor on urban economic policy and was law clerk to U.S. Supreme Court Justice Thurgood Marshall and Judge Abner Mikva of the D.C. Circuit Court of Appeals. She graduated *summa cum laude* from Vanderbilt University in 1984 with a bachelor's degree in electrical engineering. A Marshall Scholar, she received a masters in English Law, with honors, from Oxford University in 1986, and a J.D., with honors, from Harvard Law School, in 1989, where she was a member of the Harvard Law Review. Cashin was born and raised in Huntsville, Alabama, where her parents were political activists.

Erwin Chemerinksy is Alston & Bird Professor of Law and Political Science at Duke University. He joined the Duke faculty in 2004 after 21 years at the University of Southern California. Chemerinsky is the author of five books and over 100 law review articles. He frequently argues appellate cases, including in the United States Supreme Court.

Lynda G. Dodd is an assistant professor of law at American University's Washington College of Law, where she teaches and specializes in constitutional law and theory, civil rights litigation, and jurisprudence. Professor Dodd graduated from Yale Law School and earned her PhD in Politics from Princeton University. She is currently working on a book manuscript, tentatively titled *Securing the Blessings of Liberty*, which examines the history of Section 1983, from its origins in the Civil Rights Act of 1871 to the contemporary era, with a special focus on the political debates regarding civil rights enforcement strategies.

William N. Eskridge, Jr. is the John A. Garver Professor of Jurisprudence at the Yale Law School. He is the author of the forthcoming study of the rise and fall of consensual sodomy laws, *Dishonorable Passions: Sodomy Law in America, 1861–2003* (Viking, 2008), the research for which formed the primary basis for his contribution to this volume. Professor Eskridge has also published *Dynamic Statutory Interpretation* (Harvard 1994); *The Case for Same–Sex Marriage* (Free Press, 1996); *Gaylaw: Challenging the Apartheid of the Closet* (Harvard 1999); *Equality Practice: Civil Unions and the Future of Gay Rights* (Routledge 2002); and *Gay Marriage: For Better or For Worse?* (Oxford, 2006) (with Darren Spedale); *Super-Statutes: America's constitution of Statutes* (Yale also forthcoming 2008).

Myriam Gilles is a Professor at the Benjamin N. Cardozo School of Law, where she teaches courses on civil rights law, equality, and national security & civil liberties. Professor Gilles has written extensively on police misconduct litigation, structural reform injunctions, and the deterrent effect of civil rights damage awards on governmental actors. Professor Gilles earned her undergraduate degree at Harvard College and her law degree at Yale.

Risa L. Goluboff is Professor of Law and History at the University of Virginia. A legal historian, her scholarly interests include civil rights, constitutional law, and labor law. In addition to numerous law review articles and book chapters, in 2007 Goluboff published *The Lost Promise of Civil Rights* (Harvard University Press). Goluboff received her A.B. *summa cum laude* from Harvard in 1994 and spent the following year teaching at the University of Cape Town (South Africa) as a Fulbright Scholar. She received her law degree from Yale Law School, and an M.A. with distinction and a Ph.D. in history, both from Princeton University. Goluboff clerked for the Honorable Guido Calabresi of the U.S. Court of Appeals for the Second Circuit and for Supreme Court Justice Stephen G. Breyer.

Serena Mayeri is an Assistant Professor of Law at the University of Pennsylvania Law School, where she teaches legal history, family law, and employment discrimination. She is the author of several articles on civil rights and women's rights, including "The Strange Career of Jane Crow: Sex Segregation and the Transformation of Anti–Discrimination Discourse," in the *Yale Journal of Law and the Humanities* (2006), and "Constitutional Choices: Legal Feminism and the Historical Dynamics of Change," in the *California Law Review* (2004). She received her A.B.

from Harvard College, and earned a J.D. and a Ph.D. from Yale, where her dissertation won the history department's George Washington Eggleston Prize and the Organization of American Historians' Lerner–Scott Prize. Prior to teaching at Penn, she served as a Samuel I. Golieb Fellow at New York University Law School and as a law clerk to Judge Guido Calabresi on the U.S. Court of Appeals for the Second Circuit.

Thomas B. Metzloff, Professor of Law at Duke Law School, teaches courses in Civil Procedure, Legal Ethics, Constitutional Law, and Dispute Resolution. For the past four years, he has been the Director of the "Voices of American Law" project. The purpose of the project is to interview participants in leading Supreme Court cases in order to create documentaries about the cases to be used in law schools and other educational settings. Most of the cases involve constitutional law issues.

Cornelia T.L. Pillard is a Professor at Georgetown University Law Center. Prior to joining the faculty, Professor Pillard worked as an Assistant to the Solicitor General and drafted the Supreme Court briefs for the United States in *United States v. Virginia*, as well as litigating over twenty cases before the Supreme Court. She has written extensively on gender issues, focusing on equality and reproductive choice. In 1998–2000, Professor Pillard took leave from Georgetown to work in the Department of Justice as Deputy Assistant Attorney General, Office of Legal Counsel. Professor Pillard is graduate of Yale College, where she earned her B.A., and Harvard Law School, where she earned her J.D. After law school, she served as a law clerk to the Honorable Louis H. Pollak of the U.S. District Court for the Eastern District of Pennsylvania.

Wendell Pritchett is Professor of Law and Associate Dean for Academic Affairs at the University of Pennsylvania, where he teaches property, local government law, urban policy, and legal history. Professor Pritchett received his J.D. from Yale Law School (1991) and his Ph.D. in American History from the University of Pennsylvania (1997). His first book, Brownsville, Brooklyn: Blacks, Jews and the Changing Face of the Ghetto (University of Chicago Press, 2002), explores race relations and public policy in 20th century Brooklyn. His biography of Robert Weaver, the first Secretary of Housing and Urban Development, will be published by the University of Chicago Press in 2008.

George Rutherglen is the John Barbee Minor Distinguished Professor of Law and the Edward F. Howrey Research Professor at the University of Virginia. He has written numerous articles on civil rights and employment discrimination. He has also co-authored Employment Discrimination: Law and Theory (2005), and Civil Rights Actions: Enforcing the Constitution (2d ed. 2007). Most recently, he has published Employment Discrimination: Visions of Equality in Theory and Doctrine

(2d ed. 2007). He has also written widely on admiralty and civil procedure, serving on the ABA Standing Committee on Federal Judicial Improvements. He is a graduate of the University of California at Berkeley, where he received both is A.B. and J.D. degrees, and before coming to the University of Virginia, he served as a law clerk to Judge J. Clifford Wallace on the U.S. Court of Appeals for the Ninth Circuit and to Justices William O. Douglas and John Paul Stevens on the U.S. Supreme Court.

Richard Schragger is Professor of Law and Class of 1948 Professor in Scholarly Research in Law at the University of Virginia School of Law. He teaches property, local government law, and urban law and policy, and has published a number of articles at the intersection of constitutional and local government law, including *The Limits of Localism,* 100 MICH. L. J. 371 (2001), *The Role of the Local in the Doctrine and Discourse of Religious Liberty,* 117 HARV. L. REV. 1810 (2004), and *Can Strong Mayors Empower Weak Cities? On the Power of Local Executives in a Federal System,* 115 YALE L.J. 2542 (2006). He is a *magna cum laude* graduate of Harvard Law School and served as a law clerk for Judge Dolores Sloviter on the U.S. Court of Appeals for the Third Circuit. Before coming to the University of Virginia, Professor Schragger was a Visiting Professor at the Georgetown University Law Center and the Quinnipiac University School of Law and a Visting Scholar at the Yale Law School. Before that, he was an associate with Miller, Cassidy, Larroca & Lewin in Washington, D.C.

Susan Sturm is the George M. Jaffin Professor of Law and Social Responsibility at Columbia Law School, where her principal areas of teaching and research include institutional change, structural inequality in employment and higher education, employment discrimination, public law remedies, conflict resolution, and civil procedure. She is a founding co-director of the Center for Institutional and Social Change at Columbia. Her recent publications include: Conflict Resolution and Systemic Change (with Howard Gadlin, 2007); The Law School Matrix: Reforming Legal Education in a Culture of Competition and Conformity (with Lani Guinier, 2007); Courts as Catalysts: Rethinking the Role of the Judiciary in New Governance (with Joanne Scott, 2007); The Architecture of Inclusion: Advancing Workplace Equity in Higher Education (2006); Law's Role in Addressing Complex Discrimination (2005); Equality and the Forms of Justice (2004); Lawyers and the Practice of Workplace Equity (2002); Second Generation Employment Discrimination: A Structural Approach, (2001); and Who's Qualified? (with Lani Guinier) (Beacon Press, 2001). "The Architecture of Inclusion" is the subject of the June 2007 issue of the Harvard Journal of Law and Gender. Susan also has developed a website with Lani Guinier, www.racetalks.org, on building multiracial learning communities. In 2007, she received the Presidential Teaching Award for Outstanding Teaching at Columbia.

†